MINING THE WEB
DISCOVERING KNOWLEDGE FROM HYPERTEXT DATA

The Morgan Kaufmann Series in Data Management Systems

Series Editor: Jim Gray, Microsoft Research

Mining the Web: Discovering Knowledge from Hypertext Data
Soumen Chakrabarti

Advanced SQL: 1999—Understanding Object-Relational and Other Advanced Features
Jim Melton

Database Tuning: Principles, Experiments, and Troubleshooting Techniques
Dennis Shasha and Philippe Bonnet

SQL: 1999—Understanding Relational Language Components
Jim Melton and Alan R. Simon

Information Visualization in Data Mining and Knowledge Discovery
Edited by Usama Fayyad, Georges G. Grinstein, and Andreas Wierse

Transactional Information Systems: Theory, Algorithms, and the Practice of Concurrency Control and Recovery
Gerhard Weikum and Gottfried Vossen

Spatial Databases: With Application to GIS
Philippe Rigaux, Michel Scholl, and Agnès Voisard

Information Modeling and Relational Databases: From Conceptual Analysis to Logical Design
Terry Halpin

Component Database Systems
Edited by Klaus R. Dittrich and Andreas Geppert

Managing Reference Data in Enterprise Databases: Binding Corporate Data to the Wider World
Malcolm Chisholm

Data Mining: Concepts and Techniques
Jiawei Han and Micheline Kamber

Understanding SQL and Java Together: A Guide to SQLJ, JDBC, and Related Technologies
Jim Melton and Andrew Eisenberg

Database: Principles, Programming, and Performance, Second Edition
Patrick O'Neil and Elizabeth O'Neil

The Object Data Standard: ODMG 3.0
Edited by R. G. G. Cattell and Douglas Barry

Data on the Web: From Relations to Semistructured Data and XML
Serge Abiteboul, Peter Buneman, and Dan Suciu

Data Mining: Practical Machine Learning Tools and Techniques with Java Implementations
Ian Witten and Eibe Frank

Joe Celko's SQL for Smarties: Advanced SQL Programming, Second Edition
Joe Celko

Joe Celko's Data and Databases: Concepts in Practice
Joe Celko

Developing Time-Oriented Database Applications in SQL
Richard T. Snodgrass

Web Farming for the Data Warehouse
Richard D. Hackathorn

Database Modeling & Design, Third Edition
Toby J. Teorey

Management of Heterogeneous and Autonomous Database Systems
Edited by Ahmed Elmagarmid, Marek Rusinkiewicz, and Amit Sheth

Object-Relational DBMSs: Tracking the Next Great Wave, Second Edition
Michael Stonebraker and Paul Brown, with Dorothy Moore

MINING THE WEB
DISCOVERING KNOWLEDGE FROM HYPERTEXT DATA

Soumen Chakrabarti

Indian Institute of Technology, Bombay

MORGAN KAUFMANN PUBLISHERS

An Imprint of Elsevier

AMSTERDAM   BOSTON   LONDON   NEW YORK
OXFORD   PARIS   SAN DIEGO   SAN FRANCISCO
SINGAPORE   SYDNEY   TOKYO

Senior Editor Lothlórien Homet
Publishing Services Manager Edward Wade
Editorial Assistant Corina Derman
Cover Design Ross Carron Design
Text Design Frances Baca Design
Cover Image Kimihiro Kuno/Photonica
Composition and Technical Illustration Windfall Software, using ZzTEX
Copyeditor Sharilyn Hovind
Proofreader Jennifer McClain
Indexer Steve Rath
Printer The Maple-Vail Book Manufacturing Group

Morgan Kaufmann Publishers
An Imprint of Elsevier
340 Pine Street, Sixth Floor
San Francisco, CA 94104-3205
www.mkp.com

Library of Congress Control Number: 2002107241
ISBN-13: 978-1-55860-754-5
ISBN-10: 1-55860-754-4

This book is printed on acid-free paper.

FOREWORD

Jiawei Han
University of Illinois, Urbana-Champaign

The World Wide Web overwhelms us with immense amounts of widely distributed, interconnected, rich, and dynamic hypertext information. It has profoundly influenced many aspects of our lives, changing the ways we communicate, conduct business, shop, entertain, and so on. However, the abundant information on the Web is not stored in any systematically structured way, a situation which poses great challenges to those seeking to effectively search for high quality information and to uncover the knowledge buried in billions of Web pages. Web mining-or the automatic discovery of interesting and valuable information from the Web-has therefore become an important theme in data mining.

As a prominent researcher on Web mining, Soumen Chakrabarti has presented tutorials and surveys on this exciting topic at many international conferences. Now, after years of dedication, he presents us with this excellent book. *Mining the Web: Discovering Knowledge from Hypertext Data* is the first book solely dedicated to the theme of Web mining and if offers comprehensive coverage and a rigorous treatment. Chakrabarti starts with a thorough introduction to the infrastructure of the Web, including the mechanisms for Web crawling, Web page indexing, and keyword or similarity-based searching of Web contents. He then gives a systematic description of the foundations of Web mining, focusing on hypertext-based machine learning and data mining methods, such as clustering, collaborative filtering, supervised learning, and semi-supervised learning. After that, he presents the application of these fundamental principles to Web mining itself-especially Web linkage analysis-introducing the popular PageRank and HITS algorithms that substantially enhance the quality of keyword-based Web searches.

If you are a researcher, a Web technology developer, or just an interested reader curious about how to explore the endless potential of the Web, you will find this book provides both a solid technical background and state-of-the-art knowledge on this fascinating topic. It is a jewel in the collection of data mining and Web technology books. I hope you enjoy it.

CONTENTS

PREFACE

This book is about finding significant statistical patterns relating hypertext documents, topics, hyperlinks, and queries and using these patterns to connect users to information they seek. The Web has become a vast storehouse of knowledge, built in a decentralized yet collaborative manner. It is a living, growing, populist, and participatory medium of expression with no central editorship. This has positive and negative implications. On the positive side, there is widespread participation in authoring content. Compared to print or broadcast media, the ratio of content creators to the audience is more equitable. On the negative side, the heterogeneity and lack of structure makes it hard to frame queries and satisfy information needs. For many queries posed with the help of words and phrases, there are thousands of apparently relevant responses, but on closer inspection these turn out to be disappointing for all but the simplest queries. Queries involving nouns and noun phrases, where the information need is to find out about the named entity, are the simplest sort of information-hunting tasks. Only sophisticated users succeed with more complex queries—for instance, those that involve articles and prepositions to relate named objects, actions, and agents. If you are a regular seeker and user of Web information, this state of affairs needs no further description.

Detecting and exploiting *statistical dependencies* between terms, Web pages, and hyperlinks will be the central theme in this book. Such dependencies are also called *patterns*, and the act of searching for such patterns is called *machine learning*, or *data mining*. Here are some examples of machine learning for Web applications. Given a crawl of a substantial portion of the Web, we may be interested in constructing a topic directory like Yahoo!, perhaps detecting the emergence and decline of prominent topics with passing time. Once a topic directory is available, we may wish to assign freshly crawled pages and sites to suitable positions in the directory.

In this book, the data that we will "mine" will be very rich, comprising text, hypertext markup, hyperlinks, sites, and topic directories. This distinguishes the area of Web mining as a new and exciting field, although it also borrows liberally from traditional data analysis. As we shall see, useful information on the Web is accompanied by incredible levels of noise, but thankfully, the law of large numbers kicks in often enough that statistical analysis can make sense of the confusion. Our goal is to provide both the technical background and tools and tricks of the trade of Web content mining, which was developed roughly between 1995 and 2002, although it continues to advance. This book is addressed to those who are, or would like to become, researchers and innovative developers in this area.

Prerequisites and Contents

The contents of this book are targeted at fresh graduate students but are also quite suitable for senior undergraduates. The book is partly based on tutorials at SIGMOD 1999 and KDD 2000, a survey article in SIGKDD *Explorations*, invited lectures at ACL 1999 and ICDT 2001, and teaching a graduate elective at IIT Bombay in the spring of 2001. The general style is a mix of scientific and statistical programming with system engineering and optimizations. A background in elementary undergraduate statistics, algorithms, and networking should suffice to follow the material. The exposition also assumes that the reader is a regular user of search engines, topic directories, and Web content in general, and has some appreciation for the limitations of basic Web access based on clicking on links and typing keyword queries.

The chapters fall into three major parts. For concreteness, we start with some engineering issues: crawling, indexing, and keyword search. This part also gives us some basic know-how for efficiently representing, manipulating, and analyzing hypertext documents with computer programs. In the second part, which is the bulk of the book, we focus on machine learning for hypertext: the art of creating programs that seek out statistical relations between attributes extracted from Web documents. Such relations can be used to discover topic-based clusters from a collection of Web pages, assign a Web page to a predefined topic, or match a user's interest to Web sites. The third part is a collection of applications that draw upon the techniques discussed in the first two parts.

To make the presentation concrete, specific URLs are indicated throughout, but there is no saying how long they will remain accessible on the Web. Luckily, the Internet Archive will let you view old versions of pages at *www.archive.org/*, provided *this* URL does not get dated.

Omissions

The field of research underlying this book is in rapid flux. A book written at this juncture is guaranteed to miss out on important areas. At some point a snapshot must be taken to complete the project. A few omissions, however, are deliberate. Beyond bare necessities, I have not engaged in a study of protocols for representing and transferring content on the Internet and the Web. Readers are assumed to be reasonably familiar with HTML. For the purposes of this book, you do not need to understand the *XML* (*Extensible Markup Language*) standard much more deeply than HTML. There is also no treatment of Web application services, dynamic site management, or associated networking and data-processing technology.

I make no attempt to cover natural language (NL) processing, natural language understanding, or knowledge representation. This is largely because I do not know enough about natural language processing. NL techniques can now parse relatively well-formed sentences in many languages, disambiguate polysemous words with high accuracy, tag words in running text with part-of-speech information, represent NL documents in a canonical machine-usable form, and perform NL translation. Web search engines have been slow to embrace NL processing except as an explicit translation service. In this book, I will make occasional references to what has been called "ankle-deep semantics"—techniques that leverage semantic databases (e.g., as a dictionary or thesaurus) in shallow, efficient ways to improve keyword search.

Another missing area is Web *usage* mining. Optimizing large, high-flux Web sites to be visitor-friendly is nontrivial. Monitoring and analyzing the behavior of visitors in the past may lead to valuable insights into their information needs, and help in continually adapting the design of the site. Several companies have built systems integrated with Web servers, especially the kind that hosts e-commerce sites, to monitor and analyze traffic and propose site organization strategies. The array of techniques brought to bear on usage mining has a large overlap with traditional data mining in the relational data-warehousing scenario, for which excellent texts already exist.

Acknowledgments

I am grateful to many people for making this work possible. I was fortunate to associate with Byron Dom, Inderjit Dhillon, Dharmendra Modha, David Gibson, Dimitrios Gunopulos, Jon Kleinberg, Kevin McCurley, Nimrod Megiddo, and Prabhakar Raghavan at IBM Almaden Research Center, where some of the inventions described in this book were made between 1996 and 1999. I also acknowledge the extremely stimulating discussions I have had with researchers at the then Digital System Research Center in Palo Alto, California: Krishna

Bharat, Andrei Bröder, Monika Henzinger, Hannes Marais, and Mark Najork, some of whom have moved on to Google and AltaVista. Similar gratitude is also due to Gary Flake, C. Lee Giles, Steve Lawrence, and Dave Pennock at NEC Research, Princeton. Thanks also to Pedro Domingos, Susan Dumais, Ravindra Jaju, Ronny Lempel, David Lewis, Tom Mitchell, Mandar Mitra, Kunal Punera, Mehran Sahami, Eric Saund, and Amit Singhal for helpful discussions. Jiawei Han's text on data mining and his encouragement helped me decide to write this book. Krishna Bharat, Lyle Ungar, Karen Watterson, Ian Witten, and other, anonymous, referees have greatly enhanced the quality of the manuscript.

Closer to home, Sunita Sarawagi and S. Sudarshan gave valuable feedback. Together with Pushpak Bhattacharya and Krithi Ramamritham, they kept up my enthusiasm during this long project in the face of many adversities. I am grateful to Tata Consultancy Services for their generous support through the Lab for Intelligent Internet Research during the preparation of the manuscript. T. P. Chandran offered invaluable administrative help. I thank Diane Cerra, Lothlórien Homet, Edward Wade, Mona Buehler, Corina Derman, and all the other members of the Morgan Kaufmann team for their patience with many delays in the schedule and their superb production job. I regret forgetting to express my gratitude to anyone else who has contributed to this work. The gratitude does live on in my heart. Finally, I wish to thank my wife, Sunita Sarawagi, and my parents, Sunil and Arati Chakrabarti, for their constant support and encouragement.

CHAPTER 1

INTRODUCTION

The World Wide Web is the largest and most widely known repository of hypertext. Hypertext documents contain text and generally embed hyperlinks to other documents distributed across the Web. Today, the Web comprises billions of documents, authored by millions of diverse people, edited by no one in particular, and distributed over millions of computers that are connected by telephone lines, optical fibers, and radio modems. It is a wonder that the Web works at all. Yet it is rapidly assisting and supplementing newspapers, radio, television, and telephone, the postal system, schools and colleges, libraries, physical workplaces, and even the sites of commerce and governance.

A brief history of hypertext and the Web. Citation, a form of hyperlinking, is as old as written language itself. The Talmud, with its heavy use of annotations and nested commentary, and the Ramayana and Mahabharata, with their branching, nonlinear discourse, are ancient examples of hypertext. Dictionaries and encyclopedias can be viewed as a self-contained network of textual nodes joined by referential links. Words and concepts are described by appealing to other words and concepts. In modern times (1945), Vannevar Bush is credited with the first design of a photo-electrical-mechanical storage and computing device called a Memex (for "memory extension"), which could create and help follow hyperlinks across documents. Doug Engelbart and Ted Nelson were other early pioneers; Ted Nelson coined the term *hypertext* in 1965 [160] and created the Xanadu hypertext system with robust two-way hyperlinks, version management, controversy management, annotation, and copyright management.

In 1980 Tim Berners-Lee, a consultant with CERN (the European organization for nuclear research) wrote a program to create and browse along named, typed bidirectional links between documents in a collection. By 1990, a more general proposal to support hypertext repositories was circulating in CERN, and by late 1990, Berners-Lee had started work on a graphical user interface (GUI) to hypertext, and named the program the "World Wide Web." By 1992, other GUI interfaces such as Erwise and Viola were available. The Midas GUI was added to the pool by Tony Johnson at the Stanford Linear Accelerator Center in early 1993.

In February 1993, Mark Andressen at NCSA (National Center for Supercomputing Applications, *www.ncsa.uiuc.edu/*) completed an initial version of Mosaic, a hypertext GUI that would run on the popular X Window System used on UNIX machines. Behind the scenes, CERN also developed and improved HTML, a markup language for rendering hypertext, and Http, the hypertext transport protocol for sending HTML and other data over the Internet, and implemented a server of hypertext documents called the CERN HTTPD. Although stand-alone hypertext browsing systems had existed for decades, this combination of simple content and transport standards, coupled with user-friendly graphic browsers led to the widespread adoption of this new hypermedium. Within 1993, Http traffic grew from 0.1% to over 1% of the Internet traffic on the National Science Foundation backbone. There were a few hundred Http servers by the end of 1993.

Between 1991 and 1994, the load on the first Http server (*info.cern.ch*) increased by a factor of one thousand (see Figure 1.1(a)). The year 1994 was a landmark: the Mosaic Communications Corporation (later Netscape) was founded, the first World Wide Web conference was held, and MIT and CERN agreed to set up the World Wide Web Consortium (W3C). The following years (1995–2001) featured breakneck innovation, irrational exuberance, and return to reason, as is well known. We will review some of the other major events later in this chapter.

A populist, participatory medium. As the Web has grown in size and diversity, it has acquired immense value as an active and evolving repository of knowledge. For the first time, there is a medium where the number of writers—disseminators of facts, ideas, and opinions—starts to approach the same order of magnitude as the number of readers. To date, both numbers still fall woefully short of representing all of humanity,and its languages, cultures, and aspirations. Still, it is a definitive move toward recording many areas of human thought and endeavor in a manner

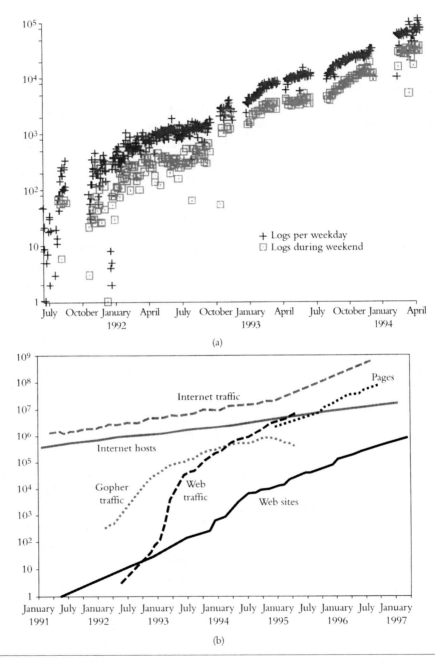

FIGURE 1.1 The early days of the Web: CERN Http traffic grows by a factor of 1000 between 1991 and 1994 (a) (image courtesy W3C); the number of servers grows from a few hundred to a million between 1991 and 1997 (b) (image courtesy Nielsen [165]).

far more populist and accessible than before. Although media moguls have quickly staked out large territories in cyberspace as well, the political system is still far more anarchic (or democratic, depending on the point of view) than conventional print or broadcast media. Ideas and opinions that would never see the light of day in conventional media can live vibrant lives in cyberspace. Despite growing concerns in legal and political circles, censorship is limited in practice to only the most flagrant violations of "proper" conduct.

Just as biochemical processes define the evolution of genes, mass media defines the evolution of memes, a word coined by Richard Dawkins to describe ideas, theories, habits, skills, languages, and artistic expressions that spread from person to person by imitation. Memes are replicators—just like genes—that are copied imperfectly and selected on the basis of viability, giving rise to a new kind of evolutionary process. Memes have driven the invention of writing, printing, and broadcasting, and now they have constructed the Internet. "Free speech online," chain letters, and email viruses are some of the commonly recognized memes on the Internet, but there are many, many others. For any broad topic, memetic processes shape authorship, hyperlinking behavior, and resulting popularity of Web pages. In the words of Susan Blackmore, a prominent researcher of memetics, "From the meme's-eye point of view the World Wide Web is a vast playground for their own selfish propagation."

The crisis of abundance and diversity. The richness of Web content has also made it progressively more difficult to leverage the value of information. The new medium has no inherent requirements of editorship and approval from authority. Institutional editorship addresses policy more than form and content. In addition, storage and networking resources are cheap. These factors have led to a largely liberal and informal culture of content generation and dissemination. (Most universities and corporations will not prevent an employee from writing at reasonable length about their latest kayaking expedition on their personal homepage, hosted on a server maintained by the employer.) Because the Internet spans nations and cultures, there is little by way of a uniform civil code. Legal liability for disseminating unverified or even libelous information is practically nonexistent, compared to print or broadcast media.

Whereas the unregulated atmosphere has contributed to the volume and diversity of Web content, it has led to a great deal of redundancy and nonstandard form and content. The lowest common denominator model for the Web is rather primitive: the Web is a set of documents, where each document is a multiset (bag) of terms. Basic search engines let us find pages that contain or do not contain specified keywords and phrases. This leaves much to be desired. For most broad queries (e.g., "java" or "kayaking") there are millions of qualifying pages. By "qualifying," all we mean is that the page contains those, or closely related, keywords. There is little support to disambiguate short queries like *java* unless embedded in a longer, more specific query. There is no authoritative information about the reliability and prestige of a Web document or a site.

Uniform accessibility of documents intended for diverse readership also complicates matters. Outside cyberspace, bookstores and libraries are quite helpful in guiding people with different backgrounds to different floors, aisles, and shelves. The amateur gardener and a horticulture professional know well how to walk their different ways. This is harder on the Web, because most sites and documents are just as accessible as any other, and conventional search services to date have little support for adapting to the background of specific users.

The Web is also adversarial in that commercial interests routinely influence the operation of Web search and analysis tools. Most Web users pay only for their network access, and little, if anything, for the published content that they use. Consequently, the upkeep of content depends on the sale of products, services, and online advertisements.[1] This results in the introduction of a large volume of ads. Sometimes these are explicit ad hyperlinks. At other times they are more subtle, biasing apparently noncommercial matter in insidious ways. There are businesses dedicated exclusively to raising the rating of their clients as judged by prominent search engines, officially called *search engine optimization*.

The goal of this book. In this book I seek to study and develop programs that connect people to the information they seek from the Web. The techniques that are examined will be more generally applicable to any hypertext corpus. I will call hypertext data *semistructured* or *unstructured*, because they do not have a compact or precise description of data items. Such a description is called a *schema*, which is mandatory for relational databases. The second major difference is that unstructured and semistructured hypertext has a very large number of attributes, if each lexical unit (word or token) is considered as a potential attribute. (We will return to a comparison of data mining for structured and unstructured domains in Section 1.6.)

---

1. It is unclear if such revenue models will be predominant even a few years from now.

The Web is used in many ways other than authoring and seeking information, but we will largely limit our attention to this aspect. We will not be directly concerned with other modes of usage, such as Web-enabled email, news, or chat services, although chances are some of the techniques we study may be applicable to those situations. Web-enabled transactions on relational databases are also outside the scope of this book.

We shall proceed from standard ways to access the Web (using keyword search engines) to relatively sophisticated analyses of text and hyperlinks in later chapters. Machine learning is a large and deep body of knowledge we shall tap liberally, together with overlapping and related work in pattern recognition and data mining. Broadly, these areas are concerned with searching for, confirming, explaining, and exploiting nonobvious and statistically significant constraints and patterns between attributes of large volumes of potentially noisy data. Identifying the main topic(s) discussed in a document, modeling a user's topics of interest, and recommending content to a user based on past behavior and that of other users all come under the broad umbrella of machine learning and data mining. These are well-established fields, but the novelty of highly noisy hypertext data does necessitate some notable innovations.

The following sections briefly describe the sequence of material in the chapters of this book.

1.1   Crawling and Indexing

We shall visit a large variety of programs that process textual and hypertextual information in diverse ways, but the capability to quickly fetch a large number of Web pages into a local repository and to index them based on keywords is required in many applications. Large-scale programs that fetch tens of thousands of Web pages per second are called *crawlers, spiders, Web robots,* or *bots.* Crawling is usually performed to subsequently index the documents fetched. Together, a crawler and an index form key components of a Web search engine.

One of the earliest search engines to be built was Lycos, founded in January 1994, operational in June 1994, and a publicly traded company in April 1996. Lycos was born from a research project at Carnegie Mellon University by Dr. Michael Mauldin. Another search engine, WebCrawler, went online in spring 1994. It was also started as a research project, at the University of Washington, by Brian Pinkerton. During the spring of 1995, Louis Monier, Joella Paquette, and Paul Flaherty at Digital Equipment Corporation's research labs developed AltaVista, one of the best-known search engines with claims to over 60 patents, the highest in this area so far. Launched in December 1995, AltaVista started fielding two million queries a day within three weeks.

Many others followed the search engine pioneers and offered various innovations. HotBot and Inktomi feature a distributed architecture for crawling and storing pages. Excite could analyze similarity between keywords and match queries to documents having no syntactic match. Many search engines started offering a "more like this" link with each response. Search engines remain some of the most visited sites today.

Chapter 2 looks at how to write crawlers of moderate scale and capability and addresses various performance issues. Then, Chapter 3 discusses how to process the data into an index suitable for answering queries. Indexing enables keyword and phrase queries and Boolean combinations of such queries. Unlike relational databases, the query engine cannot simply return all qualifying responses in arbitrary order. The user implicitly expects the responses to be ordered in a way that maximizes the chances of the first few responses satisfying the information need. These chapters can be skimmed if you are more interested in mining per se; more in-depth treatment of information retrieval (IR) can be found in many excellent classic texts cited later.

1.2 Topic Directories

The first wave of innovations was related to basic infrastructure comprising crawlers and search engines. Topic directories were the next significant feature to gain visibility.

In 1994, Jerry Yang and David Filo, Ph.D. students at Stanford University, created the Yahoo![2] directory (*www.yahoo.com/*) to help their friends locate useful Web sites, growing by the thousands each day. Srinija Srinivasan, another Stanford alum, provided the expertise to create and maintain the treelike branching hierarchies that steer people to content. By April 1995, the project that had started out as a hobby was incorporated as a company.

The dazzling success of Yahoo! should not make one forget that organizing knowledge into ontologies is an ancient art, descended from philosophy and epistemology. An ontology defines a vocabulary, the entities referred to by elements in the vocabulary, and relations between the entities. The entities may be

---

2. Yahoo! is an acronym for "Yet Another Hierarchical Officious Oracle!"

fine-grained, as in WordNet, a lexical network for English, or they may be relatively coarse-grained topics, as in the Yahoo! topic directory.

The paradigm of browsing a directory of topics arranged in a tree where children represent specializations of the parent topic is now pervasive. The average computer user is familiar with hierarchies of directories and files, and this familiarity carries over rather naturally to topic taxonomies. Following Yahoo!'s example, a large number of content portals have added support for hosting topic taxonomies. Some organizations (e.g., Yahoo!) employ a team of editors to maintain the taxonomy; others (e.g., About.com and the Open Directory Project (*dmoz.org/*) are more decentralized and work through a loosely coupled network of volunteers. A large fraction of Web search engines now incorporate some form of taxonomy-based search as well.

Topic directories offer value in two forms. The obvious contribution is the cataloging of Web content, which makes it easier to search (e.g., SOCKS as in the firewall protocol is easier to distinguish from the clothing item). Collecting links into homogeneous clusters also offers an implicit "more like this" mechanism: once the user has located a few sites of interest, others belonging to the same, sibling, or ancestor categories may also be of interest. The second contribution is in the form of quality control. Because the links in a directory usually go through editorial scrutiny, however cursory, they tend to reflect the more authoritative and popular sections of the Web. As we shall see, both of these forms of human input can be exploited well by Web mining programs.

1.3 Clustering and Classification

Topic directories built with human effort (e.g., Yahoo! or the Open Directory) immediately raise a question: Can they be constructed automatically out of an amorphous corpus of Web pages, such as collected by a crawler? We study one aspect of this problem, called *clustering,* or *unsupervised learning,* in Chapter 4. Roughly speaking, a clustering algorithm discovers groups in the set of documents such that documents within a group are more similar than documents across groups.

Clustering is a classic area of machine learning and pattern recognition [72]. However, a few complications arise in the hypertext domain. A basic problem is that different people do not agree about what they expect a clustering algorithm to output for a given data set. This is partly because they are implicitly using different similarity measures, and it is difficult to guess what their similarity measures are because the number of attributes is so large.

Hypertext is also rich in features: textual tokens, markup tags, URLs, host names in URLs, substrings in the URLs that could be meaningful words, and host IP addresses, to name a few. How should they contribute to the similarity measure so that we can get good clusterings? We study these and other related problems in Chapter 4.

Once a taxonomy is created, it is necessary to maintain it with example URLs for each topic as the Web changes and grows. Human effort to this end may be greatly assisted by supervised learning, or classification, which is the subject of Chapter 5. A classifier is first trained with a corpus of documents that are labeled with topics. At this stage, the classifier analyzes correlations between the labels and other document attributes to form models. Later, the classifier is presented with unlabeled instances and is required to estimate their topics reliably.

Like clustering, classification is also a classic operation in machine learning and data mining. Again, the number, variety, and nonuniformity of features make the classification problem interesting in the hypertext domain. We shall study many flavors of classifiers and discuss their strengths and weaknesses.

Although research prototypes abound, clustering and classification software is not as widely used as basic keyword search services. IBM's Lotus Notes text-processing system and its Intelligent Miner for Text include some state-of-the-art clustering and classification packages. Verity's K2 text-processing product also includes a text categorization tool. We will review other systems in the respective chapters.

Clustering and classification are at two opposite extremes with regard to the extent of human supervision they need. Real-life applications are somewhere in between, because unlabeled data is easy to collect but labeling data is onerous. In our preliminary discussion above, a classifier trains on labeled instances and is presented unlabeled test instances only after the training phase is completed. Might it help to have the test instances available while training? In a different setting specific to hypertext, if the labels of documents in the link neighborhood of a test document are known, can that help determine the label of the test document with higher accuracy? We study such issues in Chapter 6.

1.4 Hyperlink Analysis

Although classic information retrieval has provided extremely valuable core technology for Web searching, the combined challenges of abundance, redundancy, and misrepresentation have been unprecedented in the history of IR. By 1996, it was clear that relevance-ranking techniques from classic IR were not sufficient for Web searching. Web queries were very short (two to three terms) compared with IR benchmarks (dozens of terms). Short queries, unless they include highly selective keywords, tend to be broad because they do not embed enough information to pinpoint responses. Such broad queries matched thousands to millions of pages, but sometimes missed the best responses because there was no direct keyword match. The entry pages of Toyota and Honda do not explicitly say that they are Japanese car companies. At one time, the query "Web browser" failed to match the entry pages of Netscape Corporation or Microsoft's Internet Explorer page, but there were thousands of pages with hyperlinks to these sites with the term *browser* somewhere close to the link.

It was becoming clear that the assumption of a flat corpus, common in IR, was not taking advantage of the structure of the Web graph. In particular, relevance to a query is not sufficient if responses are abundant. In the arena of academic publications, the number of citations to a paper is an indicator of its prestige. In the fall of 1996, Larry Page and Sergey Brin, Ph.D. students at Stanford University, applied a variant of this idea to a crawl of 60 million pages to assign a prestige score called PageRank (after Page). Then they built a search system called Backrub. In 1997, Backrub went online as Google (*www.google.com/*). Around the same time, Jon Kleinberg, then a researcher at IBM Research, invented a similar system called HITS (for *hyperlink induced topic search*). HITS assigned *two* scores to each node in a hypertext graph. One was a measure of authority, similar to Google's prestige, the other was a measure of a node being a comprehensive catalog of links to good authorities.

Chapter 7 is a study of these and other algorithms for analyzing the link structure of hypertext graphs. The analysis of social networks is quite mature, and so is one special case of social network analysis, called *bibliometry,* which is concerned with the bibliographic citation graph of academic papers. The initial specifications of these pioneering hyperlink-assisted ranking systems have close cousins in social network analysis and bibliometry, and have elegant underpinnings in the linear algebra and graph-clustering literature. The PageRank and HITS algorithms have led to a flurry of research activity in this area (by now known generally as *topic distillation*) that continues to this day. This book follows this literature in some detail and shows how topic-distillation algorithms are adapting to the idioms of Web authorship and linking styles. Apart from algorithmic research, the book covers techniques for Web measurements and notable results therefrom.

1.5 Resource Discovery and Vertical Portals

Despite their great sophistication, Web search tools still cannot match an experienced librarian or researcher finding relevant papers in a research area. At some stage, it seems inevitable that the "shallow" syntactic and statistical analysis will fall short of representing and querying knowledge.

Unfortunately, language analysis does not scale to billions of documents yet. We can counter this by throwing more hardware at the problem. One way to do this is to use federations of crawling and search services, each specializing in specific topical areas. Domain specialists in those areas can best help build the lexicon and tune the algorithms for the corresponding communities.

Each member of such a federation needs to be a goal-driven information forager. It needs to locate sites and pages related to its broad umbrella of topics, while minimizing resources lost on fetching and inspecting irrelevant pages. Information thus collected may be used to host "vertical portals" that cater to a special-interest group, such as "kayaking" or "high-end audio equipment."

Chapter 8 presents several recent techniques for goal-driven Web resource discovery that build upon the crawling and learning techniques developed in earlier chapters.

Much remains to be done beyond a statistical analysis of the Web. Clearly the goal is substantial maturity in extracting, from syntactic features, semantic knowledge in forms that can be manipulated automatically. Important applications include structured information extraction (e.g., "monitor business news for acquisitions, or maintain an internal portal of competitors' Web sites") and processing natural language queries (e.g., "even though I updated /etc/lilo.conf and /etc/fstab, my computer uses /dev/sda1 rather than /dev/sdb1 as the boot partition—why?"). For some of these problems, no practical solution is in sight; for others, progress is being made. We will briefly explore the landscape of ongoing research in the final Chapter 9.

1.6 Structured vs. Unstructured Data Mining

Is there a need for a separate community and literature on Web mining? I have noted that Web mining borrows heavily from IR, machine learning, statistics, pattern recognition, and data mining, and there are dozens of excellent texts and conferences in those areas. Nevertheless, I feel that the new medium of Web publishing has resulted in, and will continue to inspire, significant innovations over and above the contribution of the classic research areas.

Large volumes of easily accessible data are crucial to the success of any data analysis research. Although there is a decades-old community engaged in hyper-text research, most of the exciting developments traced in this book were enabled only after Web authorship exploded. Even traditional data mining researchers are increasingly engaging in Web analysis because data is readily available, the data is very rich in features and patterns, and the positive effects of successful analysis are immediately evident to the researcher, who is also often an end user.

In traditional data mining, which is usually coupled with data warehousing systems, data is structured and relational in nature, having well-defined tables, attributes (columns), tuples (rows), keys, and constraints. Most data sets in the machine learning domain (e.g., the well-known University of California at Irvine data set) are structured as tables as well.

A feature that is unique to the Web is the spontaneous formation and evolution of topic-induced graph clusters and hyperlink-induced communities in the Web graph. Hyperlinks add significant amounts of useful information beyond text for search, relevance ranking, classification, and clustering,

Another feature is that well-formed HTML pages represent a tree structure, with text and attributes embedded in the nodes. A properly parsed HTML page gives a *tag-tree,* which may reveal valuable clues to content-mining algorithms through layout and table directives. For example, the entry page of an online newspaper undergoes temporal changes in a very interesting fashion: the masthead is static, the advertisements change almost every time the page is accessed, and breaking news items drift slowly through the day. Links to prominent sections remain largely the same, but their content changes maybe once a day. The tag-tree is a great help in "taking the page apart" and selecting and analyzing specific portions, as we shall see in Chapters 7 and 8.

In a perfectly engineered world, Web pages will be written in a more sophisticated markup language with a universally accepted metadata description format. XML (*www.w3.org/XML/*) and RDF (*Resource Description Framework*; *www.w3.org/RDF/*) have made great strides in that direction, especially in specific domains like e-commerce, electronic components, genomics, and molecular chemistry. I believe that the Web will always remain adventurous enough that its most interesting and timely content can never be shoehorned into rigid schemata. While I am by no means downplaying the importance of XML and associated standards, this book is more about *discovering* patterns that are spontaneously driven by semantics, rather than *designing* patterns by fiat.

1.7 **Bibliographic Notes**

The Web is befittingly a great source of information on its history. The W3C Web site (*www.w3c.org/*) and the Internet Society (*www.isoc.org/internet-history/*) have authoritative material tracing the development of the Web's greatest innovations. Nielsen records many such events from 1990 to 1995 as well [165]. Search Engine Watch (*searchenginewatch.com/*) has a wealth of details about crawler and search engine technology. Vannevar Bush proposed the Memex in his seminal paper "As We May Think" [29]. Details about Xanadu can be found at *www.xanadu.net/* and Nelson's book *Literary Machines* [161]. The references to memetics are from the intriguing books by Dawkins [62] and Blackmore [19].

CRAWLING THE WEB

The World Wide Web, or the Web for short, is a collection of billions of documents written in a way that enables them to cite each other using *hyperlinks*, which is why they are a form of *hypertext*. These documents, or *Web pages*, are typically a few thousand characters long, written in a diversity of languages, and cover essentially all topics of human endeavor. Web pages are served through the Internet using the *hypertext transport protocol* (Http) to client computers, where they can be viewed using *browsers*. Http is built on top of the *transport control protocol* (TCP), which provides reliable data streams to be transmitted from one computer to another across the Internet.

Throughout this book, we shall study how automatic programs can analyze hypertext documents and the networks induced by the hyperlinks that connect them. To do so, it is usually necessary to fetch the pages to the computer where those programs will be run. This is the job of a *crawler* (also called a *spider*, *robot*, or *bot*). In this chapter we will study in detail how crawlers work. If you are more interested in how pages are indexed and analyzed, you can skip this chapter with hardly any loss of continuity.

I will assume that you have basic familiarity with computer networking using TCP, to the extent of writing code to open and close sockets and read and write data using a socket. We will focus on the organization of large-scale crawlers, which must handle millions of servers and billions of pages.

2.1   **HTML and HTTP Basics**

Web pages are written in a tagged markup language called the *hypertext markup language* (HTML). HTML lets the author specify layout and typeface, embed diagrams, and create hyperlinks. A hyperlink is expressed as an *anchor* tag with an href attribute, which names another page using a *uniform resource locator* (URL), like this:

```
<a href="http://www.cse.iitb.ac.in/">The IIT Bombay
Computer Science Department</a>
```

In its simplest form, the target URL contains a protocol field (http), a server hostname (*www.cse.iitb.ac.in*), and a file path (/, the "root" of the published file system).

A Web browser such as Netscape Communicator or Internet Explorer will let the reader *click* the computer mouse on the hyperlink. The click is translated transparently by the browser into a network request to fetch the target page using Http.

A browser will fetch and display a Web page given a complete URL like the one above, but to reveal the underlying network protocol, we will (ab)use the telnet command available on UNIX machines, as shown in Figure 2.1. First the telnet client (as well as any Web browser) has to resolve the server hostname *www.cse.iitb.ac.in* to an Internet address of the form 144.16.111.14 (called an *IP address*, IP standing for *Internet protocol*) to be able to contact the server using TCP. The mapping from name to address is done using the *Domain Name Service* (DNS), a distributed database of name-to-IP mappings maintained at known servers [202]. Next, the client connects to port 80, the default Http port, on the server. The underlined text is entered by the user (this is transparently provided by Web browsers). The *slanted* text is called the *MIME header*. (MIME stands for *multipurpose Internet mail extensions*, and is a metadata standard for email and Web content transfer.) The ends of the request and response headers are indicated by the sequence CR-LF-CR-LF (double newline, written in C/C++ code as "\r\n\r\n" and shown as the blank lines).

Browsing is a useful but restrictive means of finding information. Given a page with many links to follow, it would be unclear and painstaking to explore them in search of a specific information need. A better option is to *index* all the text so that information needs may be satisfied by keyword searches (as in library catalogs). To perform indexing, we need to fetch all the pages to be indexed using a crawler.

```
% telnet www.cse.iitb.ac.in 80
Trying 144.16.111.14...
Connected to www.cse.iitb.ac.in.
Escape character is 'Ĵ'.
GET / Http/1.0

Http/1.1 200 OK
Date: Sat, 13 Jan 2001 09:01:02 GMT
Server: Apache/1.3.0 (Unix) PHP/3.0.4
Last-Modified: Wed, 20 Dec 2000 13:18:38 GMT
ETag: "5c248-153d-3a40b1ae"
Accept-Ranges: bytes
Content-Length: 5437
Connection: close
Content-Type: text/html
X-Pad: avoid browser bug

<html>
<head><title>IIT Bombay CSE Department Home Page</title></head>
<body>...<a href="http://www.iitb.ac.in">IIT Bombay</a>...
</body></html>
Connection closed by foreign host.
%
```

FIGURE 2.1   Fetching a Web page using telnet and Http.

2.2 Crawling Basics

How does a crawler fetch "all" Web pages? Before the advent of the Web, traditional text collections such as bibliographic databases and journal abstracts were provided to the indexing system directly, say, on magnetic tape or disk. In contrast, there is no catalog of all accessible URLs on the Web. The only way to collect URLs is to scan collected pages for hyperlinks to other pages that have not been collected yet. This is the basic principle of crawlers. They start from a given set of URLs, progressively fetch and scan them for new URLs (*outlinks*), and then fetch these pages in turn, in an endless cycle. New URLs found thus represent potentially pending work for the crawler. The set of pending work expands quickly as the crawl proceeds, and implementers prefer to write this data to disk to relieve main memory as well as guard against data loss in the event of a crawler crash. There is no guarantee that all accessible Web pages will be located in

this fashion; indeed, the crawler may never halt, as pages will be added continually even as it is running. Apart from outlinks, pages contain text; this is submitted to a text indexing system (described in Section 3.1) to enable information retrieval using keyword searches.

It is quite simple to write a basic crawler, but a great deal of engineering goes into industry-strength crawlers that fetch a substantial fraction of all accessible Web documents. Web search companies like AltaVista, Northern Light, Inktomi, and the like do publish white papers on their crawling technologies, but piecing together the technical details is not easy. There are only a few documents in the public domain that give some detail, such as a paper about AltaVista's Mercator crawler [108] and a description of Google's first-generation crawler [26]. Based partly on such information, Figure 2.2 should be a reasonably accurate block diagram of a large-scale crawler.

The central function of a crawler is to fetch many pages at the same time, in order to overlap the delays involved in

1. Resolving the hostname in the URL to an IP address using DNS

2. Connecting a socket to the server and sending the request

3. Receiving the requested page in response

together with time spent in scanning pages for outlinks and saving pages to a local document repository. Typically, for short pages, DNS lookup and socket connection take a large portion of the processing time, which depends on round-trip times on the Internet and is generally unmitigated by buying more bandwidth.

The entire life cycle of a page fetch, as listed above, is managed by a logical *thread* of control. This need not be a thread or process provided by the operating system, but may be specifically programmed for this purpose for higher efficiency. In Figure 2.2 this is shown as the "Page fetching context/thread," which starts with DNS resolution and finishes when the entire page has been fetched via Http (or some error condition arises). After the fetch context has completed its task, the page is usually stored in compressed form to disk or tape and also scanned for outgoing hyperlinks (hereafter called "outlinks"). Outlinks are checked into a work pool. A load manager checks out enough work from the pool to maintain network utilization without overloading it. This process continues until the crawler has collected a "sufficient" number of pages. It is difficult to define "sufficient" in general. For an intranet of moderate size, a complete crawl may well be possible. For the Web, there are indirect estimates of the number

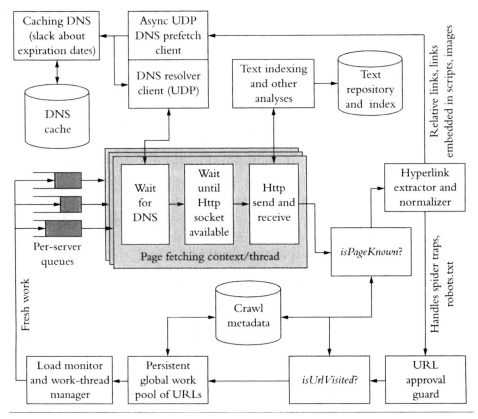

FIGURE 2.2 Typical anatomy of a large-scale crawler.

of publicly accessible pages, and a crawler may be run until a substantial fraction is fetched. Organizations with less networking or storage resources may need to stop the crawl for lack of space, or to build indices frequently enough to be useful.

2.3 Engineering Large-Scale Crawlers

In the previous section we discussed a basic crawler. Large-scale crawlers that send requests to millions of Web sites and collect hundreds of millions of pages need a great deal of care to achieve high performance. In this section we will discuss the important performance and reliability considerations for a large-scale crawler. Before we dive into the details, it will help to list the main concerns:

- Because a single page fetch may involve several seconds of network latency, it is essential to fetch many pages (typically hundreds to thousands) at the same time to utilize the network bandwidth available.

- Many simultaneous fetches are possible only if the DNS lookup is streamlined to be highly concurrent, possibly replicated on a few DNS servers.

- Multiprocessing or multithreading provided by the operating system is not the best way to manage the multiple fetches owing to high overheads. The best bet is to explicitly encode the state of a fetch context in a data structure and use asynchronous sockets, which do not block the process/thread using it, but can be polled to check for completion of network transfers.

- Care is needed to extract URLs and eliminate duplicates to reduce redundant fetches and to avoid "spider traps"—hyperlink graphs constructed carelessly or malevolently to keep a crawler trapped in that graph, fetching what can potentially be an infinite set of "fake" URLs.

2.3.1   **DNS Caching, Prefetching, and Resolution**

Address resolution is a significant bottleneck that needs to be overlapped with other activities of the crawler to maintain throughput. In an ordinary local area network, a DNS server running on a modest PC can perform name mappings for hundreds of workstations. A crawler is much more demanding as it may generate dozens of mapping requests per second. Moreover, many crawlers avoid fetching too many pages from one server, which might overload it; rather, they spread their access over many servers at a time. This lowers the locality of access to the DNS cache. For all these reasons, large-scale crawlers usually include a customized DNS component for better performance. This comprises a custom client for address resolution and possibly a caching server and a prefetching client.

First, the DNS caching server should have a large cache that should be persistent across DNS restarts, but residing largely in memory if possible. A desktop PC with 256 MB of RAM and a disk cache of a few GB will be adequate for a caching DNS, but it may help to have a few (say, two to three) of these. Normally, a DNS cache has to honor an expiration date set on mappings provided by its upstream DNS server or peer. For a crawler, strict adherence to expiration dates is not too important. (However, the DNS server should try to keep its mapping as up to date as possible by remapping the entries in cache during relatively idle time intervals.) Second, many clients for DNS resolution are coded poorly. Most UNIX systems provide an implementation of gethostbyname (the DNS client

API—application program interface), which cannot concurrently handle multiple outstanding requests. Therefore, the crawler cannot issue many resolution requests together and poll at a later time for completion of individual requests, which is critical for acceptable performance. Furthermore, if the system-provided client is used, there is no way to distribute load among a number of DNS servers. For all these reasons, many crawlers choose to include their own custom client for DNS name resolution. The Mercator crawler from Compaq System Research Center reduced the time spent in DNS from as high as 87% to a modest 25% by implementing a custom client. The ADNS asynchronous DNS client library[1] is ideal for use in crawlers.

In spite of these optimizations, a large-scale crawler will spend a substantial fraction of its network time not waiting for Http data transfer, but for address resolution. For every hostname that has not been resolved before (which happens frequently with crawlers), the local DNS may have to go across many network hops to fill its cache for the first time. To overlap this unavoidable delay with useful work, *prefetching* can be used. When a page that has just been fetched is parsed, a stream of HREFs is extracted. Right at this time, that is, even before any of the corresponding URLs are fetched, hostnames are extracted from the HREF targets, and DNS resolution requests are made to the caching server. The prefetching client is usually implemented using UDP (*user datagram protocol*, a connectionless, packet-based communication protocol that does not guarantee packet delivery) instead of TCP, and it does not wait for resolution to be completed. The request serves only to fill the DNS cache so that resolution will be fast when the page is actually needed later on.

2.3.2 Multiple Concurrent Fetches

Research-scale crawlers fetch up to hundreds of pages per second. Web-scale crawlers fetch hundreds to thousands of pages per second. Because a single download may take several seconds, crawlers need to open many socket connections to different Http servers at the same time. There are two approaches to managing multiple concurrent connections: using multithreading and using nonblocking sockets with event handlers. Since crawling performance is usually limited by network and disk, multi-CPU machines generally do not help much.

---

1. See *www.chiark.greenend.org.uk/~ian/adns/*.

Multithreading

After name resolution, each logical thread creates a client socket, connects the socket to the Http service on a server, sends the Http request header, then reads the socket (by calling recv) until no more characters are available, and finally closes the socket. The simplest programming paradigm is to use *blocking* system calls, which suspend the client process until the call completes and data is available in user-specified buffers.

This programming paradigm remains unchanged when each logical thread is assigned to a physical thread of control provided by the operating system, for example, through the pthreads multithreading library available on most UNIX systems [164]. When one thread is suspended waiting for a connect, send, or recv to complete, other threads can execute. Threads are not generated dynamically for each request; rather, a fixed number of threads is allocated in advance. These threads use a shared concurrent work-queue to find pages to fetch. Each thread manages its own control state and stack, but shares data areas. Therefore, some implementers prefer to use processes rather than threads so that a disastrous crash of one process does not corrupt the state of other processes.

There are two problems with the concurrent thread/process approach. First, mutual exclusion and concurrent access to data structures exact some performance penalty. Second, as threads/processes complete page fetches and start modifying the document repository and index concurrently, they may lead to a great deal of interleaved, random input-output on disk, which results in slow disk seeks.

The second performance problem may be severe. To choreograph disk access and to transfer URLs and page buffers between the work pool, threads, and the repository writer, the numerous fetching threads/processes must use one of shared memory buffers, interprocess communication, semaphores, locks, or short files. The exclusion and serialization overheads can become serious bottlenecks.

Nonblocking sockets and event handlers

Another approach is to use *nonblocking* sockets. With nonblocking sockets, a connect, send, or recv call returns immediately without waiting for the network operation to complete. The status of the network operation may be polled separately. In particular, a nonblocking socket provides the select system call, which lets the application suspend and wait until more data can be read from or written to the socket, timing out after a prespecified deadline. select can in fact monitor several sockets at the same time, suspending the calling process until *any one* of the sockets can be read or written.

Each active socket can be associated with a data structure that maintains the state of the logical thread waiting for some operation to complete on that socket, and callback routines that complete the processing once the fetch is completed. When a select call returns with a socket identifier, the corresponding state record is used to continue processing. The data structure also contains the page in memory as it is being fetched from the network. This is not very expensive in terms of RAM. One thousand concurrent fetches on 10 KB pages would still use only 10 MB of RAM.

Why is using select more efficient? The completion of page fetching threads is *serialized*, and the code that completes processing the page (scanning for outlinks, saving to disk) is not interrupted by other completions (which may happen but are not detected until we explicitly select again). Consider the pool of freshly discovered URLs. If we used threads or processes, we would need to protect this pool against simultaneous access with some sort of mutual exclusion device. With selects, there is no need for locks and semaphores on this pool. With processes or threads writing to a sequential dump of pages, we need to make sure disk writes are not interleaved. With select, we only append complete pages to the log, again without the fear of interruption.

2.3.3 Link Extraction and Normalization

It is straightforward to search an HTML page for hyperlinks, but URLs extracted from crawled pages must be processed and filtered in a number of ways before throwing them back into the work pool. It is important to clean up and canon-icalize URLs so that pages known by different URLs are not fetched multiple times. However, such duplication cannot be eliminated altogether, because the mapping between hostnames and IP addresses is many-to-many, and a "site" is not necessarily the same as a "host."

A computer can have many IP addresses and many hostnames. The reply to a DNS request includes an IP address and a *canonical hostname*. For large sites, many IP addresses may be used for load balancing. Content on these hosts will be mirrors, or may even come from the same file system or database. On the other hand, for organizations with few IP addresses and a need to publish many logical sites, *virtual hosting* or *proxy pass* may be used[2] to map many different sites (hostnames) to a single IP address (but a browser will show different content for

---

2. See the documentation for the Apache Web server at *www.apache.org/*.

the different sites). The best bet is to avoid IP mapping for canonicalization and stick to the canonical hostname provided by the DNS response.

Extracted URLs may be *absolute* or *relative*. An example of an absolute URL is `http://www.iitb.ac.in/faculty/`, whereas a relative URL may look like `photo.jpg` or `/~soumen/`. Relative URLs need to be interpreted with reference to an absolute *base* URL. For example, the absolute form of the second and third URLs with regard to the first are `http://www.iitb.ac.in/faculty/photo.jpg` and `http://www.iitb.ac.in/~soumen/` (the starting "/" in /~soumen/ takes you back to the root of the Http server's published file system). A completely canonical form including the default Http port (number 80) would be `http://www.iitb.ac.in:80/faculty/photo.jpg`.

Thus, a canonical URL is formed by the following steps:

1. A standard string is used for the protocol (most browsers tolerate Http, which should be converted to lowercase, for example).

2. The hostname is canonicalized as mentioned above.

3. An explicit port number is added if necessary.

4. The path is normalized and cleaned up, for example, `/books/../papers/sigmod1999.ps` simplifies to `/papers/sigmod1999.ps`.

2.3.4   Robot Exclusion

Another necessary step is to check whether the server prohibits crawling a normalized URL using the `robots.txt` mechanism. This file is usually found in the Http root directory of the server (such as `http://www.iitb.ac.in/robots.txt`). This file specifies a list of path prefixes that crawlers should *not* attempt to fetch. The `robots.txt` file is meant for crawlers only and does not apply to ordinary browsers. This distinction is made based on the `User-agent` specification that clients send to the Http server (but this can be easily spoofed). Figure 2.3 shows a sample `robots.txt` file.

2.3.5   Eliminating Already-Visited URLs

Before adding a new URL to the work pool, we must check if it has already been fetched at least once, by invoking the *isUrlVisited?* module, shown in Figure 2.2. (Refreshing the page contents is discussed in Section 2.3.11.) Many sites are quite densely and redundantly linked, and a page is reached via many paths; hence, the *isUrlVisited?* check needs to be very quick. This is usually achieved by computing a hash function on the URL.

```
# AltaVista Search
User-agent: AltaVista Intranet V2.0 W3C Webreq
Disallow: /Out-Of-Date

# exclude some access-controlled areas
User-agent: *
Disallow: /Team
Disallow: /Project
Disallow: /Systems
```

FIGURE 2.3 A sample robots.txt file.

For compactness and uniform size, canonical URLs are usually hashed using a hash function such as MD5. (The MD5 algorithm takes as input a message of arbitrary length and produces as output a 128-bit *fingerprint* or *message digest* of the input. It is conjectured that it is computationally hard to produce two messages having the same message digest, or to produce any message having a prespecified message digest value. See *www.rsasecurity.com/rsalabs/faq/3-6-6.html* for details.) Depending on the number of distinct URLs that must be supported, the MD5 may be collapsed into anything between 32 and 128 bits, and a database of these hash values is maintained. Assuming each URL costs just 8 bytes of hash value (ignoring search structure costs), a billion URLs will still cost 8 GB, a substantial amount of storage that usually cannot fit in main memory.

Storing the set of hash values on disk unfortunately makes the *isUrlVisited?* check slower, but luckily, there is some locality of access on URLs. Some URLs (such as *www.netscape.com/*) seem to be repeatedly encountered no matter which part of the Web the crawler is traversing. Thanks to relative URLs within sites, there is also some spatiotemporal locality of access: once the crawler starts exploring a site, URLs within the site are frequently checked for a while.

To exploit locality, we cannot hash the whole URL to a single hash value, because a good hash function will map the domain strings uniformly over the range. This will jeopardize the second kind of locality mentioned above, because paths on the same host will be hashed over the range uniformly. This calls for a two-block or two-level hash function. The most significant bits (say, 24 bits) are derived by hashing the hostname plus port only, whereas the lower-order bits (say, 40 bits) are derived by hashing the path. The hash values of URLs on the same host will therefore match in the 24 most significant bits. Therefore, if

the concatenated bits are used as a key in a B-tree that is cached at page level, spatiotemporal locality is exploited.

Finally, the qualifying URLs (i.e., those whose hash values are not found in the B-tree) are added to the pending work set on disk, also called the *frontier* of the crawl. The hash values are also added to the B-tree.

2.3.6 Spider Traps

Because there is no editorial control on Web content, careful attention to coding details is needed to render crawlers immune to inadvertent or malicious quirks in sites and pages. Classic lexical scanning and parsing tools are almost useless. I have encountered a page with 68 KB of null characters in the middle of a URL that crashed a lexical analyzer generated by flex.[3] Hardly any page follows the HTML standard to a level where a context-free parser like yacc or bison can parse it well. Commercial crawlers need to protect themselves from crashing on ill-formed HTML or misleading sites. HTML scanners have to be custom-built to handle errors in a robust manner, discarding the page summarily if necessary.

Using soft directory links and path remapping features in an Http server, it is possible to create an infinitely "deep" Web site, in the sense that there are paths of arbitrary depth (in terms of the number of slashes in the path or the number of characters). CGI (*common gateway interface*) scripts can be used to generate an infinite number of pages dynamically (e.g., by embedding the current time or a random number). A simple check for URL length (or the number of slashes in the URL) prevents many "infinite site" problems, but even at finite depth, Http servers can generate a large number of dummy pages dynamically. The following are real URLs encountered in a recent crawl:

- *www.troutbums.com/Flyfactory/hatchline/hatchline/hatchline/flyfactory/flyfactory /hatchline/flyfactory/flyfactory/flyfactory/flyfactory/flyfactory/flyfactory/flyfactory /flyfactory/hatchline/hatchline/flyfactory/flyfactory/hatchline/*

- *www.troutbums.com/Flyfactory/flyfactory/flyfactory/hatchline/hatchline/flyfactory /hatchline/flyfactory/hatchline/flyfactory/flyfactory/flyfactory/hatchline/flyfactory /hatchline/*

- *www.troutbums.com/Flyfactory/hatchline/hatchline/flyfactory/flyfactory/flyfactory /flyfactory/hatchline/flyfactory/flyfactory/flyfactory/flyfactory/flyfactory/flyfactory /hatchline/*

---

3. Available online at *www.gnu.org/software/flex/*.

Certain classes of traps can be detected (see the following section), but no automatic technique can be foolproof. The best policy is to prepare regular statistics about the crawl. If a site starts dominating the collection, it can be added to the *guard* module shown in Figure 2.2, which will remove from consideration any URL from that site. Guards may also be used to disable crawling active content such as CGI form queries, or to eliminate URLs whose data types are clearly not textual (e.g., not one of HTML, plain text, PostScript, PDF, or Microsoft Word).

2.3.7 Avoiding Repeated Expansion of Links on Duplicate Pages

It is desirable to avoid fetching a page multiple times under different names (e.g. , u_1 and u_2), not only to reduce redundant storage and processing costs but also to avoid adding a relative outlink v multiple times to the work pool as u_1/v and u_2/v. Even if u_1 and u_2 have been fetched already, we should control the damage at least at this point. Otherwise there could be quite a bit of redundancy in the crawl, or worse, the crawler could succumb to the kind of spider traps illustrated in the previous section.

Duplicate detection is essential for Web crawlers owing to the practice of *mirroring* Web pages and sites—that is, copying them to a different host to speed up access to a remote user community. If u_1 and u_2 are exact duplicates, this can be detected easily. When the page contents are stored, a digest (e.g., MD5) is also stored in an index. When a page is crawled, its digest is checked against the index (shown as *isPageKnown?* in Figure 2.2). This can be implemented to cost one seek per test. Another way to catch such duplicates is to take the contents of pages u_1 and u_2, hash them to $h(u_1)$ and $h(u_2)$, and represent the relative link v as tuples $(h(u_1), v)$ and $(h(u_2), v)$. If u_1 and u_2 are aliases, the two outlink representations will be the same, and we can avoid the *isPageKnown?* implementation.

Detecting exact duplicates this way is not always enough, because mirrors may have minor syntactic differences, for example, the date of update, or the name and email of the site administrator may be embedded in the page. Unfortunately, even a single altered character will completely change the digest. *Shingling*, a more complex and robust way to detect *near* duplicates, is described in Section 3.3.2. Shingling is also useful for eliminating annoying duplicates from search engine responses.

2.3.8 Load Monitor and Manager

Network requests are orchestrated by the load monitor and thread manager shown in Figure 2.2. The load monitor keeps track of various system statistics:

- Recent performance of the *wide area network* (WAN) connection, say, latency and bandwidth estimates. Large crawlers may need WAN connections from multiple *Internet service providers* (ISPs); in such cases their performance parameters are individually monitored.

- An operator-provided or estimated maximum number of open sockets that the crawler should not exceed.

- The current number of active sockets.

The load manager uses these statistics to choose units of work from the pending work pool or frontier, schedule the issue of network resources, and distribute these requests over multiple ISPs if appropriate.

2.3.9 Per-Server Work-Queues

Many commercial Http servers safeguard against *denial of service* (DoS) attacks. DoS attackers swamp the target server with frequent requests that prevent it from serving requests from bona fide clients. A common first line of defense is to limit the speed or frequency of responses to any fixed client IP address (to, say, at most three pages per second). Servers that have to execute code in response to requests (e.g., search engines) are even more sensitive; frequent requests from one IP address are in fact actively penalized.

As an Http client, a crawler needs to avoid such situations, not only for high performance but also to avoid legal action. Well-written crawlers limit the number of active requests to a given server IP address at any time. This is done by maintaining a queue of requests for each server (see Figure 2.2). Requests are removed from the head of the queue, and network activity is initiated at a specified maximum rate. This technique also reduces the exposure to spider traps: no matter how large or deep a site is made to appear, the crawler fetches pages from it at some maximum rate and distributes its attention relatively evenly between a large number of sites.

From version 1.1 onward, Http has defined a mechanism for opening one connection to a server and keeping it open for several requests and responses in succession. Per-server host queues are usually equipped with Http version 1.1 persistent socket capability. This reduces overheads of DNS access and Http connection setup. On the other hand, to be polite to servers (and also because servers protect themselves by closing the connection after some maximum number of transfers), the crawler must move from server to server often. This tension

between access locality and politeness (or protection against traps) is inherent in designing crawling policies.

2.3.10 Text Repository

The crawler's role usually ends with dumping the contents of the pages it fetches into a repository. The repository can then be used by a variety of systems and services which may, for instance, build a keyword index on the documents (see Chapter 3), classify the documents into a topic directory like Yahoo! (see Chapter 5), or construct a hyperlink graph to perform link-based ranking and social network analysis (see Chapter 7). Some of these functions can be initiated within the crawler itself without the need for preserving the page contents, but implementers often prefer to decouple the crawler from these other functions for efficiency and reliability, provided there is enough storage space for the pages. Sometimes page contents need to be stored to be able to provide, along with responses, short blurbs from the matched pages that contain the query terms.

Page-related information is stored in two parts: metadata and page contents. The metadata includes fields like content type, last modified date, content length, Http status code, and so on. The metadata is relational in nature but is usually managed by custom software rather than a relational database. Conventional relational databases pay some overheads to support concurrent updates, transactions, and recovery. These features are not needed for a text index, which is usually managed by bulk updates with permissible downtime.

HTML page contents are usually stored compressed using, for example, the popular compression library zlib. Since the typical text or HTML Web page is 10 KB long[4] and compresses down to 2 to 4 KB, using one file per crawled page is ruled out by file block fragmentation (most file systems have a 4 to 8 KB file block size). Consequently, page storage is usually relegated to a custom storage manager that provides simple access methods for the crawler to add pages and for programs that run subsequently (e.g., the indexer) to retrieve documents.

For small-scale systems where the repository is expected to fit within the disks of a single machine, one may use the popular public domain storage manager Berkeley DB (available from *www.sleepycat.com/*), which manages disk-based databases within a single file. Berkeley DB provides several access methods. If pages need to be accessed using a key such as their URLs, the database can

---

4. Graphic files may be longer.

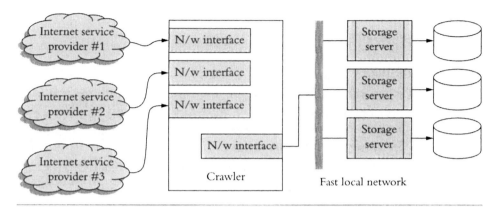

FIGURE 2.4 Large-scale crawlers often use multiple ISPs and a bank of local storage servers to store the pages crawled.

be configured as a hash table or a B-tree, but updates will involve expensive disk seeks, and a fragmentation loss between 15% and 25% will accrue. If subsequent page processors can handle pages in any order, which is the case with search engine indexing, the database can be configured as a sequential log of page records. The crawler only appends to this log, which involves no seek and negligible space overhead. It is also possible to first concatenate several pages and then compress them for a better compression factor.

For larger systems, the repository may be distributed over a number of storage servers connected to the crawler through a fast local network (such as gigabit Ethernet), as shown in Figure 2.4. The crawler may hash each URL to a specific storage server and send it the URL and the page contents. The storage server simply appends it to its own sequential repository, which may even be a tape drive, for archival. High-end tapes can transfer over 40 GB per hour,[5] which is about 10 million pages per hour, or about 200 hours for the whole Web (about 2 billion pages) at the time of writing. This is comparable to the time it takes today for the large Web search companies to crawl a substantial portion of the Web. Obviously, to complete the crawl in as much time requires the aggregate network bandwidth to the crawler to match the 40 GB per hour number, which is about 100 Mb per second, which amounts to about two T3-grade leased lines.

---

5. I use B for byte and b for bit.

```
% telnet www.cse.iitb.ac.in 80
Trying 144.16.111.14...
Connected to surya.cse.iitb.ac.in.
Escape character is 'Ĵ'.
GET / HTTP/1.0
If-modified-since: Sat, 13 Jan 2001 09:01:02 GMT

HTTP/1.1 304 Not Modified
Date: Sat, 13 Jan 2001 10:48:58 GMT
Server: Apache/1.3.0 (Unix) PHP/3.0.4
Connection: close
ETag: "5c248-153d-3a40b1ae"
Connection closed by foreign host.
%
```

FIGURE 2.5 Using the If-modified-since request header to check if a page needs to be crawled again. In this specific case it does not.

2.3.11 Refreshing Crawled Pages

Ideally, a search engine's index should be *fresh*—that is, it should reflect the most recent version of all documents crawled. Because there is no general mechanism of updates and notifications, the ideal cannot be attained in practice. In fact, a Web-scale crawler never "completes" its job; it is simply stopped when it has collected "enough" pages. Most large search engines then index the collected pages and start a fresh crawl. Depending on the bandwidth available, a round of crawling may run up to a few weeks. Many crawled pages do not change during a round—or ever, for that matter—but some sites may change many times.

Figure 2.5 shows how to use the Http protocol to check if a page changed since a specified time and, if so, to fetch the page contents. Otherwise the server sends a "not modified" response code and does not send the page. For a browser this may be useful, but for a crawler it is not as helpful, because, as I have noted, resolving the server address and connecting a TCP socket to the server already take a large chunk of crawling time.

When a new crawling round starts, it would clearly be ideal to know which pages have changed since the last crawl and refetch only those pages. This is possible in a very small number of cases, using the Expires Http response header (see Figure 2.6). For each page that did not come with an expiration date, we have to guess if revisiting that page will yield a modified version. If the crawler

```
% telnet vancouver-webpages.com 80
Trying 216.13.169.244...
Connected to vancouver-webpages.com (216.13.169.244).
Escape character is '^]'.
HEAD/cgi-pub/cache-test.pl/exp=in+1+minute&mod=Last+Night&rfc=1123 HTTP/1.0

HTTP/1.1 200 OK
Date: Tue, 26 Feb 2002 04:56:09 GMT
Server: Apache/1.3.6 (Unix)  (Red Hat/Linux) mod_perl/1.19
Expires: Tue, 26 Feb 2002 04:57:10 GMT
Last-Modified: Tue, 26 Feb 2002 04:56:10 GMT
Connection: close
Content-Type: text/html
```

FIGURE 2.6   Some sites with time-sensitive information send an Expires attribute in the Http response header.

had access to some sort of score reflecting the probability that each page has been modified, it could simply fetch URLs in decreasing order of that score. Even a crawler that runs continuously would benefit from an estimate of the expiration date of each page that has been crawled.

We can build such an estimate by assuming that the recent update rate will remain valid for the next crawling round—that is, that the recent past predicts the future. If the average interval at which the crawler checks for changes is smaller than the intermodification times of a page, we can build a reasonable estimate of the time to the next modification. The estimate could be way off, however, if the page is changed more frequently than the poll rate: we might have no idea how many versions successive crawls have missed. Another issue is that in an expanding Web, more pages appear young as time proceeds. These issues are discussed by Brewington and Cybenko [24], who also provide algorithms for maintaining a crawl in which most pages are fresher than a specified epoch. Cho [50] has also designed incremental crawlers based on the same basic principle.

Most search engines cannot afford to wait for a full new round of crawling to update their indices. Between every two complete crawling rounds, they run a crawler at a smaller scale to monitor fast-changing sites, especially related to current news, weather, and the like, so that results from this index can be patched into the master index. This process is discussed in Section 3.1.2.

2.4 Putting Together a Crawler

The World Wide Web Consortium (*www.w3c.org/*) has published a reference implementation of the Http client protocol in a package called w3c-libwww. It is written in C and runs on most operating systems. The flexibility and consequent complexity of the API may be daunting, but the package greatly facilitates the writing of reasonably high-performance crawlers. Commercial crawlers probably resemble crawlers written using this package up to the point where storage management begins.

Because the details of commercial crawlers are carefully guarded, I will focus on the design and use of the w3c-libwww library instead. This section has two parts. In the first part, I will discuss the internals of a crawler built along the same style as w3c-libwww. Since w3c-libwww is large, general, powerful, and complex, I will abstract its basic structure through pseudocode that uses C++ idioms for concreteness. In the second part, I will give code fragments that show how to use w3c-libwww.

2.4.1 Design of the Core Components

It is easiest to start building a crawler with a core whose only responsibility is to copy bytes from network sockets to storage media: this is the Crawler class. The Crawler's contract with the user is expressed in these methods:

```
class Crawler {
  void setDnsTimeout(int milliSeconds);
  void setHttpTimeout(int milliSeconds);
  void fetchPush(const string& url);
  virtual boolean fetchPull(string& url); // set url, return success
  virtual void fetchDone(const string& url,
    const ReturnCode returnCode, // timeout, server not found, ...
    const int httpStatus,        // 200, 404, 302, ...
    const hash_map<string, string>& mimeHeader,
      // Content-type = text/html
      // Last-modified = ...
    const unsigned char * pageBody,
    const size_t pageSize);
};
```

The user can push a URL to be fetched to the Crawler. The crawler implementation will guarantee that within a finite time (preset by the user using

setDnsTimeout and setHttpTimeout) the termination callback handler fetchDone will be called with the same URL and associated fields as shown. (I am hiding many more useful arguments for simplicity.) fetchPush inserts the URL into a memory buffer: this may waste too much memory for a Web-scale crawler and is volatile. A better option is to check new URLs into a persistent database and override fetchPull to extract new work from this database. The user also overrides the (empty) fetchDone method to process the document, usually storing page data and metadata from the method arguments, scanning pageBody for outlinks, and recording these for later fetchPulls. Other functions are implemented by extending the Crawler class. These include retries, redirections, and scanning for outlinks. In a way, "Crawler" is a misnomer for the core class; it just fetches a given list of URLs concurrently.

Let us now turn to the implementation of the Crawler class. We will need two helper classes called DNS and Fetch. Crawler is started with a fixed set of DNS servers. For each server, a DNS object is created. Each DNS object creates a UDP socket with its assigned DNS server as the destination. The most important data structure included in a DNS object is a list of Fetch contexts waiting for the corresponding DNS server to respond:

```
class DNS {
  list<Fetch*> waitForDns;
  :
  :  //other members
  :
}
```

A Fetch object contains the context required to complete the fetch of one URL using asynchronous sockets. waitForDns is the list of Fetches waiting for this particular DNS server to respond to their address-resolution requests.

Apart from members to hold request and response data and methods to deal with socket events, the main member in a Fetch object is a state variable that records the current stage in retrieving a page:

```
typedef enum {
  STATE_ERROR = -1, STATE_INIT = 0,
  STATE_DNS_RECEIVE, STATE_HTTP_SEND, STATE_HTTP_RECEIVE, STATE_FINAL
} State;
State state;
```

For completeness I also list a set of useful ReturnCodes. Most of these are self-explanatory; others have to do with the innards of the DNS and Http protocols.

```
typedef enum {
  SUCCESS = 0,
  //------------------------------------------------------------------------
  DNS_SERVER_UNKNOWN,
  DNS_SOCKET, DNS_CONNECT, DNS_SEND, DNS_RECEIVE, DNS_CLOSE, DNS_TIMEOUT,
  // and a variety of error codes DNS_PARSE_... if the DNS response
  // cannot be parsed properly for some reason
  //------------------------------------------------------------------------
  HTTP_BAD_URL_SYNTAX, HTTP_SERVER_UNKNOWN,
  HTTP_SOCKET, HTTP_CONNECT, HTTP_SEND, HTTP_RECEIVE,
  HTTP_TIMEOUT, HTTP_PAGE_TRUNCATED,
  //------------------------------------------------------------------------
  MIME_MISSING, MIME_PAGE_EMPTY, MIME_NO_STATUS_LINE,
  MIME_UNSUPPORTED_HTTP_VERSION, MIME_BAD_CHUNK_ENCODING
} ReturnCode;
```

The remaining important data structures within the Crawler are given below.

```
class Crawler {
  deque<string> waitForIssue;
    // Requests wait here to limit the number of network connections.
    // When resources are available, they go to...
  hash_map<SocketID, DNS*> dnsSockets;
    // There is one entry for each DNS socket, i.e., for each DNS server.
    // New Fetch record entries join the shortest list.
    // Once addresses are resolved, Fetch records go to...
  deque<Fetch*> waitForHttp;
    // When the system can take on a new Http connection, Fetch records
    // move from waitForHttp to...
  hash_map<SocketID, Fetch*> httpSockets;
    // A Fetch record completes its lifetime while attached to an Http socket.
    // To avoid overloading a server, we keep a set of IP addresses that
    // we are nominally connected to at any given time
  hash_set<IPAddr> busyServers;
    :
    :   //rest of Crawler definition
    :
}
```

```
1: Crawler::start()
2: while event loop has not been stopped do
3:    if not enough active Fetches to keep system busy then
4:       try a fetchPull to replenish the system with more work
5:       if no pending Fetches in the system then
6:          stop the event loop
7:       end if
8:    end if
9:    if not enough Http sockets busy and
       there is a Fetch f in waitForHttp whose server IP address ∉ busyServers then
10:      remove f from waitForHttp
11:      lock the IP address by adding an entry to busyServers (to be polite
         to the server)
12:      change f.state to STATE_HTTP_SEND
13:      allocate an Http socket s to start the Http protocol
14:      set the Http timeout for f
15:      set httpSockets[s] to the Fetch pointer
16:      continue the outermost event loop
17:   end if
18:   if the shortest waitForDns is "too short" then
19:      remove a URL from the head of waitForIssue
20:      create a Fetch object f with this URL
21:      issue the DNS request for f
22:      set f.state to STATE_DNS_RECEIVE
23:      set the DNS timeout for f
24:      put f on the laziest DNS's waitForDns
25:      continue the outermost event loop
26:   end if
27:   collect open SocketIDs from dnsSockets and httpSockets
28:   also collect the earliest deadline over all active Fetches
29:   perform the select call on the open sockets with the earliest deadline
      as timeout
```

FIGURE 2.7   The Crawler's event loop. For simplicity, the normal workflow is shown, hiding many conditions where the state of a Fetch ends in an error.

The heart of the Crawler is a method called Crawler::start(), which starts its *event loop*. This is the most complex part of the Crawler and is given as a pseudocode in Figure 2.7. Each Fetch object passes through a workflow. It first

```
30:    if select returned with a timeout then
31:        for each expired Fetch record f in dnsSockets and httpSockets do
32:            remove f
33:            invoke f.fetchDone(...) with suitable timeout error codes
34:            remove any locks held in busyServers
35:        end for
36:    else
37:        find a SocketID s that is ready for read or write
38:        locate a Fetch record f in dnsSockets or httpSockets that was waiting on s
39:        if a DNS request has been completed for f then
40:            move f from waitForDns to waitForHttp
41:        else
42:            if socket is ready for writing then
43:                send request
44:                change f.state to STATE_HTTP_RECEIVE
45:            else
46:                receive more bytes
47:                if receive completed then
48:                    invoke f.fetchDone(...) with successful status codes
49:                    remove any locks held in busyServers
50:                    remove f from waitForHttp and destroy f
51:                end if
52:            end if
53:        end if
54:    end if
55: end while
```

FIGURE 2.7   *(continued)*

joins the waitForDNS queue on some DNS object. When the server name resolution step is completed, it goes into the waitForHttp buffer. When we can afford another Http connection, it leaves waitForHttp and joins the httpSockets pool, where there are two major steps: sending the Http request and filling up a byte buffer with the response. Finally, when the page content is completely received, the user callback function fetchDone is called with suitable status information. The user has to extend the Crawler class and redefine fetchDone to parse the page and extract outlinks to make it a real crawler.

2.4.2 **Case Study: Using** w3c-libwww

So far we have seen a simplified account of how the internals of a package like w3c-libwww is designed; now we will see how to use it. The w3c-libwww API is extremely flexible and therefore somewhat complex, because it is designed not only for writing crawlers but for general, powerful manipulation of distributed hypertext, including text-mode browsing, composing dynamic content, and so on. Here we will sketch a simple application that issues a batch of URLs to fetch and installs a fetchDone callback routine that just throws away the page contents. We start with the main routine in Figure 2.8.

Unlike the simplified design presented in the previous section, w3c-libwww can process responses as they are streaming in and does not need to hold them in a memory buffer. The user can install various processors through which the incoming stream has to pass. For example, we can define a handler called hrefHandler to extract HREFs, which would be useful in a real crawler. It is registered with the w3c-libwww system as shown in Figure 2.8. Many other objects are mentioned in the code fragment below, but most of them are not key to understanding the main idea. hrefHandler is shown in Figure 2.9.

The method fetchDone, shown in Figure 2.10, is quite trivial in our case. It checks if the number of outstanding fetches is enough to keep the system busy; if not, it adds some more work. Then it just frees up resources associated with the request that has just completed and returns. Each page fetch is associated with an HTRequest object, similar to our Fetch object. At the very least, a termination handler should free this request object. If there is no more work to be found, it stops the event loop.

2.5 **Bibliographic Notes**

Details of the TCP/IP protocol and its implementation can be found in the classic work by Stevens [202]. Precise specifications of hypertext-related and older network protocols are archived at the World Wide Web Consortium (W3C Web site *www.w3c.org/*). Web crawling and indexing companies are rather protective about the engineering details of their software assets. Much of the discussion of the typical anatomy of large crawlers is guided by an early paper discussing the crawling system [26] for Google, as well as a paper about the design of Mercator, a crawler written in Java at Compaq Research Center [108]. There are many public-domain crawling and indexing packages, but most of them do not handle

```
vector<string> todo;
int tdx = 0;
  //...global variables storing all the URLs to be fetched...
int inProgress=0;
  //...keep track of active requests to exit the event loop properly...
int main(int ac, char ** av) {
  HTProfile_newRobot("CSE@IITBombay", "1.0");
  HTNet_setMaxSocket(64); // ...keep at most 64 sockets open at a time
  HTHost_setEventTimeout(40000);  //...Http timeout is 40 seconds
  //...install the hrefHandler...
  HText_registerLinkCallback(hrefHandler);
  //...install our fetch termination handler...
  HTNet_addAfter(fetchDone, NULL, NULL, HT_ALL, HT_FILTER_LAST);
  //...read URL list from file...
  ifstream ufp("urlset.txt");
  string url;
  while ( ufp.good() && ( ufp >> url ) && url.size() > 0 )
    todo.push_back(url);
  ufp.close();
  //...start off the first fetch...
  if ( todo.empty() ) return;
  ++inProgress;
  HTRequest * request = HTRequest_new();
  HTAnchor * anchor = HTAnchor_findAddress(todo[tdx++].c_str());
  if ( YES == HTLoadAnchor(anchor, request) ) {
    //...and enter the event loop...
    HTEventList_newLoop();
  }
  //...control returns here when event loop is stopped
}
```

FIGURE 2.8 Sketch of the main routine for a crawler using w3c-libwww.

the scale that commercial crawlers do. w3c-libwww is an open implementation suited for applications of moderate scale.

Estimating the size of the Web has fascinated Web users and researchers alike. Because the Web includes dynamic pages and spider traps, it is not easy to even define its size. Some well-known estimates were made by Bharat and Bröder [16] and Lawrence and Lee Giles [133]. The Web continues to grow, but not

```
void hrefHandler(HText * text,
                int element_number,
                int attribute_number,
                HTChildAnchor * anchor,
                const BOOL * present,
                const char ** value)
{
  if ( !anchor ) return;
  HTAnchor * childAnchor = HTAnchor_followMainLink((HTAnchor*)anchor);
  if ( !childAnchor ) return;
  char * childUrl = HTAnchor_address((HTAnchor*) childAnchor);
  //...add childUrl to work pool, or issue a fetch right now...
  HT_FREE(childUrl);
}
```

FIGURE 2.9 A handler that is triggered by w3c-libwww whenever an HREF token is detected in the incoming stream.

```
#define LIBWWW_BATCH_SIZE 16
        //...number of concurrent fetches...
int fetchDone(HTRequest * request, HTResponse * response,
            void * param, int status)
{
  if ( request == NULL ) return -1;
  //...replenish concurrent fetch pool if needed...
  while ( inProgress < LIBWWW_BATCH_SIZE && tdx < todo.size() ) {
    ++inProgress;
    string newUrl(todo[tdx]);
    ++tdx;
    HTRequest * nrq = HTRequest_new();
    HTAnchor * nax = HTAnchor_findAddress(newUrl.c_str());
    (void) HTLoadAnchor(nax, nrq);
  }
  //...process the just-completed fetch here...
  inProgress--;
  const bool noMoreWork = ( inProgress <= 0 );
  HTRequest_delete(request);
  if ( noMoreWork )
    HTEventList_stopLoop();
  return 0;
}
```

FIGURE 2.10 Page fetch completion handler for the w3c-libwww–based crawler.

at as heady a pace as in the late 1990s. Nevertheless, some of the most accessed sites change frequently. The Internet Archive (*www.archive.org/*) started to archive large portions of the Web in October 1996, in a bid to prevent most of it from disappearing into the past [120]. At the time of this writing, the archive has about 11 billion pages, taking up over 100 terabytes. Storage at such a scale is not unprecedented: a music radio station holds about 10,000 records, or about 5 terabytes of uncompressed data, and the U.S. Library of Congress contains about 20 million volumes, or an estimated 20 terabytes of text. The Internet Archive is available to researchers, historians, and scholars. An interface called the Wayback Machine lets users access old versions of archived Web pages.

WEB SEARCH AND INFORMATION RETRIEVAL

This chapter discusses how Web search engines work. Search engines have their roots in *information retrieval* (IR) systems, which prepare a keyword index for the given corpus and respond to keyword queries with a ranked list of documents. The query language provided by most search engines lets us look for Web pages that contain (or do not contain) specified words and phrases. Conjunctions and disjunctions of such clauses are also permitted. Mature IR technology predates the Web by at least a decade. One of the earliest applications of rudimentary IR systems to the Internet was Archie, which supported title search across sites serving files over the *File Transfer Protocol* (FTP). It was only in the mid-1990s that IR was widely applied to Web content by early adopters such as AltaVista. The new application revealed several issues peculiar to hypertext and Web data: Web pages have internal tag structure, they are connected to each other in semantically meaningful ways, they are often duplicated, and they sometimes lie about their actual contents to rate highly in keyword queries. We will review classical IR and discuss some of the new problems and their solutions.

3.1 Boolean Queries and the Inverted Index

The simplest kind of query one may ask involves relationships between terms and documents, such as

1. Documents containing the word "Java"

2. Documents containing the word "Java" but not the word "coffee"

3.   Documents containing the phrase "Java beans" or the term "API"

4.   Documents where "Java" and "island" occur in the same sentence

The last two queries are called *proximity queries* because they involve the lexical distance between tokens. These queries can be answered using an *inverted index*. This section describes how inverted indices are constructed from a collection of documents.

Documents in the collection are *tokenized* in a suitable manner. For ASCII text without markups, tokens may be regarded as any nonempty sequence of characters not including spaces and punctuation. For HTML, one may choose to first filter away all tags delimited by the < and > characters.[1] Each distinct token in the corpus may be represented by a suitable integer (typically 32 bits suffice). A document is thus transformed into a sequence of integers.

There may be a deliberate slight loss of information prior to this step, depending on the needs of the application. For example, terms may be downcased, and variant forms (*is, are, were*) may be conflated to one canonical form (*be*), or word endings representing parts of speech may be "stemmed" away (*running* to *run*).

At this point a document is simply a sequence of integer tokens. Consider the following two documents:

d_1: $\text{My}_1 \text{ care}_2 \text{ is}_3 \text{ loss}_4 \text{ of}_5 \text{ care}_6 \text{ with}_7 \text{ old}_8 \text{ care}_9 \text{ done}_{10}$.

d_2: $\text{Your}_1 \text{ care}_2 \text{ is}_3 \text{ gain}_4 \text{ of}_5 \text{ care}_6 \text{ with}_7 \text{ new}_8 \text{ care}_9 \text{ won}_{10}$.

Here the subscripts indicate the position where the token appears in the document. The same information (minus case and punctuation) can be represented in the following table, called POSTING:

tid	did	pos
my	1	1
care	1	2
is	1	3
⋮		
new	2	8
care	2	9
won	2	10

---

1. However, some search engines pay special attention to the contents of META tags.

Here tid, did, and pos signify token ID, document ID, and position, respectively. (For clarity I will use strings rather than integers for tid.) Given a table like this, it is simple to answer the sample queries mentioned above using SQL queries, as so:

1. `select did from POSTING where tid = 'java'`

2. `(select did from POSTING where tid = 'java') except (select did from POSTING where tid = 'coffee')`

3.
```
with
   D_JAVA (did, pos) as (select did, pos from POSTING where tid = 'java'),
   D_BEANS(did, pos) as (select did, pos from POSTING where tid = 'beans'),
   D_JAVABEANS(did) as
     (select D_JAVA.did from D_JAVA, D_BEANS
        where D_JAVA.did = D_BEANS.did
        and D_JAVA.pos + 1 = D_BEANS.pos),
   D_API(did) as (select did from POSTING where tid = 'api'),
   (select did from D_JAVABEANS) union (select did from D_API)
```

If sentence terminators are well defined, one can keep a sentence counter (apart from a token counter as above) and maintain sentence positions as well as token positions in the POSTING table. This will let us search for terms occurring in the same or adjacent sentences, for example (query 4).

Although the three-column table makes it easy to write keyword queries, it wastes a great deal of space. A straightforward implementation using a relational database uses prohibitive amounts of space, up to 10 times the size of the original text [79]. Furthermore, access to this table for all the queries above show the following common pattern: given a term, convert it to a tid, then use that to probe the table, getting a set of (did, pos) tuples, sorted in lexicographic order. For queries not involving term position, discard pos and sort the set by did, which is useful for finding the union, intersection, and differences of sets of dids. One can thus reduce the storage required by mapping tids to a lexicographically sorted buffer of (did, pos) tuples. If fast proximity search is not needed, we can discard the position information and reduce storage further. Both forms of indices are shown in Figure 3.1 for the two sample documents. In effect, indexing takes a document-term matrix and turns it into a term-document matrix, and is therefore called *inverted* indexing, although *transposing* might be a more accurate description.

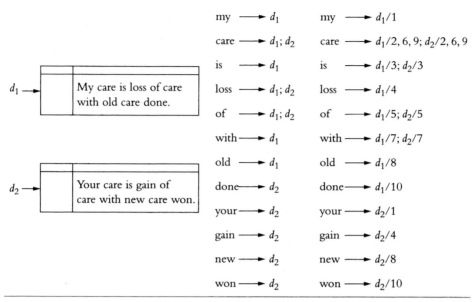

FIGURE 3.1 Two variants of the inverted index data structure, usually stored on disk. The simpler version in the middle does not store term offset information; the version to the right stores term offsets. The mapping from terms to documents and positions (written as "document/position") may be implemented using a B-tree or a hash table.

As with managing the document repository (discussed in Section 2.3.10), a storage manager such as Berkeley DB (available from *www.sleepycat.com/*) is again a reasonable choice to maintain mappings from tids to document records. However, Berkeley DB is most useful for dynamic corpora where documents are frequently added, modified, and deleted. For relatively static collections, more space-efficient indexing options are discussed in Section 3.1.3.

3.1.1 Stopwords and Stemming

Most natural languages have so-called function words and connectives such as articles and prepositions that appear in a large number of documents and are typically of little use in pinpointing documents that satisfy a searcher's information need. Such words (e.g., *a, an, the, on* for English) are called *stopwords*.

Search engines will usually not index stopwords, but will replace them with a placeholder so as to remember the offset at which stopwords occur. This enables searching for phrases containing stopwords, such as "gone with the wind"

(although there is a small chance of different phrases being aliased together). Reducing index space and improving performance are important reasons for eliminating stopwords. However, some queries such as "to be or not to be" can no longer be asked. Other surprises involve polysemy (a word having multiple senses depending on context or part of speech): *can* as a verb is not very useful for keyword queries, but *can* as a noun could be central to a query, so it should not be included in the stopword list.

Stemming or *conflation* is another device to help match a query term with a morphological variant in the corpus. In English, as in some other languages, parts of speech, tense, and number are conveyed by word inflections. One may want a query containing the word *gaining* to match a document containing the word *gains*, or a document containing the word *went* to respond to a query containing the word *goes*. Common stemming methods use a combination of morphological analysis (For example, Porter's algorithm [179]) and dictionary lookup (e.g., WordNet [151]). Stemming can increase the number of documents in the response, but may at times include irrelevant documents. For example, Porter's algorithm stems both *university* and *universal* to *univers*. When in doubt, it is better not to stem, especially for Web searches, where aliases and abbreviations abound: a community may be *gated*, but so is the UNIX router demon; a *sock* is worn on the foot, but *SOCKS* more commonly refers to a firewall protocol; and it is a bad idea to stem *ides* to *IDE*, the hard disk standard. Owing to the variety of abbreviations and names coined in the technical and commercial sectors, polysemy is rampant on the Web. Thanks to inherent biases in Web authorship, any polysemous or ambiguous query has a chance of retrieving documents related to the commercial or technical sense in lieu of the sense intended by the user.

3.1.2 Batch Indexing and Updates

For large-scale indexing systems (such as those that are used in Web search engines) the mappings shown in Figure 3.1 are not constructed incrementally as documents are added to the collection one by one, because this would involve random disk I/O and therefore be very time-consuming. Moreover, as the postings grow, there could be a high level of disk block fragmentation.

With some amount of extra space, one can replace the indexed update of variable-length postings with simple sort-merges. When documents are scanned, the postings table is naturally sorted in (d, t) order. The basic operation of "inverting" the index involves transposing the sort order to (t, d), as shown in

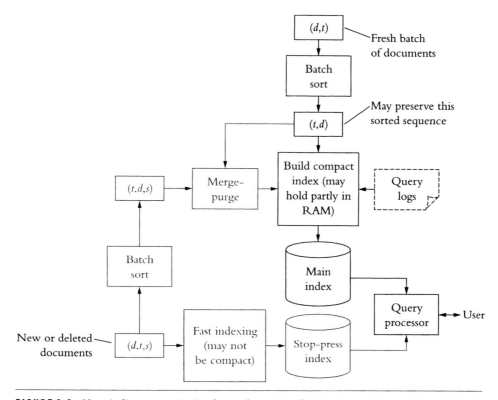

FIGURE 3.2   How indices are maintained over dynamic collections.

Figure 3.2. Once the postings records are in (t, d) order (together with offset information) the data structures shown in Figure 3.1 may be created easily.

For a dynamic collection where documents are added, modified, or deleted, a single document-level change may need to update hundreds to thousands of records. (If position information is kept, many term offsets are likely to change after any modification is made to a document.) As we shall also see in Section 3.1.3, the data structures illustrated in Figure 3.1 may be compressed, but this makes in-place updates very difficult.

Figure 3.2 offers a simpler solution. Initially, a static compact index is made out of the (t, d)–sorted postings. This is the main index used for answering queries. Meanwhile documents are added or deleted; let's call these the "documents

in flux." (In this discussion, we can model document modification as deletion followed by insertion for simplicity.) Documents in flux are represented by a *signed* (d, t) record shown as (d, t, s), where s is a bit to specify if the document has been deleted or inserted.

The (d, t, s) records are indexed to create a *stop-press* index. A user query is sent to both the main index and the stop-press index. Suppose the main index returns a document set D_0. The stop-press index returns two document sets: one, D_+, is the set of documents not yet indexed in D_0 that match the query, and the other, D_-, is the set of documents matching the query that have been removed from the collection since D_0 was constructed. The final answer to the query is $D_0 \cup D_+ \setminus D_-$.

The stop-press index has to be created quickly and therefore may not be built as carefully and compactly as the main index. (See the next section for details on compressing inverted indices.) When the stop-press index gets too large, the signed (d, t, s) records are sorted in (t, d, s) order and merge-purged into the master (t, d) records. The result is used to rebuild the main index, and now the stop-press index can be emptied. The compact main index may be partly cached in memory for speed; usually this involves analyzing query logs for frequent keywords and caching their inverted records preferentially.

3.1.3 Index Compression Techniques

The reader may notice that modulo missing stopwords, cases, and punctuation, an inverted index with position information can be used to reconstruct the documents in a collection. Therefore, the size of the index can be substantial compared to the size of the corpus. Despite some benefits from caching, large disk-resident indices will lead to a great deal of random I/O. Therefore, for large, high-performance IR installations (as with Web search engines), it is important to compress the index as far as possible, so that much of it can be held in memory.

A major portion of index space is occupied by the document IDs. The larger the collection, the larger the number of bits used to represent each document ID. At least 32 bits are needed to represent document IDs in a system crawling a large fraction of the 2+ billion pages on the Web today.

The easiest way to save space in storing document IDs is to sort them in increasing order and to store the first ID in full, and subsequently only the difference from the previous ID, which we call the *gap*. This is called *delta encoding*.

For example, if the word *bottle* appears in documents numbered 5, 30, and 47, the record for *bottle* is the vector $(5, 25, 17)$.

For small examples this may not seem like much savings, but consider that for frequent terms the average inter-ID gap will be smaller, and rare terms don't take up too much space anyway, so both cases work in our favor. Furthermore, for collections crawled from the Web, the host ID remains fixed for all pages collected from a single site. Since the unique ID of the page is the concatenation of a host ID and a path ID (see Section 2.3.5), unique IDs from different hosts do not interleave. Sites are usually semantically focused and coherent: pages within a site tend to reuse the same terms over and over. As a result, the sorted document ID vector for a given term tends to be highly clustered, meaning that inter-ID gaps are mostly small.

The next issue is how to encode these gaps in a variable number of bits, so that a small gap costs far fewer bits than a document ID. The standard binary encoding, which assigns the same length to all symbols or values to be encoded, is optimal[2] when all values are equally likely, which is not the case for gaps. Another extreme is the unary code (where a gap x is represented by $x - 1$ ones followed by a terminating marker), which favors short gaps *too* strongly (it is optimal if the gap follows a distribution given by $\Pr(X = x) = 2^{-x}$, that is, the probability of large gaps decays exponentially). Somewhere in the middle is the *gamma code,* which represents gap x as

1.   Unary code for $1 + \lfloor \log x \rfloor$, followed by
2. $x - 2^{\lfloor \log x \rfloor}$ represented in binary, costing another $\lfloor \log x \rfloor$ bits.

Thus gap x is encoded in roughly $1 + 2 \log x$ bits—for example, the number 9 is represented as "1110001." A further enhancement to this idea results in *Golomb codes* [215].

In contrast to the methods discussed so far, one may also employ *lossy* compression mechanisms that trade off space for time. A simple lossy approach is to collect documents into *buckets*. Suppose we have a million documents, each with a 20-bit ID. We can collect them into a thousand buckets with a thousand documents in each bucket. Bucket IDs will cost us only 10 bits.

---

2. If the number of bits in the code for value x is $L(x)$, the cost of this code is $\sum_x \Pr(x)L(x)$, the expected number of bits to transmit one symbol. An optimal code minimizes this cost.

In the simpler variant, an inverted index is constructed from terms to bucket IDs, which saves a lot of space because the "document" IDs have shrunk to half their size. But when a bucket responds to a query, all documents in that bucket need to be scanned, which consumes extra time. To avoid this, a second variant of this idea indexes documents in each bucket separately. Glimpse (*webglimpse.org/*) uses such techniques to limit space usage.

Generally, an index that has been compressed to the limit is also very messy to update when documents are added, deleted, or modified. For example, if new documents must be added to the inverted index, the posting records of many terms will expand in size, leading to storage allocation and compaction problems. These can be solved only with a great deal of random I/O, which makes large-scale updates impractical.

3.2 Relevance Ranking

Relational databases have precise schema and are queried using SQL (*structured query language*). In relational algebra, the response to a query is always an *unordered set* of qualifying tuples. Keyword queries are not precise, in the sense that a Boolean decision to include or exclude a response is unacceptable. A safer bet is to rate each document for how likely it is to satisfy the user's information need, sort in decreasing order of this score, and present the results in a ranked list.

Since only a part of the user's information need is expressed through the query, there can be no algorithmic way of ensuring that the ranking strategy always favors the information need. However, mature practice in IR has evolved a *vector-space model* for documents and a broad class of ranking algorithms based on this model. This combination works well in practice. In later years, the empirical vector-space approach has been rationalized and extended with probabilistic foundations. I will first describe how the accuracy of IR systems is assessed and then discuss the document models and ranking techniques that aim to score well with regard to such assessment measures.

3.2.1 Recall and Precision

The queries we have studied thus far are answered by a *set* of documents. A document either belongs to the response set or does not. The response set may be reported in any order. Although such a Boolean query has a precise meaning (like

SQL queries), an unordered response is of little use if the response set is very large (e.g., by recent estimates, over 12 million Web pages contain the word "java").

The set-valued response is of little use in such cases: no one can inspect all documents selected by the query. It might be argued that in such cases a longer, more selective query should be demanded from the user, but for nonprofessional searchers this is wishful thinking. The search system should therefore try to guess the user's information need and *rank* the responses so that satisfactory documents are found near the top of the list. Before one embarks on such a mission, it is important to specify how such rankings would be evaluated.

A benchmark is specified by a corpus of n documents D and a set of queries Q. For each query $q \in Q$, an exhaustive set of relevant documents $D_q \subseteq D$ is identified manually. Let us fix the query for the rest of this discussion. The query is now submitted to the query system, and a ranked list of documents $(d_1, d_2, \ldots, d_n)$ is returned. (Practical search systems only show the first several items on this complete list.) Corresponding to this list, we can compute a 0/1 relevance list $(r_1, r_2, \ldots, r_n)$, where $r_i = 1$ if $d_i \in D_q$ and 0 otherwise.

For this query q, the *recall* at rank $k \geq 1$ is defined as

$$\text{recall}(k) = \frac{1}{|D_q|} \sum_{1 \leq i \leq k} r_i \tag{3.1}$$

that is, the fraction of all relevant documents included in $(d_1, \ldots, d_k)$, and the *precision* at rank k is defined as

$$\text{precision}(k) = \frac{1}{k} \sum_{1 \leq i \leq k} r_i \tag{3.2}$$

that is, the fraction of the top k responses that are actually relevant. Another figure of merit is the *average precision*:

$$\text{average precision} = \frac{1}{|D_q|} \sum_{1 \leq k \leq |D|} r_k \times \text{precision}(k) \tag{3.3}$$

The average precision is the sum of the precision at each relevant hit position in the response list, divided by the total number of relevant documents. The average precision is 1 only if the engine retrieves all relevant documents and ranks them ahead of any irrelevant document.

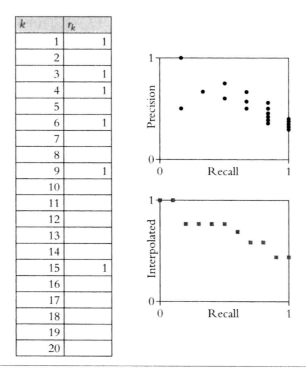

k	r_k
1	1
2	
3	1
4	1
5	
6	1
7	
8	
9	1
10	
11	
12	
13	
14	
15	1
16	
17	
18	
19	
20	

FIGURE 3.3 Precision and interpolated precision plotted against recall for the given relevance vector. Missing r_ks are zeros.

To combine precision values from multiple queries, *interpolated precision*[3] is used for a set of standard recall values, usually $0, 0.1, 0.2, \ldots, 1$. For a given query, to interpolate precision at standard recall value ρ, we take the maximum precision obtained for the query for any experimental recall greater than or equal to ρ. Having obtained the interpolated precision for all the queries at each recall level, we can average them together to draw the precision-vs.-recall curve for the benchmark. A sample relevance list and its associated plots of precision and interpolated precision against recall are shown in Figure 3.3. Interpolated precision cannot increase with recall.

Generally, there is a trade-off between recall and precision. If $k = 0$, precision is by convention equal to 1 but recall is 0. (Interpolated precision at recall

---

3. Technically, this is not interpolation.

level 0 may be less than 1.) To drive up recall, we can inspect more and more documents (increasing k), but we will start encountering more and more irrelevant documents, driving down the precision. A search engine with a good ranking function will generally show a negative relation between recall and precision. It will provide most of the relevant results early in the list. Therefore, a plot of precision against recall will generally slope down to the right. The curve of a better search engine will tend to remain above that of a poorer search engine.

We should note in passing that the recall and precision measures are not without their limitations. For a large corpus in rapid flux, such as the Web, it is impossible to determine D_q. Precision can be estimated using a great deal of manual labor. Furthermore, as we shall see in Chapter 7, precision or relevance are not the only criteria by which users expect to see search responses ranked; measures of authority are also useful. Despite these shortcomings, the recall precision framework is a useful yardstick for search engine design.

3.2.2 The Vector-Space Model

In the vector-space model, documents are represented as vectors in a multidimensional Euclidean space. Each axis in this space corresponds to a term (token). The coordinate of document d in the direction corresponding to term t is determined by two quantities:

Term frequency TF(d, t). This is simply $n(d, t)$, the number of times term t occurs in document d, scaled in any of a variety of ways to normalize document length. For example, one may normalize the sum of term counts, in which case $\text{TF}(d, t) = n(d, t) / \sum_{\tau} n(d, \tau)$; or one may set $\text{TF}(d, t) = n(d, t) / \max_{\tau} n(d, \tau)$. Other forms are also known; for example, the Cornell SMART system uses

$$\text{TF}(d, t) = \begin{cases} 0 & \text{if } n(d, t) = 0 \\ 1 + \log(1 + \log(n(d, t))) & \text{otherwise} \end{cases} \tag{3.4}$$

Inverse document frequency IDF(t). Not all axes in the vector space are equally important. Coordinates corresponding to function words such as *a, an,* and *the* will be large and noisy irrespective of the content of the document. IDF seeks to scale down the coordinates of terms that occur in many documents. If D is the document collection and D_t is the set of documents containing t, then

one common form of IDF weighting (used by SMART again) is

$$\text{IDF}(t) = \log \frac{1 + |D|}{|D_t|} \tag{3.5}$$

If $|D_t| \ll |D|$ the term t will enjoy a large IDF scale factor and vice versa. Other variants are also used; like the formula above, these are mostly dampened functions of $|D|/|D_t|$.

TF and IDF are combined into the complete vector-space model in the obvious way: the coordinate of document d in axis t is given by

$$d_t = \text{TF}(d, t)\, \text{IDF}(t) \tag{3.6}$$

We will overload the notation to let $\vec{d}$ represent document d in TFIDF-space. A query q is also interpreted as a document and transformed to $\vec{q}$ in the same TFIDF-space defined by D. (Negations and phrases in the query are handled in ways discussed in Section 3.2.5.)

The remaining issue is how to measure the proximity between $\vec{q}$ and $\vec{d}$ for all $d \in D$. One possibility is to use the magnitude of the vector difference, $|\vec{d} - \vec{q}|$. If this measure is used, document vectors must be normalized to unit length in the L_1 or L_2 metric prior to the similarity computation. (Otherwise, if document d_2 is a five-fold replication of document d_1, the distance $|d_1 - d_2|$ will be significant, which is not semantically intuitive.) Because queries are usually short, they tend to be at large distances from long documents, which are thus unduly penalized. Another option is to measure the similarity between d and q as the cosine of the angle between $\vec{d}$ and $\vec{q}$. This could have the opposite bias: short documents naturally overlap with fewer query terms, and thereby get lower scores. Even so, IR systems generally find cosine more acceptable than distance.

Summarizing, a TFIDF-based IR system first builds an inverted index with TF and IDF information, and given a query (vector) lists some number of document vectors that are most similar to the query.

3.2.3 Relevance Feedback and Rocchio's Method

The initial response from a search engine may not satisfy the user's information need if the query is incomplete or ambiguous. The average Web query is only two words long. Users can rarely express their information need within two words in sufficient detail to pinpoint relevant documents right away. If the response list has at least some relevant documents, sophisticated users can *learn* how to modify their

queries by adding or negating additional keywords. Relevance feedback automates this query refinement process. Initial ranked responses are presented together with a rating form (which can be generated easily in HTML). Usually a simple binary useful/useless opinion is all that is asked for. The user, after visiting some of the reported URLs, may choose to check some of these boxes.

This second round of input (called *relevance feedback*) from the user has been found to be quite valuable in "correcting" the ranks to the user's taste. In Chapter 5 we shall discuss various techniques that can exploit such "training" by the user for better relevance judgments. One particularly successful and early technique for "folding in" user feedback was *Rocchio's method*, which simply adds to the original query vector $\vec{q}$ a weighted sum of the vectors corresponding to the relevant documents D_+, and subtracts a weighted sum of the irrelevant documents D_-:

$$\vec{q'} = \alpha \vec{q} + \beta \sum_{D_+} \vec{d} - \gamma \sum_{D_-} \vec{d} \tag{3.7}$$

where α, β, and γ are adjustable parameters. D_+ and D_- may be provided manually by the user, or they may be generated automatically, in which case the process is called *pseudo-relevance feedback* or PRF. PRF usually collects D_+ by assuming that a certain number of the most relevant documents found by the vector-space method are relevant. γ is commonly set to zero (that is, D_- not used) unless human-labeled irrelevant documents are available. In the Cornell SMART system, the top 10 documents reported by the first-round query execution are included in D_+. It is also unsafe to let *all* words found in D_+ and D_- contribute to (3.7): a bad word may offset the benefits of many good words. It is typical to pick the top 10 to 20 words in decreasing IDF order.

Relevance feedback is not a commonly available feature on Web search engines. Apparently, this is partly because Web users want instant gratification with searches: they are not patient enough to give their feedback to the system. Another possible reason is system complexity. Major search engines field millions of queries per hour, and therefore have to dispose of each query in only a few milliseconds. Depending on the size of the vocabulary gleaned from D_+ in PRF, executing the second-round query may be much slower than the original query.

3.2.4   Probabilistic Relevance Feedback Models

Thanks to a great deal of empirical work with standard benchmarks, vector-space–based IR technology is extremely mature. Even so, the vector-space model is *operational*: it gives a precise recipe for computing the relevance of a document

with regard to the query, but does not attempt to justify *why* the relevance should be defined thus, based on some *statistical* model for the generation of documents and queries. This might be very useful if, for instance, we could propose generative models for corpora relating to different topics, and found that the best way to tune the IR system was closely related to parameters of our models that can be estimated easily.

Contributions from both operational and statistical viewpoints are needed to understand the behavior of practical IR systems, and in particular, to extend them to new domains such as hypertext. Because the judgment of relevance is inherently variable and uncertain, it is natural that probabilistic models be used to estimate the relevance of documents. Another potential advantage is that once a model of relevance is built in this manner, additional kinds of features, like hyperlinks, may be folded in without much effort.

Consider document d, which we may represent as a binary term vector $\vec{d}$, and a given query q. Let R be a Boolean random variable that represents the relevance of document d with regard to query q. A reasonable order for ranking documents is their *odds ratio* for relevance:

$$\frac{\Pr(R|q, \vec{d})}{\Pr(\bar{R}|q, \vec{d})} = \frac{\Pr(R, q, \vec{d})/\Pr(q, \vec{d})}{\Pr(\bar{R}, q, \vec{d})/\Pr(q, \vec{d})} = \frac{\Pr(R|q)\,\Pr(\vec{d}|R, q)}{\Pr(\bar{R}|q)\,\Pr(\vec{d}|\bar{R}, q)} \tag{3.8}$$

We will approximate $\Pr(\vec{d}|R, q)$ and $\Pr(\vec{d}|\bar{R}, q)$ by the product of the probabilities of individual terms in d—that is, we will assume that term occurrences are independent *given* the query and the value of R. (Similar simplifications will be made in Chapter 5 and elsewhere.) If $\{t\}$ is a universe of terms, and $x_{d,t} \in \{0, 1\}$ reflects whether the term t appears in document d or not, then the last expression can be approximated as

$$\frac{\Pr(\vec{d}|R, q)}{\Pr(\vec{d}|\bar{R}, q)} \approx \prod_t \frac{\Pr(x_t|R, q)}{\Pr(x_t|\bar{R}, q)} \tag{3.9}$$

Let $a_{t,q} = \Pr(x_t = 1|R, q)$ and $b_{t,q} = \Pr(x_t = 1|\bar{R}, q)$. Simple manipulations on the last formula show that

$$\frac{\Pr(\vec{d}|R, q)}{\Pr(\vec{d}|\bar{R}, q)} \propto \prod_{t \in d} \frac{a_{t,q}(1 - b_{t,q})}{b_{t,q}(1 - a_{t,q})} \tag{3.10}$$

Responses can be sorted in decreasing order of odds ratio. The only parameters involved here are $a_{t,q}$ and $b_{t,q}$. The simplest way to estimate these parameters is

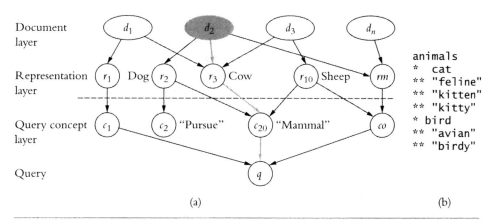

FIGURE 3.4 Bayesian inference network for relevance ranking. A document is relevant to the extent that setting its corresponding belief node to *true* lets us assign a high degree of belief in the node corresponding to the query (a). Manual specification of mappings between terms to approximate concepts (b).

from relevance feedback, but that requires too much effort on the part of the searcher, who has to rate some responses before the probabilistic ranking system can kick in.

A more general probabilistic retrieval framework casts the problem of finding documents relevant to a query as a *Bayesian inference problem*, represented by the directed acyclic graph in Figure 3.4(a). (This is a simplified version of a general model proposed by Turtle and Croft [204], with some layers missing. More details about Bayesian inference networks are to be found in Section 5.6.2.) The nodes correspond to various entities like documents, terms, "concepts" (which we will never precisely define), and the query.

The representation layer may use any feature that can be extracted from the documents, like words and phrases. Multiple nodes may be allocated to the same word because it is polysemous, or it appears in titles, author names, or other document fields. Nodes may also be added for synthesized features. For example, scholarly articles in many fields tend to use more sophisticated words and sentences. If the user is trying to discriminate between beginner material and scholarly research, the number of syllables in a word may be a useful feature. We will return to such issues in Chapter 5.

For basic vector-space IR systems, the concept and representation layers are the same: each token approximates a concept, although synonymy, polysemy, and

other term relations may confound searches. More mature IR systems, such as Verity's Search97 (see *www.verity.com/* for details) allow administrators and users to define hierarchies of concepts in files that resemble the format shown in Figure 3.4(b). The concept layer and its connections to the representation layer usually need to be designed explicitly with human input, as in Search97.

Each node is associated with a random Boolean variable, and we have some *belief* between 0 and 1 that the Boolean variable is true; for brevity I also call this the *belief* of the node. The directed arcs signify that the belief of a node is a function of the belief of its immediate parents (which depend in turn on its parents, etc.). If a node v has k parents $u_1, \ldots, u_k$, each of which is associated with a Boolean variable, we need a table of size 2^k, which, for each combination of parent variables, gives the probability that the variable at v is true. Aliasing a node and its Boolean variable, the table contains entries $\Pr(v = \text{true}|u_1, \ldots, u_k)$ for all combinations of $u_1, \ldots, u_k$.

Obviously, the model hinges on the construction of the graph and the design of the functions relating the belief of a node to the belief of its parents. Suppose v has three parents u_1, u_2, u_3 with the corresponding beliefs. v may be designed as an *or*-node, in which case $v = 1 - (1 - u_1)(1 - u_2)(1 - u_3)$. Other Boolean functions follow similar rules resembling fuzzy logic.

The relevance of a document d with regard to the query is estimated by setting the belief of the corresponding document node to 1 and all other document beliefs to 0, and then computing the belief of the query. The document nodes are thus "activated" one at a time, evaluating each document. Finally the documents are ranked in decreasing order of belief that they induce in the query.

Although probabilistic retrieval models have been studied deeply in the research literature, they are used rarely compared to standard vector-space IR engines.

3.2.5 Advanced Issues

In this section I briefly review a number of issues that need to be handled by hypertext search engines. Some of these are peculiar to hypertext and the Web.

Spamming

In classical IR corpora, document authors were largely truthful about the purpose of the document; terms found in the document were broadly indicative of content. Economic reality on the Web and the need to "capture eyeballs" has led to quite a different culture. Spammers are authors who (among other things)

surreptitiously add popular query terms to pages unrelated to those terms. They may add the terms "Hawaii vacation rental," for example, to a page about Internet gambling in a way that will go unnoticed by human readers of the page while still being noted by search engines—e.g., by making the font color the same as the background color. Human readers could not see such an addition, but a search engine would duly index this hypothetical page about Internet gambling under the terms "Hawaii," "vacation," and "rental."

In the early days of the Web, the skirmish between search engines and spammers was entertaining to watch. It was a veritable war, with search engines using many clues, such as font color, position, and repetition to eliminate some words from the index. They guarded their secrets zealously, for knowing those secrets would enable spammers to beat the system again easily enough.

With the invention of hyperlink-based ranking techniques for the Web, which I shall discuss in detail in Chapter 7, spamming went through a setback phase. The number and popularity of sites that cited a page started to matter quite strongly in determining the rank of that page in response to a query, sometimes more so than the text occurring on the page itself. However, when we revisit this topic, I will point out renewed efforts to spam even link-based ranking mechanisms.

Titles, headings, metatags, and anchor text

Although specific implementations may well include various bells and whistles, the standard TFIDF framework treats all terms uniformly. On the Web, valuable information may be lost this way, because the authorship idioms for the Web are quite different from the genres in classical IR benchmarks (news articles, financial news, medical abstracts). Web pages may also be shorter than a typical document in IR benchmarks, and depend on frames, menu bars, and other hypertext navigation aids for exposition. Most search engines respond to these different idioms by assigning weights to text occurring in titles (`<title>...</title>`), headings (`<h2>...</h2>`), font modifiers (`<strong>... </strong>`, `<b>...</b>`, `<em>...</em>`, `<font ...>...</font>`), and metatags (see Figure 3.5).

As the HTML standard matured, the metatag was introduced to help page writers identify the HTML version that the page follows, to insert descriptive keywords in a relatively structured format without having to cloak them, and to control caching and expiration parameters to be honored by browsers and crawlers (see Section 2.3.11). Figure 3.5 shows an example. For a while this scheme worked well, and some search engines started to use metatags for indexing and presenting

```
<HEAD>
<TITLE>Philately</TITLE>
<META name="description" content="Everything you wanted to know
about stamps, from prices to history.">
<META name="keywords" content="stamps, stamp collecting, stamp
history, prices, stamps for sale">
<META http-equiv="expires" content="Wed, 26 Feb 1997 08:21:57 GMT">
<META http-equiv="Pragma" content="no-cache">
</HEAD>
```

FIGURE 3.5 Use of HTML metatags.

blurbs alongside responses. Gradually, however, metatags became fertile grounds for spammers to run amok. Subsequently, search engines became more wary of paying attention to metatags for indexing.

On the other hand, the Web's rich hyperlink structure came to the rescue. Succinct descriptions of the content of a page or site v may often be found in the text of pages u that link to v. The text in and near the "anchor" or HREF construct may be especially significant, as in the following page fragment:

```
<h2>Japanese car companies</h2>
<ul>
<li><a href="http://www.toyota.com">Toyota</a></li>
<li><a href="http://www.mazda.com">Mazda</a></li>
</ul>
```

In fact, Toyota may never say it is a Japanese car company on its homepage, and *www.ibm.com* may not mention that the company manufactures mainframe computers.

In the World Wide Web Worm system, McBryan built an index where page v, which had not been fetched by the crawler, would be indexed using anchor text on pages u that link to v [143]. At that time, this was done primarily to enable some limited form of search and retrieval over pages not covered by the crawler, effectively increasing its "reach" by one link's worth. Lycos (*www.lycos.com/*) and Google (*www.google.com/*) adopted the same approach, increasing their reach by almost a factor of two. As we shall see in Chapter 7, (near) anchor text on u offers valuable editorial judgment about v as well. Consensus among many authors of pages like u about what terms to use as (near) anchor text is valuable in fighting spam and returning better-ranked responses.

Ranking for complex queries including phrases

Many search systems permit the query to contain single words, phrases, and word inclusions and exclusions, (e.g., socks -shoes +"network protocol"). Search engines differ in how they perform vector-space ranking in the presence of phrases, inclusions, and exclusions. Explicit inclusions and exclusions using + and - are hard Boolean predicates; all responses must satisfy these. Hard clauses involving phrases are dealt with similarly. With operators and phrases, the query (or the documents) can no longer be treated as ordinary points in vector space.

Suppose we had access to a dictionary of phrases while indexing the collection. The simplest approach is to construct two separate indices: one for single terms and another for phrases. Basically, we can regard the phrases as new dimensions added to the vector space [154]. If necessary, while computing similarity to the query, we can use a suitable scale factor (apart from IDF) for the axes representing the phrases. This approach is useful when query phrases are found in the dictionary. Otherwise, computing the IDF of a query phrase would require a subquery by itself, which may slow down the search.

The phrase dictionary could be cataloged manually, or derived from the corpus itself using statistical techniques. To decide if "t_1 t_2" occurs more often as a phrase than their individual rates of occurrence would lead us to expect, we build their contingency table:

$k_{00} = k(\bar{t}_1\ \bar{t}_2)$	$k_{01} = k(\bar{t}_1\ t_2)$
$k_{10} = k(t_1\ \bar{t}_2)$	$k_{11} = k(t_1\ t_2)$

Here $\bar{t}$ means a term other than t, and $k(\ )$ is the count of the respective events in the corpus. Let us propose and test the null hypothesis that the occurrences of t_1 and t_2 are independent, in which case we should observe $\Pr(t_1\ t_2) = \Pr(t_1)\Pr(t_2)$. To the extent the pair violates the null hypothesis, it is likely to be a phrase. If the null hypothesis holds, we need only two parameters, $\Pr(t_1)$ and $\Pr(t_2)$, whereas if it does not, the alternative hypothesis holds, and we need the four probabilities corresponding to each cell—that is, three parameters (because the four probabilities add up to 1).

We can use the well-known "likelihood ratio test." A hypothesis has *parameters* p taken from a parameter space Π and *observations* k, and the likelihood of the hypothesis is denoted $H(p; k)$. The likelihood ratio of the hypothesis is

$$\lambda = \frac{\max_{p \in \Pi_0} H(p; k)}{\max_{p \in \Pi} H(p; k)} \tag{3.11}$$

where Π is the entire parameter space and Π_0 is the parameter space corresponding to the null hypothesis. Because $\Pi_0 \subseteq \Pi$, $\lambda \leq 1$. It is known that $-2 \log \lambda$ is asymptotically χ^2-distributed with degree of freedom equal to the difference in the dimensions of Π_0 (in our example, 2) and Π (3). If occurrences of t_1 and t_2 are independent, λ is almost 1, and $-2 \log \lambda$ is almost 0. The larger the value of $-2 \log \lambda$, the stronger the dependence. In the Bernoulli trial setting that we have used,

$$H(p_{00}, p_{01}, p_{10}, p_{11}; k_{00}, k_{01}, k_{10}, k_{11}) \propto p_{00}^{k_{00}} p_{01}^{k_{01}} p_{10}^{k_{10}} p_{11}^{k_{11}} \tag{3.12}$$

whereas

$$\begin{aligned} H(p_1, p_2; k_{00}, k_{01}, k_{10}, k_{11}) \propto\ & ((1 - p_1)(1 - p_2))^{k_{00}} \ ((1 - p_1)p_2)^{k_{01}} \\ & \times (p_1(1 - p_2))^{k_{10}} \ (p_1 p_2)^{k_{11}} \end{aligned} \tag{3.13}$$

It is easy to maximize these probabilities through suitable choices of the parameters: for example, for the null hypothesis, $p_1/(1 - p_1)$ should equal $(k_{10} + k_{11})/(k_{01} + k_{00})$ to maximize the probability. Now one can sort the entries by $-2 \log \lambda$ and compare the top rankers against a χ^2 table to note the confidence with which the null hypothesis is violated. Dunning [75] reports the following top candidates from some common English text:

$-2 \log \lambda$	Phrase
271	the swiss
264	can be
257	previous year
167	mineral water
$\vdots$	

We will return to more tools for finding statistically significant dependence later in this book, notably in Chapter 5.

Approximate string matching

Even though a large fraction of Web pages are written in English, many other languages are also used. Dialects of English or transliteration from other languages may make many word spellings nonuniform. Often an exact character-by-character match between the query terms entered by the user and the keys in the inverted index may miss relevant matches.

Broadly speaking, there are two ways to reduce this problem. The first is to use an aggressive conflation mechanism that will collapse variant spellings into the same token. Soundex is one such conflation scheme that takes phonetics and pronunciation details into account [159], and has been used with great success in indexing and searching last names in census and telephone directory data. For example, *bradley*, *bartle*, *bartlett*, and *brodley* all share the soundex code *B634*. Soundex works well with western names, but cannot conflate, for example, *chiang* and *gong*, two transliterations of a Chinese word meaning "river."

The other approach is to decompose terms into a sequence of q-grams or sequences of q characters. For example, *wong* decomposes into the 2-grams *wo*, *on*, and *ng*, whereas *yang* decomposes into *ya*, *an*, and *ng*, and they now overlap in one out of three 2-grams. (If all vowels are conflated ahead of time, the terms become *w@ng* and *y@ng*, and the overlap is 2/3.) Depending on the language and the number of characters in a typical syllable, q is usually set between 2 and 4.

Looking up the inverted index now becomes a two-stage affair: first a different, smaller index of q-grams is consulted to expand each query term into a set of slightly distorted query terms, then all these terms are submitted to the regular index. An overlap threshold tunes the recall-precision trade-off. A similar idea has been used to find near duplicate Web pages; this technique will be discussed in Section 3.3.2. Approximate term matching in its general form is not very common in search engines. Some search engines like AltaVista permit query words to end with the wildcard character "$\star$": *univ$\star$* will match "universe" and "university." Recently, Google has started suggesting variant spellings of query terms. We conjecture that these variants are found from frequent queries in query logs using q-gram techniques.

Metasearch systems

Web IR as we have seen so far brings the documents to a central indexing and query processing system. The crawler turns the distributed document repository into a local one, on which IR systems can work. However, we can, to some

extent, take the search engine to the document rather than take the document to the search engine. More precisely, a *metasearch system*[4] forwards queries to many geographically distributed repositories, each with its own search service, and consolidates their responses.

Metasearch systems are fairly popular because they add value in a number of ways. Some of them perform nontrivial query rewriting to suit a single user query to many search engines with different query syntaxes. The overlap between the crawls collected by the major Web search engines is curiously small [16]. A metasearch system improves recall and thereby becomes a one-stop shop for many users.

Apart from providing a common query interface, metasearch systems must combine and present responses from multiple underlying search engines. The function has to go beyond just eliminating duplicates. Generally, each constituent search engine has a different, unpublished ranking algorithm. The metasearch system can generally depend only on the rank ordering. Web search services usually do not provide standard scores that can be combined by middleware easily and meaningfully. Rank consolidation is a simpler problem for intranet settings because all the constituent search engines and the metasearch system can be designed to work with each other.

3.3 Similarity Search

The "cluster hypothesis" in IR states that documents similar to documents that you have found relevant are also likely to be relevant. Many search engines provide a "more like this" or "find similar" button or hyperlink accompanying each search result. In this section I will first discuss efficient ways to provide a "find similar" service in the context of the vector-space model.

On the Web, a naive implementation of "find similar" is likely to bring up many copies of the query document. Many Web pages and sites are copied for faster and robust access worldwide in the face of poor or unpredictable network performance. Copying a single page is called *replication* or *duplication*, whereas copying an entire site is usually called *mirroring*. We will use these terms interchangeably where there is no danger of confusion.

---

4. They are sometimes wrongly called *metacrawlers*, although they generally do not do any crawling.

For a Web search engine, avoiding replicated documents and sites is desirable for a number of reasons: the index becomes smaller, searches get faster, and users are not annoyed by several identical responses to a query (keyword or "find similar"). In addition, as we have seen in Chapter 2, detecting duplicate pages also helps us delete duplicate outlinks during crawling, which can lead to significant savings in network and storage systems.

3.3.1   Handling "Find-Similar" Queries

In the vector-space model, queries and documents are both represented using unit-length, TFIDF vectors. Therefore, we can simply define the "find-similar" problem as, Given a "query" document d_q, find some small number (say, 10 to 20) of documents d from the corpus D having the largest value of $d_q \cdot d$ among all documents in D, where $\cdot$ is the dot-product.

To simplify the discussion, I will pick a slightly simpler measure. An alternative representation of a document d is a *set* of tokens $T(d)$. While discussing basic indexing, we have already seen how a document may be tokenized so that it can be represented as a sequence of tokens. Depending on the application, similarity searching may need more detailed preprocessing. For example, financial documents copied to different countries may choose to customize money amounts in units of local currency, in which case the currency symbol as well as the amounts change. One may choose to replace all currency symbols with a single token and all digit sequences following a currency symbol with another single token for such an application. Apart from these comments, we leave the specification of the tokenization step deliberately incomplete.

Using $T(d)$, one may define a similarity measure called the *Jaccard coefficient*:

$$r'(d_1, d_2) = \frac{|T(d_1) \cap T(d_2)|}{|T(d_1) \cup T(d_2)|} \tag{3.14}$$

r' would forgive any number of occurrences and any permutations of the terms. $r'(d, d) = 1$ and $r'(d_1, d_2) = r'(d_2, d_1)$, but r' does not satisfy the triangle inequality. A slightly different measure of *distance*, $1 - r'(d_1, d_2)$, is a metric.

It is easiest to precompute the nearest documents for each document, because d_q will be a rather long query otherwise, and the precomputed result is only linear in the size of the corpus and very small compared to, say, the inverted index itself. So our modified problem is, Given a large corpus D, find and store, for each $d \in D$, some small number of other documents most similar to d as per the measure r'.

```
 1: for each document d in the collection do
 2:     for each term t ∈ d do
 3:         write out record (t, d) to a file f₁.
 4:     end for
 5: end for
 6: sort the file f₁ in (t, d) order
 7: aggregate records from f₁ into the form (t, Dₜ), where Dₜ is the set of
    documents that contain t
 8: for each term t scanned from f₁ do
 9:     for each pair d₁, d₂ ∈ Dₜ do
10:         write out record (d₁, d₂, 1) to another file f₂
11:     end for
12: end for
13: sort and aggregate f₂ on key (d₁, d₂) to compute a map from (d₁, d₂)
    to the number of terms shared between d₁ and d₂
14: find r′ for qualifying document pairs
15: report document pairs with large r′
```

FIGURE 3.6 Using sketches to detect near duplicates.

For large D (such as a Web crawl) we cannot afford to score all pairs of documents, but the extreme sparsity of document vectors may save us. Two documents need to share at least one term to figure in the rankings. Also, we can a priori eliminate very frequent terms that occur, say, in more than 50% of the documents, because they are not very indicative of content (an IDF consideration). Next we can scan the inverted index of qualifying terms, compiling document *pairs* that share each term. Sorting on the document pair as the key lets us easily estimate the number of terms shared between all pairs of documents with nonzero overlap. Pseudocode for these steps is shown in Figure 3.6.

This procedure is still at the mercy of the data: frequent terms can mess up the running time even though the output size is linear in the number of documents. Part of the problem is that the obvious algorithm seeks to estimate every $r′$ exactly, which is unnecessary; a fixed error threshold would be quite adequate. This leads us to a randomized approach that I describe next. The main idea is to reduce the two term sets to two numbers using a carefully chosen random function, such that the two numbers match with a probability equal to the Jaccard coefficient between the two sets. In what follows, remember that each document d is now simply a *set* $T(d)$ of term IDs.

Suppose the universe of distinct term IDs is $N = \{1, 2, \ldots, n\}$, and let $\pi : N \to N$ be a permutation from N to N chosen uniformly at random from the $n!$ available permutations. Let $A, B \subseteq N$ and let $\pi(X) \subseteq N$ denote the set of numbers obtained by applying π elementwise on $X \subseteq N$. How many permutations out of the $n!$ available permutations satisfy

$$\min(\pi(A)) = \min(\pi(B)) \tag{3.15}$$

It is easy to see that if $x = \min(\pi(A)) = \min(\pi(B))$, then $\pi^{-1}(x)$ must belong to $A \cap B$. Thus the question simplifies to, How many permutations map some element of $A \cap B$ to the minimum image of all elements in $A \cup B$? To construct such a permutation

1. We can pick from N the range to which $A \cup B$ is mapped in $\binom{n}{|A \cup B|}$ ways.

2. The remaining $n - |A \cup B|$ elements that were not chosen may be permuted every way, that is, in $(n - |A \cup B|)!$ ways.

3. The element to be mapped to the minimum value in the range can be chosen in $|A \cap B|$ ways.

4. The remaining elements in $A \cup B$ can be permuted in $(|A \cup B| - 1)!$ ways.

Multiplying these together, we get

$$\binom{n}{|A \cup B|} (n - |A \cup B|)! \, |A \cap B| \, (|A \cup B| - 1)! = \frac{|A \cap B|}{|A \cup B|} n! \text{ ways} \tag{3.16}$$

Therefore, if a permutation π were picked uniformly at random from the $n!$ available permutations,

$$\Pr_\pi \left(\min(\pi(A)) = \min(\pi(B)) \right) = \frac{|A \cap B|}{|A \cup B|} \tag{3.17}$$

This suggests a simple technique for estimating the Jaccard coefficient $r'(d_1, d_2)$ using more than one random permutation, shown in Figure 3.7. The choice of m, the number of permutations, is guided by the precision sought in estimating r'.

To convert the pairwise test to a more efficient batch process over all documents, we would organize the computation as shown in Figure 3.8. The number of (d_1, d_2) entries over all the g streams, divided by m, gives the desired estimate of $r'(d_1, d_2)$ where this is positive. For each d_1, we can now retain a small number of d_2s that have sufficiently large $r'(d_1, d_2)$.

1: generate a set of m random permutations $\{\pi\}$
2: **for** each π **do**
3:      compute $\pi(T(d_1))$ and $\pi(T(d_2))$
4:      check if min $\pi(T(d_1)) = $ min $\pi(T(d_2))$
5: **end for**
6: if equality was observed in k cases, estimate $r'(d_1, d_2) = k/m$.

FIGURE 3.7 Using a random permutation to estimate the Jaccard coefficient.

1: **for** each random permutation π **do**
2:      create a file f_π
3:      **for** each document d **do**
4:          write out $\langle s = $ min $\pi(T(d)), d\rangle$ to f_π
5:      **end for**
6:      sort f_π using key s—this results in contiguous blocks with fixed s containing all associated ds
7:      create a file g_π
8:      **for** each pair (d_1, d_2) within a run of f_π having a given s **do**
9:          write out a **document pair** record (d_1, d_2) to g_π
10:     **end for**
11:     sort g_π on key (d_1, d_2)
12: **end for**
13: merge g_π for all π in (d_1, d_2) order, counting the number of (d_1, d_2) entries

FIGURE 3.8 Using random permutations for fast similarity search.

3.3.2 Eliminating Near Duplicates via Shingling

The "find-similar" algorithm described thus far will (correctly) report all duplicates of a query document d_q as being most similar to d_q, which will likely not be very satisfying to the user. One way to eliminate these duplicate pages in the response is to maintain a checksum with every page in the corpus, and throw out from the response any page whose checksum also matches the checksum of d_q.

Comparing simple checksums of entire pages (see Section 2.3.7) may, however, fail to detect replicated documents in many cases. The contents of replicated documents are often slightly dissimilar from the source. Replicated pages may include URLs that contain different hostnames, even if the file paths look similar. The anchors may be modified to suit the organization of the site where the copy is stored, a site maintainer's name or the latest update time may be added to the bottom of the page. The source page may change after the copying is completed or between copying instants. Formatting may be customized across sites.

Instead of depending on exact equality of checksums, one can define and measure some graded notion of dissimilarity between pages. A standard approach to measuring the dissimilarity between two strings is the *edit distance* between them: the number of character insertions, deletions, and replacements required to transform one string to the other [56]. The time taken to compute the edit distance between two strings is proportional to the product of their lengths, which would be a little slow for whole Web documents, which are typically a few kilobytes long. More problematic is the need to compare documents pairwise. If a crawler fetches a billion documents, finding the edit distance between all pairs of documents would be impractical.

Note that our implicit assumption is that an overlap in the *set* of keywords used by two documents hints at semantic similarity, whereas sharing entire *sequences* of words is a sign of plagiarism or duplication. A simpler way to catch plagiarism than edit distance is the so-called q-gram approach, which we study now.

A *q-gram*, also called a *shingle*, is a contiguous subsequence of tokens taken from a document. $S(d, w)$ is the *set* of distinct shingles of width w contained in document d. When w is fixed, we shall shorthand this to $S(d)$. (Note that $T(d) = S(d, 1)$.) As with single tokens, one may represent a shingle by a fixed-length integer. $S(d)$ is thus just a set of integers. For example, if each token is represented by a 32-bit ID, and $w = 4$, a shingle is a 128-bit number, and $S(d)$ is an unordered set of 128-bit numbers. In practice, $w = 10$ has been found suitable.

Using the shingled document representation, one may again define the *resemblance* between documents d_1 and d_2 as the Jaccard coefficient

$$r(d_1, d_2) = \frac{|S(d_1) \cap S(d_2)|}{|S(d_1) \cup S(d_2)|} \tag{3.18}$$

Hereafter, we can plug in the technique for finding similar documents that we studied in the previous section. In effect, we take all document pairs that look similar, then eliminate those that look *too* similar. While running the algorithm on shingles, we can use the results of the first run to limit the number of candidate document pairs written out in Figure 3.8.

It might be useful to run these algorithms even during crawling. Detecting replicated pages may also help us identify mirror sites and use this information to streamline subsequent crawls. Replication is one aspect of Web IR that is almost nonexistent in classic IR. Unfortunately, not all Web search engines do high-quality near duplicate elimination, possibly to avoid the computational complexity. Google is a notable exception.

3.3.3 Detecting Locally Similar Subgraphs of the Web

Interestingly, similarity search and duplicate elimination can be applied not only on text but also on the graph structure of the Web. Collapsing locally similar Web subgraphs can improve the quality of hyperlink-assisted ranking in Web search engines. In this chapter we have reviewed text-based IR for the most part. In Chapter 7 we shall see that for a hypertext repository such as the Web, hyperlinks are a valuable indicator of the authority of a page, which may be used as a supplementary ranking device. As a crude measure, the total number of citations to a page may be considered an indicator of its popularity. Deliberate or inadvertent spamming is not limited to terms alone; knowledge of link-based ranking algorithms lets site designers synthesize Web subgraphs that are favored by search engines using such ranking algorithms. In fact, there are many businesses whose exclusive portfolio is to improve search engine rankings for their customers. One common trick they use is to build tightly knit hyperlink communities between their customers' sites, using a number of replicated pages and sites hosted in diverse Internet domains. If the pages u that link to a page v are extensively replicated without independent editorial judgment based on page contents, current link-based ranking algorithms are likely to rate page v more popular than may be regarded as fair. Therefore, the ability to collapse similar regions of the Web graph can also improve link-based ranking algorithms.

In this section we will review a few approaches to detecting mirrored sites (as opposed to replicated single documents). The first approach involves repeatedly finding pages with nearly identical outlink sequences, collapsing the names of these pages, and replacing links to these pages by canonical, collapsed names.

Given a large collection of HTML pages, such as obtained from a crawler, the first step is to collect a database of HREF targets and turn them into a canonical form, such as by using the default hostname using a DNS resolution, adding a default port number, and adding trailing slashes if needed. (Obtaining the effective URI, *universal resource identifier,* for each page by an actual fetch might be too slow.) The cleaned URLs are listed and sorted to find duplicates and near duplicates, and each set of equivalent URLs is assigned a unique token ID. Each page is now stripped of all text and represented as a sequence of these outlink IDs alone.

Suppose u_1 links to v_1, and u_2 links to v_2, and v_1 and v_2 pass our test for being duplicates. For example, v_1 could be http://www.yahoo.com/ and v_2 could be http://dir.yahoo.com/. (At the time of writing, most outlinks in http://www.yahoo.com/ are relative, and their corresponding outlinks in http://dir.yahoo.com/ are relative to http://www.yahoo.com/ using an <a base=...>

directive.) In u_1 and u_2, we can now replace the HREFs by a common name v'. Observe that this makes the link sequences in u_1 and u_2 look more similar than before; in particular, they may now be regarded as duplicates. This process can be started using textual duplicate detection and then continued using the link sequence representation, until no further collapse of multiple URLs is possible.

The second approach, somewhat similar to the first, is to identify single nodes that are near duplicates, using text shingling, for instance, and then to *extend* single-node mirrors to two-node mirrors, and continue to larger and larger graphs that are likely mirrors of one another. Both of these are bottom-up approaches, requiring page contents to be analyzed for candidate replicas.

The third approach uses regularity in URL strings to identify host pairs that are mirrors, hopefully before many of the corresponding pages need to be fetched. Building upon the notion of near duplication of pages, two hosts are said to be mirrors if a large fraction of paths (the portions of the URL after the hostname, see Section 2.1) are valid on both Web sites, and these common paths link to pages that are near duplicates.

The algorithm proceeds by identifying candidate host pairs that might be mirrors and then performing a more thorough check. The raw data for each host is simply a set of known URL paths on it. Since our candidate detection must be fast, we need to design a suitable set of features to extract from this set of paths. To this end, we

1. Convert host and path to all lowercase characters

2. Let any punctuation or digit sequence be a token separator

3. Tokenize the URL into a sequence of tokens, for example, *www6.infoseek.com* gives *www, infoseek, com*

4. Eliminate stop terms such as *htm, html, txt, main, index, home, bin, cgi*

5. Form positional bigrams from the token sequence, for example, `/cell-block16/inmates/dilbert/personal/foo.htm` yields bigrams (*cellblock,inmates,*0), (*inmates,dilbert,*1), (*dilbert,personal,*2), and (*personal, foo,*3)

Once hosts are represented as sets of such positional bigrams, we can use the same sort of algorithms as shown in Figure 3.6 or Figure 3.8 to flag potentially mirrored hosts. Subsequent tests can involve matching textual similarity between pages hosted at the candidate mirrors.

3.4 **Bibliographic Notes**

There exist several authoritative and comprehensive texts about text indexing and vector-space searching that cover the area in more depth than possible in this chapter. Interested readers are referred to the classic texts by Salton and McGill [186]; Keith van Reijsbergen (*Information Retrieval*, available online at *www.dcs.gla.ac.uk/Keith/Preface.html* and *www.dcs.gla.ac.uk/~iain/keith/index.htm*); Frakes and Baeza-Yates [82]; and Witten, Moffat, and Bell [215] for details of indexing and searching. The SMART IR system from Cornell University (*ftp://ftp.cs.cornell.edu/pub/smart/*) is, after decades, still a definitive code base for IR research. The Glimpse system from the University of Arizona (*glimpse.cs.arizona.edu/*) has also seen wide circulation for efficient crawling and indexing of medium-scale Web servers for intranet use. In the commercial domain, Verity and PLS are well-known vendors of text indexing systems. The ACM Special Interest Group for IR (*www.acm.org/sigir/*) and TREC, the Text REtrieval Conference (*trec.nist.gov/*) publish the performance of IR systems on many standard corpora.

The compression of indices and their use for fast IR have been researched extensively; much of that work is accessible via Witten, Moffat, and Bell's book. I note a few issues here. Search engines try hard to order the execution plan so that the active result size is cut down as fast as possible. Consider a simple and query involving terms t_1, t_2, and t_3. The engine starts by probing the index with these three terms and gets three sorted lists of document IDs. A simple strategy is to start with the smallest document ID list. Furthermore, an IR system has to answer so-called iceberg queries: in principle, given the query q, it has to evaluate the similarity between q and each candidate document d in the collection, and then discard all but the k most similar documents. If k is small (typically 10 to 20) and the corpus is large (typically one-half to one billion), the computational effort in similarity computation is out of proportion compared to the size of the useful output. (The user is searching for the "tip of the iceberg" but the system computes the whole iceberg.) In cosine-based ranking, any document having even one word in common with the query will have a positive similarity score and needs to be considered for ranking. However, low-IDF terms may contribute little to the final ranking and may be possible to prune while the query execution is in progress. An elegant algorithm for bulk queries is given by Cohen and Lewis [52].

Some of the early work in probabilistic IR is reported by Sparck Jones, Robertson, and Walker [183, 200], Ponte and Croft [177], and Turtle and Croft [204]. The probabilistic retrieval models described in this chapter may be regarded

as supervised learners (see Chapter 5), which need labels (relevant or irrelevant) from the user to be able to estimate parameters such as *a* and *b* discussed before. To apply probabilistic techniques to ad hoc queries more effectively, we need to reuse relevance feedback across queries, using what is called the *description-oriented approach* [92, 86]. The idea is to synthesize several query-neutral attributes on the (q, d) pair and let probabilistic inferencing techniques learn from relevance feedback which attributes are useful for ranking. The advantage of query-neutral attribute synthesis is that each query can potentially improve the system for any future query if there are terms shared between these queries. Description-oriented approaches are thus a practical compromise between domain knowledge and purely data-driven learning.

For Web search engines, the Web is the best source of current information. Search Engine Watch (*searchenginewatch.com/*) has extremely informative articles about coverage, ranking technology, and anecdotes about major search engines. Bharat and Bröder made early estimates of the relative coverage of major Web search engines [16]. Lawrence and Lee Giles made estimates of the number of functioning Http servers and the number of pages therein [133]. Document fingerprinting and hashing are classic topics, but in the context of the Web, the shingling idea discussed in Section 3.3.2 was first proposed by Bröder and others [27]. The technique described in Section 3.3.3 for collapsing near duplicate subgraphs of the Web was used by Kumar and others [128]. The bottom–up cluster-growing approach is due to Cho et al. [51]. Bharat, Bröder, and others proposed and evaluated a top–down mirror detection approach [17] based on URL paths; I have briefly mentioned some salient features of their approach.

Indexing high-dimensional data is a classic difficult problem. For low-dimensional data it is possible to index one or more attributes for faster range and proximity search, as is done using B-trees or kd-trees for relational databases. However, as the number of dimensions increases, these data structures become less effective. This problem is not peculiar to text searches alone, but also occurs in indexing and searching images or speech where, too, the number of features is large. Recent work by Kleinberg [123] and Gionis et al. [90] provide new algorithms for similarity searches in high dimension. Whether they can outperform inverted index-based methods depends on the typical number of terms in a query (for Web queries, two terms on average) and the typical number of documents containing a query term. If the inverted index is sparse and the query is short, the standard inverted index approach may be quite efficient.

PART I

INFRASTRUCTURE

PART II

LEARNING

CHAPTER 4

SIMILARITY AND CLUSTERING

Keyword query processing and response ranking, described in Chapter 3, depend on computing a measure of *similarity* between the query and documents in the collection. Although the query is regarded at par with the documents in the vector-space model, it is usually much shorter and prone to ambiguity (the average Web query is only two to three words long). For example, the query *star* is highly ambiguous, retrieving documents about astronomy, plants and animals, popular media and sports figures, and American patriotic songs. Their vector-space similarity (see Chapter 3) to the single-word query may carry no hint that documents pertaining to these topics are highly dissimilar. However, if the search *clusters* the responses along the lines of these topics, as shown in Figure 4.1, the user can quickly disambiguate the query or drill down into a specific topic.

Apart from visualization of search results, clustering is useful for taxonomy design and similarity search. Topic taxonomies such as Yahoo! and the Open Directory (*dmoz.org/*) are constructed manually, but this process can be greatly facilitated by a preliminary clustering of large samples of Web documents. Clustering can also assist fast similarity search, described in Section 3.3.1. Given a precomputed clustering of the corpus, the search for documents similar to a query document d_q may be efficiently limited to a small number of clusters that are most similar to d_q, quickly eliminating a large number of documents that we can safely surmise would rank poorly.

Similarity, in a rather general way, is fundamental to many search and mining operations on hypertext and is central to most of this book. In this chapter we will study how measures of similarity are used to cluster a collection of documents into

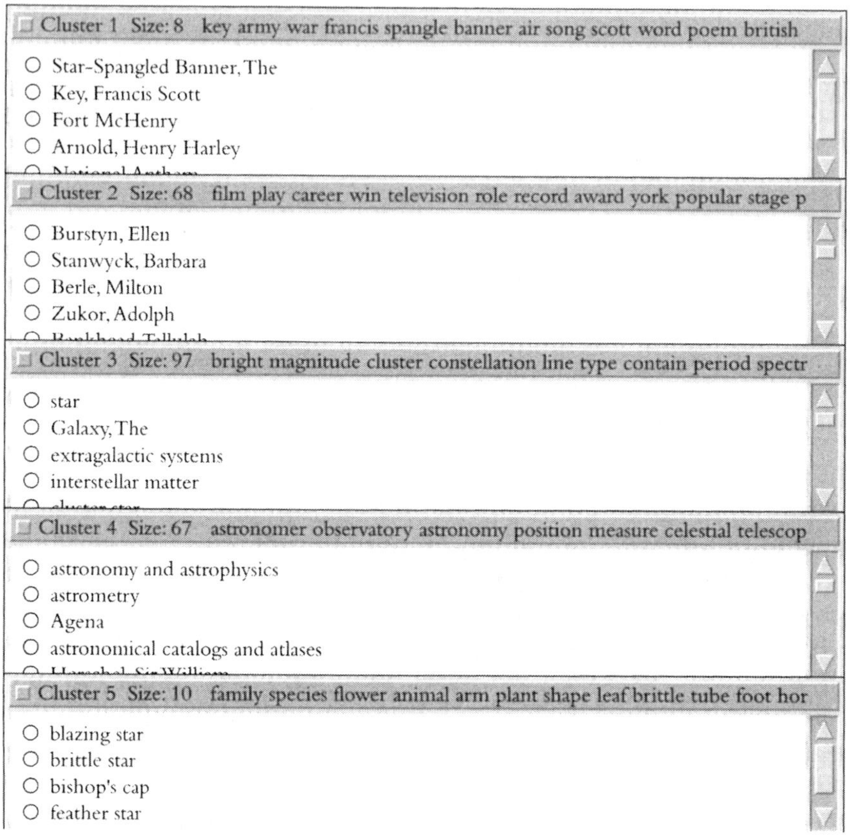

FIGURE 4.1 Scatter/Gather, a text clustering system, can separate salient topics in response to keyword queries. (Image courtesy of Hearst [101].)

groups within which interdocument similarity is large compared to the similarity between documents chosen from different groups. The utility of clustering for text and hypertext information retrieval lies in the so-called *cluster hypothesis*: given a "suitable" clustering of a collection, if the user is interested in document *d*, she is likely to be interested in other members of the cluster to which *d* belongs.

The cluster hypothesis is not limited to documents alone. If documents are similar because they share terms, terms can also be represented as bit-vectors representing the documents in which they occur, and these bit-vectors can be used to cluster the terms. As with terms and documents, we can set up a bipartite relation for people liking documents, and use this to cluster both people and documents, with the premise that similar people like similar documents, and vice versa. This important ramification of clustering is called *collaborative filtering*.

This chapter is organized as follows: I start with an overview of basic formulations and approaches to clustering (Section 4.1). Then I describe two important clustering paradigms: a bottom-up agglomerative technique (Section 4.2.1), which collects similar documents into larger and larger groups, and a top-down partitioning technique (Section 4.2.2), which divides a corpus into topic-oriented partitions. These are followed by a slew of clustering techniques that can be broadly classified as *embeddings* of the corpus in a low-dimensional space so as to bring out the clustering present in the data (Section 4.3). Next, I discuss probabilistic models and algorithms in Section 4.4, and end the chapter with a discussion of collaborative filtering.

4.1 Formulations and Approaches

Formulations of clustering problems range from combinatorial to fuzzy, and no single objective serves all applications. Most of the combinatorial definitions are intractable to optimize. Clustering is a classic applied art where a great deal of experience with data must supplement stock algorithms. It is beyond the scope of a single chapter to cover the entire breadth of the subject, but there are many classic books on it. My goal is to highlight broad classes of algorithms and the specific issues that arise when one seeks to find structure in text and hypertext domains.

I first propose a few formal specifications of the clustering problem and outline some basic approaches to clustering. We are given a collection D of documents (in general, entities to be clustered). Entities either may be characterized by some *internal* property, such as the vector-space model for documents, or they may be characterized only *externally*, via a measure of distance (dissimilarity) $\delta(d_1, d_2)$ or resemblance (similarity) $\rho(d_1, d_2)$ specified between any two pairs of documents. For example, we can use the Euclidean distance between length-normalized document vectors for δ and cosine similarity for ρ. These measures have been discussed earlier, in Chapter 3.

4.1.1 Partitioning Approaches

One possible goal that we can set up for a clustering algorithm is to *partition* the document collection into k subsets or clusters $D_1, \ldots, D_k$ so as to minimize the intracluster distance $\sum_i \sum_{d_1, d_2 \in D_i} \delta(d_1, d_2)$ or maximize the intracluster resemblance $\sum_i \sum_{d_1, d_2 \in D_i} \rho(d_1, d_2)$. If an internal representation of documents is available, then it is also usual to specify a representation of clusters with regard to that same model. For example, if documents are represented using the vector-space model, a cluster of documents may be represented by the centroid (average) of the document vectors. When a cluster representation is available, a modified goal could be to partition D into $D_1, \ldots, D_k$ so as to minimize $\sum_i \sum_{d \in D_i} \delta(d, \vec{D}_i)$ or maximize $\sum_i \sum_{d \in D_i} \rho(d, \vec{D}_i)$, where $\vec{D}_i$ is the vector-space representation of cluster i.

One could think of assigning document d to cluster i as setting a Boolean variable $z_{d,i}$ to 1. This can be generalized to *fuzzy* or *soft* clustering where $z_{d,i}$ is a real number between zero and one. In such a scenario, one may wish to find $z_{d,i}$ so as to minimize $\sum_i \sum_{d \in D} z_{d,i} \delta(d, \vec{D}_i)$ or maximize $\sum_i \sum_{d \in D} z_{d,i} \rho(d, \vec{D}_i)$.

Partitions can be found in two ways. We can start with each document in a group of its own, and collapse together groups of documents until the number of partitions is suitable; this is called *bottom-up* clustering. Alternatively, we can declare the number of partitions that we want a priori, and assign documents to partitions; this is called *top-down* clustering. I will discuss both variants in Section 4.2.

4.1.2 Geometric Embedding Approaches

The human eye is impressive at noticing patterns and clusters in data presented as points embedded in two or three dimensions, as borne out by the naming of constellations and archipelagoes. If there is natural clustering in the data, and we manage to embed or project the data points to two or three dimensions without losing the clustering property, the resulting "map" may itself be an adequate clustering aid.

I will discuss several approaches to creating clusters in low-dimensional space. In one approach, called *self-organizing maps*, clusters are laid out on a plane in a regular grid, and documents are iteratively assigned to regions of the plane. For this approach we need documents to be specified using an internal description. In another approach, called *multidimensional scaling*, the system input is the pairwise (dis-)similarity between documents. The algorithm seeks to embed the documents as points in 2D to 3D space with the minimum distortion of pairwise distances. Both of these approaches are heuristic in nature; there is no general guarantee that all collections can be rendered well. Another technique, called *latent semantic indexing,* uses techniques from linear algebra to factor the term-document matrix. The factors can be used to derive a low-dimensional representation for documents as well as terms. This representation can also be used for ad hoc searching.

A different form of partition-based clustering is to identify *dense regions* in space. As an extreme example, we can start with a 1D space with a finite extent and a finite number of points, and claim that a cluster is demarcated by endpoints within which the number of points per unit length (density) is higher than (some multiple of) the average global density. Such a density-based notion of clustering can be readily extended to more dimensions. In particular, there may be no discernible clustering when the points are considered in the original space, but clusters may emerge when the points are projected to a subspace with a smaller number of dimensions. We can look for density-based clusters in a simple bottom-up fashion. The basic observation is that if a region is dense in k dimensions, then all projections of this region are dense. Therefore, the algorithm first finds 1D dense "regions," tries to compose them into 2D regions, discarding those that fail the density test, and so on. Unfortunately this method would not scale to textual data with tens of thousands of dimensions. The only way around seems to be to propose simple *generative distributions* for documents, discussed next.

4.1.3 Generative Models and Probabilistic Approaches

In the approaches outlined thus far, the measures of (dis-)similarity are provided by the user. Carelessly designed measures can easily damage the quality of clustering. The probabilistic approach seeks to model the document collection as being generated by a random process following a specific set of distributions. For example, we can assume that each cluster that we seek is associated with a distribution over the terms in our lexicon. Given the collection, we must estimate the number of distributions, and the parameters defining these distributions. Indeed, estimating these distributions can be *defined* as the clustering problem. We will study several techniques for estimating cluster distributions. Initially we will assume that each document is generated from exactly one distribution. However, in the common situation that clusters correspond to *topics*, a single-topic-per-document model is not entirely realistic: documents are often *mixtures* of multiple topics. The more advanced techniques that we will study can estimate models in this more general setting. (This part of the chapter is key to understanding many later chapters.)

Estimating a term distribution over documents is difficult. There is little hope of capturing the joint distribution between terms or term sequences, given the large number of terms in the vocabulary (tens to hundreds of thousands for many standard collections). Most practical models need to assume that term occurrences are independent of each other. Even if each term is associated with a simple Boolean event (the term occurs or does not occur in a document), the number of event combinations is astronomical compared to the size of any document collection that we are likely to encounter.

4.2   Bottom-Up and Top-Down Partitioning Paradigms

We will now study one bottom-up clustering technique that will repeatedly merge groups of similar documents until the desired number of clusters is attained, and a top-down technique that will iteratively refine the assignment of documents to a preset number of clusters. The former method is somewhat slower, but may be used on a small sample of the corpus to "seed" the initial clusters before the latter algorithm takes over.

4.2.1   Agglomerative Clustering

Although many formulations of the clustering problem are intractable, a simple, intuitive heuristic is to start with all the documents and successively combine them into groups within which interdocument similarity is high, collapsing down to as many groups as desired. This style is called *bottom-up, agglomerative,* or *hierarchical agglomerative clustering* (HAC) and is characterized by the broad pseudocode shown in Figure 4.2. HAC is widely used in document clustering and other IR applications [180, 213].

1: let each document d be in a singleton group $\{d\}$
2: let G be the set of groups
3: **while** $|G| > 1$ **do**
4:     choose $\Gamma, \Delta \in G$ according to some measure of similarity $s(\Gamma, \Delta)$
5:     remove Γ and Δ from G
6:     let $\Phi = \Gamma \cup \Delta$
7:     insert Φ into G
8: **end while**

FIGURE 4.2   Basic template for bottom-up hierarchical agglomerative clustering.

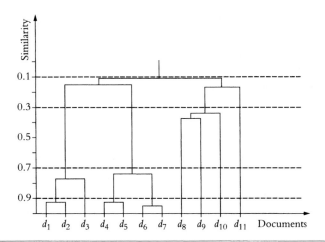

FIGURE 4.3 A dendrogram presents the progressive, hierarchy-forming merging process pictorially. The user can cut across the dendrogram at a suitable level of similarity to get the desired number of clusters. (Taken from [141].)

The hierarchical merging process leads to a tree called a *dendrogram*, drawn in the specific style shown in Figure 4.3. Typically, the earlier mergers happen between groups with a large similarity $s(\Gamma \cup \Delta)$. This value becomes lower and lower for later merges. The user can "cut across" the dendrogram at a suitable level to "read off" any desired number of clusters.

Algorithms differ as to how they compute the figure of merit for merging Γ and Δ. One commonly used measure is the *self-similarity* of $\Gamma \cup \Delta$. The self-similarity of a group of documents Φ is defined as the average pairwise similarity between documents in Φ

$$s(\Phi) = \frac{1}{\binom{|\Phi|}{2}} \sum_{d_1,d_2 \in \Phi} s(d_1, d_2) = \frac{2}{|\Phi|(|\Phi| - 1)} \sum_{d_1,d_2 \in \Phi} s(d_1, d_2) \qquad (4.1)$$

where the TFIDF cosine measure is commonly used for interdocument similarity $s(d_1, d_2)$. Other merger criteria exist. One may choose to merge that pair of clusters (Γ, Δ), which maximizes $\min_{d_1 \in \Gamma, d_2 \in \Delta} s(d_1, d_2)$, $\max_{d_1 \in \Gamma, d_2 \in \Delta} s(d_1, d_2)$, or $(\sum_{d_1 \in \Gamma, d_2 \in \Delta} s(d_1, d_2))/(|\Gamma| |\Delta|)$.

In this section, we will denote a document as d and its corresponding vector-space representation as $\vec{d}$, which we will sometimes simplify to d if there is no chance for confusion. If documents are already normalized to unit length in the L_2 norm, $s(d_1, d_2)$ is simply the dot-product, $\langle d_1, d_2 \rangle$.

By maintaining carefully chosen statistics, the dendrogram can be computed in about quadratic time and space. For any group Φ of documents, we maintain an unnormalized group profile vector

$$p(\Phi) = \sum_{d \in \Phi} \vec{d} \tag{4.2}$$

which is simply the sum of the document vectors belonging to that group, together with the number of documents in the group. It is easy to verify that

$$s(\Phi) = \frac{\langle p(\Phi), p(\Phi) \rangle - |\Phi|}{|\Phi|(|\Phi| - 1)} \tag{4.3}$$

and

$$p(\Gamma \cup \Delta) = \langle p(\Gamma), p(\Gamma) \rangle + \langle p(\Delta), p(\Delta) \rangle + 2 \langle p(\Gamma), p(\Delta) \rangle \tag{4.4}$$

Thus, in Figure 4.2, to compute $s(\Gamma \cup \Delta)$ from $p(\Gamma)$ and $p(\Delta)$ will cost just the time to do a few dot-products. For the moment we will assume that dimensionality of documents and group profiles are fixed, and therefore we can calculate a dot-product in constant time. (We will return to this issue.) Not much changes on each merge, so we would also like to maintain with each group Γ a *heap* [56] of partner groups Δ ordered by largest $s(\Gamma \cup \Delta)$. Thus, for each group, we can access its best partner (together with the score) in constant time. With n groups to start with, we precompute all pairwise similarities in $O(n^2)$ time, and insert them in heaps in $O(n^2 \log n)$ time. Now we can pick the best pair of groups to merge in $O(n)$ time, delete these groups from each of the heaps in $O(\log n)$ time, compute the similarity of the merger with old groups in $O(n)$ time, and update all heaps in $O(n \log n)$ time. Since there are $n - 1$ merges, the total time is $O(n^2 \log n)$, and all the heaps together consume $O(n^2)$ space.

Earlier we assumed that documents and group profile vectors are embedded in a space with a fixed number of dimensions. This is true, but the number of dimensions is rather large, running into tens of thousands. Moreover, the time taken to compute a dot-product is not really proportional to the number of dimensions, but only the number of nonzero coordinates, assuming a sparse vector representation is used (as it should be). For example, the Reuters collection [139] has about 22,000 financial news articles, a typical article having a few dozen to a few hundred distinct terms, whereas the total number of unique terms in the collection is over 30,000. As a result, dot–product computations near the leaves of the dendrogram would be very fast, but would get slower as the group profiles become denser, until near the root, profile vectors are almost entirely dense. A simple way to reduce the running time is to *truncate* document and group profile vectors to a fixed number (e.g., 1000) of the largest magnitude coordinates. In theory, this may lead to a clustering output that is different from what would be computed with a full representation, but empirical evidence suggests that the quality of clustering remains unaffected [60, 191].

4.2.2   The *k*-Means Algorithm

Bottom–up clustering, used directly, takes quadratic time and space and is not practical for large document collections. If the user can preset a (small) number *k* of desired clusters, a more efficient top–down partitioning strategy may be used. The best–known member of this family of algorithms is the *k*-means algorithm. We will discuss two forms of the *k*-means algorithm here. One makes "hard" (0/1) assignments of documents to clusters. The other makes "soft" assignments, meaning documents belong to clusters with a fractional score between 0 and 1.

k-means with "hard" assignment

In its common form, *k*-means uses internal representations for both the objects being clustered and the clusters themselves. For documents, the vector–space representation is used, and the cluster is represented as the centroid of the documents belonging to that cluster.

The initial configuration is arbitrary (or chosen by a heuristic external to the *k*-means algorithm), consisting of a grouping of the documents into *k* groups, and *k* corresponding vector–space centroids computed accordingly. Thereafter, the algorithm proceeds in alternating half–steps, as shown in Figure 4.4.

The basic step in *k*-means is also called *move-to-nearest,* for obvious reasons. A variety of criteria may be used for terminating the loop. One may exit when the assignment of documents to clusters ceases to change (much), or when cluster centroids move by negligible distances in successive iterations.

k-means with "soft" assignment

Rather than make any specific assignment of documents to clusters, the "soft" variant of *k*-means represents each cluster *c* using a vector μ_c in term space. Since there is no explicit assignment of documents to clusters, μ_c is not directly related to documents—for example, it is not necessarily the centroid of some documents.

1: initialize cluster centroids to arbitrary vectors
2: **while** further improvement is possible **do**
3:    **for** each document d **do**
4:       find the cluster c whose centroid is **most similar** to d
5:       assign d to this cluster c
6:    **end for**
7:    **for** each cluster c **do**
8:       recompute the centroid of cluster c based on documents assigned to it
9:    **end for**
10: **end while**

FIGURE 4.4   The k-means algorithm.

The goal of "soft" k-means is to find a μ_c for each c so as to minimize the *quantization error,* $\sum_d \min_c |d - \mu_c|^2$.

A simple strategy to iteratively reduce the error is to bring the mean vectors closer to the documents that they are closest to. We scan repeatedly through the documents, and for each document d, accumulate a "correction" $\Delta\mu_c$ for that μ_c that is closest to d:

$$\Delta\mu_c = \sum_d \begin{cases} \eta(d - \mu_c), & \text{if } \mu_c \text{ is closest to } d \\ 0 & \text{otherwise} \end{cases} \tag{4.5}$$

After scanning once through all documents, all the μ_cs are updated in a batch by setting all $\mu_c \leftarrow \mu_c + \Delta\mu_c$. η is called the *learning rate*. It maintains some memory of the past and stabilizes the system. Note that each d moves only one μ_c in each batch.

The contribution from d need not be limited to only that μ_c that is closest to it. The contribution can be shared among many clusters, the portion for cluster c being directly related to the current similarity between μ_c and d. For example, we can soften (4.5) to

$$\Delta\mu_c = \eta \frac{1/|d - \mu_c|^2}{\sum_\gamma 1/|d - \mu_\gamma|^2}(d - \mu_c)$$

or

$$\Delta\mu_c = \eta \frac{\exp(-|d - \mu_c|^2)}{\sum_\gamma \exp(-|d - \mu_\gamma|^2)}(d - \mu_c) \tag{4.6}$$

Many other update rules, similar in spirit, are possible. Soft assignment does not break close ties to make documents contribute to a single cluster that wins narrowly. It is easy to show that some variants of soft k-means are special cases of the EM algorithm (see Section 4.4.2), which can be proved to converge to local optima.

Running time

In both variants of k-means, for each round, n documents have to be compared against k centroids, which will take $O(kn)$ time. The number of rounds is usually not too strongly dependent on n or k, and may be regarded as fixed.

Bottom-up clustering is often used to "seed" the k-means procedure. If k clusters are sought, the strategy is to randomly select $O(\sqrt{kn})$ documents from the collection of n documents and subject them to bottom-up clustering until there are k groups left. This will take $O(kn \log n)$ time. Once this step is over, the centroids of the k clusters, together with the remaining points, are used to seed a k-means procedure, which takes $O(kn)$ time. The total time over the two phases is thus $O(kn \log n)$.

4.3 Clustering and Visualization via Embeddings

Visualization of results from IR systems is a key driving force behind clustering algorithms. Of the two clustering techniques we have studied so far, HAC lends itself more readily to visualization, because trees and hierarchies are ubiquitous as user interfaces. Although k-means collects documents into clusters, it has no mechanism to represent the clusters visually, in a small number of dimensions.

In this section we will study a few clustering approaches that directly represent the documents as points in a given number of dimensions (two to three if direct visualization is desired). We start with *Kohonen* or *self-organizing maps* (SOMs), a close cousin of k-means. Next, we study multidimensional scaling (MDS), which gives an explicit optimization objective: we wish to minimize the error or distortion of interpoint distances in the low-dimensional embedding as compared to the dissimilarity given in the input data. This is a satisfying formulation, but usually intractable to exact optimization. The third category of techniques uses linear transformations to reduce the number of dimensions, and some of these approximately but provably preserve important properties related to interdocument similarity.

In all these cases, the ability to reduce the data to points in a 2D or 3D space that can be visualized directly is very valuable. The human eye is great at detecting clusters in low dimensions, and techniques that transform the data to such a format without losing important similarity information from the original data are very useful for analyzing text collections.

4.3.1 Self-Organizing Maps (SOMs)

Self-organizing, or Kohonen, maps are a close cousin to k-means, except that unlike k-means, which is concerned only with determining the association between clusters and documents, the SOM algorithm also embeds the clusters in a low-dimensional space right from the beginning and proceeds in a way that places related clusters close together in that space.

As in "soft" k-means, the SOM is built by associating a representative vector μ_c with each cluster c, and iteratively refining these representative vectors. Unlike k-means, each cluster is also represented as a point in a low-dimensional space. Clusters might be represented by nodes in a triangular or square grid, for example. Figure 4.5 shows a triangular grid. A large number of clusters can be initialized even if many regions are to remain devoid of documents in the end. In Figure 4.5, the background intensity shows the local density of documents assigned to each grid point. By extracting frequent words and phrases from the documents assigned to each cluster, we can "name" regions of the map as shown in Figure 4.5.

Based on the low-dimensional embedding, a *neighborhood* $N(c)$ is defined for each cluster c; for the square grid, $N(c)$ might be chosen as all nodes within two hops of c. We also design a *proximity* function $h(\gamma, c)$, which tells us how close a node γ is to the node c. $h(c, c) = 1$, and h decays with distance (e.g., the number of links on the shortest path connecting γ and c in the grid). In fact, we don't really need $N(c)$; we can simply let $h(\gamma, c)$ be 0 for $\gamma \notin N(c)$.

The update rule for an SOM will be generalized straight from Equation (4.5) by adding one new feature: if document d matches cluster c_d best, the update contribution from d should apply not only to c_d but to all $\gamma \in N(c_d)$ as well. SOMs are a kind of neural network where data item d "activates" the neuron c_d and some other closely neighboring neurons. The overall algorithm initializes all μ to random vectors and repeatedly picks a random document d from the collection and updates the model at each neuron until the model vectors stop changing significantly. The update rule for node γ under the influence of d is thus written as

$$\mu_\gamma \leftarrow \mu_\gamma + \eta h(\gamma, c_d)(d - \mu_\gamma) \tag{4.7}$$

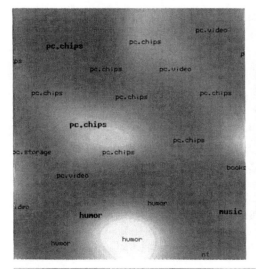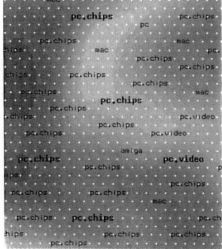

FIGURE 4.5   SOM computed from over a million documents taken from 80 Usenet news groups. Light areas have a high density of documents. The region shown is near groups pc.chips and pc.video, and closer inspection shows a number of URLs in this region that are about PC videocards.

Here, as before, η is a learning rate, which may be folded into h. An example of an SOM of over a million documents from 80 Usenet news groups is shown in Figure 4.5, together with the result of drilling down into the collection. Another example involving Web documents is shown in Figure 4.6, where the regions chalked out by SOM are in broad agreement with the human catalogers working on the Open Directory Project (*http://dmoz.org/*). The topic names in Figure 4.6 were generated manually once the correspondence with named DMoz.org topics was clear.

4.3.2   Multidimensional Scaling (MDS) and FastMap

In the case of k-means and SOM, documents have a specified internal representation, namely, the vector-space representation. In other applications, documents may be characterized only by a distance to other documents. Even in cases where an internal representation is available, one may use it for generating pairwise distances. Doing this may help in incorporating coarse-grained user feedback in clustering, such as "documents i and j are quite dissimilar" or "document i is more similar to j than k." These can be translated into a distance measure that

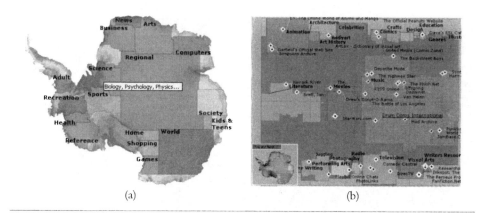

(a)   (b)

FIGURE 4.6 Another example of SOM at work: the sites listed in the Open Directory Project have been organized within a map of Antarctica, at *antarcti.ca/* (a). Clicking on a region maintains context (inset) and zooms in on more specific topics (b). Documents are located at the cluster to which they are most similar.

overrides that computed from internal representations as the user provides more feedback.

The goal of MDS is to represent documents as points in a low-dimensional space (often 2D to 3D) such that the Euclidean distance between any pair of points is as close as possible to the distance between them specified by the input. Let $d_{i,j}$ be a (symmetric) user-defined measure of distance or dissimilarity between documents i and j, and let $\hat{d}_{i,j}$ be the Euclidean distance between the point representations of documents i and j picked by our MDS algorithm. The *stress* of the embedding is given by

$$\text{stress} = \frac{\sum_{i,j}(\hat{d}_{i,j} - d_{i,j})^2}{\sum_{i,j} d_{i,j}^2} \tag{4.8}$$

We would like to minimize the stress.

This formulation is very appealing but is not easy to optimize. Iterative stress relaxation, that is, hill climbing, is the most used strategy to minimize the stress. Here I shall talk about documents and points interchangeably. Initially, all points are assigned coordinates randomly or by some external heuristic. Then, each point in turn is moved by a small distance in a direction that locally reduces its stress.

With n points to start with, this procedure involves $O(n)$ distance computations for moving each point, and so $O(n^2)$ distance computations per relaxation step. A much faster approach called FastMap, due to Faloutsos and Lin [76], pretends that the original documents are indeed points in some unknown high-dimensional space, and finds a projection to a space with a smaller number k of dimensions. The heart of the FastMap algorithm is to find a carefully selected line onto which the points are projected to obtain their first dimension, then project the points to a hyperplane perpendicular to the line, and recursively find the remaining $k - 1$ coordinates. There are thus three key subproblems: (1) how to find a good direction or line, (2) how to "project" the original points onto the line (given that we have no internal representation of the documents), and (3) how to project the points to the hyperplane.

Because there is no internal representation available, the only way in which a direction or line can be specified is via a pair of points. Let a and b be two points defining the line, called the *pivots*. We can arbitrarily let a be the origin. Consider another point x for which we wish to compute the first coordinate x_1. Using the cosine law, we get

$$d_{b,x}^2 = d_{a,x}^2 + d_{a,b}^2 - 2x_1 d_{a,b}$$

$$\Rightarrow \qquad x_1 = \frac{d_{a,x}^2 + d_{a,b}^2 - d_{b,x}^2}{2\, d_{a,b}} \qquad (4.9)$$

This 1D projection does preserve some distance information: all points x close to a will have small x_1 and hence be close to each other in the projected space, and vice versa. This also gives a clue to finding a good line: informally, a line is good if projecting onto it helps spread out the points, that is, the point set has high variance in the direction of the line. This is difficult to ensure without exhaustive checking, so Faloutsos and Lin pick pivots that are far apart as a heuristic.

The next step is to project all points to the hyperplane perpendicular to the pivot line. Again, this "projection" cannot give us an internal representation of the original points, because we have not started with any. The only purpose of the "projection" is to correct interpoint distances by taking into account the component already accounted for by the first pivot line. Consider points x and y with distance $d_{x,y}$, first coordinates x_1 and y_1, and projections x', y' (with unknown internal properties) on the hyperplane. By the Pythagorean theorem, it is easy to see that the new distance d' on the hyperplane is

$$d'_{x',y'} = \sqrt{d_{x,y}^2 - (x_1 - y_1)^2} \qquad (4.10)$$

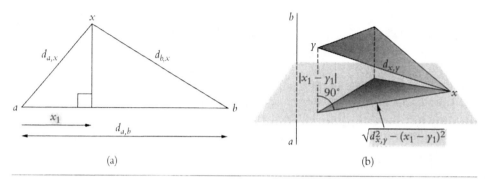

FIGURE 4.7 FastMap: projecting onto the pivot line (a), and projecting to a subspace with one less dimension (b).

At this point, we have derived the first dimension of all points and reduced the problem to one exactly like the original problem, except $k - 1$ additional dimensions remain to be computed. Therefore, we can simply call the routine recursively, until we go down to 1D space where the problem is trivially solved. The end product is a vector $(x_1, \ldots, x_k)$ for each point x in the original data set. It can be verified that FastMap runs in $O(nk)$ time. For visualization tasks, k is usually a small constant. Therefore, FastMap is effectively linear in the size of the point set. Figure 4.8 shows a fly-through 2D rendering of a 3D embedding of documents returned by a search engine in response to the query "tony bennett," which are clearly separated into two clusters. Closer inspection shows those clusters are about "country" and "jazz" music.

4.3.3 Projections and Subspaces

In many of the clustering algorithms we have discussed so far, including HAC and k-means style clustering, a significant fraction of the running time is spent in computing (dis-)similarities between documents and clusters. The time taken for one similarity calculation is proportional to the total number of nonzero components of the two vectors involved. One simple technique to speed up HAC or k-means is to *truncate* the document vectors to retain only some of the largest components. (We can retain either a fixed number of components or the smallest number of components that make up, say, at least 90% of the original vector's norm.) Truncation was introduced earlier, in Section 4.2.1; it has been

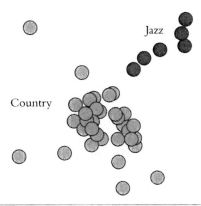

Jazz

Country

FIGURE 4.8 FastMap in action: clustering documents about country and jazz music.

experimentally evaluated by Schutze and Silverstein [191]. For the clustering task, it turns out that cutting down from tens of thousands to barely 50 dimensions has no significant negative impact on the quality of clusters generated by a clustering algorithm. Truncation to 50 axes per vector was comparable even to a more sophisticated global projection algorithm, discussed in Section 4.3.4.

One problem with orthogonal subspace projection is that one does not know if 50 or 100 coordinates are enough except by judging the outcome of clustering. Certain non-orthogonal projections have provable guarantees that the distortion that they force on inter-document distances are mild [168, 9]. Specifically, for any $0 < \epsilon > 1$ and any integer $n > 0$, choose any

$$k \geq \frac{4}{\epsilon^2/2 - \epsilon^3/3} \ln n.$$

Then for any set V of n vectors in $\mathbb{R}^d$, there is a map $f : \mathbb{R}^d \to \mathbb{R}^k$, computable in randomized polynomial time, such that for all pairs $\vec{x}, \vec{y} \in V$,

$$(1 - \epsilon)||\vec{x} - \vec{y}||^2 \leq ||f(\vec{x}) - f(\vec{y})||^2 \leq (1 + \epsilon)||\vec{x} - \vec{y}||^2.$$

While this represents a powerful theoretical property, the mapping f involves random rotations in the original space, which may destroy sparseness: document vectors which were very sparse in the original space may be mapped to dense vectors by f, reducing the performance gain from the apparently simpler

1: select, say, k^3 documents out of n uniformly at random
2: use HAC or move-to-nearest to cluster these to k^2 clusters
3: note the k^2 centroid vectors
4: for each document d, find the projection of $\vec{d}$ onto each of the centroid vectors
5: use this vector of k^2 real numbers as a representaton of d
6: with the new k^2-dimensional representation of all d, run a conventional clustering algorithm

FIGURE 4.9   Data-sensitive random projections.

representation. For example, with $\epsilon = 1/2$ and $n = 100000$, which could be quite typical in an application, we need $k \geq 32 \ln 100000 \approx 368$. If the average document has fewer than 368 terms, projection may not really simplify our document representation and therefore may not speed up clustering substantially. An effective heuristic to retain sparsity (at the cost of losing the theoretical distortion guarantee) is shown in Figure 4.9.

Hopefully, if the average document density is more than k^2, the second-round clustering will be much faster because of the speedup in distance computation. Note that this transformation is not linear. The intuition is that a uniform random selection will pick more documents from dense regions and few from unpopulated ones, with the result that fewer directions for projections will be needed to keep the clusters apart.

4.3.4   Latent Semantic Indexing (LSI)

Projections to orthogonal subspaces, that is, a subset of dimensions, may not reveal clustering structure in the best possible way. For example, the clusters may be formed by multiple correlated attributes. In this section I will characterize attribute redundancy more systematically in terms of linear algebraic operations on the term-document matrix.

Let the term-document matrix be A where the entry $A[t, d]$ may be a 0/1 value denoting the occurrence or otherwise of term t in document d. More commonly, documents are transformed into TFIDF vectors and each column of A is a document vector.

In the vector-space model, we allocated a distinct orthogonal direction for each token. The obvious intuition is that there is no need for so many (tens of thousands) of orthogonal directions because there are all sorts of latent relationships between the corresponding tokens. *Car* and *automobile* are likely to occur in similar documents, as are *cows* and *sheep*. Thus, documents as points in this space are not likely to nearly "use up" all possible regions, but are likely to occupy semantically meaningful subspaces of it. Another way of saying this is that A has a much lower rank than $\min\{|D|, |T|\}$. (See the standard text by Golub and van Loan [91] for definitions of rank and matrix factoring and decomposition.)

One way to reveal the rank of A is to compute its *singular value decomposition* (SVD). Without going into the details of how the SVD is computed, which is standard, I will write down the decomposed form of A as

$$A_{|T|\times|D|} = U_{|T|\times r} \begin{pmatrix} \sigma_1 & \cdots & 0 \\ \vdots & \ddots & \vdots \\ 0 & \cdots & \sigma_r \end{pmatrix} V^T_{r\times|D|} \tag{4.11}$$

where r is the rank of A, U and V are column-orthonormal ($U^T U = V^T V = \mathbf{I}$, the identity matrix), and the diagonal matrix Σ in the middle can be organized (by modifying U and V) such that $\sigma_1 \geq \ldots \geq \sigma_r > 0$.

The standard cosine measure of similarity between documents can be applied to the A matrix: the entries of $(A^T A)_{|D|\times|D|}$ may be interpreted as the pairwise document similarities in vector space. The situation is completely symmetric with regard to terms, and we can regard the entries of $(AA^T)_{|T|\times|T|}$ as the pairwise term, similarity based on their co–occurrence in documents. (In Chapter 7, I will return to defining similarity using such matrix products, where the matrices will be node adjacency matrices of hyperlink graphs.)

The tth row of A may therefore be regarded as a $|D|$-dimensional representation of term t, just as the dth column of A is the $|T|$-dimensional vector-space representation of document d. Because A has redundancy revealed by the SVD operation, we can now use a "better" way to compute document-to-document similarities as $(V\Sigma^2 V^T)_{|D|\times|D|}$ and term-to-term similarities as $(U\Sigma^2 U^T)_{|T|\times|T|}$. In other words, the tth row of U is a refined representation of term t, and the dth row of V is a refined representation of document d. Interestingly, both representations are vectors in an r-dimensional subspace, and we can therefore talk about the similarity of a term with a document in this subspace.

In *latent semantic indexing (LSI)*, the corpus is first used to precompute the matrices U, Σ, and V. A query is regarded as a document. When a query "q" is submitted, it is first projected to the r-dimensional "LSI space" using the transformation

$$\hat{q} = \Sigma^{-1}_{r\times r} U^T_{r\times|T|} q_{|T|} \tag{4.12}$$

At this point $\hat{q}$ becomes comparable with the r-dimensional document representations in LSI space. Now one can look for document vectors close to the transformed query vector.

In LSI implementations, not all r singular values are retained. A smaller number k, roughly 200 to 300, of the top singular values are retained—that is, A is approximated as

$$A_k = \sum_{1 \le i \le k} \vec{u}_i \sigma_i \vec{v}_i^T \tag{4.13}$$

where $\vec{u}_i$ and $\vec{v}_i$ are the ith columns of U and V. How good an approximation is A_k? The Frobenius norm of A is given by

$$|A|_F = \sqrt{\sum_{t,d} A[t, d]^2} \tag{4.14}$$

It can be shown that

$$|A|_F^2 = \sigma_1^2 + \cdots + \sigma_r^2, \tag{4.15}$$

and

$$\min_{\text{rank}(B)=k} |A - B|_F^2 = |A - A_k|_F^2 = \sigma_{k+1}^2 + \cdots + \sigma_r^2 \tag{4.16}$$

That is, A_k is the best rank-k approximation to A under the Frobenius norm.

The above results may explain why retrieval based on LSI may be close to vector-space quality, despite reduced space and perhaps query time requirements (although the preprocessing involved is quite time-consuming). Interestingly, in practice, LSI does *better,* in terms of recall/precision, than TFIDF retrieval. Heuristic explanations may be sought in signal-processing practice, where SVD has been used for decades, with the experience that the dominating singular values capture the "signal" in A, leaving the smaller singular values to account for the "noise." In IR terms, LSI maps synonymous and related words to similar vectors, potentially bridging the "syntax gap" in traditional IR and thus improving recall. Although a complete discussion is outside our scope here, LSI may also be able to exploit correlations between terms to resolve polysemy in some situations, improving precision as well.

More rigorous theories seeking to explain the improved accuracy of LSI have been proposed by Papadimitriou et al. [170] and by Azar et al. [9]. Papadimitriou et al. assume that documents are generated from a set of topics with disjoint vocabularies, and after the resulting low-rank block matrix A is slightly perturbed, LSI can recover the block structure and hence the topic information. Azar et al. generalized this result to the case where A is not necessarily close to a block matrix but is approximated well by some low-rank matrix.

Thus far, we have discussed LSI/SVD as a device for dimensionality reduction, noise filtering, and ad hoc retrieval. But it can also be used for visualization (choose $k = 2$ or 3) or clustering, by using any of the other algorithms in this chapter after applying SVD. An example of a 2D embedding via LSI is shown in Figure 4.10. LSI can run in minutes to hours on corpora in the rough range of 10^3 to 10^4 documents, but is not very practical at the scale of the Web. At the time of this writing, I know of no public-domain SVD package that can work efficiently without storing the whole input matrix in memory. This can lead to an unacceptable memory footprint for a large collection.

4.4 Probabilistic Approaches to Clustering

Although the vector-space representation has been very successful for ad hoc retrieval, using it for clustering leaves a few unresolved issues. Consider HAC as discussed in Section 4.2.1. The document and group profile vectors were determined by a single IDF computation before the agglomerative process. Perhaps it makes more sense to compute IDF with regard to $\Gamma \cup \Delta$, not the entire corpus, when evaluating the self-similarity of $\Gamma \cup \Delta$. However, such a policy would interfere with the optimizations I have described.

Given a corpus with various salient topics, documents are likely to include terms highly indicative of one or relatively few topics, together with noise terms selected from a common set. A major function of IDF is to downplay noise-words, but we may get the same effect by identifying that a document is composed of these separate distributions, and attribute similarity only to overlap in terms generated from distributions other than the noise distribution. Continuing on this line of thought, documents assigned to some node c in a topic taxonomy such as Yahoo! may be thought of as picking up vocabulary from distributions associated with nodes on the path from the root up to c, inclusive. Note that the notion of a noise-word becomes context-dependent in the hierarchical setting: the word *can*, used largely as a verb, has low information content at the root node of Yahoo!, but in the subtree rooted at /Environment/Recycling, *can* is used mostly as a noun and should not be attributed to the noise distribution.

Label	Titles
B1	A Course on Integral Equations
B2	Attractors for Semigroups and Evolution Equations
B3	Automatic Differentiation of Algorithms: Theory, Implementation, and Application
B4	Geometrical Aspects of Partial Differential Equations
B5	Ideals, Varieties, and Algorithms –An Introduction to Computational Algebraic Geometry and Commutative Algebra
B6	Introduction to Hamiltonian Dynamical Systems and the N-Body Problem
B7	Knapsack Problems: Algorithms and Computer Implementations
B8	Methods of Solving Singular Systems of Ordinary Differential Equations
B9	Nonlinear Systems
B10	Ordinary Differential Equations
B11	Oscillation Theory for Neutral Differential Equations with Delay
B12	Oscillation Theory of Delay Differential Equations
B13	Pseudodifferential Operators and Nonlinear Partial Differential Equations
B14	Sync Methods for Quadrature and Differential Equations
B15	Stability of Stochastic Differential Equations with Respect to Semi-Martingales
B16	The Boundary Integral Approach to Static and Dynamic Contact Problems
B17	The Double Mellin-Barnes Type Integrals and Their Applications to Convolution Theory

(a)

FIGURE 4.10 Subtopics are clearly separated by LSI in this collection of mathematical abstracts (a). The query "application theory" and a cone around it is shown shaded on page 101 (b). (Image courtesy Berry et al. [15].)

In this section, we are interested in proposing and validating generative models of documents that move away from the paradigm of assigning importance to terms, or defining similarity or distance measures, by fiat. Instead, we propose random processes that generate documents, and characterize clustering as *discovering* the random processes and associated parameters that are (most) likely to have generated a given collection of documents. Several desirable ramifications will follow:

- There will be no need for IDF to determine the importance of a term.

- Some of the models we will study can directly and naturally capture the notion of stopwords vs. content-bearing words.

- There is no need to define distances or similarities between entities.

- Assignment of entities to clusters need not be "hard"; it is probabilistic.

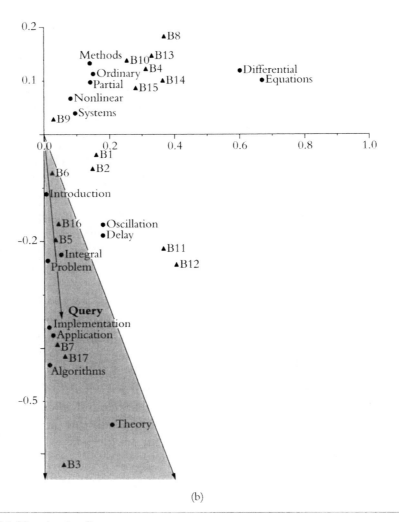

(b)

FIGURE 4.10   *(continued)*

4.4.1 Generative Distributions for Documents

Statistical pattern recognition and IR algorithms are built on the premise that the patterns (documents, images, audio) that we observe are generated by random processes that follow specific distributions. The observations let us estimate various parameters pertaining to those distributions, which in turn let us design strategies for analyzing the patterns, by way of clustering, indexing, or classification.

This may sound clean and appealing, but proposing credible distributions that can generate natural language is very difficult. Even if some limited success can be achieved in this quest, the computation involved is usually heavy-duty. We must be content to model only a few aspects of the observed data, hoping that they will suffice for the application at hand.

The aspects that are almost always axed by the need for simplicity and efficiency are *dependencies* and *ordering* between terms. To appreciate why dependencies are difficult to capture, consider the Reuters collection [139], which has about 22,000 news articles, using over 30,000 unique tokens. Even if each attribute (axis) in the vector space had just two possible values (0/1), there would be $2^{30,000} \approx 10^{10,000}$ possible documents. Clustering is intimately tied to estimating the density of the distribution being sampled, so the chances of finding a decent estimate in a space this size with only 22,000 documents is out of the question.

In a bid to reduce the severity of the problem, we can make the drastic assumption that term occurrences are *independent* events. To start with, let us make the further assumption that term counts are unimportant, that is, the event associated with a term and a document is a 0/1 random variable. This is called the *multivariate binary* model, or the *binary model* for short. A document *event* is just a bit-vector with a 0/1 slot for each term in the vocabulary W, and the bit corresponding to a term t is flipped on with probability ϕ_t, and off with probability $1 - \phi_t$. All the ϕ_ts are collected into the parameter set for this model, called Φ. Given Φ, the probability of generating document d is given by

$$\Pr(d|\Phi) = \prod_{t \in d} \phi_{c,t} \prod_{t \in W, t \notin d} (1 - \phi_{c,t}) \tag{4.17}$$

Since typically $|W| \gg |d|$, short documents are discouraged by this model. Also, the second product makes strong independence assumptions and is likely to greatly underestimate $\Pr(d|\Phi)$ for many not-so-unlikely documents. On the other hand, assuming all $\phi_t > 0$ and $\phi_t < 1$, all the $2^{|W|}$ possible documents, some of them essentially impossible in real life, have positive probability. Thus, this model smooths out the probability over too large a space, depriving the more likely regions.

In our second attempt, we will model term counts. The modified generative process is as follows: the writer first decides the total term count (including repetitions) of the document d to be generated by drawing a random positive integer L from a suitable distribution $\Pr(\ell)$; suppose the instantiated event is ℓ_d. Next, the writer gets a die: it has $|W|$ faces, one face for each term in the vocabulary. When tossed, the face corresponding to term t comes up with probability θ_t ($\sum_t \theta_t = 1$). We represent by Θ all parameters needed to capture the length distribution and all θ_ts. The author tosses this die ℓ_d times and writes down the terms that come up. Suppose term t turns up $n(d, t)$ times, with $\sum_\tau n(d, \tau) = \ell_d$. The document *event* in this case comprises ℓ_d and the set of counts $\{n(d, t)\}$. The probability of this compound event is given by

$$\Pr(\ell_d, \{n(d, t)\}|\Theta) = \Pr(L = \ell_d|\Theta)\,\Pr(\{n(d, t)\}|\ell_d, \Theta)$$

$$= \Pr(L = \ell_d|\Theta)\binom{\ell_d}{\{n(d, t)\}}\prod_{t \in d} \theta_t^{n(d,t)} \qquad (4.18)$$

where $\binom{\ell_d}{\{n(d,t)\}} = \frac{\ell_d!}{n(d,t_1)!\,n(d,t_2)!\cdots}$ is the multinomial coefficient. We will abbreviate the compound event on the lhs by $\Pr(d|\Theta)$. This is called the *multinomial* model. The length distribution is vital; without it, the empty document would have probability 1.

The multinomial model does not fix the term–independence assumption. In fact, it assumes that occurrences of a given term are also independent of each other, which is another assumption that is clearly wrong. Reading a document from left to right, if you see the word *Pentium* five times, you are not really surprised to see it a sixth time, unlike what the additional factor of θ_t in Equation (4.18) suggests. Even so, the multinomial model, in preserving term count information, turns out to be somewhat superior for most text mining tasks.

From a linguist's perspective, such models are insufferably crude: there is not a shade of grammar or semantic sense in these characterizations; there is not even a hint of the strong short-range dependence that is commonly seen between terms. (For example, the word *spite* is quite likely to follow the word *in* and precede the word *of*.) We offer no defense, but note that these models are approximations to physical reality, make parameter estimation tractable, and produce acceptable experimental results for machine learning tasks in the text domain.

4.4.2 Mixture Models and Expectation Maximization (EM)

The notion of generative distributions makes it easy and elegant to express the clustering problem, perhaps a little more elegantly than the formulations in Section 4.1. Consider a given collection of documents, for example, a set of pages crawled from the Web. It is possible to estimate Θ_{Web} for this collection, and then calculate the probability $\Pr(d|\Theta_{\text{Web}})$ of all Web documents d with regard to Θ_{Web}. But we may not really believe that a single multinomial model suffices for the whole Web. Suppose a set of topics, such as arts, science, and politics, were given to us ahead of time, and we can identify which topic a document talks about. (Until Section 4.4.3 we will assume that a document is about exactly one topic.) We can estimate, in lieu of a single Θ_{Web}, specialized parameter sets Θ_{arts}, Θ_{science}, Θ_{politics}, and so on, and for a document belonging to a topic y, evaluate $\Pr(d|\Theta_y)$. Intuitively, we would expect this to be generally much larger than $\Pr(d|\Theta_{\text{Web}})$, because Θ_y may correctly capture that some terms are rare or frequent in documents about topic y, compared to a random document from the Web at large.

The preceding discussion reveals the essence of the clustering problem and leads us to the following *mixture model* for document generation. Suppose there are m topics (also called *components* or *clusters*). The author of a page has to first decide what topic he wishes to write about. This may be done using a multinomial m-way *selector* distribution with probabilities $\alpha_1, \ldots, \alpha_m$, where $\alpha_1 + \cdots + \alpha_m = 1$. Once a topic y is decided upon, the author uses Θ_y, the distribution for that topic, to generate the document. For example, we can use the binary or the multinomial distribution for each component. We can even use different distributions for different components.

In preparation for the rest of this section, I will simplify the notation. For each component y, there are many parameters $\theta_{y,t}$, one for each term t. I collect all these parameters, all the α_is, as well as the number of clusters m, into a global parameter space. I reuse Θ to name this parameter space:

$$\Theta = (m; \alpha_1, \ldots, \alpha_m; \{\theta_{y,t} \; \forall y, t\})$$

It is conventional to denote the data points as x rather than d, which I will follow for the rest of this section. Lastly, I will illustrate the EM algorithm not with the multinomial component distribution but with a simple distribution characterized by just one parameter per component: the Poisson distribution with mean μ characterized by $\Pr(X = x) = e^{-\mu}\mu^x/x!$, for $x = 0, 1, 2, \ldots$. Accordingly, we will have m parameters $\mu_1, \ldots, \mu_m$, and our simplified parameter space will be

$$\Theta = (m; \alpha_1, \ldots, \alpha_m; \mu_1, \ldots, \mu_m)$$

With the setup as described so far, we see that

$$\Pr(x|\Theta) = \sum_{j=1}^{m} \alpha_j \Pr(x|\mu_j) \tag{4.19}$$

Note that x is multivariate in general—certainly for text—although for the Poisson distribution, it is just a real number.

For the clustering task, we are given n independent, identically distributed (iid.) observations $X = \{x_1, \ldots, x_n\}$, and we need to estimate Θ—that is, we would like to find Θ so as to maximize

$$\Pr(X|\Theta) = \prod_{i=1}^{n} \Pr(x_i|\Theta) \quad \triangleq \quad L(\Theta|X) \tag{4.20}$$

and thus

$$\log L(\Theta|X) = \sum_{i} \log \left(\sum_{j} \alpha_j \Pr(x_i|\mu_j) \right) \tag{4.21}$$

For the moment we will assume that m is provided as an input. Our estimation of Θ will therefore concern the α and μ parameters.

If the component y_i ($1 \leq y_i \leq m$) from which each observation x_i has been generated were known, this would be a trivial problem. The challenge is that $Y = \{y_i\}$ is a set of *hidden* random variables. The component distributions define the clusters, and Y indicates the cluster to which each data point belongs.

Since Y is unknown, it must be modeled as a random variable, and we can assign data points to clusters only in a probabilistic sense. The classic approach to solving the problem is to maximize L (see Equation (4.21)) explicitly with regard to both X and Y: $L(\Theta|X, Y) = \Pr(X, Y|\Theta)$. Since we do not know Y, we must take the expectation of L over Y. Unfortunately, estimating the distribution of Y requires knowledge of Θ. To break the cycle, we start with a suitable guess Θ^g. Let the "complete data likelihood" be

$$Q(\Theta, \Theta^g) = E_Y \left(\log L(\Theta|X, Y) \big| X, \Theta^g \right) \tag{4.22}$$

$$= \sum_Y \{\Pr(Y|X, \Theta^g)\}\{\log \Pr(X, Y|\Theta)\} \tag{4.23}$$

$$= \sum_Y \{\Pr(Y|X, \Theta^g)\}\{\log(\Pr(Y|\Theta) \Pr(X|Y, \Theta))\} \tag{4.24}$$

$$= \sum_{y_1=1}^{m} \cdots \sum_{y_n=1}^{m} \left\{ \prod_{j=1}^{n} \Pr(y_j|x_j, \Theta^g) \right\} \left\{ \sum_{i=1}^{n} \log(\alpha_{y_i} \Pr(x_i|\mu_{y_i})) \right\} \tag{4.25}$$

The last expression can be simplified to

$$Q(\Theta, \Theta^g) = \sum_{\ell=1}^{m} \sum_{i=1}^{n} \Pr(\ell|x_i, \Theta^g) \, \log \left(\alpha_\ell \Pr(x_i|\mu_\ell) \right) \tag{4.26}$$

Because Q is an expectation over Y, this step is called the *expectation,* or E, step.

How should we pick a refined value of Θ? It seems reasonable to choose the next estimate of Θ so as to maximize $Q(\Theta, \Theta^g)$. This step is called the *maximization,* or M, step. There is one constraint to the maximization, namely, $\sum_i \alpha_i = 1$, and we perform a standard Lagrangian optimization:

$$\frac{\partial}{\partial \alpha_k} \left[\sum_{\ell=1}^{m} \sum_{i=1}^{n} \{\log \alpha_i + \cdots\} \Pr(\ell|x_i, \Theta_g) - \lambda \sum_i \alpha_i \right] = 0 \tag{4.27}$$

which yields

$$\alpha_k = \frac{1}{\lambda} \sum_{i=1}^{n} \Pr(k|x_i, \Theta^g) \tag{4.28}$$

From the constraint we can now show that $\lambda = n$.

We must also find the new values of μ_i, $i = 1, \ldots, m$. For concreteness I have picked a specific one-parameter distribution, a Poisson distribution with mean μ_i for the ith component. (It is not necessary for all components to follow the same distribution for the algorithm to work.) The Poisson distribution is characterized as $\Pr(x|\mu) = e^{-\mu}\mu^x/x!$ for integer $x = 0, 1, 2, \ldots$. Thus, our second set of derivatives is

$$\frac{\partial}{\partial \mu_k} \left[\sum_{\ell=1}^{m} \sum_{i=1}^{n} \Pr(\ell|x_i, \Theta^g) \left(-\mu_\ell + x_i \log \mu_\ell \right) \right] = 0 \tag{4.29}$$

which yields

$$\sum_{i=1}^{n} \left(-1 + \frac{x_i}{\mu_k} \right) \Pr(k|x_i, \Theta^g) = 0 \qquad (4.30)$$

Simplifying,

$$\mu_k = \frac{\sum_{i=1}^{n} x_i \Pr(k|x_i, \Theta^g)}{\sum_{i=1}^{n} \Pr(k|x_i, \Theta^g)} \qquad (4.31)$$

The complete algorithm, called *expectation maximization* (EM), is shown in Figure 4.11. It can be shown that the maximization step guarantees that $L(\Theta)$ never decreases, and must therefore reach a local maximum.

In general, finding a suitable value of m is a nontrivial task. For some applications, m may be known, and in addition, for some documents i, y_i (the cluster to which that document belongs) may also be specified. A common example would be the assignment of Web documents to Yahoo!-like clusters, where a few documents have been manually assigned to clusters but most documents are not assigned. This is an instance of a *semisupervised* learning problem, which we will study in Chapter 6. Completely supervised learning or classification is the topic of Chapter 5. There the classifier is given a fixed set of labels or classes and sample documents with each class.

When m is not specified, there are two broad techniques to estimate it. The first is to hold out some of the data, build the mixture model on the rest, then find the likelihood of the held-out data given the mixture parameters. This process is repeated while increasing the number of clusters until the likelihood ceases to increase. (Note that this would not work without the held-out data; if training data were used, the system would prefer an inordinately large value of m, a phenomenon called *overfitting*, discussed in Section 5.5.) This approach has been proposed by Smyth [197].

1: Initialize $\Theta^{(0)}$, $i = 0$
2: **while** $L(\Theta|X, Y)$ can be increased **do**
3:    Estimate $\vec{\alpha}^{(i+1)}$ using (4.28)
4:    Estimate $\vec{\mu}^{(i+1)}$ using (4.31)
5:    $i \leftarrow i + 1$
6: **end while**

FIGURE 4.11   The EM algorithm.

A different approach is to constrain the model complexity using a *prior distribution* over the model parameters that makes complex models unlikely (see Sections 4.4.5 and 5.6.1 for more details on prior distributions). This is the approach adopted in the well-known AutoClass clustering package by Cheeseman and others [47].

A criticism of the standard mixture model as applied to text is that many documents are relevant to multiple topics. In fact, the term *mixture model* may be misleading in this context, because after a generating distribution is selected probabilistically, a data point is generated from only one distribution after all. Operationally, this means that each distribution has to "compete on its own" with other distributions for a share of α, that is, they cannot collude to generate documents. In the next two sections, I will discuss two approaches to address this limitation.

4.4.3 Multiple Cause Mixture Model (MCMM)

If a document is (partially or wholly) about a topic, the topic *causes* certain words to become more likely to appear in the document. Let c be the topics or clusters and t be terms. Let $\gamma_{c,t}$ ($0 \leq \gamma_{c,t} \leq 1$) denote a normalized measure (not to be interpreted as a probability) of causation of t by c. Suppose the extent to which topic c is "activated" in writing a given document d is $a_{d,c}$ ($0 \leq a_{d,c} \leq 1$). Then the belief that term t will appear in the document d is given by a *soft disjunction*, also called a *noisy OR*:

$$b_{d,t} = 1 - \prod_c (1 - a_{d,c}\, \gamma_{c,t}), \qquad (4.32)$$

That is, the term does not appear only if it is not activated by any of the classes under consideration. Let the document d be represented by the binary model where $n(d, t)$, the number of times term t appears in it, is either zero or one. Then the goodness of the beliefs in various term activations is defined as a log likelihood:

$$g(d) = \log \left(\prod_{t \in d} b_{d,t} \prod_{t \notin d} (1 - b_{d,t}) \right)$$

$$= \sum_t \log \left(n(d, t)\, b_{d,t} + (1 - n(d, t))(1 - b_{d,t}) \right) \qquad (4.33)$$

For a document collection $\{d\}$ the aggregate goodness is $\sum_d g(d)$.

Like other iterative clustering algorithms, we somehow set a number of clusters, and the iterations proceed in pairs of half-steps. In each iteration, the first half-step fixes $\gamma_{c,t}$ and improves on the choice of $a_{d,c}$. The second half-step fixes $a_{d,t}$ and improves on the choice of $\gamma_{c,t}$. In both half-steps, the search for improved parameter values is done by local hill climbing, that is, finding $\partial \sum_d g(d)/\partial a_{d,c}$ or $\partial \sum_d g(d)/\partial \gamma_{c,t}$ and taking a short step along the gradient.

MCMMs can be used in a supervised learning setting, too (see Chapter 5); in that case, the activations $a_{d,c}$ are provided for documents d in the training set, and the system needs to estimate only the coupling matrix $\gamma_{c,t}$. When given a new document q, the coupling matrix is kept fixed and $a_{q,c}$ estimated so as to maximize $g(q)$. This information can be used to tag documents with labels from a predefined set of labels with examples that have been used to train or supervise the system.

MCMMs are thus a very flexible and simple model, useful for both unsupervised and supervised learning. Their only drawback is speed. The representation of the coupling matrix is dense, and hill climbing is slow. With a few hundred terms, a thousand documents, and about 10 clusters, supervised runs take a few minutes and unsupervised runs take a few hours on stock hardware. For larger document collections with tens of thousands of terms, aggressive elimination of terms (see Section 5.5) is required.

4.4.4   Aspect Models and Probabilistic LSI

Hofmann has proposed a new generative model for multitopic documents [109, 110]. We start with the raw term counts in a given document collection, in the form of a matrix in which entry $n(d, t)$ denotes the frequency of term t in document d. Put another way, each pair (d, t) has a *binary event* associated with it. The *number of times* this event occurs is the observed data $n(d, t)$. Note the subtle distinction between this model and the multinomial model discussed in Section 4.4.1. In the multinomial model, given a document length, the frequencies of individual terms apportion this quota of total count. Here the total event count over all (d, t) is set in advance, and the (d, t) events must apportion this total count. This means that the corpus must be fixed in advance and that analyzing a new document from outside the corpus takes some special steps, unlike the multinomial model.

When an author starts composing a document, she induces a probability distribution $\Pr(c)$ over topics or clusters. For example, she may set a probability of 0.3 for writing (using terms) about politics and 0.7 for petroleum. Different clusters *cause* event (d, t) with different probabilities. To find the overall $\Pr(d, t)$, we condition and sum over clusters:

$$\Pr(d, t) = \sum_c \Pr(c) \Pr(d, t|c) \tag{4.34}$$

The main approximation in the aspect model is to assume conditional independence between d and t given c, which gives us

$$\Pr(d, t) = \sum_c \Pr(c) \Pr(d|c) \Pr(t|c) \tag{4.35}$$

The important parameters of this characterization are $\Pr(c)$, $\Pr(d|c)$, and $\Pr(t|c)$. An EM-like procedure can be used to estimate these parameters, together with the E-step parameter $\Pr(c|d, t)$, which may be interpreted as a grade of evidence that event (d, t) was caused by cluster c.

$$\Pr(c|d, t) = \frac{\Pr(c, d, t)}{\Pr(d, t)}$$

$$= \frac{\Pr(c) \Pr(d, t|c)}{\sum_\gamma \Pr(\gamma, d, t)}$$

$$= \frac{\Pr(c) \Pr(d|c) \Pr(t|c)}{\sum_\gamma \Pr(\gamma) \Pr(d|\gamma) \Pr(t|\gamma)} \tag{4.36}$$

$$\Pr(c) = \frac{\sum_{d,t} n(d, t) \Pr(c|d, t)}{\sum_\gamma \sum_{d,t} n(d, t) \Pr(\gamma|d, t)} \tag{4.37}$$

$$\Pr(d|c) = \frac{\sum_t n(d, t) \Pr(c|d, t)}{\sum_\delta \sum_t n(\delta, t) \Pr(c|\delta, t)} \tag{4.38}$$

$$\Pr(t|c) = \frac{\sum_d n(d, t) \Pr(c|d, t)}{\sum_\tau \sum_d n(d, \tau) \Pr(c|d, \tau)} \tag{4.39}$$

As in EM, the user has to fix the number of clusters ahead of time or use validation with a held-out set. Hofmann also describes an enhanced EM procedure. The number of clusters is akin to the number of singular values retained in the LSI (SVD) decomposition discussed in Section 4.3.4; we may use held-out data for cross-validation to determine a suitable number of clusters.

The factor model can be used as a probabilistic version of LSI, dubbed *probabilistic LSI,* or *PLSI.* A text collection is first subjected to the PLSI analysis and the four sets of parameters estimated as specified. Now for each document d and each cluster c, we precompute

$$\Pr(c|d) = \frac{\Pr(c)\,\Pr(d|c)}{\sum_\gamma \Pr(\gamma)\,\Pr(d|\gamma)} \tag{4.40}$$

where all the quantities on the right-hand side are estimated parameters. A query q (regarded as a bag of words, like documents) has to be *folded* into the system. The precalculated parameters are frozen, and new parameters $\Pr(c|q, t)$ for all c, t, $\Pr(q|c)$ for all c are estimated as

$$\Pr(c|q, t) = \frac{\Pr(c)\underline{\Pr(q|c)}\,\Pr(t|c)}{\sum_\gamma \Pr(\gamma)\underline{\Pr(q|\gamma)}\,\Pr(t|\gamma)} \tag{4.41}$$

$$\Pr(q|c) = \frac{\sum_t n(q, t)\underline{\Pr(c|q, t)}}{\sum_t n(q, t)\underline{\Pr(c|q, t)} + \sum_d \sum_t n(d, t)\,\Pr(c|d, t)} \tag{4.42}$$

This is itself an iterative procedure with the coupling shown by the underlined variables.

Once $\Pr(c|q)$ and $\Pr(c|d)$ are known for all d, one may use the vector of posterior class probabilities as a surrogate representation, just as the projection via U or V^T is used in LSI. That is, the similarity between q and d may be defined in a number of reasonable ways, for example, $\sum_c \Pr(c|q)\,\Pr(c|d)$, or $\sum_c \Pr(c)\,\Pr(d|c)\,\Pr(q|c)$, for both of which the similarity-finding operations remains a dot–product of vectors.

PLSI has been evaluated using four standard IR collections: MED (1033 abstracts from medical journals), CRAN (1400 documents on aeronautics), CACM (3204 abstracts from a computer science periodical), and CISI (1460 abstracts related to library science). As shown in Figure 4.12, PLSI compares favorably in terms of recall precision with standard TFIDF cosine-based ranking. The vector-space ranking used in comparison is a simple one-shot process. The best vector-space–based contenders today use two enhancements. First, it is a two-shot process: some number of top-ranking results are assumed to be relevant, and a second query is generated including certain words from those top-ranking documents; the final response set is the result of this second query. Second, the TFIDF weights are adjusted to reflect diverse document lengths; this may lead to favorable scoring of documents that match a query in only a few local regions.

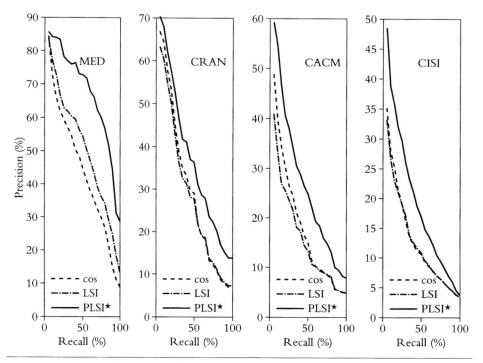

FIGURE 4.12 PLSI shows a significant improvement beyond standard one-shot TFIDF vector-space retrieval as well as standard LSI for several well-known data sets.

It would be interesting to compare PLSI with the length-adjusted, two-round variants of TFIDF search engines.

4.4.5 Model and Feature Selection

Clustering is also called *unsupervised learning* because topic-based clusters emerge as a result of the learning process, and are not specified ahead of time. As we have seen, (dis-)similarity measures are central to many forms of unsupervised learning. With a large number of dimensions where many dimensions are noisy and correlated, the similarity measure gets distorted rather easily. For example, noise-words or stopwords are integral to any language. A precompiled list of stopwords, or even a corpus-dependent IDF weighting, may fail to capture semantic emptiness in certain terms. Failing to eliminate or play down these dimensions sufficiently results in all similarity scores being inflated by some random, noisy amount. In bottom-up clustering, this noise often manifests itself in unbalanced, stringy dendrograms—once a cluster becomes large, there is no stopping it from gathering more mass.

A possible approach is to launch a search for a subset of terms that appears to be "noisy" in the sense that the clusters found all share a common distribution over these terms, together with per-cluster distribution over useful "signal" terms. Let D be the set of documents and D^T, D^N, and D^S be the representation of documents in the entire term space T, a noisy subset of term N, and the complement signal space $S = T \setminus N$. Using standard independence assumptions, we can approximate

$$\Pr(D^T|\Theta) = \Pr(D^N|\Theta)\,\Pr(D^S|\Theta) \tag{4.43}$$

$$= \prod_{d \in D} \Pr(d^N|\Theta^N)\,\Pr(d^S|\Theta^S)$$

$$= \prod_{d \in D} \Pr(d^N|\Theta^N)\,\Pr(d^S|\Theta^S_{c(d)}) \tag{4.44}$$

where Θ^S is composed of per-cluster parameters Θ^S_c for a set of clusters $\{c\}$, $c(d)$ is the cluster to which d belongs, and d^N (respectively, d^S) are documents projected to the noise (respectively, signal) attributes.

If $|T|$ ranges into tens of thousands, it can be daunting to partition it every way into N and S. An obvious technique is to cluster the terms in T according to their occurrence in documents, the process being called *distributional clustering*. (One can use the U matrix in LSI for doing this, for instance.) The hope is to collect the term set into a manageable number of groups, each of which is then tested for membership or otherwise in S as a whole.

MCMM and PLSI may achieve the same effect via a slightly different route. In MCMM, we can designate one cluster node to take care of the noise terms, and we can do likewise with one factor in PLSI. We can seed these clusters suitably (with, say, known stopwords) so that they gravitate toward becoming a generator of noise terms. It would be interesting to compare how well MCMM and PLSI achieve signal and noise separation compared to the feature subset search approach.

There is another useful way to look at the search for S and N in Equation (4.43): we would like to maximize $\Pr(D^T|\Theta)$, while at the same time *share* the cost of the parameters for the N subspace over all clusters—there is only one set of parameters Θ^N, whereas the Θ^S is diversified over each cluster. In other words, we wish to *factor out* Θ^N from all the clusters. Why is this desirable?

The medieval English philosopher and Franciscan monk William of Ockham (c. 1285–1349) proposed that "plurality should not be posited without necessity" ("*pluralitas non est ponenda sine neccesitate*"). This utterance has since been called *Occam's razor, the principle of parsimony*, and *the principle of simplicity*, and it has had profound influence on statistical analysis of noisy data.

In data analysis, Occam's razor would favor the simplest model that "explains" the data as well as any other. More formally, if under some assumptions about the space of generative models, two models generate the data with equal probability, then we should prefer the simpler model. This is not merely a normative stand. As we shall see in Chapter 5, picking simple models helps us generalize what we have learned from limited samples to yet-unseen data. If we do not control the complexity of the models we accept, we are in danger of learning chance artifacts from our sample data, a phenomenon called *overfitting*.

The *Minimum Description Length* (MDL) principle [182] is a ramification of Occam's razor that helps us control model complexity. MDL expresses the goodness of fit of models to data by composing a cost measure that has two components: *model cost* and *data cost*. The model cost is the number of bits $L(\Theta)$ needed to express an efficient encoding of the model Θ. The data cost $L(\mathbf{x}|\Theta)$ is the number of bits needed to express the data $\mathbf{x}$ with regard to a specified model (not necessarily a mixture model). Shannon's classic work on information and coding theory [57] lets us approximate $L(\mathbf{x}|\Theta) \approx -\log \Pr(\mathbf{x}|\Theta)$, the entropy lower bound, in most cases. Clustering thus amounts to finding

$$
\begin{aligned}
\Theta^* &= \arg \min_{\Theta} \{L(\Theta) + L(\mathbf{x}|\Theta)\} \\
&= \arg_{\Theta} \min \left\{ L(\Theta) - \log \Pr(\mathbf{x}|\Theta) \right\}
\end{aligned}
\tag{4.45}
$$

$L(\Theta)$ is the coding cost for the model and its parameters. The coding cost of parameters that take values from finite, discrete sets is easily determined by assuming a prior distribution over the parameters. For example, we may assume a prior distribution for m, the number of components in a mixture model (see Section 4.4.2) of the form $\Pr(M = m) = 2^{-m}$ for $m \geq 1$. Now we can use Shannon's theorem again to encode the parameter with regard to the prior distribution with a cost close to the entropy of the prior distribution. For continuous-valued parameters, some form of discretization is needed. A complete description of continuous parameter spaces is beyond this book's scope.

4.5 Collaborative Filtering

Throughout this chapter, we have studied how to cluster documents based on the terms they contain. However, the relation between documents and terms may be used, for example, in the opposite direction as well: we may wish to cluster terms based on documents in which they appear. In general terms, whenever we have a source of data that is bipartite or dyadic, coupling two kinds of entities, techniques similar to EM, LSI, or PLSI may be employed to build models fitting the data. One interesting form of dyadic data is user preferences for Web pages, books, songs, and the like. People form one set of entities, and the items of their likes and dislikes (Web pages, books, songs) form the other. The relation "document contains term" is replaced by "person likes item."

4.5.1 Probabilistic Models

The input to the system is a sparse, incomplete matrix Y where rows correspond to people and columns correspond to items, say, movies. Most entries are missing, because most people have not seen most movies. The few entries that are filled in may represent preferences in some simple graded manner; $Y_{ij} = 1$ if person i liked movie j, and 0 otherwise. (There is a semantic distinction between not seeing a movie and disliking it, but I will ignore this to keep the current discussion simple.)

The central question in *collaborative filtering* (CF) is, Given a new row (person) with only a few entries available, can we accurately and efficiently estimate the missing columns for that person, using the collective experience of other people recorded in the rest of the preference matrix? This will let us propose movies that the person is very likely to enjoy.

Some early CF systems represented each person as a vector over their preference for movies, then clustered people using this vector representation using any of the methods studied so far (k-means is commonly used). The early systems did not use the symmetry in the relationship between people and items.

Here is an elegant generative model for CF that extends mixture models to two kinds of entities:

- Let the input matrix Y have m people and n movies. We assume that people can be clustered into m' clusters and movies can be clustered into n' clusters. The properties of these clusters are a priori unknown.

- The probability that a random person belongs to people-cluster i' is $p_{i'}$.

1: guess m' and n', the number of clusters
2: start with an arbitrary hard assignment of people and movies to clusters
3: **repeat**
4:      pick a person (movie) at random
5:      find the probability $\pi_{i \to i'}$ ($\pi_{j \to j'}$) of it belonging to each person- (movie-) cluster i' (j')
6:      make a new hard assignment of the person (movie) to a person- (movie-) cluster i' (j') with probability proportional to $\pi_{i \to i'}$ ($\pi_{j \to j'}$)
7:      based on all the current hard assignments, reestimate the maximum likelihood values of all $p_{i'}$, $p_{j'}$, and $p_{i'j'}$
8: **until** parameter estimates are satisfactory

FIGURE 4.13   Estimation of collaborative filtering parameters using Gibbs sampling.

- The probability that a random movie belongs to movie-cluster j' is $p_{j'}$.

- The probability that a person belonging to people-cluster i' will like a movie in movie-cluster j' is $p_{i'j'}$.

These parameters can be estimated from the preference matrix using the EM-like Monte Carlo estimation procedure shown in Figure 4.13, called *Gibbs sampling*.

The estimates of $\pi_{i \to i'}$ ($\pi_{j \to j'}$) depend on the current estimates of $p_{i'}, p_{j'}, p_{i'j'}$ and the row (column) corresponding to the selected entity. Consider the case where person i has been picked at random, corresponding to the ith row of Y. Consider the movie corresponding to column j in this row. Suppose movie j is currently assigned to movie-cluster $\ell(j)$. Then $\pi_{i \to i'}$ can be estimated as

$$\pi_{i \to i'} = p_{i'} \prod_j \begin{cases} p_{i'\ell(j)} & \text{if } Y_{ij} = 1 \\ 1 - p_{i'\ell(j)} & \text{if } Y_{ij} = 0 \end{cases} \tag{4.46}$$

This is basically the same binary model as described in Section 4.4.1. A symmetric formula is used if a movie is selected at random instead of a person. Using the current assignment of people and movies to clusters, it is relatively straightforward to refine the estimates of p'_i, p'_j, and $p_{i'j'}$ for all i', j'.

Note that the model discussed above has *two kinds* of clusters (also called *two-sided clustering*), unlike the basic aspect model studied in Section 4.4.4 where the assumption is that *one* kind of clustering induces a joint distribution on documents and terms. This is why a standard EM procedure cannot be used for this formulation.

4.5.2 Combining Content-Based and Collaborative Features

Recommender systems may suffer from the *cold-start* syndrome: there is scant user preference data available when a system is first deployed, possibly leading to poor recommendations, which may keep potential users away. This problem is usually countered by supplementing preference data with attributes of the items (books, songs, movies, or Web pages).

Web pages provide an especially interesting scenario because of the rich variety of features that can be extracted from them. A few kinds of reasonable features are listed below; many others are possible.

- The set of users who visited each page (this is the standard preference input).
- The set of terms that appear on each page, possibly with term counts.
- The hostname and/or domain where the page is hosted, for example, *www.mit.edu*.
- The set of users who have visited at least one page on these hosts.
- The URLs, hostnames, and text on pages that belong to the hyperlink neighborhood of pages rated by users.

Text and markup on pages may be regarded as content-based input, and user visits are collaborative inputs. Links embedded in pages may be regarded as both content-based and collaborative input. As you can see, the space of possible features is essentially boundless. Alexa Internet (*info.alexa.com/*) distributes a Web browser "toolbar" that can send the user's click-trail to a server to enable a number of useful services, one of which is a "find related pages" service, which depends on unpublished combinations of clues from hyperlink structure, click data, and text on the pages.

Clustering in traditional, structured data domains enjoys a certain simplicity lacking in hypertext. In the former case, the entities being clustered may be modeled as *rows* or tuples in a single relational table. Each row is self-contained and has a set of *values* corresponding to the *attributes* or columns of the table. In the simplest cases, the attributes are continuous, and clustering has a simple geometric interpretation. It is more difficult to define a notion of distance or similarity involving categorical or set-valued attributes. The traditional vector-space representation, as well as associated clustering algorithms, seeks to reduce textual entities into (sparse) relational ones. As we have seen in this chapter, this reduction works reasonably well if clustering flat text is our goal.

We will consider two examples to illustrate the issues involved in clustering hypertext with collaborative information. In the first example, the collaborative information is in the form of hyperlinks. In the second example, the collaborative information is presented as the organization of URLs into topic-based bookmark folders by multiple users, each possibly using a custom, personalized topic structure.

Hyperlinks as similarity indicators

Consider clustering hypertext documents that are connected using hyperlinks, which hint that documents at the endpoint of a hyperlink are somehow related. This information should influence clustering decisions.

If hypertext were modeled using only the link graph, a variety of classic graph clustering and partitioning techniques could be brought to bear [104]. However, we would like to exploit textual similarity in conjunction with graph proximity. HyPursuit [211] is a "content-link" clustering system that is prototypical of most known approaches to scenarios involving diverse feature types. It uses a hybrid similarity function between any pair of documents d_1, d_2 that is sensitive to the following factors:

- The length of the shortest path between d_1 and d_2 following hyperlinks. The specific similarity function is $1/2^{|d_1 \rightsquigarrow d_2|} + 1/2^{|d_2 \rightsquigarrow d_1|}$, where $|u \rightsquigarrow v|$ denotes the number of links on the shortest path from u to v.

- The existence of common ancestors x of d_1 and d_2, which is a generalization of co-citation (a single other document citing d_1 and d_2 directly, see Section 7.1.3). In particular, HyPursuit uses the factor $\sum_x 1/2^{|x \rightsquigarrow d_1| + |x \rightsquigarrow d_2|}$, where the shortest paths must not include d_1 or d_2 as intermediate nodes.

- Common descendants reachable from d_1 and d_2 in a symmetric fashion.

- Textual similarity between d_1 and d_2 measured in conventional TFIDF similarity.

The overall similarity is the maximum of textual similarity and a weighted sum of link-based similarity. While HyPursuit has performed satisfactorily on some data sets, acceptable performance is clearly dependent on careful tuning.

Topic-based collaborative input

As a second example, Web users often maintain *bookmarks* of URLs useful to them. Popular browsers have utilities to maintain bookmarks in user-defined *folders,* which are usually delineated along topics. However, individuals differ greatly in their delineation of topics and agree on neither the naming nor the contents of their folders. Folders contain documents (in the form of URLs). This is a many-to-many relation: a folder usually contains a number of documents, and a document may be included in many folders. Furthermore, documents contain terms; this is also a many-to-many relation. Thus the two relations involved here are

includes(f, d)

contains(d, t)

where f is a folder, d is a document, and t is a term. Traditional document clustering uses only the contains relation, whereas there is valuable information also in the includes relation, which we seek to use. There are now many sources of clues regarding similarity:

- If folders f_1 and f_2 both include a common document, they are similar.
- If documents d_1 and d_2 belong to the same folder, they are similar.
- If two documents share terms, they are similar.
- If two terms are contained in the same document, they are similar. (This notion of similarity is statistical, not necessarily semantic.)

Of course, these similarity cues reinforce each other, for example, documents belonging to similar folders are similar and terms belonging to similar documents are similar. The data may be pictured as a tripartite graph with layers F (folders), D (documents), and T (terms). Figure 4.14(a) shows the F and D layers.

The problem is to cluster documents in this setting, combining all the sources of information regarding similarity in a suitable manner. (One may end up clustering folders and terms as side effects.)

Given the clustering algorithms we have studied thus far, at this stage it is quite unclear how best to enhance or design the entity (document, folders) representation to reflect the many sources of information about similarity. A simple strategy is to mark each folder using a unique token (distinct from any term occurring in the documents) and pretend that the folder tokens are included in the documents like other terms (i.e., the includes relation is encoded in the contains relation). Such a representation is unlikely to succeed: if the documents have many ordinary terms, these may crowd out the information in the includes relation. Intuitively, the event of a user including a document in a folder should carry more importance than a page author using a term in a document.

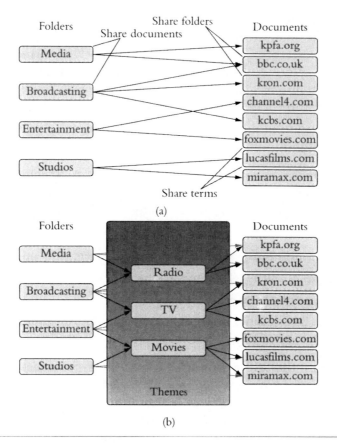

FIGURE 4.14 Algorithms for clustering the documents *D* should pay attention to the folder layer *F* as well as the text contained in documents (a). The goal of clustering is to interpose a third layer of *themes* or clusters *C* to simplify the graph while distorting the folder-to-document mappings minimally (b).

We characterize the clustering task as interposing a layer *C* of *theme* nodes and mapping *F* to *D* through the *C* layer (see Figure 4.14(b)). The *C* layer is supposed to "simplify" the graph [35]. For example, if two folders contain the exact same set of *x* URLs, these can be collected under a single theme node, which is shared between the two folders, using $x + 2$ edges rather than $2x$. Obviously, simplifying the graph is not the only goal. While doing this we must also ensure that the document set included in each folder does not change too much. When we must do so, we should ensure that the textual contents of the new folder are "close" to the original one. In Figure 4.14(a), the folder called *Studios* includes *lucasfilms.com* and *miramax.com*. Introducing the middle layer of theme nodes also includes *foxmovies.com*.

The MDL principle can be applied in this setting, too. Given the initial mapping between folders and documents, each folder f maps to a set of documents D_f. Documents in D_f induce a distribution Θ_f in term space. Choosing the maximum likelihood (ML) estimate for Θ_f (that is, that Θ_f that maximizes $\Pr(D_f|\Theta_f)$) lets us encode documents in D_f most efficiently. The clustering process builds a potentially worse model with regard to which D_f needs to be encoded. Let the graph after introducing a suitable C layer be G'. In the new graph, folder f maps to document set D'_f, whose corresponding ML parameter set is Θ'_f. Encoding D_f with regard to Θ'_f may not be as efficient as encoding D_f with regard to Θ_f. Specifically, we will need about $-\log \Pr(D_f|\Theta'_f)$ bits instead of $-\log \Pr(D_f|\Theta_f)$ bits, the minimum possible. We call $(-\log \Pr(D_f|\Theta'_f)) - (-\log \Pr(D_f|\Theta_f))$ the *distortion*. Such a sacrifice in encoding documents may be worthwhile if the graph G' that maps from folders to documents through C is much simpler than the original graph G. Summarizing, we seek

$$G^* = \arg \min_{G'} \left\{ L(G') - \sum_f \log \Pr(D_f|\Theta'_f) \right\} \tag{4.47}$$

The complexity of G may be measured by considering the degree of nodes to design an efficient code (popular link endpoints get smaller codes). Figure 4.15 shows the clear trade-off between $L(G')$ and text coding distortion for some real-life data from bookmark files.

4.6 Bibliographic Notes

Clustering is a classic area of pattern recognition, statistics, machine learning, and data mining. I cannot hope to do justice to the entire field of unsupervised structure discovery from data, so I have focused on issues that are specific to text and hypertext. The comprehensive introductory text by Jain and Dubes [114] has a wealth of information on applications, models, and algorithms, although scalability issues are not often in the forefront. Han and Kamber [96] and Hand, Manilla, and Smyth [97] also describe classic data clustering in some detail.

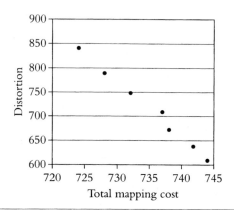

FIGURE 4.15 Trade-off between describing G' and distortion of folder term distributions (in relative number of bits). The simpler the mapping graph, the greater the term distribution distortion. Clustering seeks to minimize the sum of these two costs.

The database community has been concerned with high-performance clustering algorithms for large disk-resident data sets that do not fit in memory. The k-means paradigm is amenable to scalable implementations because it involves sequential scans over the point set. BIRCH is a well-known scalable clustering algorithm that collects cluster statistics on a cleverly adjusted number of clusters given limited main memory [220]. Bradley and others have also considered how to collect sufficient statistics for clustering tasks using few sequential passes over input data [23]. The density-based, bottom-up algorithm to detect dense subspaces (see Section 4.1.2) is by Agrawal and others [2].

Willet [213] and Rasmussen [180] survey a variety of algorithms suitable for text clustering, and Macskassy and others evaluate human performance on clustering tasks [142]. Maarek et al. [141] propose the use of HAC for organizing browser bookmarks. They propose using correlated word bigrams rather than single words as features to reduce noise in the similarity comparisons. HAC and k-means have been used in conjunction in the well-known Scatter/Gather system built by Cutting and others [59, 60]. Another clustering/visualization tool suitable for text is CViz (*www.alphaworks.ibm.com/tech/cviz/*).

SVD is a standard operation in linear algebra; see, for example, the classic text by Golub and van Loan [91]. Deerwester et al. [66] and Berry, Dumais, and O'Brien [15] give a detailed account of LSI. The treatment of EM is standard; see, for example, Mitchell's standard text [153]. The AutoClass system builds upon EM and adds heuristics for searching for and constraining the complexity of proposed models [47]. For an extensive treatment of self-organizing maps together with applications to Web and news group data see Kohonen et al. [125] and visit *http://websom.hut.fi/websom/*. Partitioning features into noisy and useful sets has been proposed by Dom et al. [207]. The application of MCMM to text is by Saund and others [184, 187]. The application of aspect models to text and collaborative dyadic data is by Hofmann and others [109, 110, 111]. The dyadic framework has been extended to handle content-based and collaborative analysis by Popescul and others [178].

CHAPTER 5

SUPERVISED LEARNING

Organizing human knowledge into related areas is nearly as old as human knowledge itself, as is evident in writings from many ancient civilizations. In modern times, the task of organizing knowledge into systematic structures is studied by ontologists and library scientists, resulting in such well-known structures as the Dewey decimal system, the Library of Congress catalog, the AMS Mathematics Subject Classification, and the U.S. Patent Office subject classification [11, 68]. Subject-based organization routinely permeates our personal lives as we organize books, CDs, videos, and email.

The evolution of the Web has followed this familiar history. Around the same time as ad hoc keyword search engines like AltaVista became popular, the Yahoo! (*www.yahoo.com*) topic directory was launched. Since then, many other Web catalogs have appeared. The Open Directory Project (*dmoz.org*) and About.com are some of the best known at present.

Topic directories are some of the most popular sites on the Web. There is a wealth of information in the manner in which humans have assigned structure to an otherwise haphazard collection of Web pages. Earlier, directories were used mainly for browsing, assisted with some simple search capability on the few lines of description associated with resource links, not the contents of the external pages themselves. Of late, well-known search portals such as Google (*www.google.com/*) return with search responses the "topic path" of a response (such as /Arts/Painting), if the response URL has been associated with one or more topics in the Open Directory. Because the Open Directory is manually maintained, it does not capture all URLs; therefore only a fraction of Google responses are tagged with topics.[1]

Topic tagging improves the search experience in many ways. They are a great warning for queries gone astray or ambiguous queries [48], and they are an indirect means for finding similar documents. Whereas most "find-similar" utilities look for pairwise syntactic similarities with the query document (see Section 3.3.1), a topic-based search first maps the query document to a class (or a few classes), thus greatly enhancing the vocabulary. Then it finds similar documents with respect to this enhanced vocabulary. Topic tagging can also be used to assist hierarchical visualization and browsing aids [101].

News tracking provides another example of the utility of detecting predefined topics in text. Most online news sites provide tools to customize "front pages" as per reader taste. URL- or keyword-based selection is often inadequate, for the same reasons that make keyword-based searching imperfect. Systems have been built to capture URL clicks and to use them to report similar pages. Further applications to topic tagging can be found in organizing email [1] and bookmarks by content [140, 141].

Assigning topic labels to documents is but one of many general uses of supervised learning for text. Text classification has been used to narrow down authors of anonymous documents by learning the writing style (stylometry), as with the *Federalist Papers* written by Alexander Hamilton, John Jay, and James Madison and published anonymously under the pen name Publius [156]. The Flesch-Kincaid index is a hand-tuned "classifier" of sorts, combining the number of syllables per word and number of words per sentence into an index of difficulty of reading technical documents [78]. Yet another application is to classify the purpose of hyperlinks. Documents are connected via hyperlinks and citations for a variety of reasons, including elaboration, citation of supporting material, critique, and so on. Machine learning can be used to guess the (main) purpose of creating a hyperlink.

5.1 The Supervised Learning Scenario

Library scientists undergo extensive training to be able to tag publications with correct and comprehensive topic labels. Can a computer program attain even a fraction of their learning capability? This is an important question in view of the

---

1. It is possible that Google also uses automatic classification to some extent.

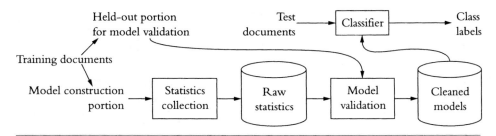

FIGURE 5.1 A typical supervised text-learning scenario.

growing volume of the Web, together with its vastly reduced editorial control and resulting diversity. Learning to assign objects to classes given examples is called *classification* or *supervised learning*, and is the subject of this chapter.

In supervised learning, the *learner* (also called the *classifier*) first receives training data in which each item (document or Web page, in our setting) is marked with a label or class from a discrete finite set. (Sometimes these labels may be related through a taxonomic structure, such as a hierarchical topic catalog. Except in Section 5.7, we will be largely concerned with "flat" sets of class labels.) The learning algorithm is trained using this data. It is common to "hold out" part of the labeled data to tune various parameters used in the classifier. Once the classifier is trained, it is given unlabeled "test" data and has to guess the label. Figure 5.1 illustrates the process at a high level.

Supervised learning has been intensively studied for several decades in AI, machine learning, and pattern recognition, and of late in data warehousing and mining. In those domains, the data is usually more "structured" than text or hypertext. Structured data usually comes in relational tables with well-defined data types for a moderate number of columns. For example, many data sets in the well-known U.C. Irvine repository [20] have between 5 and 50 features. Furthermore, the semantic connection between these columns and the class label is often well understood, at least qualitatively; for example, smoking and cancer risk, age and rash driving, or income and credit card fraud.

In this chapter, our goal is to study supervised learning specifically for text and hypertext documents. Text, as compared to structured data, has a very large number of potential features, of which many are irrelevant. If the vector-space model is used, each term is a potential feature. Furthermore, there are many features that show little information content individually, but in conjunction are vital inputs for learning.

Unlike structured tables with a uniform number of columns[2] per instance, documents can have a diverse number of features. There is little hope of precisely characterizing the joint distribution of the relevant features, owing to sparsity of data as well as computational limitations. The number of distinct class labels is much larger than structured learning scenarios. Finally, the classes may be related by hierarchical relationships, commonly seen in topic directories on the Web.

The models that we shall study in this chapter, although mostly restricted to text alone, will form building blocks for more complex models that couple hyperlink structure with topics, discussed in Chapters 6 and 7. Hypertext classification is at the core of many resource discovery systems that start from pages related to a specified topic and locate additional relevant pages. We will study such systems in Chapters 7 and 8. Supervised learning and its variants are also used for extracting structured snippets of information from unstructured text, which we will discuss in Chapter 9.

5.2 Overview of Classification Strategies

I will present a number of techniques for text classification and comment on their features, strengths, and weaknesses.

Given a typical IR system based on vector-space similarity (see Chapter 3), it is very easy to build a *nearest neighbor* (NN) classifier. An NN classifier (Section 5.4) simply indexes all the training set documents, remembering their class labels. A test document is submitted as a query to the IR system, and the distribution of labels on the training documents most similar to it are used to make a decision.

The vector-space model assigns large weights to rare terms, without regard to the frequency with which terms occur across documents from different classes. The process of *feature selection* (Section 5.5) removes terms in the training documents that are statistically uncorrelated with the class labels, leaving behind a reduced subset of terms to be used for classification. Feature selection can improve both speed and accuracy.

Next we study *Bayesian classifiers* (Section 5.6), which fit a generative term distribution $\Pr(d|c)$ (see Section 4.4.1) to each class c of documents $\{d\}$. While testing, the distribution most likely to have generated a test document is used to label it. This is measured as $\Pr(c|d)$ and derived from $\Pr(d|c)$ using Bayes's rule.

---

2. To be sure, structured tabular data may have entries such as "null," "unknown," or "not applicable," but these are usually modeled as categorical attribute values.

Another approach is to estimate a *direct* distribution $\Pr(c|d)$ from term space to the probability of various classes. *Maximum entropy classifiers* (Section 5.8) are an example of this approach. We may even represent classes by numbers (for a two-class problem, -1 and $+1$, say) and construct a direct function from term space to the class variable. *Support vector machines* (Section 5.9.2) are an example of this approach.

For hypertext applications, it is sometimes necessary to assemble features of many different kinds into a document representation. We may wish to combine information from ordinary terms, terms in titles, headers and anchor text, the structure of the HTML tag-tree in which terms are embedded, terms in pages that are link neighbors of the test page, and citation to or from a page with a known class label, to name a few. We will discuss *rule induction* over such diverse features in Section 5.10.2.

As with ad hoc query processing in IR systems, care with tokenization and feature extraction may be important for classification tasks. For example, replacing monetary amounts, four-digit years, and time in the form "hh:mm" by a special token for each type of string has been known to improve accuracy. For words that can be associated with multiple senses or parts of speech, we have seen part-of-speech or sense disambiguation improve accuracy slightly. In another application, abbreviation of phrases was key: for example, some documents mentioned "mild steel" while others used "M.S." or "M/S." In a different context, "M.S." may be mistaken for an academic degree. Clearly, designing a suitable token representation for a specific classification task is a practiced art. Automating feature extraction and representation for specific tasks is an interesting area of research.

5.3 Evaluating Text Classifiers

There are several criteria to evaluate classification systems:

* Accuracy, the ability to predict the correct class labels most of the time. This is based on comparing the classifier-assigned labels with human-assigned labels.
* Speed and scalability for training and applying/testing in batch mode.
* Simplicity, speed, and scalability for document insertion, deletion, and modification, as well as moving large sets of documents from one class to another.
* Ease of diagnosis, interpretation of results, and adding human judgment and feedback to improve the classifier.

Ideally, I would like to compare classifiers with regard to all of these criteria, but simplicity and ease of use are subjective factors, and speed and scalability change with evolving hardware. Therefore, I will mainly focus on the issue of accuracy, with some comments on performance where appropriate.

5.3.1   Benchmarks

The research community has relied on a few labeled collections, some of which have by now become de facto benchmarks. I describe a few of them below.

Reuters: The Reuters corpus has roughly 10,700 labeled documents with 30,000 terms and 135 categories. The raw text takes about 21 MB. There is a predefined division of the labeled documents into roughly 7700 training and 3000 test documents. About 10% of the documents have multiple class labels. It appears that a document's membership in some of the classes is predicated simply on the occurrence of a small, well-defined set of keywords in the document.

OHSUMED: This corpus comprises 348,566 abstracts from medical journals, having in all around 230,000 terms and occupying 400 MB. It is mostly used to benchmark IR systems on ad hoc queries, but it can also be used for classification. Each document is tagged with one or more *Medical Subject Headings* (MeSH) terms from a set of over 19,000 MeSH terms, which may be regarded as labels.

20NG: This corpus has about 18,800 labeled Usenet postings organized in a directory structure with 20 topics. There are about 94,000 terms. The raw concatenated text takes up 25 MB. The labeled set is usually split randomly into training and test sets, with, say, 75% chosen as training documents. The class labels are in a shallow hierarchy with five classes at the first level and 20 leaf classes.

WebKB: The WebKB corpus has about 8300 documents in 7 categories. About 4300 pages on 7 categories (faculty, project, and the like) were collected from four universities, and about 4000 miscellaneous pages were collected from other universities. For each classification task, any one of the four university pages are selected as test documents and the rest as training documents. The raw text is about 26 MB.

Industry: This is a collection of about 10,000 home pages of companies from 105 industry sectors (e.g., `advertising`, `coal`, `railroad`, `semiconductors`, etc.). The industry sector names are the class labels. There is a shallow hierarchy over the labels. The first level has about 80 classes, and there are 105 leaves. The labeling is published on *www.marketguide.com*.

5.3.2 Measures of Accuracy

Depending on the application, one of the following assumptions is made:

* Each document is associated with *exactly one* class.
* Each document is associated with a *subset* of classes.

For most topic-based applications, the total number of classes is usually more than two. This is not a problem in the "exactly one" scenario. In this setting, a *confusion matrix* M can be used to show the classifier's accuracy. Entry $M[i, j]$ gives the number of test documents belonging to class i that were assigned to class j by the classifier. If the classifier were perfect, only diagonal elements $M[i, i]$ would be nonzero. If M is large, it is difficult to evaluate a classifier at a glance, so sometimes the ratio of the sum of diagonals to the sum of all elements in the matrix is reported as an accuracy score. The closer this ratio is to 1 the better the classifier.

To avoid searching over the power set of class labels in the "subset" scenario, many systems create a two-class problem for every class. For example, if the original data specified a class *Sports*, a classifier with classes *Sports* and *Not-sports* would be created. Documents labeled *Sports* would be examples of the positive class; all other documents would be examples of the negative class *Not-sports*. A test document would be submitted to all these classifiers to get a class subset. This is also called the *two-way ensemble* or the *one-vs.-rest* technique.

Ensemble classifiers are evaluated on the basis of *recall* and *precision,* similar to ad hoc retrieval (see Chapter 3). Let test document d be hand tagged[3] with a set of classes C_d, and suppose the classifier outputs its estimated set of classes C'_d. Here $C_d, C'_d \subseteq \mathcal{C}$, the universe of class labels.

The recall for class c is the fraction of test documents hand tagged with c that were also tagged with c by the classifier. The precision for class c is the fraction of test documents tagged with c by the classifier that were also hand tagged with c. As in ad hoc retrieval, there is a trade-off between recall and precision.

---

3. By "hand tagged," I mean that these labels are the "ground truth" against which the classifier is evaluated.

Classifier for c_1		
	Guess	
	$\bar{c_1}$	c_1
True $\bar{c_1}$	70	10
c_1	5	15

Classifier for c_2		
	Guess	
	$\bar{c_2}$	c_2
True $\bar{c_2}$	40	20
c_2	14	26

Classifier for c_3		
	Guess	
	$\bar{c_3}$	c_3
True $\bar{c_3}$	61	9
c_3	19	11

Precision $P_1 = 15/(15 + 10)$ $P_2 = 26/(26 + 20)$ $P_3 = 11/(11 + 9)$
Recall $R_1 = 15/(15 + 5)$ $R_2 = 26/(26 + 14)$ $R_3 = 11/(11 + 19)$

Microaveraged precision: $\dfrac{15+26+11}{(15+10)+(26+20)+(11+9)}$

Microaveraged recall: $\dfrac{15+26+11}{(15+5)+(26+14)+(11+19)}$

Macroaveraged precision: $\frac{1}{3}(P_1 + P_2 + P_3)$

Macroaveraged recall: $\frac{1}{3}(R_1 + R_2 + R_3)$

FIGURE 5.2   How to evaluate the accuracy of classifiers. "True" is the hand-assigned class label any; "Guess" is the classifier output. See text for details.

Here is a simple notation to understand recall and precision in a precise manner. For each c and each d, we define a 2×2 contingency matrix $M_{d,c}$, as follows (the expression $[E]$ means 1 if the predicate E is true and 0 otherwise):

$$M_{d,c}[0, 0] = [c \in C_d \text{ and classifier outputs } c]$$
$$M_{d,c}[0, 1] = [c \in C_d \text{ and classifier does not output } c] \quad \text{(loss of recall)}$$
$$M_{d,c}[1, 0] = [c \notin C_d \text{ and classifier outputs } c] \qquad \text{(loss of precision)} \quad (5.1)$$
$$M_{d,c}[1, 1] = [c \notin C_d \text{ and classifier does not output } c]$$

Thus for each (d, c), $M_{d,c}$ has exactly one nonzero entry out of four.

The *microaveraged* contingency matrix is defined as $M_\mu = \sum_{d,c} M_{d,c}$. The microaveraged *recall* is defined as $\frac{M_\mu[0,0]}{M_\mu[0,0]+M_\mu[0,1]}$. The microaveraged *precision* is defined as $\frac{M_\mu[0,0]}{M_\mu[0,0]+M_\mu[1,0]}$. All this is exactly analogous to ad hoc recall and precision. Consider a three-class problem. For each class $c = c_1, c_2, c_3$, we train one classifier with classes c and $\bar{c}$. Let the total number of test documents be 100, and suppose the three classifiers perform as shown Figure 5.2. The micro- and macroaveraged recall and precision are shown in the same figure.

Microaveraging makes the overall precision and recall depend most on the accuracy observed for the classes with the largest number of (positive) documents: the accuracy can be poor for classes with few positive examples without affecting the overall numbers much. One may also look at the data aggregated by specific classes, $M_c = \sum_d M_{c,d}$. This will give the recall and precision for each class separately. Suppose M_c is scaled so the four entries add up to one, giving M'_c. The *macroaveraged* contingency matrix can be defined as $(1/|C|) \sum_c M'_c$. The macroaveraged recall and precision can then be defined in the usual way. Macroaveraged measures pay equal importance to each class, whereas microaveraged measures pay equal importance to each document.

For most classifiers, various parameters can be tuned so that the set of classes returned for a test document may be made to trade off recall for precision or vice versa. It is common to report classifier performance by plotting a graph of (micro- or macroaveraged) precision against recall. A better classifier has a higher curve (see Figure 5.14 for an example). One may also plot the line $y = x$ on this graph and note where this intersects the recall-precision plot. This point is called the *break-even point*. Also used is the so-called F_1 *score*, which is defined as the harmonic mean of recall and precision:

$$F_1 = \frac{2 \times \text{recall} \times \text{precision}}{\text{recall} + \text{precision}}$$

where recall and precision may be defined in the various ways mentioned above. The harmonic mean discourages classifiers that sacrifice one measure for another too drastically.

5.4 Nearest Neighbor Learners

The basic intuition behind nearest neighbor (NN) classifiers is that similar documents are expected to be assigned the same class label. The vector-space model introduced in Chapter 3 and the cosine measure for similarity lets us formalize the intuition.

At training time, we simply index each document (as described in Chapter 3) and remember its class label. Given a test document d_q, we use it as a query and let the IR system fetch us the k training documents most similar to d_q (k is a tuned constant). The class that occurs the largest number of times among these k training documents is reported as the class of the test document d_q (see Figure 5.3).

As a refinement, rather than accumulate raw counts of classes, we can accumulate *weighted* counts. If training document d has label c_d, c_d accumulates a score of $s(d_q, d)$, the vector-space similarity between d_q and d, on account of d. The class with the maximum score wins. Yet another refinement is to use a per-class

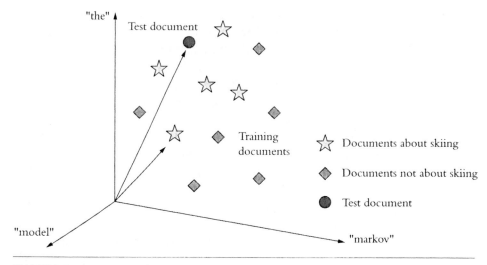

FIGURE 5.3 Nearest neighbor classification.

offset b_c, which is tuned by testing the classifier on a portion of training data held out for this purpose. Combining these ideas, the score of class c for test document d_q is given as

$$\text{score}(c, d_q) = b_c + \sum_{d \in k\text{NN}(d_q)} s(d_q, d) \tag{5.2}$$

where $k\text{NN}(d_q)$ is the set of k training documents most similar to d_q.

Because NN classifiers do very little at training time, they are also called *lazy learners*. Like b_c, the parameter k can be tuned by setting aside a portion of the labeled documents for validation (see Figure 5.1) and trying out various values of k, a process called *cross-validation*. Another approach would be to cluster the training set using some technique from Chapter 4 and choosing a value of k that is related to the size of small clusters.

5.4.1 Pros and Cons

An NN learner has several advantages and disadvantages. The biggest advantage is that very often it comes for free; there may already be an inverted index on the collection to support full-text searching that can be reused for classification. This also makes collection updates trivial to handle (because the classifier is "lazy" and does nothing but indexing at training time). With properly tuned values of k and

b_c for each label c, k-NN classifiers are comparable in accuracy to the best-known classifiers.

On the other hand, classifying a test document d_q involves as many inverted index lookups as there are distinct terms in d_q, followed by scoring the (possibly large number of) candidate documents that overlap with d_q in at least one word, sorting by overall similarity, and picking the best k documents, where k could be very small compared to the number of candidates. Such queries are called *iceberg queries* (because the user is looking for the tip of the iceberg) and are difficult to answer in time that is comparable to output size. In contrast, in the case of naive Bayesian classifiers (introduced in Section 5.6.1), each inverted list has length related to the number of *classes*, which is much smaller than the number of training documents.

A related problem with NN classifiers is the space overhead and redundancy in storing the training information, which is recorded at the level of individual documents. The classifier, being "lazy," does not distill this data into simpler "class models," unlike many of the more sophisticated classifiers we will study later on.

In practice, to reduce space requirements, as well as speed up classification, lazy learners are made to work a little harder at training time. For example, we may find clusters in the data (see Chapter 4) and store only a few statistical parameters per cluster. A test document is first compared with a few cluster representatives and then with the documents in only the most promising clusters. Unfortunately this strategy often leads to various ad hoc choices, for example, number and size of clusters and parameters. In addition, choosing k is a practiced art and the best choice can be sensitive to the specific corpus at hand.

5.4.2   Is TFIDF Appropriate?

Recall that in the computation of similarity s in Equation (5.2), each dimension or term was assigned an inverse document frequency with respect to the *whole* corpus. This may fail to exploit correlations between class labels and the term frequencies. An example with two classes, each having 100 training documents, will make this clear. Consider two terms. One term t_1 occurs in 10 documents in each class, that is, in 10% of the overall corpus. The other term t_2 occurs in 40 documents in the first class but none in the second class, that is, in 20% of the corpus. Thus, t_1 is "rarer," and IDF scoring will downplay the role of t_2 in the distance measure.

Clearly, class labels on training documents should play a central role in making judgments about how well a term can help discriminate between documents from different classes. Terms that occur *relatively* frequently in some classes compared to others should have higher importance; overall rarity in the corpus is not as important. In the next section, I shall introduce several techniques for estimating the importance of features.

5.5 Feature Selection

We can make a reasonable estimate of a distribution over features when the number of training instances is substantially larger than the number of features. Unfortunately, this is not the case with text. Let us revisit the binary document model where word counts are ignored (see Section 4.4.1). With a vocabulary set W, there are $2^{|W|}$ possible documents. For the Reuters data set, that number would be $2^{30,000} \approx 10^{10,000}$, whereas there are only about 10,300 documents available. In any set of training documents, we will witness a very tiny fraction of these possible documents. Therefore, any estimate of the joint probability distribution over all terms will be very crude.

If we abandon trying to estimate the *joint* distribution of all terms and restrict ourselves, as in Section 4.4.1, to estimating the *marginal* distribution of each term (in each class), the situation improves drastically. However, it may still be nontrivial to judge, from a limited training collection, whether a given term appears more frequently in one class compared to another.

We clarify the issue using a simple two-class example. Let there be N training documents sampled from each class, and fix a term t. Drawing a document and checking if it contains t is like tossing a coin. For the two classes, we can imagine two coins, with $\Pr(\text{head}) = \phi_1$ and ϕ_2, each of which has been tossed N times and produced k_1 and k_2 heads, respectively. It is possible that $\phi_1 < \phi_2$ but $k_1 > k_2$, especially if N is small. If N is too small for us to believe that $\phi_1 < \phi_2$ or $\phi_1 > \phi_2$ with sufficient confidence, it may be better not to use t for classification rather than build an unreliable model, which may lead us to wrong decisions on an ulimited number of test documents. Building an unreliable model that fits limited training data closely, but fails to generalize to unforeseen test data is called *overfitting*.

Feature selection can be heuristic, guided by linguistic and domain knowledge, or statistical. Many classifiers eliminate standard stopwords like *a*, *an*, *the*, and so on. We have seen this to improve classification accuracy a little, even though some stopwords appear to be correlated with the class label. Some classifiers also perform quick-and-dirty approximations to feature selection by ignoring terms that are "too frequent" or "too rare" according to empirically chosen thresholds, which may be corpus- and task-sensitive.

As data sets become larger and more complex, these simple heuristics may not suffice. The challenge looms large especially for hierarchical topic directories, because as one surfs down into detailed topics, terms that would be excellent discriminators with respect to English start resembling stopwords with respect to the specialized collection. Furthermore, in settings such as the Web, jargon and multilingual content makes stopwording difficult.

Feature selection is desirable not only to avoid overfitting and thus *improve* accuracy but also to *maintain* accuracy while discarding as many features as possible, because a great deal of space for storing statistics is saved in this manner. The reduction in space usually results in better classification performance. Sometimes, the reduced class models fit in main memory; even if they don't, caching becomes more effective.

The "perfect" algorithm for feature selection would be goal-directed: it would pick all possible subsets of features, and for each subset train and test a classifier, and retain that subset that resulted in the highest accuracy. For common text collections this is a computational impossibility. Therefore, the search for feature subsets has to be limited to a more manageable extent.

In this section we will study two basic strategies for feature selection. One starts with the empty set and includes good features; the other starts from the complete feature set and excludes irrelevant features.

5.5.1 Greedy Inclusion Algorithms

The most commonly used class of algorithms for feature selection in the text domain share the following outline:

1. Compute, for each term, a measure of discrimination among classes.

2. Arrange the terms in decreasing order of this measure.

3. Retain a number of the best terms or features for use by the classifier.

Often, the measure of discrimination of a term is computed independently of other terms—this is what makes the procedure "greedy." It may result in some terms appearing to be useful that actually add little value given certain other terms that have already been included. In practice, this overinclusion often has mild effects on accuracy.

Several measures of discrimination have been used. The choice depends on the model of documents used by the classifier, the desired speed of training (feature selection is usually considered a part of training), and the ease of updates to documents and class assignments. Although different measures will result in somewhat different term ranks, the *sets* included for acceptable accuracy will tend to have large overlap. Therefore, most classifiers will tend to be insensitive to the specific choice of discrimination measures. I describe a few commonly used discrimination measures next.

The χ^2 test

Classic statistics provides some standard tools for testing if the class label and a single term are "significantly" correlated with each other. For simplicity, let us consider a two-class classification problem and use the *binary* document model (see Section 4.4.1). Fix a term t, let the class labels be 0 and 1, and let

$k_{i,0}$ = number of documents in class i not containing term t

$k_{i,1}$ = number of documents in class i containing term t

This gives us a 2×2 contingency matrix

		I_t	
		0	1
C	0	k_{00}	k_{01}
	1	k_{10}	k_{11}

where C and I_t denote Boolean random variables and $k_{\ell m}$ denotes the number of observations where $C = \ell$ and $I_t = m$. We would like to test if these random variables are independent or not. Let $n = k_{00} + k_{01} + k_{10} + k_{11}$. We can estimate the marginal distributions as

$$\Pr C = 0 = (k_{00} + k_{01})/n,$$
$$\Pr(C = 1) = 1 - \Pr(C = 0) = (k_{10} + k_{11})/n,$$
$$\Pr(I_t = 0) = (k_{00} + k_{10})/n, \text{ and}$$
$$\Pr(I_t = 1) = 1 - \Pr(I_t = 0) = (k_{01} + k_{11})/n$$

If C and I_t were independent we would expect $\Pr(C = 0, I_t = 0) = \Pr(C = 0) \Pr(I_t = 0)$. Our empirical estimate of $\Pr(C = 0, I_t = 0)$ is k_{00}/n. The same holds for the three other cells in the table. We expect cell (ℓ, m) to have value $n \Pr(C = \ell, I_t = m)$, and its observed value is $k_{\ell m}$. The χ^2 measure aggregates the deviations of observed values from expected values (under the independence hypothesis), as follows:

$$\chi^2 = \sum_{\ell,m} \frac{\left(k_{\ell m} - n \Pr(C = \ell) \Pr(I_t = m)\right)^2}{n \Pr(C = \ell) \Pr(I_t = m)}$$

This can be simplified to

$$\chi^2 = \frac{n(k_{11}k_{00} - k_{10}k_{01})^2}{(k_{11} + k_{10})(k_{01} + k_{00})(k_{11} + k_{01})(k_{10} + k_{00})} \tag{5.3}$$

The larger the value of χ^2, the lower is our belief that the independence assumption is upheld by the observed data. Statisticians use precompiled tables to determine the confidence with which the independence assumption is refuted. This test is similar to the likelihood ratio test, described in Section 3.2.5, for detecting phrases.

For feature selection, it is adequate to sort terms in decreasing order of their χ^2 values, train several classifiers with a varying number of features (picking the best ones from the ranked list), and stopping at the point of maximum accuracy. See Figures 5.4 and 5.5 for details.

Mutual information

This measure from information theory is useful when the multinomial document model (see Section 4.4.1) is used, term occurrences are regarded as discrete events, documents are of diverse length (as is usual), and no length scaling is performed.

If X and Y are discrete random variables taking specific values denoted x, y, then the *mutual information* (MI) between them is defined as

$$\mathrm{MI}(X, Y) = \sum_x \sum_y \Pr(x, y) \log \frac{\Pr(x, y)}{\Pr(x) \Pr(y)} \tag{5.4}$$

where the marginal distributions are denoted $\Pr(x)$ and $\Pr(y)$, shorthand for $\Pr(X = x)$ and $\Pr(Y = y)$ as usual.

MI measures the extent of dependence between random variables, that is, the extent to which $\Pr(x, y)$ deviates from $\Pr(x) \Pr(y)$ (which represents the independence assumption), suitably weighted with the distribution mass at (x, y). (Therefore, deviations from independence at rare values of (x, y) are played down in the measure.) If X and Y are independent, then $\Pr(x, y)/\Pr(x) \Pr(y) = 1$ for all x, y and therefore $\mathrm{MI}(X, Y) = 0$. It can also be shown that $\mathrm{MI}(X, Y)$ is zero only if X and Y are independent. The more positive it is, the more correlated X and Y are.

There are several instructive ways to interpret MI. One interpretation is that it is the *reduction* in the entropy of X if we are told the value of Y, or equivalently, the reduction in the entropy of Y given X. The entropy of a random variable X taking on values from a discrete set of symbols $\{x\}$ is given

by $H(X) = -\sum_x \Pr(x) \log \Pr(x)$. The conditional entropy $H(X|Y)$ is given by
$-\sum_{x,y} \Pr(x, y) \log \Pr(x|y) = -\sum_{x,y} \log \frac{\Pr(x,y)}{\Pr(y)}$. It is easy to verify that

$$MI(X, Y) = H(X) - H(X|Y) = H(Y) - H(Y|X) \tag{5.5}$$

If the difference in entropy is large, the value of X tells us a lot about the conditional distribution of Y and vice versa.

Another interpretation of MI uses the Kullback-Leibler (KL) distance [57] between distributions. The KL distance from distribution Θ_1 to Θ_2, each defined over a random variable Z taking values from the domain $\{z\}$, is defined as

$$KL(\Theta_1 \| \Theta_2) = \sum_z \Pr_{\Theta_1}(z) \log \frac{\Pr_{\Theta_1}(z)}{\Pr_{\Theta_2}(z)}$$

The KL distance gives the average number of bits wasted by encoding events from the "correct" distribution Θ_1 using a code based on a not-quite-right distribution Θ_2. In our case, $Z = (X, Y)$, $z = (x, y)$, and the model $\Theta_2 = \Theta_{\text{independent}}$ corresponds to the hypothesis that X and Y are independent, that means that $\Pr(x, y) = \Pr(x) \Pr(y)$, whereas $\Theta_1 = \Theta_{\text{true}}$ makes no such assumption. Thus,

$$KL(\Theta_{\text{true}} \| \Theta_{\text{independent}}) = \sum_{x,y} \Pr(x, y) \log \frac{\Pr(x, y)}{\Pr(x) \Pr(y)} = MI(X, Y) \tag{5.6}$$

If $MI(X, Y)$ turns out to be zero, $\Theta_{\text{independent}}$ was a perfectly accurate approximation to Θ_{true}. To the extent $MI(X, Y)$ is large, X and Y are dependent.

To apply MI to feature selection, we will map the above definition to document models in a natural way. Fix a term t and let I_t be an event associated with that term. The definition of the event will vary depending on the document model. For the binary model, $i_t \in \{0, 1\}$, whereas for the multinomial model, i_t is a nonnegative integer. $\Pr(i_t)$ is the empirical fraction of documents in the training set in which event i_t occurred. For example, in the multinomial model, $\Pr(I_t = 2)$ is the empirical fraction of documents in which term t occurred twice. Let c range over the set of classes. $\Pr(i_t, c)$ is the empirical fraction of training documents that are in class c with $I_t = i_t$. $\Pr(c)$ is the fraction of training documents belonging to class c.

For the binary document model and two classes (as in the case of the χ^2 test), the MI of term t with regard to the two classes can be written as

$$MI(I_t, C) = \sum_{\ell,m \in \{0,1\}} \frac{k_{\ell,m}}{n} \log \frac{k_{\ell,m}/n}{(k_{\ell,0} + k_{\ell,1})(k_{0,m} + k_{1,m})/n^2} \tag{5.7}$$

A possible problem with this approach is that document lengths are not normalized. If a term occurs roughly at the same rate (say, five times per 10,000 words) in two classes, but one class has longer documents than the other, the term may appear to be a good feature using this measure. For this reason, length-normalized feature selection algorithms are sometimes preferred.

Fisher's discrimination index

This measure is useful when documents are scaled to constant length, and therefore, term occurrences are regarded as fractional real numbers. For simplicity let us again consider a two-class learning problem. Let X and Y be the sets of document vectors corresponding to the two classes. The components of these document vectors may be raw term counts scaled to make each document vector unit length, or we may already have applied some term-weighting scheme.

Let $\mu_X = (\sum_X x)/|X|$ and $\mu_Y = (\sum_Y y)/|Y|$ be the mean vectors, or centroids, for each class. Each document vector and these mean vectors are column vectors in $\mathbb{R}^m$, say. Further, let the respective covariance matrices be $S_X = (1/|X|) \sum_X (x - \mu_X)(x - \mu_X)^T$ and $S_Y = (1/|Y|) \sum_Y (y - \mu_Y)(y - \mu_Y)^T$. The covariance matrices are $m \times m$ in size.

Fisher's discriminant seeks to find a column vector $\alpha \in \mathbb{R}^m$ such that the ratio of the square of the difference in mean vectors projected onto it, that is, $(\alpha^T(\mu_X - \mu_Y))^2$, to the average projected variance $\frac{1}{2}\alpha^T(S_X + S_Y)\alpha$, is maximized. Noting that both the numerator and denominator are scalar numbers, and that $\alpha^T S_X \alpha$ is a simple way of writing $(1/|X|) \sum_X \alpha^T(x - \mu_X)(x - \mu_X)^T \alpha$, we can write

$$\alpha^* = \arg\max_{\alpha} J(\alpha) = \arg\max_{\alpha} \frac{(\alpha^T(\mu_X - \mu_Y))^2}{\alpha^T(S_X + S_Y)\alpha} \tag{5.8}$$

Informally, Fisher's discriminant finds a projection of the data sets X and Y onto a line such that the two projected centroids are far apart compared to the spread of the point sets projected onto the same line.

With $S = (S_X + S_Y)/2$, it can be shown that $\alpha = S^{-1}(\mu_X - \mu_Y)$ achieves the extremum when S^{-1} exists. (We will omit the "2" where it won't affect the optimization.) Also, if X and Y for both the training and test data are generated from multivariate Gaussian distributions with $S_X = S_Y$, this value of α induces the optimal (minimum error) classifier by suitable thresholding on $\alpha^T q$ for a test point q.

Fisher's discriminant in the above form has been used in signal-processing applications, in which the number of dimensions in the x and y vectors is on the order of hundreds at most. Inverting S would be unacceptably slow for tens of thousands of dimensions. To make matters worse, although the raw data set is sparse (most words occur in few documents), the linear transformations would destroy sparsity. In any case, our goal in feature selection is not to arrive at linear projections involving multiple terms but to eliminate terms from consideration.

Therefore, instead of looking for the best single direction α, we will regard each term t as providing a candidate direction α_t, which is parallel to the corresponding axis in the vector-space model. That is, $\alpha_t = (0, \ldots, 1, \ldots, 0)^T$, with a 1 in the tth position alone. We will then compute the *Fisher's index* (FI) of t, defined as

$$\text{FI}(t) = J(\alpha_t) = \frac{(\alpha_t^T (\mu_X - \mu_Y))^2}{\alpha_t^T S \alpha_t} \tag{5.9}$$

Because of the special form of α_t, the expression above can be greatly simplified. $\alpha_t^T \mu_X = \mu_{X,t}$, the tth component of μ_X, and $\alpha_t^T \mu_Y = \mu_{Y,t}$, the tth component of μ_Y. $\alpha^T S_X \alpha$ can also be simplified to $(1/|X|) \sum_X (x_t - \mu_{X,t})^2$, and $\alpha^T S_Y \alpha$ can be simplified to $(1/|Y|) \sum_Y (y_t - \mu_{Y,t})^2$. Thus we can write

$$\text{FI}(t) = \frac{(\mu_{X,t} - \mu_{Y,t})^2}{(1/|X|) \sum_X (x_t - \mu_{X,t})^2 + (1/|Y|) \sum_Y (y_t - \mu_{Y,t})^2} \tag{5.10}$$

This measure can be generalized to a set $\{c\}$ of more than two classes to yield the form

$$\text{FI}(t) = \frac{\sum_{c_1,c_2} (\mu_{c_1,t} - \mu_{c_2,t})^2}{\sum_c \frac{1}{|D_c|} \sum_{d \in D_c} (x_{d,t} - \mu_{c,t})^2} \tag{5.11}$$

where D_c is the set of training documents labeled with class c. Terms are sorted in decreasing order of $\text{FI}(t)$ and the best ones chosen as features.

Validation

Merely ranking the terms does not complete the process; we have to decide a cutoff rank such that only terms that pass the bar are included in the feature set. We can do this by validation or cross-validation. In the validation approach, a portion of the training documents are held out, the rest being used to do term ranking. Then the held-out set is used as a test set. Various cutoff ranks can be tested using

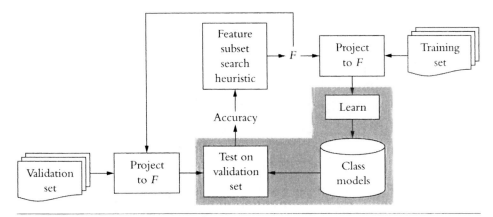

FIGURE 5.4   A general illustration of wrapping for feature selection.

the same held-out set. In *leave-one-out* cross-validation, for each document d in the training set D, a classifier is trained over $D \setminus \{d\}$ and then tested on d. If this takes too much time, a simpler form of cross-validation can be used. The training set is partitioned into a few parts. In turn, one part is taken to be the test set, and the remaining parts together form the training set. An aggregate accuracy is computed over all these trials.

The training and test sets, derived using any of the approaches described above, may be used with a *wrapper*, shown in Figure 5.4, to search for the set of features that yield the highest accuracy. A simple "search heuristic" shown in the diagram is to keep adding one feature at every step until the classifier's accuracy ceases to improve. For certain kinds of classifiers (e.g., maximum entropy classifiers, see Section 5.8, or support vector machines, see Section 5.9.2), such a search would be very inefficient: it would essentially involve training a classifier from scratch for each choice of the cutoff rank. Luckily, some other classifiers (like the naive Bayesian classifier, see Section 5.6) can be evaluated on many choices of feature sets at once.

Figure 5.5 shows the effect of feature selection on the accuracy of Bayesian classifiers, which I will discuss in detail in Section 5.6. The corpus is a selection of 9600 patents sampled from the U.S. Patent database. The terms were ordered using Fisher's discriminant. The classifiers use the binary and multinomial document models, discussed in Section 4.4.1. Only 140 out of about 20,000 raw features

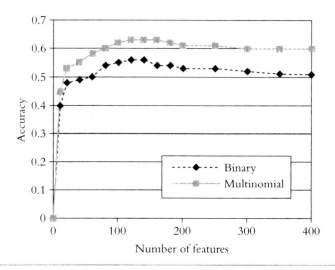

FIGURE 5.5   Effect of feature selection on Bayesian classifiers.

suffice for the best feasible accuracy, which cuts down statistics storage and access costs dramatically. For reasons given later, Bayesian classifiers cannot overfit much, although there is a visible degradation in accuracy beyond the best choice of the number of features. The accuracy varies quite smoothly in the vicinity of the maximum. Barring minor fluctuations, the accuracy increases sharply as the very best features are included one by one, then fluctuates slightly near the crest (which is quite wide) before showing a small drop-off.

5.5.2   Truncation Algorithms

Another approach to feature selection is to start from the complete set of terms T and drop terms from consideration, ending up with a feature subset $F \subseteq T$. What is the desirable property relating F to T?

Most probabilistic classifiers must, one way or another, derive a conditional probability distribution of class labels given data, which we denote as $\Pr(C|T)$, where C is the class label and T is the multivariate term vector. As a result of restricting the training data to F, the distribution changes to $\Pr(C|F)$. We would like to keep the distorted distribution $\Pr(C|F)$ as similar as possible to the original $\Pr(C|T)$ while minimizing the size of F. The similarity or distance between two distributions can be measured in various ways; a well-known measure is the KL distance discussed above.

1: **while** truncated $\Pr(C|F)$ is reasonably close to original $\Pr(C|T)$ **do**
2: **for** each remaining feature X **do**
3:   *Identify a candidate Markov blanket M:*
4:   For some tuned constant k, find the set M of k variables in $F \setminus X$ that are most strongly correlated with X
5:   *Estimate how good a blanket M is:*
6:   Estimate
$$\sum_{x_M, x} \Pr(X_M = x_M, X = x) \mathrm{KL}\big(\Pr(C|X_M = x_M, X = x),$$
$$\Pr(C|X_M = x_M)\big)$$
7: **end for**
8: Eliminate the feature having the best surviving Markov blanket
9: **end while**

FIGURE 5.6 Pseudocode for a heuristic algorithm for feature truncation.

Two random variables P and Q are said to be *conditionally independent* given R, if for any value assignments p, q, r, $\Pr(P = p|Q = q|R = r) = \Pr(P = p|R = r)$. Thus, Q gives no information about P over and above that which we gain by knowing the value of R.

Let X be a feature in T. Let $M \subseteq T \setminus \{X\}$. M is called a *Markov blanket* for $X \in T$ if X is conditionally independent of $(T \cup C) \setminus (M \cup \{X\})$, given M. Intuitively, the presence of M renders the presence of X unnecessary as a feature. It can be shown that eliminating a variable because it has a Markov blanket contained in other existing features does not increase the KL distance between $\Pr(C|T)$ and $\Pr(C|F)$. In practice, there may not be a perfect Markov blanket for any variable, but only an approximate one, and finding it may be difficult. To control the computational cost, we may limit our search for Markov blankets M to those with at most k features. As another cost-cutting heuristic, given feature X, we may restrict our search for the members of M to those features that are most strongly correlated (using tests similar to the χ^2 or MI tests) with X. A sample pseudocode is shown in Figure 5.6. In experiments with the Reuters data set, over two-thirds of T could be discarded while *increasing* classification accuracy by a few percentage points.

5.5.3 Comparison and Discussion

I have presented a variety of measures of association between terms and class labels, and two generic approaches to selecting features. The preferred choice of association measure and selection algorithm depends on the nature and difficulty of the classification task.

In my experience with several kinds of classifiers and standard benchmarks, I have found that the choice of association measures does not make a dramatic difference, provided the issue of document length is addressed properly. Although different association measures induce different orderings on the terms, by the time we have included enough terms for acceptable accuracy, the *set* of terms included under all the orderings show significant overlap.

Greedy inclusion algorithms scale nearly linearly with the number of features, whereas the Markov blanket technique is much more elaborate and general, taking time proportional to at least $|T|^k$. Markov blankets seek to improve upon greedy inclusion in two important ways, illustrated by these simplified examples:

*   The correlation between C and X_1, and between C and X_2, may be individually strong, while X_1's power to predict C may render X_2 unnecessary as a feature, or vice versa. A greedy inclusion algorithm may include them both.

*   The correlation between C and X_1, and between C and X_2, may be individually weak, but collectively, X_1, X_2 may be an excellent predictor of C. This might happen if X_1, X_2 are associated with phrases whose constituent term(s) also appear in other contexts. A greedy inclusion approach might discard both X_1 and X_2.

The first concern is primarily one of efficiency. Greedy inclusion may overestimate the number of features required. If the classifier has high quality, feature redundancy does not affect accuracy; it is purely a performance issue. Even for crude classifiers, the effect on accuracy is generally quite small (see, e.g., Figure 5.5).

The second concern is potentially more serious, but practical experience [138] seems to indicate that there is enough natural redundancy among features in text that we need not be too concerned with missing weak signals. In particular, it is rare to find X_1 and X_2 weakly correlated with C but jointly predicting C much better than other single features.

In my experience, the binary view of a feature being either useful or not is not the best possible, especially for hypertext applications where artificial features need to be synthesized out of markup or hyperlinks. As Joachims [119] and others point out, textual features are many in number, each being of low quality. Most have tiny amounts of information for predicting C, but these tiny amounts vary a great deal from one feature to another. To accommodate that view, a classifier might transform and combine features into fewer, simpler ones, rather than just discard a large number of features. A common technique is to represent the documents in vector space (see Chapter 3) and then project the document vectors to a lower-dimensional space using a variety of approaches (see Chapter 4). Investigating the effect of such transformations on classification accuracy can be an interesting area of research.

5.6 Bayesian Learners

Once feature selection is performed, nonfeature terms are removed from the training documents, and the resulting "clean" documents are used to train the learner. In this section we will study *Bayesian learners,* a practical and popular kind of statistical learner. In spite of their crude approximations, Bayesian classifiers remain some of the most practical text classifiers used in applications.

We will assume, for simplicity of exposition, that a document can belong to exactly one of a set of classes or topics. Document creation is modeled as the following process:

1. Each topic or class c has an associated *prior* probability $\Pr(c)$, with $\sum_c \Pr(c) = 1$. The author of a document first picks a topic at random with its corresponding probability.

2. There is a class–conditional document distribution $\Pr(d|c)$ for each class. Having earlier fixed a class c, its document distribution is used to generate the document.

Thus the overall probability of generating the document from class c is $\Pr(c) \Pr(d|c)$. Finally, given the document d, the *posterior* probability that d was generated from class c is seen, using Bayes's rule, to be

$$\Pr(c|d) = \frac{\Pr(c) \Pr(d|c)}{\sum_\gamma \Pr(\gamma) \Pr(d|\gamma)} \tag{5.12}$$

γ ranges over all classes so that $\Pr(c|d)$ becomes a proper probability measure.

$\Pr(d|c)$ is estimated by modeling the class–conditional term distribution in terms of a set of parameters that we can collectively call Θ. Our estimate of Θ is based on two sources of information:

*   Prior knowledge that exists before seeing any training documents for the current problem. This is characterized by a distribution on Θ itself.

*   Terms in the training documents D.

After observing the training data D, our posterior distribution for Θ is written as $\Pr(\Theta|D)$. Based on this discussion we can elaborate

$$\Pr(c|d) = \sum_{\Theta} \Pr(c|d, \Theta) \Pr(\Theta|D)$$

$$= \sum_{\Theta} \frac{\Pr(c|\Theta) \Pr(d|c, \Theta)}{\sum_{\gamma} \Pr(\gamma|\Theta) \Pr(d|\gamma, \Theta)} \Pr(\Theta|D) \tag{5.13}$$

The sum may be taken to an integral in the limit for a continuous parameter space, which is the common case. In effect, because we only know the training data for sure and are not sure of the parameter values, we are summing over all possible parameter values. Such a classification framework is called *Bayes optimal*. In practice, taking the expectation over $\Pr(\Theta|D)$ is computationally infeasible for all but the smallest number of dimensions. A common practice is to replace the integral above with the value of the integrand ($\Pr(c|d, \Theta)$) for one specific value of Θ. For example, we can choose $\arg\max_{\Theta} \Pr(\Theta|D)$, called the *maximum likelihood estimate* (MLE). MLE turns out not to work well for text classification; alternatives are suggested shortly.

5.6.1 Naive Bayes Learners

A statistical learner that is widely used for its simplicity and speed of training, applying, and updating is the *naive Bayes learner*. The epithet "naive" signifies the assumption of independence between terms—that is, that the joint term distribution is the product of the marginals. The models for the marginals depend on the document model being used. Here I will use the binary and multinomial models first introduced in Section 4.4.1.

In the *binary* model, the parameters are $\phi_{c,t}$, which indicates the probability that a document in class c will mention term t at least once. With this definition,

$$\Pr(d|c) = \prod_{t \in d} \phi_{c,t} \prod_{t \in W, t \notin d} (1 - \phi_{c,t}) \tag{5.14}$$

W being the set of features. We do not wish to calculate $\prod_{t \in W, t \notin d}(1 - \phi_{c,t})$ for every test document, so we rewrite Equation (5.14) as

$$\Pr(d|c) = \prod_{t \in d} \frac{\phi_{c,t}}{1 - \phi_{c,t}} \prod_{t \in W} (1 - \phi_{c,t})$$

precompute and store $\prod_{t \in W}(1 - \phi_{c,t})$ for all c, and only compute the first product at testing time.

In the *multinomial* model, each class has an associated die with $|W|$ faces. The $\phi_{c,t}$ parameters are replaced with $\theta_{c,t}$, the probability of the face $t \in W$ turning up on tossing the die. Let term t occur $n(d, t)$ times in document d, which is said to have *length* $\ell_d = \sum_t n(d, t)$. The document length is a random variable denoted L and assumed to follow a suitable distribution for each class. For this model,

$$\Pr(d|c) = \Pr(L = \ell_d|c) \, \Pr(d|\ell_d, c)$$

$$= \Pr(L = \ell_d|c) \binom{\ell_d}{\{n(d, t)\}} \prod_{t \in d} \theta_t^{n(d,t)} \tag{5.15}$$

where $\binom{\ell_d}{\{n(d,t)\}} = \frac{\ell_d!}{n(d,t_1)! \, n(d,t_2)! \cdots}$ is the multinomial coefficient, which can be dropped if we are just *ranking* classes, because it is the same for all c. It is also common (but questionable) to assume that the length distribution is the same for all classes and thus drop the $\Pr(L = \ell_d|c)$ term as well.

Both forms of naive Bayes classifiers multiply together a large number of small probabilities, resulting in extremely tiny probabilities as answers. Care is needed to store all numbers as logarithms and guard against unwanted underflow. Another effect of multiplying many tiny ϕ or θ values is that the class that comes out at the top wins by a huge margin, with a score very close to 1, whereas all other classes have negligible probability. The extreme score skew can be unintuitive in case two or more classes are reasonable candidates.

For two-class problems, a *logit function* is sometimes used to sanitize the scores. Let the classes be $+1$ and -1. The logit function is defined as

$$\text{logit}(d) = \frac{1}{1 + e^{-\text{LR}(d)}} \tag{5.16}$$

where

$$\text{LR}(d) = \frac{\Pr(C = +1|d)}{\Pr(C = -1|d)}$$

is the likelihood ratio. Note that as $\text{LR}(d)$ stretches from 0 to ∞, $\text{logit}(d)$ ranges from $\frac{1}{2}$ to 1. The $\text{logit}(x)$ function has a steep slope near $x = 0$ and levels off rapidly for large x. Finding a suitable threshold on the logit function may reduce the problem of score skew [175].

Parameter smoothing

MLE cannot be used directly in the naive Bayes classifier. For example, in the binary model, if a test document d_q contains a term t that never occurred in any training document in class c, $\phi_{c,t}^{\text{MLE}} = 0$. As a result $\Pr(c|d_q)$ will be zero, even if a number of other terms clearly hint at a high likelihood of class c generating the document. Unfortunately, such "accidents" are not rare at all.

There is a rich literature, dating back to Bayes in the 18th century and Laplace in the 19th century, on the issue of estimating probability from insufficient data. We can start delving into this issue by posing the following question: If you toss a coin n times and it always comes up heads, what is the probability that the $(n+1)$st toss will also come up heads? Although MLE leads to the answer 1, it is not appealing from real-life experience. Furthermore, we certainly expect the answer to change with n: if $n = 1$, we are still quite agnostic about the fairness of the coin; if $n = 1000$, we have a firmer belief. MLE cannot distinguish between these two cases.

In our setting, each coin toss is analogous to inspecting a document (in some fixed class c) to see if term t appears in it. The MLE estimate of $\phi_{c,t}$ is simply the fraction of documents in class c containing the term t. When c and/or t are omitted, they are assumed to be fixed for the rest of this section. Also for this section let k out of n documents contain the term; we denote this event by the notation $\langle k, n \rangle$.

The Bayesian approach to parameter smoothing is to posit a *prior* distribution on ϕ, called $\pi(\phi)$, before any training data is inspected. An example of π is the uniform distribution $\mathcal{U}(0, 1)$. The *posterior* distribution of ϕ is denoted by

$$\pi(\phi|\langle k, n \rangle) = \frac{\pi(\phi) \Pr(\langle k, n \rangle | \phi)}{\int_0^1 dp\, \pi(p) \Pr(\langle k, n \rangle | p)} \tag{5.17}$$

Usually, the smoothed estimate $\tilde{\phi}$ is some property of the posterior distribution $\pi(\phi|\langle k, n \rangle)$. There is a *loss function* $L(\phi, \tilde{\phi})$, which characterizes the penalty for picking a smoothed value $\tilde{\phi}$ as against the "true" value. Often, the loss is taken as the square error, $L(\phi, \tilde{\phi}) = (\phi - \tilde{\phi})^2$. For this choice of loss, the best choice of the smoothed parameter is simply the expectation of the posterior distribution on ϕ having observed the data

$$\tilde{\phi} = E(\pi(\phi|\langle k, n \rangle)) = \frac{\int_0^1 p\, dp\, \pi(p) \Pr(\langle k, n \rangle | p)}{\int_0^1 dp\, \pi(p) \Pr(\langle k, n \rangle | p)} = \frac{\int_0^1 p^{k+1}(1-p)^{n-k} dp}{\int_0^1 p^k (1-p)^{n-k} dp}$$

$$= \frac{\mathbb{B}(k+2, n-k+1)}{\mathbb{B}(k+1, n-k+1)} = \frac{\Gamma(k+2)\, \Gamma(n+2)}{\Gamma(k+1)\, \Gamma(n+3)} = \frac{k+1}{n+2} \tag{5.18}$$

where $\mathbb{B}$ and Γ are the standard beta and gamma functions. Although the derivation is nontrivial, the end result is simple in a misleading way: just "combine" a prior belief of fairness ($\frac{1}{2}$) with observed data ($\frac{k}{n}$). This is called *Laplace's law of succession*. Heuristic alternatives exist; one example is *Lidstone's law of succession*, which sets $\phi = (k + \lambda)/(n + 2\lambda)$, where λ is a tuned constant trading off between prior belief and data. (In Laplace's law, they have equal say.)

The derivation for the multinomial document model is quite similar, except that instead of two possible events in the binary model discussed above, there are $|W|$ possible events, where W is the vocabulary. Thus

$$\tilde{\theta}_{c,t} = \frac{1 + \sum_{d \in D_c} n(d,t)}{|W| + \sum_{d \in D_c, \tau \in d} n(d,\tau)} \tag{5.19}$$

Comments on accuracy and performance

The multinomial naive Bayes classifier generally outperforms the binary variant for most text-learning tasks. Figure 5.5 shows an example. A well-tuned k-NN classifier may outperform a multinomial naive Bayes classifier [217], although the naive Bayes classifier is expected to produce far more compact models and take less time to classifiy test instances.

Any Bayesian classifier partitions the multidimensional term space into regions separated by what are called *decision boundaries*. Within each region, the probability (or probability density, if continuous random variables are modeled) of one class is higher than others; on the boundaries, the probabilities of two or more classes are exactly equal. Two or more classes have comparable probabilities near the boundaries, that are therefore the regions of potential confusion. Little confusion is expected in those parts of a region that have a dense collection of examples, all from the associated class.

To make this more concrete, consider a two–class problem with training data $\{(d_i, c_i), i = 1, \ldots, n\}$, where $c_i \in \{-1, 1\}$. As we have seen before, the multinomial naive Bayes model assumes that a document is a bag or multiset of terms, and the term counts are generated from a multinomial distribution after fixing the document length ℓ_d, which, being fixed for a given document, lets us write

$$\Pr(d|c, \ell_d) = \binom{\ell_d}{\{n(d,t)\}} \prod_{t \in d} \theta_{c,t}^{n(d,t)} \tag{5.20}$$

where $n(d,t)$ is the number of times t occurs in d, and $\theta_{c,t}$ are suitably estimated multinomial probability parameters with $\sum_t \theta_{c,t} = 1$ for each c (see Section 4.4.1).

For the two–class scenario, we only need to compare $\Pr(c = -1|d)$ against $\Pr(c = 1|d)$, or equivalently, $\log \Pr(c = -1|d)$ against $\log \Pr(c = 1|d)$, which simplifies to a comparison between

$$\log \Pr(c = 1) + \sum_{t \in d} n(d, t) \log \theta_{1,t} \tag{5.21}$$

and

$$\log \Pr(c = -1) + \sum_{t \in d} n(d, t) \log \theta_{-1,t}$$

where $\Pr(c = \ldots)$, called the class *priors*, are the fractions of training instances in the respective classes. Simplifying (5.21), we see that NB is a linear classifier: it makes a decision between $c = 1$ and $c = -1$ by thresholding the value of $\alpha_{\mathrm{NB}} \cdot d + b$ for a suitable vector α_{NB} (which depends on the parameters $\theta_{c,t}$) and a constant b depending on the priors. Here d is overloaded to denote the vector of $n(d, t)$ term counts and "·" denotes a dot-product.

One notable problem with naive Bayes classifiers is their strong *bias*. A machine learning algorithm is biased if it restricts the space of possible hypotheses from which it picks a hypothesis to fit the data, before assessing the data itself. Although a naive Bayes classifier picks linear discriminants, it cannot pick from the *entire* set of possible linear discriminants, because it fixes the policy that $\alpha_{\mathrm{NB}}(t)$, the tth component of the discriminant, depends only on the statistics of term t in the corpus. In Sections 5.8 and 5.9, you shall see other classifiers that do not suffer from this form of bias.

5.6.2 Small-Degree Bayesian Networks

The naive Bayes model asserts that fixing the class label of a document imposes a class-conditional distribution on the terms that occur in the document, but that there are no other statistical dependencies between the terms themselves (which is a gross approximation). This simple dependency structure can be represented as a simple hub-and-spoke graph, shown in Figure 5.7(a). Each random variable, including the class label and each term, is a node, and dependency edges are drawn from c to t for each t. If we wish to represent additional dependencies between terms, more edges have to be introduced as shown in Figure 5.7(b), creating a *Bayesian network*.

A Bayesian network is a directed acyclic graph that represents dependencies between a set of random variables and models their joint distribution. Each node

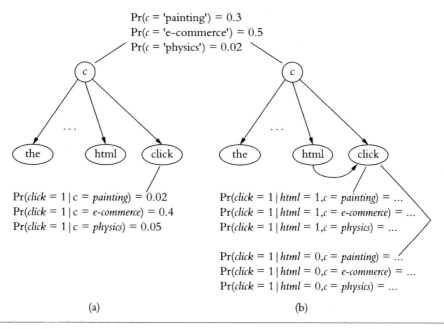

FIGURE 5.7 Bayesian networks. For the naive Bayes assumption, the only edges are from the class variable to individual terms (a). Toward better approximations to the joint distribution over terms, the probability of a term occurring may now depend on observations about other terms as well as the class variable (b).

in the graph represents a random variable. The set of nodes that are connected by directed edges to a node X are called the *parents* of X, denoted $\mathbf{Pa}(X)$. A specific set of values for these parents is denoted $\mathbf{pa}(X)$. Fixing the values of the parent variables completely determines the conditional distribution of X in the sense that information about any other variable would not affect this distribution. For discrete variables, the distribution data for X can be stored in the obvious way as a table with each row showing a set of values of the parents, the value of X, and a conditional probability.

Unlike in the naive models expressed by Equations (5.14) and (5.15), $\Pr(d|c)$ is not a simple product over all terms. Instead it is expressed as a product of conditional probabilities:

$$\Pr(\mathbf{x}) = \prod_x \Pr(x|\mathbf{pa}(X)) \tag{5.22}$$

1: Compute mutual information $MI(X_t, C)$ between class labels C and each feature X_t
2: For each pair of distinct variables X_i and X_j, calculate $MI(X_i, X_j|C)$
3: Initialize the network with class node C
4: **while** all X_t has not been added to the network **do**
5:     Find X_j with maximum $MI(X_j, C)$
6:     Add X_j to the network
7:     Add directed edge (C, X_j)
8:     **while** in-degree of X_j is less than $k + 1$ and there is an X_i not connected to X_j **do**
9:         Find an X_i with highest $MI(X_i, X_j|C)$
10:         Add directed edge (X_i, X_j)
11:     **end while**
12: **end while**

FIGURE 5.8   Inducing limited-dependence Bayesian networks.

Using Bayesian networks for text classification addresses the clearly crude approximations made by naive Bayes classifiers regarding term independence.

Given the graph structure of the network and training data, it is in principle simple to derive the probability tables. What is difficult is to derive the structure itself, especially if the number of nodes is large. One way to limit the complexity is to limit the number of parents that each node can have. In our context of text classification, a k-dependence Bayesian network has one node for the class variable C and a node X_t for each term t. There is a directed edge from C to each X_t. In addition, each X_t is permitted to have up to k incident edges from other X_t's.

Figure 5.8 shows the pseudocode for constructing such a limited-degree Bayesian network. Generally speaking, the difficult part is to get a good network *structure*. For a specified network, estimating the parameters is relatively straightforward. To enumerate all pairs of features, the algorithm takes at least quadratic time, which makes it difficult to apply this algorithm to large text corpora unless some preelimination of features is performed.

We only know of Bayesian networks designed for the binary document model; the size of the conditional probability tables (see Figure 5.7) can be prohibitive for the multinomial model. While accuracy improvements for structured machine learning data sets (from the U.C. Irvine repository) have been clearly visible, they are surprisingly mild for text data (Reuters). There is room to suspect that the test problems were too simple, and Bayesian network induction will shine in the face of more complex data sets, where it is harder to discriminate between the classes.

5.7   Exploiting Hierarchy among Topics

In standard classification problems that arise in the structured data scenario, such as data warehouses, the class labels form a discrete set. For example, credit card transactions may be classified as "normal" or "fraudulent." Sometimes there is a mild ordering between the class labels, such as high, medium, or low cancer-risk patients. In contrast, for text classification, the class labels themselves are related by a large and complex class hierarchy, sometimes called a *taxonomy* (although the term "taxonomy" is sometimes reserved for single-word or concept interrelationships). In this section, we will restrict ourselves to hierarchies that are trees. Tree-structured hierarchies are widely used in directory browsing, provide an intuitive interface for representing refinements and generalizations, and are often the output of clustering algorithms. The usual semantics of tree-structured hierarchies is *inheritance*: if class c_0 is the parent of class c_1, any training document that belongs to c_1 also belongs to c_0.

5.7.1   Feature Selection

An important issue that needs to be revisited is feature selection. The discriminating ability of a term is obviously influenced by the set of training documents involved, and therefore the ability should also be quite sensitive to the node (or class) in the hierarchy at which it is evaluated. Note that the measure of discrimination of a term can be evaluated with respect only to *internal* nodes of the hierarchy. To cite a simple example, the (ambiguous) word "can" may be a noisy word at the root node of Yahoo!, but may be a great help in classifying documents under the subtree of /Science/Environment/Recycling. (In this particular example, a part-of-speech analysis might have helped, but that is not true in general.)

5.7.2   Enhanced Parameter Estimation

The "uniform prior assumption" made in Section 5.6.1 is unrealistic. For example, in the binary model, the minimum loss parameter value would be $\phi = \frac{1}{2}$ for *all* terms in the absence of data, whereas experience with languages tells us that words are rare and differ greatly in how rare they are. I also introduced one technique toward better smoothing by exploiting document-length distributions.

Why should we expect that a class hierarchy might help in further improvements to parameter estimates? In part because our inheritance model ensures that there are more document samples at shallow classes than classes at or near the leaves. If a parameter estimate is unreliable at a node with few training documents, perhaps we can impose a strong prior from a well-trained parent to repair the estimates.

This intuition has been formalized into a procedure called *shrinkage* [147]. Consider a path $c_1, c_2, \ldots, c_n$ in the taxonomy, starting from the root c_1. Since there are many more training documents associated with c_1 than c_n, parameter estimates of c_1 are more reliable, but less specific to a topic, compared with c_n. Since shrinkage seeks to improve estimates of descendants using data from ancestors, parameter smoothing can be built naturally into the framework by simply introducing a dummy class c_0 as the parent of the root c_1, where all terms are equally likely. (Henceforth in this section, we will only consider the multinomial model.)

Fix a specific path $c_0, c_1, \ldots, c_n$. Before applying shrinkage, MLEs are computed for $\theta_{c_i,t}$ for $i = 1, \ldots, n$. ($\theta_{c_0,t}$ is set to $1/|W|$.) There is no need for Laplace or any other type of smoothing at this stage. The "shrunk" estimate $\tilde{\theta}_{c_n,t}$ is determined by a linear interpolation of the MLE parameters at the ancestor nodes up through c_0, that is,

$$\tilde{\theta}_{c_i,t} = \lambda_i \theta_{c_i,t}^{\mathrm{MLE}} + \cdots + \lambda_1 \theta_{c_1,t}^{\mathrm{MLE}} + \lambda_0 \theta_{c_0,t}^{\mathrm{MLE}} \tag{5.23}$$

where $\sum_i \lambda_i$ is scaled to 1. The best values of the mixing weights λ_i are determined empirically, by iteratively maximizing the probability of a held-out portion H_n of the training set for node c_n. (Note that this setup gives us the parameter only for class c_n. To compute the parameters for c_{n-1}, for example, we need to set up a new system and solve it.) Figure 5.9 shows the pseudocode for shrinkage. It is actually a simple form of the expectation maximization algorithm discussed in Chapter 4.

Shrinkage has been tested on the Industry and 20NG data sets, as well as a partial download of the Yahoo! science subtree with 264 leaves. Shrinkage improves accuracy beyond hierarchical naive Bayes, in one case from 59% to 64%, in another from 66% to 76%. The improvement is high when data is sparse, which is expected. Models generated using shrinkage also appear capable of utilizing many more features than naive Bayes without overfitting.

1: hold out some portion H_n of the training set for class c_n
2: using the remaining data find $\theta^{\text{MLE}}_{c_i,t}$ for $i = 1, \ldots, n$
3: initialize all λ_i to some positive value so that $\sum_i \lambda_i = 1$
4: **while** $\Pr(H_n | \{\theta_{c_n,t} \, \forall t\})$ increases **do**
5:      **for** $i = 0, 1, \ldots, n$ **do**
6:          Calculate $\beta_i = \sum_{t \in H_n} \dfrac{\lambda_i \theta^{\text{MLE}}_{c_i,t}}{\sum_j \lambda_j \theta^{\text{MLE}}_{c_i,t}}$, the degree to that the current estimate
        of class i predicts terms in the held-out set
7:      **end for**
8:      readjust the mixing weights $\lambda_i \leftarrow \beta_i / \sum_j \beta_j$ for $i = 0, 1, \ldots, n$
9:      recompute $\tilde{\theta}_{c_n,t}$ for all t using equation (5.23)
10: **end while**

FIGURE 5.9 Pseudocode for the shrinkage algorithm.

5.7.3 Training and Search Strategies

Topic trees are generally interpreted as "*is-a*" hierarchies; for example, a document belonging to /Arts/Photography automatically belongs to /Arts. All documents are relevant to the root "topic" by definition. A training document d may be marked with one or more nodes in the hierarchy. All these nodes and their ancestors up to the root node are trained with d.

Given a test document d, the goal is usually to find one or more of the most likely leaf nodes in the hierarchy. The root represents the universe of documents, so by convention, $\Pr(\text{root}|d) = 1$. In our hierarchy model, a document cannot belong to more than one path, so if $\{c_i\}, i = 1, \ldots, m$ is the set of children of c_0, then

$$\sum_i \Pr(c_i|d) = \Pr(c_0|d) \tag{5.24}$$

Several search strategies are possible; I mention two obvious ones.

Greedy search

When a test document has to be classified, the search starts at the root and decisions are made greedily. The learner regards each internal node as a stand-alone flat classification problem, picks the highest probability class, and continues at that class. The obvious shortcoming is that if a classification error is made early on in a shallow level of the tree, it can never be revoked. There is thus a guaranteed compounding of error with the depth of the tree, and deep trees are likely to yield poor accuracy.

Best-first search

Apart from the property expressed in Equation (5.24), we can write the following *chain rule*:

$$\Pr(c_i|d) = \Pr(c_0|d)\,\Pr(c_i|c_0, d) \tag{5.25}$$

Finding the leaf c_* with maximum $\Pr(c_*|d)$ is equivalent to finding the leaf with the minimum value of $-\log \Pr(c_*|d)$, that leads us to rewrite Equation (5.25) as

$$-\log \Pr(c_i|d) = (-\log \Pr(c_0|d)) + (-\log \Pr(c_i|c_0, d)) \tag{5.26}$$

Suppose the edge (c_0, c_i) is assigned a (nonnegative) edge weight of $-\log \Pr(c_i|c_0, d)$. The reader can verify that locating the most probable leaf is the same as finding the weighted shortest path from the root to a leaf. The pseudocode for finding some number m of most likely leaf classes is given in Figure 5.10.

For the best-first search to make a difference from greedy search, we need to rescale the raw probabilities generated by the naive Bayes classifier as suggested at the end of Section 5.6.1. Otherwise the best-first search may degenerate to a greedy search because the best class at each level will tend to absorb most of the probability of the parent, crowding out the competition.

1: Initialize frontier min-heap F to $\{\langle \text{root}, 0\rangle\}$
2: Initialize output leaf set L to the empty set
3: **while** $|L| < m$ and F is not empty **do**
4:     Remove $\langle c_0, \ell_0\rangle$ from F with smallest ℓ
5:     **if** c_0 is a leaf node **then**
6:         Insert c_0 into L
7:     **else**
8:         **for** each child c_i of c_0 **do**
9:             Evaluate $\Pr(c_i|c_0, d)$
10:             Insert $\langle c_i, \ell_0 - \log \Pr(c_i|c_0, d)\rangle$ into F
11:         **end for**
12:     **end if**
13: **end while**
14: Return L

FIGURE 5.10 Best-first search for the m most probable leaf class.

Patents
(950)

- Communication (200)
  - Antenna
  - Modulator
  - Demodulator
  - Telephony
- Electricity (400)
  - Transmission
  - Motors
  - Regulation
  - Heating
- Electronics (800)
  - Oscillator
  - Amplifier
  - Resistor
  - System

Classifier	Flat	Best-First
Number of features	250	Shown in parentheses
Approximate total number of parameters	2651	2649
Accuracy	0.60	0.63
Time/document	15 ms	6 ms

FIGURE 5.11 Using best-first search on a hierarchy can improve both accuracy and speed. The number of features for each internal node is tuned so that the total number of features for both flat and best-first are roughly the same (and thus the model complexity is comparable). Because each document belonged to exactly one leaf node, recall equals precision in this case and is called "accuracy."

I have experimented with a three-level U.S. Patent taxonomy with the root on level 1, three internal nodes that are fairly difficult to separate (communication, electricity, electronics) at level 2, and four subclasses for each of those three classes, for a total of 12 leaves. For this data set, improvements were noted in both accuracy and speed when a hierarchical best-first classifier was used against flattening the taxonomy (see Figure 5.11).

The semantics of hierarchical classification

There is a noticeable asymmetry in the scenario discussed in this section: a training document can be associated with any node, be it an internal or a leaf node, but a test document must be routed to a leaf, because it makes no sense to compare the probability scores of a parent with a child. There are many different reasons why we might want the classifier to assign a test document to an internal node. The classifier may find that none of the children matches the document, or that many children match the document, or that the chances of making a mistake while pushing down the test document one more level may be too high. Not all hierarchies may represent the *is-a* relation. Modeling a variety of relations between class labels and developing algorithms for such relations is an interesting area of research.

5.8 Maximum Entropy Learners

In the Bayesian framework, $\Pr(c|d)$ is determined indirectly by first modeling $\Pr(d|c)$ at training time and then appealing to Bayes's rule, Equation (5.12), at testing time. The Bayesian approach has at least two (related) problems: First, because d is represented in a high-dimensional term space, $\Pr(d|c)$ cannot be estimated accurately from a training set of limited size. Second, it is potentially dangerous to add synthesized features (e.g., phrases, or a part-of-speech or sense tag for ambiguous words) to the multinomial naive Bayes feature set. Synthesized features can be highly correlated and may "crowd out" other useful features. In this section we will study an alternative probabilistic framework that directly models $\Pr(c|d)$ from training data.

Suppose we are given training data $\{(d_i, c_i), i = 1, \ldots, n\}$. Here each d_i is a multivariate feature vector and c_i is a discrete class label. Our model for $\Pr(c|d)$ will involve a number of *indicator functions*[4] $f_j(d, c)$, indexed by j, that flag certain conditions relating d and c. The expectation of each indicator f_j is

$$E(f_j) = \sum_{d,c} \Pr(d, c) f_j(d, c) \tag{5.27}$$

But we can also express $E(f_j)$ in another way, using Bayes's rule:

$$E(f_j) = \sum_{d,c} \Pr(d) \Pr(c|d) f_j(d, c)$$

$$= \sum_d \Pr(d) \sum_c \Pr(c|d) f_j(d, c) \tag{5.28}$$

For any indicator, we naturally insist that Equation (5.27) equals Equation (5.28). We can approximate $\Pr(d, c)$ and $\Pr(d)$ with their empirical estimates from the training data, $\widetilde{\Pr}(d, c)$ and $\widetilde{\Pr}(d)$. Assuming that the training data has

---

4. Indicator functions are commonly called *features* in the literature, but I wish to avoid confusion with features as defined earlier.

no duplicate documents and that each document has only one class label, we can write our constraint for index j as

$$\sum_i \tilde{\mathrm{Pr}}(d_i, c_i) f_j(d_i, c_i) = \sum_i \tilde{\mathrm{Pr}}(d_i) \sum_c \mathrm{Pr}(c|d_i) f_j(d_i, c),$$

or

$$\sum_i \frac{1}{n} f_j(d_i, c_i) = \sum_i \frac{1}{n} \sum_c \mathrm{Pr}(c|d_i) f_j(d_i, c) \tag{5.29}$$

because a random draw from the training data will bring up document d_i with uniform probability $1/n$.

These constraints will generally not determine $\mathrm{Pr}(c|d)$ in a unique way. If all the constraints together still leave some slack, how should we choose $\mathrm{Pr}(c|d)$? In the extreme situation that the training set is empty, according to the *principle of maximum entropy* [94, 116], we should consider all classes to be *equally* likely, because that choice will maximize the entropy (see Section 5.5.1) of $\mathrm{Pr}(c|d)$. The rationale behind the maximum entropy principle is the same as that behind Occam's razor (see Section 4.4.5)—both prefer the *simplest* model to explain observed data.

We can perform a constrained maximization in general, maximizing the entropy of the model distribution $\mathrm{Pr}(c|d)$ while obeying the constraint, Equation (5.29), for all j. Using a Lagrangian variable λ_j for each indicator constraint, collectively called Λ, we wish to optimize

$$G(\mathrm{Pr}(c|d), \Lambda) = -\sum_{d,c} \mathrm{Pr}(d)\, \mathrm{Pr}(c|d) \log \mathrm{Pr}(c|d)$$

$$+ \sum_j \lambda_j \left(\sum_i f_j(d_i, c_i) - \sum_{i,c} \mathrm{Pr}(c|d_i) f_j(d_i, c) \right) \tag{5.30}$$

By differentiating G with regard to $\mathrm{Pr}(c|d)$, we can show [173] that $\mathrm{Pr}(c|d)$ has the parametric form

$$\mathrm{Pr}(c|d) = \frac{1}{Z(d)} \exp\left(\sum_j \lambda_j f_j(d, c) \right)$$

$$= \frac{1}{Z(d)} \prod_j \mu_j^{f_j(d,c)} \tag{5.31}$$

where $\mu_j = e^{\lambda_j}$ simplifies the expression and $Z(d)$ is a scale factor to make sure that $\sum_c \mathrm{Pr}(c|d) = 1$.

Fitting the distribution to the data involves two steps:

1. From prior knowledge, or trial and error, identify a set of *indicator functions.* Each indicator will correspond to one parameter variable to be estimated and one constraint equation.

2. Iteratively arrive at values for the parameters that satisfy the constraints while maximizing the entropy of the distribution being modeled.

A significant result is that maximizing the entropy subject to the above constraints is equivalent to maximizing $\sum_{d \in D} \log \Pr(c_d|d)$, that is, the probability of the class observations given the document. This result is significant in that it changes our goal from constrained optimization to a (simpler) case of likelihood maximization. A host of nonlinear techniques are available to perform the maximization [173].

As in Bayesian classifiers, it is common to pick an indicator for each (class, term) combination. The indicator function takes as input a document and a class, since $\Pr(c|d)$ is a function of those two things. Thus one may define, for the binary document model,

$$f_{c',t}(d, c) = \begin{cases} 1 & \text{if } c = c' \text{ and } t \in d \\ 0 & \text{otherwise} \end{cases} \tag{5.32}$$

where the subscript (c', t) is used to index the indicators. However, it is more common to use term frequency information, as in the multinomial model:

$$f_{c',t}(d, c) = \begin{cases} 0 & \text{if } c \neq c' \\ \dfrac{n(d,t)}{\sum_\tau n(d,\tau)} & \text{otherwise} \end{cases} \tag{5.33}$$

The promise of the maximum entropy approach is that even though its feature space has a one-to-one correspondence with naive Bayes learners, it does not suffer from the independence assumptions inherent in those methods. For example, if the terms $t_1 = \textit{machine}$ and $t_2 = \textit{learning}$ are often found together in class c, λ_{c,t_1} and λ_{c,t_2} would be suitably discounted.

The maximum entropy method outperforms naive Bayes in accuracy, but not consistently. For the WebKB data set comprising classes such as faculty, student, course, and project pages from universities, the accuracy increased from 87% to 92%. However, for the industry sector data set, accuracy dropped from 80.23% to 80.02%, and for the news group data set, accuracy dropped from 85.8% to 84.6%. The maximum entropy optimization is complex and somewhat prone to overfitting. The real promise of the maximum entropy technique seems to be in dealing with a large number of synthesized, possibly redundant features. Surprisingly, we have not seen extensive studies on the maximum entropy classifier in such applications. Some of the *discriminative* classifiers in the next section outperform maximum entropy classifiers by a modest margin, as we shall see later on.

5.9 Discriminative Classification

So far we have studied a number of classifiers based on probabilistic generative models. Bayesian classifiers estimate the $\Pr(d|c)$ distribution and use Bayes's rule to "invert" it to $\Pr(c|d)$, whereas maximum entropy classifiers directly estimate $\Pr(c|d)$. The training set was used to estimate the parameters of the models. We saw in Section 5.6.1 that naive Bayes classifiers induce hyperplanar (linear) decision boundaries between classes in the term space. Equation (5.31) for maximum entropy classification can be rewritten as

$$\log \Pr(c|d) = -\log Z_d + \sum_{t \in d} f_{c,t}(d, c) \log \mu_{c,t} \tag{5.34}$$

which shows that $\log \Pr(c|d)$ is predicted as a linear function of d's feature vector. I will now extend these observations to introduce two kinds of *discriminative* classifiers, where the goal is to directly map the feature space to class labels, encoded as numbers (e.g., $+1$ and -1 for a two-class problem). For example, we may encode document d as a suitable feature vector and try to find a vector α in feature space such that $\text{sign}(\alpha \cdot d + b)$ predicts the class, where b is a suitable constant and "$\cdot$" is the dot-product. Discriminative classifiers remain completely agnostic about any distributions generating the data. They are some of the most accurate classifiers designed for text to date.

5.9.1 Linear Least-Square Regression

As we have just discussed, there is no inherent reason for going through the modeling step as in Bayesian or maximum entropy classifiers to get a linear discriminant. In fact, we can look for some arbitrary α such that $\alpha \cdot d_i + b$ *directly* predicts the label c_i of document d_i. This would be a *linear regression* problem. A common objective in linear regression is to minimize the *square error* between the observed and predicted class variable: $\sum_i (\alpha \cdot d_i + b - c_i)^2$. The least-square optimization frequently uses gradient-descent methods, such as the Widrow-Hoff (WH) update rule. The WH approach starts with some rough estimate $\alpha^{(0)}$, considers (d_i, c_i) one by one, and updates $\alpha^{(i-1)}$ to $\alpha^{(i)}$ as follows:

$$\alpha^{(i)} = \alpha^{(i-1)} + 2\eta(\alpha^{(i-1)} \cdot d_i - c_i)d_i \tag{5.35}$$

Here η is a tuned constant called the *learning rate* that prevents α from swinging around too much. The final α used for classification is usually the average of all αs found along the way. When applying the linear classifier to a test document d, we can threshold the real number output by the classifier, predicting the class to be $\text{sign}(\alpha \cdot d + b) \in \{-1, 1\}$.

With no loss of generality, we can scale α so that $\|\alpha\| = 1$, in which case we can interpret the classifier in two equivalent ways:

- The classifier is a *hyperplane* that separates positive ($c = 1$) and negative ($c = -1$) instances as best as it can, ideally keeping only positive instances on one side and negative instances on the other.

- Documents are *projected* onto a direction α (perpendicular to the hyperplane), giving each a scalar representation. On this line, positive and negative instances are well separated.

Discriminants obtained by minimizing square error perform quite well on text data [217], outperforming naive Bayes and comparing favorably with k-NN, although still a little short of support vector machines, discussed next.

5.9.2   Support Vector Machines

With the usual assumption that the training and test population are drawn from the same distribution, a hyperplane that is close to many training data points has a greater chance of misclassifying test instances compared to a hyperplane that passes through a no-man's land clear of any training instances. This is the basic intuition behind *support vector machines* (*SVMs*), which are currently the most accurate classifiers for text.

Like naive Bayes classifiers, linear SVMs also make a decision by thresholding $\alpha_{\text{SVM}} \cdot d + b$ (the estimated class is $+1$ or -1 according to whether the quantity is greater or less than 0) for a suitable vector α_{SVM} and constant b. However, α_{SVM} is chosen far more carefully than in naive Bayes classifiers. Initially, let us assume that the n training documents (represented as vectors in $\mathbb{R}^m$) from the two classes are linearly separable by a hyperplane perpendicular to a suitable α. SVM seeks

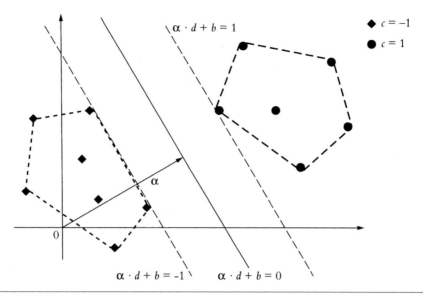

FIGURE 5.12 Illustration of the SVM optimization problem.

an α that maximizes the distance of any training point from the hyperplane; this can be written as

$$\text{Minimize} \quad \tfrac{1}{2}\alpha \cdot \alpha \quad (= \tfrac{1}{2}\|\alpha\|^2)$$

$$\text{subject to} \quad c_i(\alpha \cdot d_i + b) \geq 1 \quad \forall i = 1, \ldots, n \tag{5.36}$$

where $\{d_1, \ldots, d_n\}$ are the training document vectors and $\{c_1, \ldots, c_n\}$ their corresponding classes.

The optimal separator is orthogonal to the shortest line connecting the convex hull of the two classes, and intersects it halfway (see Figure 5.12). Since all $c_i \in \{-1, 1\}$, α and b can be scaled so that for all training documents d,

$$c_i(\alpha \cdot d_i + b) \geq 1 \tag{5.37}$$

If d_1 and d_2 are points touching the separator slab on opposite sides, it follows that

$$\alpha \cdot (d_1 - d_2) = 2 \tag{5.38}$$

and therefore

$$\frac{\alpha}{\|\alpha\|} \cdot (d_1 - d_2) = \frac{2}{\|\alpha\|} \tag{5.39}$$

The distance of any training point from the optimized hyperplane (called the *margin*) will be at least $1/\|\alpha\|$.

In real life, the classes in the training data are sometimes, but not always, separable. To handle the general case where a single hyperplane may not be able to correctly separate *all* training points, *fudge* variables $\{\xi_1, \ldots, \xi_n\}$ are introduced, and Equation (5.36) is enhanced as

$$\text{Minimize} \quad \tfrac{1}{2}\alpha \cdot \alpha + C \sum_i \xi_i \tag{5.40}$$

$$\text{subject to} \quad c_i(\alpha \cdot d_i + b) \geq 1 - \xi_i \forall i = 1, \ldots, n$$

$$\text{and} \quad \xi_i \geq 0 \quad \forall i = 1, \ldots, n$$

If d_i is misclassified, then $\xi_i \geq 1$, so $\sum_i \xi_i$ bounds from above the number of training errors, which is traded off against the margin using the tuned constant C. SVM packages solve the *dual* of Equation (5.40), involving scalars $\lambda_1, \ldots, \lambda_n$, given by

$$\text{Maximize} \quad \sum_i \lambda_i - \frac{1}{2} \sum_{i,j} \lambda_i \lambda_j c_i c_j (d_i \cdot d_j) \tag{5.41}$$

$$\text{subject to} \quad \sum_i c_i \lambda_i = 0$$

$$\text{and} \quad 0 \leq \lambda_i \leq C \quad \forall i = 1, \ldots, n$$

Formula (5.41) represents a quadratic optimization problem. SVM packages iteratively refine a few λs at a time (called the *working set*), holding the others fixed. For all but very small training sets, we cannot precompute and store all the inner products $d_i \cdot d_j$. As a scaled-down example, if an average document costs 400 bytes in RAM, and there are only $n = 1000$ documents, the corpus size is 400,000 bytes, and the inner products, stored as 4-byte floats, occupy $4 \times 1000 \times 1000$ bytes, 10 times the corpus size. Therefore, the inner products are computed on demand, with an LRU (*least recently used*) cache of recent values to reduce recomputation.

For n documents, the time taken to train an SVM is proportional to n^a, where a typically ranges between 1.7 and 2.1. The scaling of SVM for a sample from the Open Directory Project (*dmoz.org*) is shown in Figure 5.13. Recent versions of public-domain SVM packages, such as SVM light [117], have edged much closer to linear training time using clever selection of working sets.

SVMs are some of the most accurate classifiers for text; no other kind of classifier has been known to outperform it across the board over a large number of document collections. In one set of experiments with a subset of classes from the Reuters data set, the linear support vector machine (LSVM) has shown better accuracy than naive Bayes and decision tree classifiers, as shown in Figure 5.14.

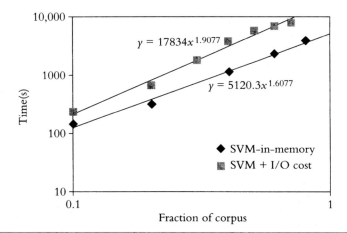

FIGURE 5.13 SVM training time variations as the training set size is increased, with and without sufficient memory to hold the training set. In the latter case, the memory is set to about a quarter of that needed by the training set.

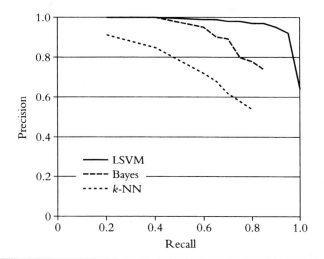

FIGURE 5.14 Comparison of LSVM with previous classifiers on the Reuters data set (data taken from Dumais [73]). (The naive Bayes classifier used binary features, so its accuracy can be improved. Also, the k-NN classifier does not use a per-class b_c, as described in Section 5.4.)

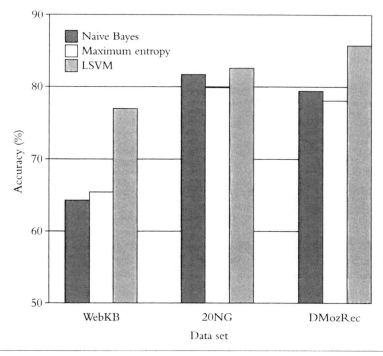

FIGURE 5.15 Comparison of accuracy across three classifiers: naive Bayes, maximum entropy and LSVM, using three data sets: 20 news groups, the *Recreation* subtree of the Open Directory, and university Web pages from WebKB.

In another set of experiments, SVM outperformed naive Bayes and maximum entropy classifiers, as shown in Figure 5.15.

Yang and Liu [217] have made comparisons between SVMs, *k*-NN, linear least-square, and naive Bayes classifiers using the Reuters data set under carefully standardized conditions. Some of their findings are shown in Table 5.1.

An interesting revelation made by SVMs is that many standard text classification tasks have classes that are perfectly or near perfectly separable using a hyperplane in feature space [118]. Therefore, linear SVMs are generally considered adequate for text classification tasks. We do not know of significant benefits from using more complex nonlinear SVMs [190].

TABLE 5.1 Comparison between several classifiers discussed in this chapter, using the Reuters collection.

Method	Microaveraged recall	Microaveraged precision	Microaveraged F1	Macroaveraged F1
Linear SVM	0.81	0.91	0.86	0.53
k-NN	0.83	0.88	0.86	0.52
Least square	0.85	0.85	0.85	0.50
Naive Bayes	0.77	0.82	0.80	0.39

5.10 Hypertext Classification

Thus far in this chapter, we have studied text classifiers without any discussion of hypertextual features. Finally, we turn to a discussion of techniques to address supervised learning for hypertext. Apart from plain text, HTML, the dominant form of hypertext on the Web, contains many different kinds of features. A well-formed HTML document is a properly nested hierarchy of regions that is represented by a tree-structured Document Object Model or DOM (*www.w3.org/DOM/*).

In a DOM tree, internal nodes are elements (such as the list-building constructs UL or LI in HTML), and some of the leaf nodes are segments of text. Some other nodes are hyperlinks to other Web pages, which can in turn be represented by DOM trees.

In this section we will discuss how to encode diverse hypertextual features in forms suitable for supervised learning. Often we will want to represent features from hypertext in the form of *relations*. None of the classification techniques we have covered so far can deal with relational training data effectively, so I will introduce the last kind of learning, called *inductive learning*, near the end of this section.

5.10.1 Representing Hypertext for Supervised Learning

In our study of keyword-based search technology, we have seen that search engines assign heuristic weights to terms that occur in specific HTML tags, such as TITLE, H1, STRONG, EM, and so on. General semistructured data, as might be transmitted in XML, can also be represented as a DOM tree (suitable cross-links are added if necessary). Paying special attention to tags can help with supervised learning as well. The following example, somewhat contrived, shows how markup context should qualify ordinary terms. A resume, written in an XML-like format, may contain the following marked-up text:

```
<resume>
    <publication>
        <title>Statistical models for Web-surfing</title>
    </publication>
    <hobbies>
        <item>Wind-surfing</item>
    </hobbies>
</resume>
```

Depending on the classification task, it could be really important to distinguish between the two occurrences of the word "surfing," a task easily achieved by prefixing each term by the sequence of tags that we need to follow from the DOM root to get to the term, such as `resume.publication.title.`*surfing* and `resume.hobbies.item.`*surfing*. We cannot really take this technique to the extreme, especially if a repeated term in different sections *should* reinforce belief in a class label (unlike in the example above).

If we intend to use an SVM or a maximum entropy classifier, we may maintain both forms of a term: plain text and prefixed as above. The general situation is far more complex, however. We may want to accumulate evidence from `resume.publication.journal.`*surfing* and `resume.publication.title.`*surfing*; one (imperfect) way to achieve this is to create many versions of each term, each with a *prefix* of the DOM paths, for example., `resume.`*surfing*, `resume.publication.`*surfing*, and so on.

Sometimes these simple tricks suffice to boost accuracy beyond classifiers depending on plain text alone. In an experiment conducted by Yi and Sundaresan [219] with 10,705 patents from the U.S. Patent Office, a plain-text classifier gave 70% errors, whereas using path-tagged terms gave only 24% errors. When they used path prefixes, the errors reduced to 17%. For a collection of 1700 resumes collected from the Web, Yi and Sundaresan report that a naive Bayes classifier applied on flattened HTML showed 53% errors, whereas using prefix-tagged terms showed 40% errors.

Notwithstanding empirical success, these representations are fairly ad hoc and somewhat inflexible. For example, the recipe does not extend easily if we also wish to add features derived from hyperlinks. *Relations* provide a uniform way to codify hypertextual features. I provide some examples below; their meanings should be clear from the names used for the relation and attribute names.

```
contains-text(domNode, term)
part-of(domNode1, domNode2)
tagged(domNode, tagName)
links-to(srcDomNode, dstDomNode)
contains-anchor-text(srcDomNode, dstDomNode, term)
classified(domNode, label)
```

In the rest of this section we will study inductive classifiers that can discover rules from a collection of relations. For example, the system might be able to come up with a rule of the form

```
classified(A, facultyPage) :-
  contains-text(A, professor), contains-text(A, phd),
  links-to(B, A), contains-text(B, faculty).
```

I use Prolog notation, where :- is read "if," and a comma implies conjunction.

5.10.2 Rule Induction

For simplicity I will focus on a two-class setting, with positive examples D_+ and negative examples D_-. The rule finder returns a set of predicate rules. If on a test instance any of these rules returns true, then the test instance is positive; otherwise it is negative. Each rule is a conjunction of (possibly negated) predicates.

Figure 5.16 shows a basic rule-induction pseudocode resembling a well-known rule learner called *FOIL* (for *first-order inductive logic*). The outer loop learns new (disjunctive) rules one at a time, removing positive examples covered by any rule generated thus far. When a new empty rule is initialized, its free variables can be bound in all possible ways, which may lead to covering many (remaining) positive and negative instances. The inner loop adds conjunctive literals to the new rule until no negative example is covered by the new rule. As we add literals, we wish to uncover all negative bindings while uncovering as few positive bindings as possible. Therefore, a reasonable heuristic is to pick a literal that rapidly increases the ratio of surviving positive to negative bindings.

(a) Rule induction:

1: Let R be the set of rules learned, initially empty
2: **while** $D_+ \neq \emptyset$ **do**
3:      *Learn a new rule*
4:      Let $r \equiv$ true be the new rule
5:      **while** some $d \in D_-$ satisfies r **do**
6:          *Add a new (possibly negated) literal to r to specialize it*
7:          Add "best possible" literal p as a conjunct to r
8:      **end while**
9:      $R \leftarrow R \cup \{r\}$
10:     Remove from D_+ all instances for which r evaluates to true
11: **end while**
12: Return R

(b) Types of literals explored:

- $X_i = X_j$, $X_i = c$, $X_i > X_j$, $X_i \geq X_j$, and so on, where X_i, X_j are variables and c is a constant.

- $Q(X_1, \ldots, X_k)$, where Q is a relation and X_i are variables, at least one of which must be already bound.

- $not(L)$, where L is a literal of the above forms.

(c) Best literal selection:

1: Suppose we are considering the addition of literal p to rule r. Let r' be the resulting rule after adding p to r.
2: Let f' be the fraction of variable bindings that make r' true, f the fraction of variable bindings that make r true, and s the number of variable bindings that satisfy both r and r'.
3: Pick that p with maximum $s(\log f' - \log f)$.

FIGURE 5.16 A rule learning system called FOIL. The overall pseudocode (a). Choice of literals (b). Ranking candidate literals (c).

This justifies the literal selection in Figure 5.16, but many other ordering heurstics are in use.[5]

An important advantage of relational learning is that just as we can learn class labels for individual pages, we can also learn relationships between them. For example, we can encode training data of the form

```
member(homePage, department)
teaches(homePage, coursePage)
advises(homePage, homePage)
writes(homePage, paper)
```

in a straightforward manner, and identify additional examples of these relations from portions of the Web graph.

Another interesting possibility is to integrate decisions made by a statistical classifier (such as naive Bayes) into the rule-learning system. This can be done by a more complex search for literals, which may involve running a naive Bayes classifier and comparing the estimated probabilities of various classes.

The labeling relation `classified(page, label)` may best be modeled as recursive. For example, the following rule

```
classified(A, facultyPage) :-
  links-to(A, B), classified(B, studentPage),
  links-to(A, C), classified(C, coursePage),
  links-to(A, D), classified(D, publicationsPage).
```

relates the label of page A in terms of the known labels of neighboring pages B, C, and D. It may be argued that the transfer of label information is not really directed: there may have been a mistake in estimating the label of page B, and an accurate guess at the label of A may help us fix the label of B in turn. I will discuss *semisupervised* learning strategies in Chapter 6, which will address this issue.

5.11 **Bibliographic Notes**

Whereas classifiers for text are relatively recent, classifiers for structured data are very well researched. Those of you unfamiliar with machine learning as a broad

---

5. FOIL's literal selection policy requires us to encode `contains-text(domNode, term)` as `contains-text-term(domNode)`, with one relation for each term, but I avoid this technicality to keep the discussion simple.

area should refer to Mitchell's classic text [153]. Learning algorithms often draw from the field of information theory. For a more detailed treatise of important concepts such as entropy and mutual information, you are encouraged to refer to the authoritative textbook by Cover and Thomas [57].

Some of the well-known early text classifiers such as the Apte–Damerau–Weiss system used a decision rule–based approach [7]. At the heart of such systems is a rule inducer such as Swap-1 [212], FOIL [58], or RIPPER [53]. One advantage of rule-based systems is noise rejection in the test document: once the system "tunes in" to the promising patterns, all other features in the test documents are simply ignored (which is not the case with statistical learners that have to smooth their term distribution parameters). Rule-based systems can even perform context-sensitive classification where the presence of some words is qualified by other words in the vicinity, as shown by Cohen and Singer [54]. Some disadvantages are that the complexity of rule induction tends to be high and updates are not simple.

Yang and Pedersen [218] and Mladenic [155] compare a variety of feature selection algorithms for text. I have reported on a scalable system for simultaneous feature selection for all nodes in a taxonomy elsewhere [37]. Sahami and Koller have studied the effect of more sophisticated feature selection and reduced the naive attribute independence assumption [126, 127]. Whereas this resulted in significantly improved accuracy for many data sets from the UCI repository, the effect on text classification accuracy was slight. Their system, as well as scalable naive learners, seems to indicate that once feature selection is made hierarchical, each decision point in the hierarchy needs very few terms as features.

Bayesian classifiers have been in use for at least several decades in other areas such as pattern recognition and signal processing. Heckerman presents an authoritative tutorial on the general subject of Bayesian networks [102, 103]. Applications of Bayesian learners to text are surprisingly recent. The CMU WebKB project and the TAPER system have used naive Bayes classifiers [37, 145]. Both have compared different document models such as binary and multinomial and arrived at similar conclusions. Lewis presents comprehensive metrics on which to evaluate classifiers [137]. Yang and Liu [217] present extensive comparisons between k-NN, naive Bayes, SVM, and least-square classifiers.

In spite of making crude independence assumptions, and therefore underestimating $\Pr(d|c)$ severely, naive Bayesian classifiers have acceptable accuracy [138]. The insight here is that classification error does not directly depend on the precision of $\Pr(d|c)$ but on the shape of the decision boundaries separating the favorable class density regions in term space, because a classifier has to merely pick $\arg\max_c \Pr(c|d)$. For such *discrete regression* settings, it is possible to have highly biased and yet effective classifiers if their variance is low, as explained by Friedman, Domingos, and Pazzani [71, 85]. Whereas their effect on classification accuracy appears to be mild, better approximations to $\Pr(d|c)$ are useful for other applications, such as clustering (see Chapter 4). "Repairing" naive estimates with a manageable number of joint distributions on highly correlated terms may be a potential solution, as proposed by Meretakis and Wuthrich [150].

Parameter estimation using shrinkage has been studied by McCallum and others [147]. Shrinkage as a general statistical tool has been discussed by Carlin, Louis, James, and Stein [32, 115, 201]. Mitchell has shown that a hierarchical naive Bayes classifier will give the same result as one that flattens the hierarchy [152]. However, it is assumed that MLE parameters are used. If the feature set is diverse across internal nodes and smoothing is performed, experimental evidence suggests that mild improvements in accuracy are possible [37]. The work on learning markup hierarchies is by Yi and Sundaresan [219].

Maximum entropy methods have been extensively used in signal processing and natural language analysis for some time. The proof of equivalence between constrained entropy maximization and likelihood maximization is by Della Pietra, Della Pietra, and Lafferty [173]. The application of this method to text learning has been made recently by Nigam, Lafferty, and McCallum [167].

As with maximum entropy, support vector machines [209] have been used in other domains before text. The application of LSVMs to text classification is by Dumais, Platt, Heckerman, and Sahami [74]. There are excellent texts and tutorial articles on SVMs: if interested, you can visit *www.kernel-machines.org* for many resources relevant to SVMs. Shashua established that the decision surface found by a linear SVM is the *same* as Fisher's discriminant for only the support vectors found by an SVM [194]. The fast *sequential minimum optimization* (*SMO*) algorithm is due to Platt [176]. Other optimizations, incorporated into the popular SVM light system, are described by Joachims [117]. However, the scaling behavior is roughly $n^{1.7}$–$n^{2.1}$, where n is the number of training instances. Ongoing work is reducing the time to be nearly linear in n, which is important to extend LSVMs to Web-scale data.

Given the excellent accuracy of k-NN, least-square, and SVM classifiers, it is natural to question the wide acceptance of naive Bayes classifiers. Naive

Bayes classifiers are very simple to understand and code, involve no iterative optimization, and can adapt essentially instantly to new or modified documents. Because they depend strongly on instances near interclass boundaries to determine separators, SVMs can be sensitive to small modifications to the training set, which may make fast document updates complicated.

CHAPTER 6

SEMISUPERVISED LEARNING

We have seen two extreme learning paradigms so far. The setting in Chapter 4 was unsupervised: only a collection of documents was provided without any labels, and the system was supposed to propose a grouping of the documents based on similarity. In contrast, Chapter 5 considered the completely supervised setting where each object was tagged with a class. Real-life applications are somewhere in between. It is generally easy to collect unsupervised data: every time Google completes a crawl, a collection of over a billion documents is created. On the other hand, labeling is a laborious job, which explains why the size and reach of Yahoo! and the Open Directory lag behind the size of the Web.

Consider a document collection D in which a subset $D^K \subset D$ (with $|D^K| \ll |D|$) has known labels, and our goal is to label the rest of the collection. The simplest approach would be to train a supervised learner or classifier using the labeled subset D^K, and apply the trained learner on the remaining documents. But will this necessarily lead to the highest accuracy?

Qualitatively, it is easy to see that there could be information in $D \setminus D^K$ that could be harnessed to enable better learning. Document $d_1 \in D^K$ may be labeled with class c_1, and document d_2 may share a number of terms with document d_3, although there may be no term overlap between d_1 and d_3. If d_2 is classified into c_1 with high confidence, we have reason to believe that d_3 may also be assigned class c_1 with low risk. Basically, the unsupervised portion of the corpus, $D \setminus D^K$, adds to our vocabulary, our knowledge about the joint distribution of terms, and unsupervised measures of interdocument similarity.

For hypertext, the situation gets more interesting. Clues about similarity and class membership come from diverse sources, such as site name, directory path, and, very importantly, hyperlinks. The fact that thousands of Web pages have HREF citations to *www.toyota.com/* and *www.honda.com/* offer ample evidence that these two pages are strongly related, and we can use this knowledge to classify one page if the other were known to be a Japanese car manufacturer's site. As another example, if u links to v, and v and w have large textual similarity, we may venture that u and w have similar topics.

The challenge is to put together multiple sources of evidence of similarity and class membership into a label-learning system. In this chapter we will study several algorithms that combine different features with partial supervision to estimate labels of unlabeled instances better than simple supervised learning.

6.1 Expectation Maximization

One simple way to make use of $D \setminus D^K$ is to first train a supervised learner on D^K, then label all documents in $D \setminus D^K$, pretend that all or some of them (the ones where the classifier was most confident, say) have been correctly labeled, retrain the classifer using these new labels, and continue until labels do not change anymore. If the classifier makes too many mistakes, the simple algorithm above may lead the term distributions of classes to drift arbitrarily badly.

A better option is to use a "soft" classification, as in the EM algorithm (see Section 4.4.2). When we used EM for clustering, we set up a fixed number of clusters with some arbitrary initial distributions, and then alternately iterated the following steps:

1. Reestimate, for each cluster c and each document d, the quantity $\Pr(c|d)$, based on the current parameters of the distribution that characterizes c.

2. Recompute the parameters of the distribution for each cluster. As in Section 4.4.2, we will use a multinomial distribution over terms.

In clustering, none of the $\Pr(c|d)$ values were known ahead of time, and each had to be estimated repeatedly. In a semisupervised scenario, the documents in D^K are labeled, and we should exploit that information. The simplest way is to set up one cluster for each class label (although this may not be the best choice; see Section 6.1.3) and estimate a class-conditional distribution that includes information from $D \setminus D^K$, simultaneously estimating the class (equivalently, cluster) memberships of these unlabeled documents.

We can combine the EM procedure (Section 4.4.2) with the multinomial naive Bayes text classifier (see Sections 4.4.1 and 5.6.1) [168]. Recall that in the multinomial naive Bayes text classifier, the key parameters were $\theta_{c,t}$, which represented, roughly speaking, the "rate" at which term t occurred in documents belonging to class c. Using Laplace's law, these parameters were estimated as in Equation (5.19)

$$\tilde{\theta}_{c,t} = \frac{1 + \sum_{d \in D_c^K} n(d, t)}{|W| + \sum_{d \in D_c^K, \tau \in d} n(d, \tau)}$$

where D_c^K is the set of training documents labeled with class c, $n(d, t)$ is the number of times term t occurs in document d, and W is the vocabulary (after a feature selection step, if any).

For semisupervised learning, we cannot say "$d \in D_c^K$" with certainty, but only have a current probability value $\Pr(c|d)$. We have to use this probability to weight the contribution of term counts from the documents to the classes. A straightforward way to do this is to modify Equation (5.19) to

$$\tilde{\theta}_{c,t} = \frac{1 + \sum_{d \in D} \Pr(c|d)\, n(d, t)}{|W| + \sum_{d \in D} \sum_{\tau} \Pr(c|d)\, n(d, \tau)} \tag{6.1}$$

where the sum is now over *all* documents. Likewise, we modify the class prior for c from $|D_c^K|/|D|$ to

$$\Pr(c) = \frac{1}{|D|} \sum_{d \in D} \Pr(c|d) \tag{6.2}$$

For each document d in the labeled set D^K, we know the class label c_d, and therefore we can set $\Pr(c_d|d) = 1$ and $\Pr(c'|d) = 0 \ \forall c' \neq c_d$. Alternatively, we can set these values before the first iteration, but then let the class probabilities of the labeled documents "smear" over other classes just like unlabeled documents. The choice depends on the faith we have in the labeling process.

The modified EM-like procedure is shown in Figure 6.1. Strictly speaking, this is not EM, because the M-step, Equation (6.1), uses a Laplace estimate, not a maximum likelihood estimate. In practice, convergence is not a problem.

6.1.1 Experimental Results

To study the semisupervised EM algorithm, we take a completely labeled (assume single label per document) corpus D and randomly select a subset as D^K. The

1: fix a set of unlabeled documents $D^U \subseteq D \setminus D^K$ for use in the EM-like steps
2: using D^K alone, build the initial model Θ_0
3: **for** $i = 0, 1, 2, \ldots$ while results are not satisfactory **do**
4:     **for** each document $d \in D^U$ **do**
5:         E-step: estimate $\Pr(c|d, \Theta_i)$ using a naive Bayes classifier
        (Section 5.6.1, Equation (5.15))
6:     **end for**
7:     **for** each c and t **do**
8:         M–like step: estimate $\theta_{c,t}$ using Equation (6.1) to build the next
        model Θ_{i+1}
9:     **end for**
10: **end for**

FIGURE 6.1 A semisupervised learning algorithm using ideas from EM and naive Bayes classification.

algorithm can only see the labels of D^K. The algorithm is also permitted to use a set $D^U \subseteq D \setminus D^K$ of unlabeled documents in the EM procedure. At the end, the algorithm must label all documents in $D \setminus D^K$ (e.g., assign them the most likely class label). A document is said to be correctly classified if the class with the largest probability matches its concealed class label. The accuracy of the learner is the fraction of documents with concealed labels that are correctly classified.

A completely supervised learner can use only D^K to train itself, that is, $D^U = \emptyset$. The lower curve in Figure 6.2 shows the effect of increasing the size of D^K while holding $D^U = \emptyset$. As $|D^K|$ increases, the accuracy improves, which is quite intuitive. More interestingly, the upper curve shows the same variation for a nonempty D^U, which clearly illustrates the value of exploiting information from unlabeled documents. Another set of numbers showing EM's superiority over naive Bayes is shown in Table 6.1.

In Figure 6.3, D^K is held fixed and accuracy is plotted against $|D^U|$. Clearly, accuracy benefits from larger collections of unlabeled documents, because these expose more details about document-to-document similarity, increase the vocabulary of the classes, and make estimates of term distributions more dense and accurate.

As expected, the largest boost to accuracy is observed in Figure 6.2 when D^K is small, because the supervised learner is then placed at maximum disadvantage compared to the semisupervised learner. For large sizes of D^K, the completely

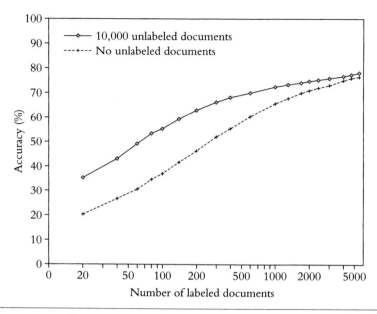

FIGURE 6.2 When D^K is small, a semisupervised learner can boost accuracy significantly by exploiting latent information about term distributions in a pool D^U of unlabeled documents taken from $D \setminus D^K$.

supervised learner is comparable to the semisupervised learner; indeed, for some data sets, it edges past the semisupervised learner.

6.1.2 Reducing the Belief in Unlabeled Documents

There can be a great deal of noise in the term distribution of documents in D^U, and the E-step in Figure 6.1 also makes mistakes. To reduce such distraction from D^U, we can attenuate the contribution from documents in D^U by an additional

Algorithm	$|D^K|$	$|D^U|$	Error
Naive Bayes	788	0	3.3%
Naive Bayes	12	0	13.0%
EM	12	776	4.3%

TABLE 6.1 EM beats naive Bayes with the same D^K, provided it is given a large D^U. $|D| = 788$ throughout.

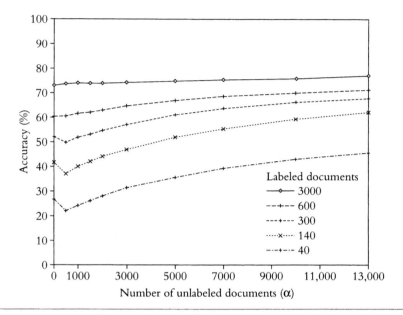

FIGURE 6.3   Increasing D^U while holding D^K fixed also shows the advantage of using large unlabeled sets in the EM-like algorithm.

factor $0 < \alpha < 1$ in Equation (6.1), turning it into

$$\theta_{c,t} = \frac{1 + \sum_{d \in D^K}[c = c_d]\, n(d, t) + \sum_{d \in D^U} \alpha \ \Pr(c|d)\, n(d, t)}{|W| + \sum_{d \in D^K, \tau}[c = c_d]\, n(d, \tau) + \sum_{d \in D^U} \alpha \ \Pr(c|d)\, n(d, \tau)} \qquad (6.3)$$

where c_d is the supervised class label of d, and $[c = c_d]$ is 1 if $c = c_d$ and 0 otherwise. Although this expression of relative distrust in unlabeled documents has no formal underpinnings, experiments show that accuracy is indeed influenced by the choice of α (see Figure 6.4).

Unfortunately, there is no lesson about the best values to pick for α. For small $|D^K|$, paying more attention to D^U by raising α closer to 1 seems to help, whereas for a larger number of labeled documents, it seems best to drive α down toward 0. This is an intuitive recipe but not a quantitative one; empirical evaluation seems inevitable.

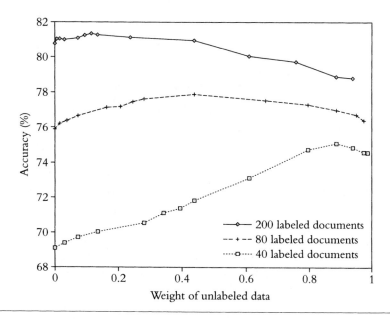

FIGURE 6.4 Attenuating the influence of unlabeled documents by a factor $0 < \alpha < 1$ leads to a boost in accuracy.

6.1.3 Modeling Labels Using Many Mixture Components

Another issue that warrants care when using the EM-like algorithm is that there need not be a one-to-one correspondence between the EM clusters and the supervised class labels. Term distributions of some classes or topics are best expressed as a *mixture* of a few simple distributions. In particular, when text classifiers are set up with a positive and a negative class, the negative class is often best modeled as a mixture. (Documents about "football" may fit a simple multinomial distribution, but documents *not* about "football" are actually about a variety of other things; an author rarely sets out to write a document merely to *not* write about something!)

Varying the number of clusters used by the EM-like algorithm shows that although the EM-like algorithm has lower accuracy with one mixture component per label compared to a naive Bayes classifier, increasing the number of clusters pushes EM accuracy beyond naive Bayes (see Figure 6.5). Eventually, increasing the number of clusters leads to overfitting and lowers accuracy.

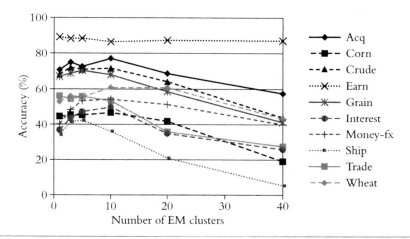

FIGURE 6.5 Allowing more clusters in the EM-like algorithm than there are class labels often helps to capture term distributions for composite or complex topics, and boosts the accuracy of the semisupervised learner beyond that of a naive Bayes classifier.

6.2 Labeling Hypertext Graphs

In the hypertext setting, there is more to unlabeled documents than exploited by the EM-like procedure described earlier. Consider the following scenarios:

- A test document is cited directly by a training document, or cites a training document.

- More generally, there is a short path between the test document and one or more training documents.

- The test document is cited by a named category in a Web directory such as Yahoo! or the Open Directory, even if our target category system is somewhat different from those of Yahoo! or the Open Directory.

- Some category of a Web directory co-cites one or more training documents along with the test document.

Consider a snapshot of the Web graph and a set of topics, for example, all the leaf nodes of a topic directory like Yahoo! or the Open Directory. Assume that through human supervision, a (small) subset of nodes V^K (extending D^K used before to the graph setting) in the Web graph have been labeled with topics taken from the predefined set. We may wish to use the supervision to label some or all nodes in $V \setminus V^K$. We could submit the documents in V^K to any of the text classifiers described in Chapter 5, as if they were isolated documents, but, as noted before, this may discard valuable information in hyperlinks.

6.2.1 Absorbing Features from Neighboring Pages

Often, a page u may have little text on it to train or apply a text classifier. Many important, exemplary sites about broad topics create and optimize an intensely graphic presentation, using images, text rendered as images, clickable image maps, JavaScript, and HTML frames. Such "features" make it impossible for a text classifier to extract tokens from which it can learn term distributions. Often, some second-level pages on these sites that u cites have usable quantities of text, but how can these features be used to characterize u to a text classifier?

Absorbing textual features

We compare a simple, text-based naive Bayes classifier with two obvious methods for absorbing text from neighboring pages:

Local+Nbr: Absorb all text from immediate neighbors (for both in- and outlinks) into the training or testing document.

Local+TagNbr: A term t absorbed from an out-neighbor is prefixed with a distinctive tag O: to become O:t, and a term t absorbed from an in-neighbor is prefixed with a distinctive tag I: to become I:t. No ordinary token starts with these special prefixes, and therefore there are three isolated token spaces that do not share counts.

Absorption of neighboring text was found to be ineffective for a collection of topic-labeled, hyperlinked patents, as well as a collection of labeled Web pages from Yahoo! Figure 6.6 shows that, at best, accuracy is unaffected; at worst, it may go down slightly. Why does adding extra information not help?

Implicit in all the variants of "absorbing neighboring text" is the assumption that the topic of a page u is likely to be the same as the topic of a page cited by u. This is not always true; the topics may be *related* but not identical. There can also be some topics ("free speech online" or "download Netscape") that crop up everywhere without regard to the desired set of class labels.

Consider, for instance, a university homepage that has relatively little text but several links. The distribution of topics of the pages cited by these first-level links could be quite distorted compared to the totality of contents available from the university site; for example, "how to get to our campus" or "recent

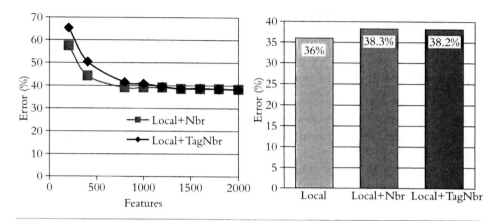

FIGURE 6.6 Absorbing text from neighboring pages in an indiscriminate manner does not help classify hyperlinked patent documents any better than a purely text-based naive Bayes classifier.

sports prowess" may figure high on the front page. If we carelessly use textual features from such pages in representing the homepage, a text-based classifier may (deservedly, you might argue) think the university is a gym or a transportation company.

Absorbing link-derived features

Given enough samples, we should be able to learn that university homepages tend to link to pages about athletic prowess, and that pages pertaining to all topics tend to link to pages about Web browsers. We can even use the fact that u points to a page about athletics to raise our belief that u is a university homepage, and learn to systematically reduce the attention we pay to the fact that a page links to the Netscape download site.

The key insight is that the *classes* of hyperlinked neighbors, rather than the *text* they contain, is a better representation of hyperlinks. Assume for the moment that all neighbors of u (which can be either a training or a test document) have been classified correctly. For example, they may have been assigned classes like /Sports/Basketball or /Computers/Software/OperatingSystems/Linux. As in the section above, these strings can be named apart from ordinary tokens by using a unique prefix (say, L@), and included as if they were terms in the document. Depending on the accuracy of classifying the neighbors (in practice, they cannot all be classified manually and perfectly), some of these link-derived features may be far more useful for classification than even the best ordinary tokens.

Another interesting issue is the representation of link-derived features for the common case where class labels are from an *is-a hierarchy*. The contribution of a link-derived feature may depend strongly on the level of detail at which the feature is represented. Returning to the college homepage example, we may find College A's homepage linked to a page about /Sports/Basketball and College B's homepage linked to a page about /Sports/Hockey/IceHockey. (Even a single college homepage can do this at different times.) Rather than encode the whole topic path, we may choose to include L@/Sports or L@/Computers/Software. Why might we expect this to work better? The evidence at the detailed topic level may be too noisy, and coarsening the topic helps collect more reliable data on the dependence between the class of the homepage and the link-derived feature.

We should not go overboard pruning these paths: as an extreme example, L@/ is not likely to be of any use as a link-derived feature, and for specific topics, even L@/Computers/Software may be far too general. There is no need for guesswork here; we can throw all prefixes of the class path into the feature pool

```
L@/
L@/Computers/
L@/Computers/Software
L@/Computers/Software/OperatingSystems
L@/Computers/Software/OperatingSystems/Linux
```

and leave the feature selection algorithm (see Section 5.5) to do its job in selecting those levels of representation from the above list that best assist classification. In my experiments, I saw that many link-derived features came out at the top after feature selection. In fact, adding too many textual features led to quick degradation of accuracy as the document model was now a single multinomial model over textual and link-derived features. As I noted in the beginning of Section 5.8, the degradation is due to redundant features with poor information content "crowding out" good features in the multinomial model.

My experiments [39] with a corpus of U.S. patents show that the prefix trick indeed pays off. This corpus has three first-level classes, each of which has four children. Each leaf topic has 800 documents, for a total of 9600 documents, shown in Figure 6.7(a). In Figure 6.7(b) *Text* is a purely text-based classifer, *Link* uses the whole (two-level) class path as link-derived features, and *Prefix* uses the prefix trick. In all cases, separate multinomial models are used for text and link-derived features. In *Text+Prefix*, these two distributions are assumed to be conditionally independent given the class of the current document.

Figure 6.7(b) shows that the prefix trick can reduce errors from 36% to 21% for this corpus, whereas a full-path encoding of link-derived features barely makes a 2% dent on the error rate of text-based classification.

6.2.2   A Relaxation Labeling Algorithm

The main limitation with features synthesized from class labels of linked neighbors is that, in practice, hardly any neighbors of a node (page) to be classified will be linked to any prelabeled node, because $|V^K| \ll |V|$. In this section I extend the EM approach to a graph, using labeled and unlabeled nodes in the link neighborhood of a page to be classified.

The basic strategy will be to start with a labeling of reasonable quality (using a text classifier, say) and refine it using a coupled distribution of text and labels of neighbors, until the labeling stabilizes.

Given a hypertext graph $G(V, E)$, where each vertex u is associated with text u_T, we seek a labeling f of all (unlabeled) vertices so as to maximize

$$\Pr(f(V)|E, \{u_T, u \in V\}) = \frac{\Pr(f(V))\ \Pr(E, \{u_T, u \in V\}|f(V))}{\Pr(E, \{u_T, u \in V\})} \qquad (6.4)$$

where

$$\Pr(E, \{u_T, u \in V\}) = \sum_{\phi} \Pr(\phi)\ \Pr(E, \{u_T, u \in V\}|\phi) \qquad (6.5)$$

is a scaling constant that is not a function of f because it sums over all possible label assignments ϕ. This is fortunate, because we do not need to evaluate it. Here E means "the event that edges were generated as per the edge list E," and the notation $\{u_T, u \in V\}$ denotes the event that the nodes in G have the respective textual contents. It is extremely unlikely that we can obtain a known function for $\Pr(E, \{u_T, u \in V\}|f(V))$, so we will need to approximate it using heuristic assumptions. Note that the text-based probabilistic classifiers discussed in Chapter 5 were concerned with estimating $\Pr(\{u_T, u \in V\}|f(V))$; that is, the event E was not considered. Because the term space $\{u_T, u \in V\}$ had thousands of dimensions, it was impractical to accurately represent the joint distribution between terms, and therefore inter-term independence was assumed.

For the same concerns of complexity, we will find it easier to assume independence between events E and $\{u_T, u \in V\}$, as well as within their components. In

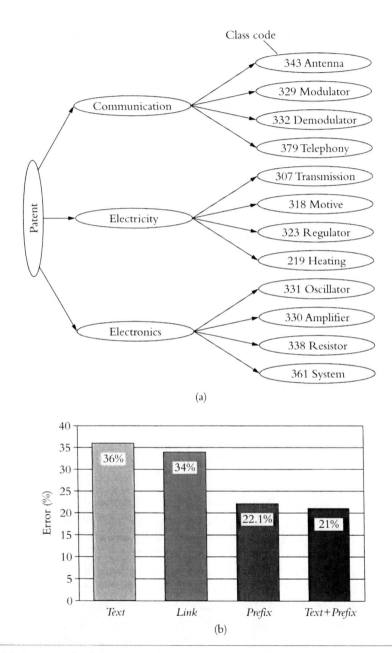

FIGURE 6.7 A two-level topic hierarchy of selected U.S. patents (a). Using prefix-encoded link features in conjunction with text can significantly reduce classification errors (b).

other words, we will assume that term occurrences are independent, link-derived features are independent, and, moreover, there is no dependence between a term and a link-derived feature. Obviously, these are flagrant departures from reality, but, as in Chapter 5, we hope that decision boundaries will remain relatively immune to errors in the probability estimates.

Extending D^K from Section 6.1, let V^K be the subset of nodes whose labels are known, and let these label assignments be denoted $f(V^K)$. To reiterate, we know the edge set E, the text representation of all nodes (which we will denote $V^T = \{u_T, u \in V\}$), and $f(V^K)$. Fix a node v whose class probabilities we wish to estimate. Let $N(v)$ be the immediate neighbors of v and $N^U(v) \subseteq N(v)$ be the unlabeled neighbors. We can write

$$
\begin{aligned}
\Pr(f(v) \mid E, V^T, f(V^K)) &= \sum_{f(N^U(v)) \in \Omega_v} \Pr\left(f(v), f(N^U(v)) \mid E, V^T, f(V^K)\right) \\
&= \sum_{f(N^U(v)) \in \Omega_v} \Pr\left(f(N^U(v)) \mid E, V^T, f(V^K)\right) \\
&\qquad \Pr\left(f(v) \mid f(N^U(v)), E, V^T, f(V^K)\right)
\end{aligned}
\tag{6.6}
$$

where $f(N^U(v))$ ranges over Ω_v, the set of all possible class assignments to unlabeled neighbors of v. If there are m class labels and v has k neighbors, then $|\Omega_v| = m^k$. Similar to naive Bayes text classifiers, we approximate the joint probability of neighbor classes by the product of the marginals:

$$
\Pr(f(N^U(v)) \mid E, V^T, f(V^K)) \approx \prod_{w \in N^U(v)} \Pr\left(f(w) \mid E, V^T, f(V^K)\right)
\tag{6.7}
$$

Equation (6.7) reflects that the class probabilities of neighboring nodes are coupled through this system of equations, which must be solved simultaneously for $f(v)$. Chances are, we will need to estimate some other $f(w)$s for $w \in V^U$ as well.

Instead of attempting a global optimization, which obtains a unique f for all nodes in V^U, we can start with greedy labeling, which pays attention only to the node-labeling cost $L(u, c)$, and then iteratively "correct" neighborhoods where the presence of edges leads to a very high penalty in terms of the edge costs. In the context of hypertext classification, the relaxation labeling algorithm first uses a text classifier to assign class probabilities to each node (page). Then it considers each page in turn and reevaluates its class probabilities in light of the latest estimates of the class probabilities of its neighbors. (This means that, similar to EM, nodes are always given a "soft" classification, not a "hard" one.)

We write the estimated class probabilities in the rth round as $\Pr_{(r)}(f(v) \mid E, V^T, f(V^K))$. For $r = 0$, the probabilities are estimated using an ordinary text classifier. Thereafter, we estimate, using Equations (6.6) and (6.7),

$$
\underline{\Pr_{(r+1)}(f(v) \mid E, V^T, f(V^K))}
$$

$$
\approx \sum_{f(N^U(v)) \in \Omega_v} \left[\prod_{w \in N^U(v)} \underline{\Pr_{(r)}\left(f(w) \,\middle|\, E, V^T, f(V^K)\right)} \right] \tag{6.8}
$$

$$
\Pr\left(f(v) \,\middle|\, f(N^U(v)), E, V^T, f(V^K)\right)
$$

Here the underlined parts show the induction on timestep that is used to break the circular definition. The theory of *Markov Random Fields* (MRFs), of which this is a special case, suggests that the above recurrences will converge provided the seed values $\Pr_{(0)}(f(v) \mid E, V^T, f(V^K))$ are reasonably accurate [49, 171, 173]. The product in Equation (6.8) can also be quite large, but it turns out that only few configurations from Ω_v have any significant probability mass to contribute to the sum [39].

The last piece to fill in is $\Pr\left(f(v) \mid f(N^U(v)), E, V^T, f(V^K)\right)$. To make the above expression more manageable, we invoke the assumption of a "limited range of influence." Thus, we approximate

$$
\Pr\left(f(v) \,\middle|\, f(N^U(v)), E, V^T, f(V^K)\right) \approx \Pr\left(f(v) \,\middle|\, f(N^U(v)), E, V^T, f(N^K(v))\right)
$$

$$
= \Pr\left(f(v) \,\middle|\, f(N(v)), V^T\right) \tag{6.9}
$$

where $N^K(v) = N(v) \cap V^K$. E is dropped because "it has already done its job" in providing information about $N(v)$. Because we have already taken the graph structure into account via E and $N(v)$, we can assume that the text of nodes other than v contain no information about $f(v)$, so we can further simplify

$$
\Pr\left(f(v) \,\middle|\, f(N(v)), V^T\right) \approx \Pr\left(f(v) \,\middle|\, f(N(v)), v^T\right) \tag{6.10}
$$

Summarizing, we need to estimate the class (probabilities) of v given the text v^T on that page and the classes of the neighbors of v. We can use Bayes's rule to invert that goal to building distributions for $(f(N(v)), v^T)$ conditioned on $f(v)$.

1: **Input:** Test node v
2: construct a suitably large *vicinity graph* around and containing v
3: **for** each w in the vicinity graph **do**
4:      assign $\Pr_{(0)}(f(v) \mid E, V^T, f(V^K))$ using a text classifier
5: **end for**
6: **while** label probabilities do not stabilize ($r = 1, 2, \ldots$) **do**
7:      **for** each node w in the vicinity graph **do**
8:          update to $\Pr_{(r+1)}(f(v) \mid E, V^T, f(V^K))$ using Equation (6.8)
9:      **end for**
10: **end while**

FIGURE 6.8   The HyperClass algorithm.

(The probabilistic text classifiers in Chapter 5 estimated $\Pr(v^T \mid f(v))$ alone.) We have already solved this estimation problem (albeit crudely, using the ubiquitous independence assumptions that plague naive Bayes classifiers) in Section 6.2.1. Now we have all the pieces we need to propose the complete testing algorithm in Figure 6.8.

I experimented with the U.S. patent corpus mentioned before and two versions of HyperClass. In one version (dubbed *Link*), the update step only used the coupling between $f(v)$ and $f(N(v))$. In the other version, called *Text+Link*, the joint distribution of $f(N(v))$ and v^T was used. I randomly elided the labels of a fraction of nodes in the 9600-node graph, ran the relaxation algorithm shown in Figure 6.8, and checked the fraction of nodes w for which $\arg\max_{f(w)} \Pr(f(w) \mid \ldots)$ was the "true" label.

The results are shown in Figure 6.9. The text-based classifer has $V^U = \emptyset$, so its error is fixed. Adding semisupervised hyperlink information cuts down errors by as much as 42%. More important, the benefits are seen even when only a small fraction of the neighborhood of a test page has known labels, and the accuracy varies gracefully as the extent of supervision changes. The most interesting feature in the graph is the small gap between *Link* and the text-based classifier when the test neighborhood is completely unlabeled. What extra information does *Link* tap to achieve a lower error? The gain is from the implicit bias in our model that "pages tend to link to pages with a related class label."

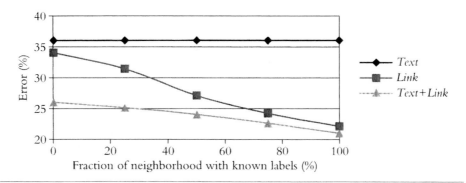

FIGURE 6.9 Semisupervised learning using relaxation labeling. The *x*-axis shows the fraction of nodes whose labels were *not* concealed. The *y*-axis shows accuracy for three classifiers: *Text,* which uses text alone, *Link,* which uses the coupling between $f(v)$ and $f(N(v))$, and *Text+Link,* which combines v^T and $f(N(v))$ assuming feature independence.

6.2.3 A Metric Graph-Labeling Problem

It turns out that relaxation labeling is an approximate procedure to optimize a global objective function on the hypertext graph whose nodes are being labeled or colored. I will describe the graph-coloring framework in this section. In principle, what a learner can infer about the topic of page *u* depends not only on immediate neighbors of *u* but possibly on the entire Web. However, no reasonable computational procedure can take into account the entire Web to process one page. It is also unclear if such far-flung influences are significant or whether capturing them is useful.

Most Web surfers know that, starting at a page with a specific topic, it is very easy to lose one's way among pages of diverse topics within very few clicks (see Section 8.3). Therefore, we would expect significant clues regarding the topic of a page *u* to be limited to a neighborhood of limited radius around *u*. As an extreme simplification, we can assume that the only *direct* clue or influence is limited to a radius of just one link.

To simplify the discussion, let us consider a hypertext graph where nodes (documents) can belong to exactly one of two topics or classes, which we can call

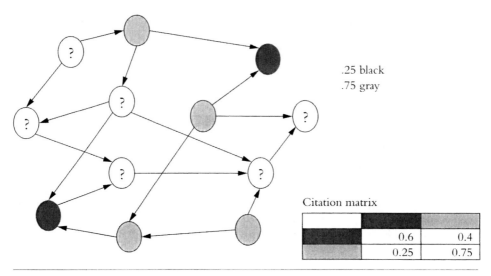

.25 black
.75 gray

Citation matrix

	0.6	0.4
	0.25	0.75

FIGURE 6.10 *Semisupervised hypertext classification represented as a problem of completing a partially colored graph subject to a given set of cost constraints.*

black and gray. We are given a graph where a (typically small) subset of nodes have known colors (i.e., topics). We are also given two other items of information:

♦   The marginal distribution of topics, that is, what the probability is of a randomly picked node being black or gray.

♦   A 2 × 2 *topic citation matrix*, which gives the probability of a black (respectively, gray) node linking to a black (respectively gray) node.

The goal is to find a maximally likely coloring f of the uncolored nodes in the graph (nodes marked with "?" in Figure 6.10). The model generalizes naturally to the multitopic scenario.

Maximizing $\Pr(f(V \setminus V^K))$ is equivalent to minimizing $-\log \Pr(f(V \setminus V^K))$. Assuming node labels/colors are picked as iid random variables from the label distribution, the cost of assigning label $f(u)$ to node u is $-\log \Pr(f(u)|u)$, which we can rewrite as $L(u, f(u))$. Generally, if c is a label, then labeling a node u with color or topic c has a specified cost $L(u, c)$. This part of the cost may be based on text alone. Similarly, the probability of assigning a specific pair of labels across an edge can be turned into a cost. Let an *affinity* $A(c_1, c_2)$ be defined between all pairs of colors. Labeling the endpoints of a link (u, v) with colors c_u, c_v has an associated cost $A(c_u, c_v)$. The goal is to find a labeling $f(u)$ for all unlabeled u so as to minimize

$$Q(f) = \sum_u L(u, f(u)) + \sum_{(u,v) \in E} A(f(u), f(v)) \tag{6.11}$$

Kleinberg and Tardos [124] show that this problem is NP-complete and give approximation algorithms (involving rounding the results of linear programs) with a cost that is within a $O(\log k \log \log k)$ multiplicative factor of the minimal cost, where k is the number of distinct class labels.

6.3 Co-training

A problem that arises in practice while applying metric or relaxation labeling is the possible imbalance of power between the two parts of the cost function in Equation (6.11): the node part and the edge part. As discussed in Chapters 4 and 5, representing accurate joint distributions over thousands of terms is not practical in terms of space, time, and availability of training data; it is difficult also for several hundred classes. Naive models, which assume class-conditional attribute independence, are therefore used widely. We have seen an example in the relaxation labeling algorithm discussed in Section 6.2.2.

The main problem with naive models is that although the feature probabilities $\Pr(d|c)$ may be correctly ordered over the classes, their absolute values may be quite noisy and arbitrary. This would not be a problem for ordinary classification, but two such probability values (one, $\Pr(v^T|f(v))$, from a text-based classifier and the other, $\Pr(f(N(v))|f(v))$, from a link-based classifier) may have widely different ranges of values. Generally, because the dimensionality for the textual subproblem is higher than the link subproblem, $\Pr(v^T|f(v))$ tends to be lower in magnitude than $\Pr(f(N(v))|f(v))$. Care must be taken to ensure that one component does not overwhelm the overall score. This is usually done by aggressive pruning of textual features.

Co-training, a new semisupervised learning method proposed by Blum and Mitchell [22], avoids the above problem by letting the classifiers maintain *disjoint* feature spaces. The classifiers are isolated so that their scores are never directly compared or compounded. Instead, the scores are used by each classifer to train the other, hence the name of the algorithm. Figure 6.11 shows the pseudocode. In practice, you need not limit the recommendation from one classifier to another to just one document per class, but can instead pick small batches.

1: partition the feature space F into two disjoint subsets F_A and F_B
2: initialize two supervised learners $\mathcal{L}_A$ and $\mathcal{L}_B$
3: **for** each document d **do**
4:     project d to the two subspaces forming d_A and d_B
5:     train $\mathcal{L}_A$ with d_A and $\mathcal{L}_B$ with d_B
6: **end for**
7: **while** accuracy improves **do**
8:     $\mathcal{L}_A$ teaches $\mathcal{L}_B$:
9:     **for** each class label c **do**
10:         $\mathcal{L}_A$ picks that unlabeled document d_A that best classifies as label c
11:         $\mathcal{L}_B$ adds d_B to the training set for class c
12:     **end for**
13:     $\mathcal{L}_B$ teaches $\mathcal{L}_A$:
14:     **for** each class label c **do**
15:         $\mathcal{L}_B$ picks that unlabeled document d_B that best classifies as label c
16:         $\mathcal{L}_A$ adds d_A to the training set for class c
17:     **end for**
18:     retrain $\mathcal{L}_A$ and $\mathcal{L}_B$ with new training sets
19: **end while**

FIGURE 6.11 Outline of the co-training algorithm.

At the beginning of Section 6.1, I proposed a "hard" variant to EM, in which the classifier can be trained on D^K and used to classify documents in $D \setminus D^K$, which will then join the training set for subsequent iterations. I noted that if the classifier made too many errors, the term distributions could drift and get progressively worse. Co-training is similar to this simple scheme, except for the important distinction that it uses *two* classifiers. Why would we expect co-training to compare favorably with "hard" or regular EM?

Blum and Mitchell made a few assumptions about the data. Suppose $\mathcal{L}_A$ ($\mathcal{L}_B$) is trying to learn a target function f_A (f_B). First, there must be no instance d for which $f_A(d_A) \neq f_B(d_B)$. Second, d_A is conditionally independent of d_B (and vice versa) given the label of d. The intuition is that when $\mathcal{L}_A$ is used to generate instances for $\mathcal{L}_B$, these instances appear randomly distributed to $\mathcal{L}_B$ (and vice versa, owing to the conditional independence assumption). If $\mathcal{L}_A$ and $\mathcal{L}_B$ can each learn in the presence of some noise in the training data, their accuracy should improve.

A natural way to test co-training is to represent each document d with two sets of features: d_A is the usual bag of words generated from the text on d, and d_B

Error %	$\mathcal{L}_A$	$\mathcal{L}_B$	Combined
$D^U = \emptyset$	12.9	12.4	11.1
Co-training	6.2	11.6	5.0

(a)

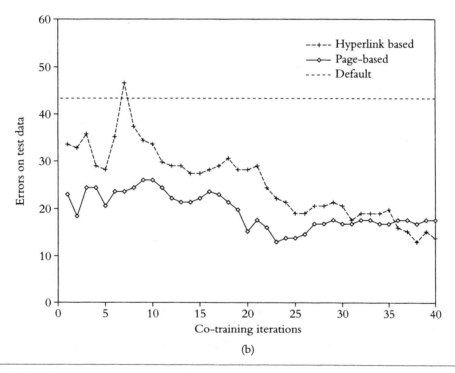

(b)

FIGURE 6.12 Co-training reduces classification error (a). Reduction in error against the number of mutual training rounds (b).

is another bag of words generated from all the available anchor text from HREF tags that target d. These are not really independent, and yet the co-training algorithm does well, reducing the error below the levels of both $\mathcal{L}_A$ and $\mathcal{L}_B$ individually, as shown in Figure 6.12. For $D^U = \emptyset$, the "combined" classifier picks a class c by maximizing $\Pr(c|d_A, d_B)$, which is assumed to be $\Pr(c|d_A)\Pr(c|d_B)$.

6.4 **Bibliographic Notes**

The application of EM to semisupervised text topic learning is by Nigam et al. [168]. The semisupervised HyperClass algorithm has been tested only on patents. It would be of interest to implement a practical version of it for Web data and compare its accuracy and performance with simpler heuristics, such as absorbing terms from targets of same-site links. I know of no attempt to apply the Kleinberg and Tardos algorithm to real-life hypertext data; it would be interesting to know if and by what margin the global optimization improves beyond iterative relaxation labeling heuristics. It would also be of interest, for Web topic directories, to measure the benefits from unsupervised text against the use of link-derived features—which is more valuable?

All the hypertext-oriented algorithms assume, correctly, that link structure and content are highly correlated and that there is a great deal of topical locality in hypertext and the Web. See Section 8.3 for a more detailed discussion of content-based locality in hypertext, as well as recent measurements of such properties by Davison [61] and Menczer [148].

A first-order Markov Random Field (MRF) has been used throughout this chapter for both ease of exposition and efficiency of implementation. However, learning higher-order MRFs may be useful in some situations. For example, it is useful to know that "computer science department homepages often link to a list of faculty homepages, that in turn list papers, some of which could be about robotics." There may even be backward links involved, such as "homepages of oil and energy-producing companies are often cited by pages about environmental awareness, which in turn cite articles about the ozone hole." Learning such higher-order patterns while preventing combinatorial blowup would be valuable.

The alert reader would have noticed in Section 6.2.1 that the tokens synthesized using the prefix trick were all thrown into a multinomial bag-of-words model (see Section 4.4.1), which will share and distort the probability of events, because events subsuming one another (L@/Computers subsumes L@/) are definitely not independent. The binary model is better at handling synthesized features, but losing term frequency information usually makes it less accurate than a classifier based on the multinomial model. The maximum entropy classifier (see Section 5.8) could combine the robustness of the binary model to synthesized features with the better accuracy of the multinomial model, and needs further study in this context.

The aspect model proposed by Hofmann [109, 110] and discussed in Section 4.4.4 uses a few cluster or aspect variables to "bottleneck" the dependence among terms. Similar aspect variables can be used to model the dependence between text- and link-based features. As mentioned in Section 6.1.3, it will be important to adapt the aspect model to supervised learning by mapping between aspects and class labels.

Blum and Mitchell conduct a detailed analysis of the conditions under which co-training performs well, in the PAC (probabilistically approximately correct) setting first proposed by Valiant [208]. Similar to the situation with naive Bayes assumptions, co-training seems to work well even when the assumptions required for accuracy boost are not met. Nigam and Ghani [166] perform further extensive experiments to reveal the importance of various assumptions, as well as to compare co-training with EM.

PART III

APPLICATIONS

CHAPTER 7

SOCIAL NETWORK ANALYSIS

The size of the Web and the reach of search engines were both increasing rapidly by late 1996, but there was growing frustration with traditional IR systems applied to Web data. IR systems work with finite document collections, and the worth of a document with regard to a query is intrinsic to the document. Documents are self-contained units, and are generally descriptive and truthful about their contents.

In contrast, the Web resembles an indefinitely growing and shifting universe. Recall, an important notion in classic IR (see Section 3.2.1), has relatively little meaning for the Web; in fact, we cannot even measure recall because we can never collect a complete snapshot of the Web. Most Web search engines present the best 10 to 20 responses on the first page, most users stop looking after the second page, and all that seems to matter is the number of relevant "hits" within the first 20 to 40 responses—in other words, the precision at low recall.

Focusing on precision is not a great help, either. On one hand, Web documents are not always descriptive or truthful. Site designers use nontextual content such as images and Flash (*www.macromedia.com*/) to project the desired look and feel. Entire businesses are built on stuffing pages with invisible keywords to lure search engines to index pages under common queries. Often, the match between a query and a Web page can be evaluated only by looking at the link graph neighborhood of the page. On the other hand, the Web is also afflicted with the "abundance problem." For most short queries (such as "Java") there are millions of relevant responses. Most Web queries are two words long. How can we hope to identify the best 40 documents matching a query from among a million documents if documents are not self-complete and truthful?

Apart from the sheer flux and populist involvement, the most important features that distinguish hypertext from a text collection for IR research are hyperlinks. Hyperlinks address the needs of amplification, elaboration, critique, contradiction, and navigation, among others. The hyperlink graph of the Web evolves organically, without any central coordination, and yet shows rich global and local properties. Hyperlink graph information is a rich supplement to text, sometimes even beating text in terms of information quality.

Starting around 1996, a frenzy of research efforts has sought to understand the structure of the Web and to exploit that understanding for better IR. Research has proceeded in a few major directions:

- Hyperlinks were used in conjunction with text for better topic classification. We have seen examples of such efforts in Chapter 6.

- For broad queries that elicited large response sets from keyword search engines, hyperlinks were used to estimate popularity or authority of the responses. Google is a prime example of such techniques. This chapter in large part deals with such techniques.

- Independent of specific applications, researchers made comprehensive measurements on the Web and on the reach of search engines. They formulated models of creation, modification, and destruction of nodes and links that closely predicted observed data. The last part of this chapter deals with this area.

This chapter deals with a variety of link-based techniques for analyzing social networks that enhance text-based retrieval and ranking strategies. As we shall see, social network analysis was well established long before the Web, in fact, long before graph theory and algorithms became mainstream computer science. Therefore, later developments in evolution models and properties of random walks, mixing rates, and eigen systems [157] may make valuable contributions to social network analysis, especially in the context of the Web.

7.1 Social Sciences and Bibliometry

The Web is an example of a *social network*. Social networks have been extensively researched long before the advent of the Web. Perhaps coincidentally, between 1950 and 1980, around the same time that Vannevar Bush's proposed hyper-medium called *Memex* [29] was gaining acceptance, social sciences made great strides in measuring and analyzing social networks. (See the authoritative text by Wasserman and Faust [210] for details.)

Networks of social interaction are formed between academics by co-authoring, advising, and serving on committees; between movie personnel by directing and acting; between musicians, football stars, friends, and relatives; between people by making phone calls and transmitting infections; between countries via trading relations; between papers through citation; and between Web pages by hyperlinking to other Web pages.

Social network theory is concerned with properties related to connectivity and distances in graphs, with diverse applications like epidemiology, espionage, citation indexing, and the like. In the first two examples, one might be interested in identifying a few nodes to be removed to significantly increase average path length between pairs of nodes. In citation analysis, one may wish to identify influential or central papers.

7.1.1 Prestige

Using edge-weighted, directed graphs to model social networks has been quite common. With this model, it has been clear that in-degree is a good first-order indicator of *status* or *prestige*. More interestingly, as early as 1949, Seeley realized the recursive nature of prestige in a social network [192, pages 234–35]:

> . . . we are involved in an "infinite regress": [an actor's status] is a function of the status of those who choose him; and their [status] is a function of those who choose them, and so *ad infinitum*.

Consider the node (vertex) adjacency matrix E of the document citation graph, where $E[i,j] = 1$ if document i cites document j, and zero otherwise. Every node v has a notion of prestige $p[v]$ associated with it, which is simply a positive real number. Over all nodes, we represent the prestige score as a vector $\mathbf{p}$. Suppose we want to confer to each node v the sum total of prestige of all u that links to v, thus computing a new prestige vector $\mathbf{p}'$. This is easily written in matrix notation as

$$\mathbf{p}' = E^T \mathbf{p} \qquad\qquad (7.1)$$

because

$$p'[v] = \sum_u E^T[v, u] p[u]$$
$$= \sum_u E[u, v] p[u]$$

To reach a *fixpoint* for the prestige vector, one can simply start with $\mathbf{p} = (1, \ldots, 1)^T$ and turn Equation (7.1) into an iterative *assignment* $\mathbf{p} \leftarrow E^T \mathbf{p}$, interleaved with normalizing $\|\mathbf{p}\|_1 = \sum_u p[u]$ to 1, to avoid numeric overflow. This process will lead to a convergent solution for $\mathbf{p}$ and is called *power iteration* in linear algebra [91]. The convergent value of $\mathbf{p}$, the fixpoint, is called the *principal eigenvector* (i.e., the eigenvector associated with the eigenvalue having the largest magnitude) of the matrix E^T. Clearly, work by Seeley and others between 1949 and 1970 firmly established this eigen analysis paradigm. Enhancements such as an attenuation factor ($\mathbf{p}' = \alpha E^T \mathbf{p}$) are also known.

7.1.2 Centrality

Various graph-based notions of centrality have been proposed in the social network literature. The *distance* $d(u, v)$ between two nodes u and v in a graph without edge weights is the smallest number of links via which one can go from u to v. (One can add up the edge weights in the case of a weighted graph to derive the path length.) The *radius* of node u is $r(u) = \max_v d(u, v)$. The *center* of the graph is $\arg\min_u r(u)$, the node that has the smallest radius. One may look for influential papers in an area of research by looking for papers u with small $r(u)$, which means that most papers in that research community have a short citation path to u.

For other applications, different notions of centrality are useful. In the case of trading partners and cartels, or in the study of epidemics, espionage, or suspected terrorist communication on telephone networks, it is often useful to identify *cuts*:

a (small) number of edges that, when removed, disconnect a given pair of vertices. Or one may look for a small set of vertices that, when removed (together with edges incident with them), will decompose the graph into two or more connected components.

The variations of graph-based formulations and measures that have been used in the social sciences are too numerous to cover in detail; I will conclude this section with the observation that no single measure is suited for all applications and that the repertoire of measures is already quite mature.

7.1.3 Co-citation

If document u cites documents v and w, then v and w are said to be *co-cited* by u. Documents v and w being co-cited by many documents like u is evidence that v and w are somehow related to each other. Consider again the node (vertex) adjacency matrix E of the document citation graph, where $E[i,j] = 1$ if document i cites document j, and zero otherwise. Then

$$
\begin{aligned}
(E^T E)[v, w] &= \sum_u E^T[v, u]E[u, w] \\
&= \sum_u E[u, v]E[u, w] \\
&= |\{u : (u, v) \in E, (u, w) \in E\}|
\end{aligned}
\tag{7.2}
$$

The entry (v, w) in the $(E^T E)$ matrix is the *co-citation index* of v and w and an indicator of relatedness between v and w. One may use this pairwise relatedness measure in a clustering algorithm, such as *multidimensional scaling* (MDS), discussed in Chapter 4. MDS uses the document-to-document similarity (or distance) matrix to embed the documents represented as points in a low-dimensional Euclidean space (such as the 2D plane) while "distorting" interpoint distances as little as possible. Visualizing clusters based on co–citation reveals important social structures between and within link communities. Such studies have been performed on academic publications several years back [144] and later by Larson on a small collection from the Web [132] concerning geophysics, climate, remote sensing, and ecology. A sample MDS map is shown in Figure 7.1.

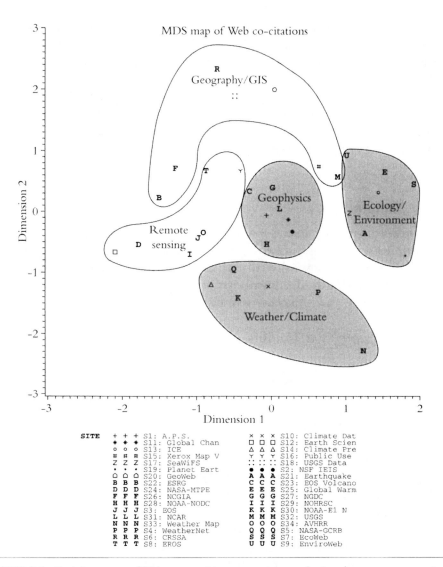

FIGURE 7.1 Social structure of Web communities concerning geophysics, climate, remote sensing, and ecology. The cluster labels are generated manually. This image is taken from Larson [132].

7.2 **PageRank and HITS**

Two algorithms for ranking Web pages based on links, PageRank and HITS (hyperlink induced topic search), were developed around the fall of 1996 at Stanford University by Larry Page[1] and Sergey Brin, and at IBM Almaden by Jon Kleinberg. Both sought to remedy the "abundance problem" inherent in broad queries, supplementing precision with notions related to prestige in social network analysis.

In PageRank, each page on the Web has a measure of *prestige* that is independent of any information need or query. Roughly speaking, the prestige of a page is proportional to the sum of the prestige scores of pages linking to it. In HITS, a query is used to select a subgraph from the Web. From this subgraph, two kinds of nodes are identified: *authoritative* pages to which many pages link, and *hub* pages that consist of comprehensive collections of links to valuable pages on the subject.

Although there are technical differences, all three measures are defined recursively: prestige of a node depends on the prestige of other nodes, and the measure of being a good hub depends on how good neighboring nodes are as authorities (and vice versa). Both procedures involve computing eigenvectors for the adjacency matrix, or a matrix derived thereof, of the Web or a suitably relevant subgraph of the Web. In this section we will study these algorithms and take a careful look at their strengths and weaknesses.

7.2.1 **PageRank**

Assume for the moment that the Web graph is strongly connected—that is, from any node u there is a directed path to node v. (It is not; we come back to this issue a little later.) Consider a Web surfer clicking on hyperlinks forever, picking a link uniformly at random on each page to move on to the next page. Suppose the surfer starts from a random node in accordance with a distribution $\vec{p}_0$, with probability $p_0[u]$ of starting from node u, where $\sum_u p_0[u] = 1$. Let the adjacency matrix of the Web be E, where $E[u, v] = 1$ if there is a hyperlink $(u, v) \in E$, and zero otherwise. We overload E to denote both the edge set and its corresponding matrix.

After clicking once, what is the probability $p_1[v]$ that the surfer is on page v? To get to v, the surfer must have been at some node u with a link to v in the previous step, and then clicked on the specific link that took her from u to v.

---

1. PageRank is named after Larry Page, a founder of Google.

Given E, the out-degree of node u is given simply by

$$N_u = \sum_v E[u, v] \tag{7.3}$$

or the sum of the uth row of E. Assuming parallel edges (multiple links from u to v) are disallowed, the probability of the latter event given the former (i.e., being at u) is just $1/N_u$. Combining,

$$p_1[v] = \sum_{(u,v) \in E} \frac{p_0[u]}{N_u} \tag{7.4}$$

Let us derive a matrix L from E by normalizing all row-sums to one, that is,

$$L[u, v] = \frac{E[u, v]}{\sum_\beta E[u, \beta]} = \frac{E[u, v]}{N_u} \tag{7.5}$$

With L defined as above, Equation (7.4) can be recast as

$$p_1[v] = \sum_u L[u, v] p_0[u] \tag{7.6}$$

or

$$\mathbf{p}_1 = L^T \mathbf{p}_0 \tag{7.7}$$

The form of Equation (7.7) is identical to that of Equation (7.1) except for the edge weights used to normalize the degree. After the ith step, we will get

$$\mathbf{p}_{i+1} = L^T \mathbf{p}_i \tag{7.8}$$

We will initially assume that nodes with no outlinks have been removed a priori. If E and therefore L are *irreducible* (i.e., there is a directed path from every node to every other node) and *aperiodic* (i.e., for all u, v, there are paths with all possible number of links on them, except for a finite set of path lengths that may be missing), the sequence $(\mathbf{p}_i)$, $i = 0, 1, 2, \ldots$ will converge to the principal eigenvector of L^T, that is, a solution to the matrix equation $\mathbf{p} = L^T \mathbf{p}$, also called the *stationary distribution* of L. The prestige of node u, denoted $p[u]$, is also called its PageRank. Note that the stationary distribution is independent of $\mathbf{p}_0$.

For an infinitely long trip made by the surfer, the converged value of $\mathbf{p}$ is simply the relative rate at that the surfer hits each page. There is a close correspondence to the result of the "aimless surfer" model above and the notion of prestige in bibliometry: a page v has high prestige if the visit rate is high, which happens if there are many neighbors u with high visit rates leading to v.

The simple surfing model above does not quite suffice, because the Web graph is not strongly connected and aperiodic. An analysis of a significant portion of the Web graph (a few hundred million nodes) in 2000 showed that it is not strongly connected as a whole [28]. Only a fourth of the graph is strongly connected. Obviously, there are many pages without any outlinks, as well as directed paths leading into a cycle, where the walk could get trapped.

A simple fix is to insert fake, low-probability transitions all over the place. In the new graph, the surfer first makes a two-way choice at each node:

1. With probability d, the surfer jumps to a random page on the Web.
2. With probability $1 - d$, the surfer decides to choose, uniformly at random, an out-neighbor of the current node as before.

d is a tuned constant, usually chosen between 0.1 and 0.2. Because of the random jump, Equation(7.7) changes to

$$\mathbf{p}_{i+1} = (1 - d)L^T\mathbf{p}_i + d \begin{pmatrix} 1/N & \cdots & 1/N \\ \vdots & \ddots & \vdots \\ 1/N & \cdots & 1/N \end{pmatrix} \mathbf{p}_i$$

$$= \left((1 - d)L^T + \frac{d}{N}\boxed{\mathbf{1}_N} \right) \mathbf{p}_i$$

simplifying notation,

$$= (1 - d)L^T\mathbf{p}_i + \frac{d}{N}(1, \ldots, 1)^T \tag{7.9}$$

where N is the number of nodes in the graph. $p[u]$ is the PageRank of node u. Given the large number of edges in E, direct solution of the eigen system is usually not feasible. A common approach is to use *power iterations* [91], which involves picking an arbitrary nonzero $\mathbf{p}_0$ (often with all components set to $1/N$), repeated multiplication by $(1 - d)L^T + \frac{d}{N}\boxed{\mathbf{1}_N}$, and intermittent scaling $|\mathbf{p}_i|$ to one. Since notions of popularity and prestige are at best noisy, numeric convergence is usually not necessary in practice, and the iterations can be terminated as soon as there is relative stability in the ordering of the set of prestige scores.

There are two ways to handle nodes with no outlink. You can jump with probability one in such cases, or you can first preprocess the graph, iteratively removing all nodes with an out-degree of zero (removing some nodes may lead to the removal of more nodes), computing the PageRanks of surviving nodes, and propagating the scores to the nodes eliminated during the preprocessing step.

In this application, the exact values of $\mathbf{p}_i$ are not as important as the ranking they induce on the pages. This means that we can stop the iterations fairly quickly. Page et al. [169] report acceptable convergence ranks in 52 iterations for a crawl with 322 million links.

In Google, the crawled graph is first used to precompute and store the PageRank of each page. Note that the PageRank is independent of any query or textual content. When a query is submitted, a text index is used to first make a selection of possible response pages. Then an undisclosed ranking scheme that combines PageRank with textual match is used to produce a final ordering of response URLs. All this makes Google comparable in speed, at query time, to conventional text-based search engines.

PageRank is an important ranking mechanism at the heart of Google, but it is not the only one: keywords, phrase matches, and match proximity are also taken into account, as is anchor text on pages linking to a given page. Search Engine Watch (*www.searchenginewatch.com/*) reports that during some weeks in 1999, Google's top hit to the query "more evil than Satan" returned *www.microsoft.com/*, probably because of anchor text spamming. This embarrassment was fixed within a few weeks. The next incident occurred around November 2000, when Google's top response to a rather offensive query was *www.georgewbushstore.com/*. This was traced to *www.hugedisk.com/*, which hosted a page that had the offensive query words as anchor text for a hyperlink to *www.georgewbushstore.com/*.

Although the details of Google's combined ranking strategy are unpublished, such anecdotes suggest that the combined ranking strategy is tuned using many empirical parameters and checked for problems using human effort and regression testing. The strongest criticism of PageRank is that it defines prestige via a single random walk uninfluenced by a specific query. A related criticism is of the artificial decoupling between relevance and quality, and the ad hoc manner in which the two are brought together at query time, for the sake of efficiency.

7.2.2 HITS

In hyperlink induced topic search (HITS), proposed by Kleinberg [122], a query-dependent graph is chosen for analysis, in contrast to PageRank. Specifically, the query q is sent to a standard IR system to collect what is called a *root set R* of nodes in the Web graph. For reasons to be explained shortly, any node u that neighbors any $r \in R$ via an inbound or outbound edge—that is, $(u, r) \in E$ or $(r, u) \in E$—is included as well (E is the edge set for the Web). The additional

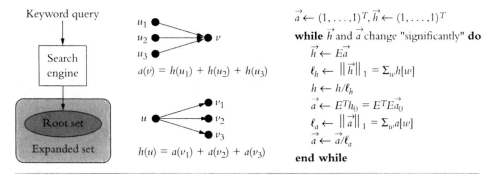

FIGURE 7.2 The HITS algorithm. ℓ_h and ℓ_a are L_1 vector norms.

nodes constitute the *expanded set* and, together with the root set, form the *base set* V_q. Edges that connect nodes from the same host are now eliminated because they are considered "navigational" or "nepotistic" (also see Section 7.3.1). Let us call the remaining edges E_q. We thus construct the query-specific graph $G_q = (V_q, E_q)$ (see Figure 7.2). (I will drop the subscript q where clear from context.)

Kleinberg observed that as in academic literature, where some publications (typically in conferences) initiate new ideas and others consolidate and survey significant research (typically in journals or books), the Web includes two flavors of prominent or popular pages: *authorities,* which contain definitive high-quality information, and *hubs,* which are comprehensive lists of links to authorities. Every page is, to an extent, both a hub and an authority, but these properties are graded. Thus, every page u has two distinct measures of merit, its hub score $h[u]$ and its authority score $a[u]$. Collectively, the scores over all the nodes in G_q are written as vectors $\vec{a}$ and $\vec{h}$, with the uth vector component giving the score for node u.

As in the case of PageRank, the quantitative definitions of hub and authority scores are recursive. The authority score of a page is proportional to the sum of hub scores of pages linking to it, and conversely, its hub score is proportional to the authority scores of the pages to which it links. In matrix notation, this translates to the following pair of equations:

$$\vec{a} = E^T \vec{h} \tag{7.10}$$

$$\vec{h} = E\vec{a} \tag{7.11}$$

Again, power iterations may be used to solve this system of equations iteratively, as shown in the pseudocode in Figure 7.2. When $\vec{a}$ attains convergence, it will be the principal eigenvector of $E^T E$. $\vec{h}$ will converge to the principal eigenvector of EE^T. Typically, runs with several thousand nodes and links "converge" in 20 to 30 iterations, in the sense that the rankings of hubs and authorities stabilize.

Summarizing, the main steps in HITS are

1. Send query to a text-based IR system and obtain the root set.
2. Expand the root set by radius one to obtain an expanded graph.
3. Run power iterations on the hub and authority scores together.
4. Report top-ranking authorities and hubs.

The entire process is generically called *topic distillation*. User studies [40] have shown that reporting hubs is useful over and above reporting authorities, because they provide useful annotations and starting points for users to start exploring a topic.

HITS cannot precompute hub and authority scores because the graph G_q can only be computed after query "q" is known. This is both a strength and a weakness. The model of conferring authority through linkage clearly makes more sense when restricted to a subgraph of the Web that is relevant to a query, and therefore we expect HITS to need fewer ranking tweaks than PageRank once the scores are computed. Haveliwala [98] has proposed to precompute a few topic-specific PageRanks to address this limitation. The flip side is that HITS has to undertake an eigenvector computation per query.

Bipartite subgraphs are key to the reinforcement process in HITS. Consider Figure 7.2. If in some transfer step node v_1 collects a large authority score, in the next reverse transfer, the hub u will collect a large hub score, which will then diffuse to siblings v_2 and v_3 of node v_1. Many times, such diffusion is crucial to the success of HITS, but it can be overdone. Some causes and remedies are discussed in Sections 7.3 and 7.4.

The key distinction of HITS from PageRank is the modeling of hubs. Page-Rank has no notion of a hub, but (Google) users seem not to regard this as a major handicap to searching, probably because on the Web, great hubs soon accumulate inlinks and thereby high prestige, thus becoming good authorities as well.

Higher-order eigenvectors and clustering

If the query is ambiguous (e.g., "Java" or "jaguar") or polarized (e.g., "abortion" or "cold fusion"), the expanded set will contain a few, almost disconnected, link communities. In each community there may be dense bipartite subgraphs. In

```
1: while X does not converge do
2:     X ← MX
3:     for i = 1, 2, . . . do
4:         for j = 1, 2, . . . , i − 1 do
5:             X(i) ← X(i) − (X(i) · X(j))X(i)
                {orthogonalize X(i) with regard to column X(j)}
6:         end for
7:         normalize X(i) to unit L₂ norm
8:     end for
9: end while
```

FIGURE 7.3 Finding higher-order eigenvectors in HITS using power iterations.

such cases, the highest-order eigenvectors found by HITS will reveal hubs and authorities in the largest near-bipartite component. One can tease out the structure and ranking within smaller components by calculating not only the principal eigenvector but also a few more. The iterations expressed in Equation (7.10) find the *principal eigenvectors* of EE^T and $E^T E$. Other eigenvectors can also be found using the iterative method. Given an $n \times n$ matrix M ($= E^T E$, say) for which we wish to find k eigenvectors, we initialize an $n \times k$ matrix X (generalizing the $n \times 1$ vector before) with positive entries. Let $X(i)$ be the ith column of X. The iterations are generalized to the steps shown in Figure 7.3 [91].

Similar to Larson's study (Figure 7.1), higher-order eigenvectors can reveal clusters in the graph structure. In the a or h vector, each graph node had only one number as a representation. Thanks to using X, each node now has k hub scores and k authority scores. These should not be interpreted as just more scores for ranking but as a multidimensional geometric embedding of the nodes. For example, if $k = 2$, one can plot each node as a point in the plane using its authority (or hub) score row-vector. For a polarized issue like "abortion," there are two densely linked communities on the Web, with sparse connections in between, mostly set up via eclectic hubs. A low-dimensional embedding and visualization may bring out community clustering graphically in case a query matches multiple link communities.

The connection between HITS and LSI/SVD

There is a direct mapping between finding the singular value decomposition (SVD) of E, as described in Section 4.3.4, and the eigensystem of EE^T or $E^T E$. Let the SVD of E be $U\Sigma V^T$, where $U^T U = \mathbf{I}$ and $V^T V = \mathbf{I}$ and Σ is a diagonal matrix $\text{diag}(\sigma_1, \ldots, \sigma_r)$ of singular values, where r is the rank of E, and $\mathbf{I}$ is an identity matrix of suitable size. Then $EE^T = U\Sigma V^T V\Sigma U^T = U\Sigma\mathbf{I}\Sigma U^T = U\Sigma^2 U^T$, which implies that $EE^T U = U\Sigma^2$. Here if E is $n \times n$ with rank r, then U is $n \times r$; Σ and Σ^2 are $r \times r$. Specifically, $\Sigma^2 = \text{diag}(\sigma_1^2, \ldots, \sigma_r^2)$. $U\Sigma^2$ is $n \times r$ as well. If $U(j)$ is the jth column of U, we can write $EE^T U(j) = \sigma_j^2 U(j)$, which means that $U(j)$ is an eigenvector of EE^T with corresponding eigenvalue σ_j^2, for $j = 1, \ldots, r$. If Σ^2 is arranged such that $\sigma_1^2 \geq \ldots \sigma_r^2$, it turns out that finding the hub scores for E is the same as finding $U(1)$, and more generally, finding multiple hubs/authorities corresponds to finding many singular values of EE^T and $E^T E$.

Thus, the HITS algorithm is equivalent to running SVD on the hyperlink relation (source,target) rather than the (term,document) relation to which SVD is usually applied. Recall that SVD finds us vector representations for terms and documents in "latent semantic space." As a consequence of the equivalence shown above, a HITS procedure that finds multiple hub and authority vectors also finds a multidimensional representation for nodes in a hypertext graph. We can either present the SVD representation visually to aid clustering, or use one of the many clustering algorithms discussed in Chapter 4 on this representation of documents.

7.2.3   Stochastic HITS and Other Variants

Several subsequent studies have provided deeper analysis and comparison of HITS and PageRank. I provide here several observations that improve our understanding of how these algorithms work.

HITS is sensitive to local topology. The two graphs in Figure 7.4(a) differ only in the insertion of one node (5) to turn a single edge into a chain of two edges, something that frequently happens on the Web owing to a redirection or reorganization of a site. You can verify that this edge splitting upsets the scores for HITS quite significantly, whereas it leaves PageRanks relatively unaffected. More specifically, the update equations for authorities change from the system

$$a_2 \leftarrow 2a_2 + a_4 \tag{7.12}$$

$$a_4 \leftarrow a_2 + a_4 \tag{7.13}$$

to the new system

$$a_2 \leftarrow 2a_2 + a_4 \tag{7.14}$$

$$a_4 \leftarrow a_4 \tag{7.15}$$

$$a_5 \leftarrow a_2 + a_5 \tag{7.16}$$

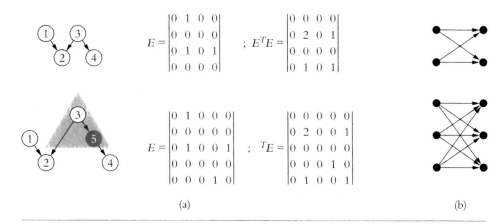

FIGURE 7.4 Minor perturbations in the graph may have dramatic effects on HITS scores (a). The principal eigenvector found by HITS favors larger bipartite cores (b).

Thus, node 5 takes the place of node 4, the mutual reinforcement between the authority scores of nodes 2 and 4 is lost, and node 4's authority score vanishes to zero compared to those of nodes 2 and 5.

HITS needs *bipartite cores* in the score reinforcement process. Consider the graph in Figure 7.4(b): it has two connected components, each of which is a complete bipartite graph, with 2×2 and 2×3 nodes. Let us assign all hub scores to 1 and start HITS iterations. After the first iteration, each authority score in the smaller component will be 2 and each authority score in the larger component will be 3. The scores will progress as follows:

Iteration	h_{small}	a_{small}	h_{large}	a_{large}
0	1	0	1	0
1a	1	2	1	3
1h	4	2	9	3
2a	4	8	9	27
2h	16	8	81	27

Here I ignore score scaling, because the relative magnitude of the scores illustrates the point. In general, after $i > 0$ full iterations, we can show that $a_{small} = 2^{2i-1}$ and $a_{large} = 3^{2i-1}$. Thus their ratio is $a_{large}/a_{small} = (3/2)^{2i-1}$, which grows without bound as i increases. Thus, in the principal eigenvector, the smaller component finds absolutely no representation. In contrast, it can be verified that PageRank will not be so drastic; the random jump will ensure some positive scores for the prestige of all nodes.

Many researchers have sought to improve HITS by removing some of these anomalies. Lempel and Moran [135] proposed *SALSA, a stochastic algorithm for link structure analysis*. The goal of SALSA was to cast bipartite reinforcement in the random surfer framework. They proposed and analyzed the following random surfer specification while maintaining the essential bipartite nature of HITS:

1.   At a node v, the random surfer chooses an inlink (that is, an incoming edge (u, v)) uniformly at random and moves to u.

2.   Then, from u, the surfer takes a random forward link (u, w) uniformly at random.

Thus, the transition probability from v to w is

$$p(v, w) = \frac{1}{\text{InDegree}(v)} \sum_{(u,v),(u,w)\in E} \frac{1}{\text{OutDegree}(u)} \tag{7.17}$$

This may be regarded as the authority-to-authority transition; a symmetric formulation (follow an outlink and then an inlink) handles hub-to-hub transitions.

SALSA does not succumb to tightly knit communities to the same extent as HITS. In fact, the steady-state node probabilities of the authority-to-authority transition (assuming it is irreducible and ergodic) have a very simple form:

$$\pi_v \propto \text{InDegree}(v) \tag{7.18}$$

That is, the SALSA authority score is proportional to the in-degree. Although the sum in Equation (7.17) suggests a kind of sibling link reinforcement, the probabilities are chosen such that the steady-state node probabilities do not reflect any nonlocal prestige diffusion. It might be argued that a total absence of long-range diffusion is at the opposite extreme from HITS, and an intermediate level of reinforcement is better than either extreme.

A recent study by Ng et al. [162] shows that HITS's long-range reinforcement is bad for *stability*: random erasure of a small fraction (say, 10%) of nodes or edges can seriously alter the ranks of hubs and authorities. It turns out that PageRank is much more stable to such perturbations, essentially because of its random jump step. Ng et al. propose to recast HITS as a bidirectional random walk by a "random surfer" similar to PageRank: Every timestep, with probability d, the surfer jumps to a node in the base set uniformly at random. With the remaining probability $1 - d$:

- If it is an odd timestep, the surfer takes a random outlink from the current node.
- If it is an even timestep, the surfer goes backward on a random inlink leading to the current node.

Ng et al. showed that this variant of HITS with random jumps has much better stability in the face of small changes in the hyperlink graph, and that the stability improves as d is increased. (They also showed this to be the case with PageRank.) Obviously, $d = 1$ would be most stable but useless for ranking: scores would diffuse all over. There is no recipe known for setting d based on the graph structure alone. It is clear that, at some stage, page content must be reconciled into graph models of the Web to complete the design of Web IR systems [98].

7.3 Shortcomings of the Coarse-Grained Graph Model

Both HITS and PageRank use a coarse-grained model of the Web, where each page is a node in a graph with a few scores associated with it. The model takes no notice of either the text or the markup structure on each page. (HITS leaves the selection of the base set to an external IR algorithm.)

In real life, Web pages are more complex than the coarse-grained model suggests. An HTML page sports a tag-tree structure, which is rendered by browsers as roughly rectangular regions with embedded text and hyperlinks. Unlike HITS or PageRank, human readers do not pay equal attention to all the links on a page. They use the position of text and links (and their interpretation of the text, of course) to carefully judge where to click to continue on their (hardly random) surfing.

Algorithms that do not model the behavior of human information foragers may fall prey to many artifacts of Web authorship, which I illustrate in this section. In the next section, I will describe several enhancements to the model and algorithms that avoid such pitfalls.

7.3.1 Artifacts of Web Authorship

The central assumption in PageRank and HITS is that a hyperlink confers authority. Obviously, this holds only if the hyperlink was created as a result of editorial judgment based on the contents of the source and target pages, as is largely the case with social networks in academic publications. Unfortunately, that central assumption is increasingly being violated on the Web.

Much has changed about authoring Web pages ever since those algorithms were proposed. HTML is increasingly generated by programs, not typed in by hand. Pages are often generated from templates and/or dynamically from relational and semistructured databases (e.g., Zope; *zope.org/*). There are sites designed by companies whose mission is to increase the number of search engine hits for their customers. Their common strategies include stuffing irrelevant words in pages and linking up their customers in densely connected cliques, even if those customers have nothing in common. The creation and dissemination of hypertext happens at an unprecedented scale today and is inexorably coupled with commerce and advertising. I will describe three related ways in that these authoring idioms manifest themselves.

Nepotistic links

Kleinberg summarily discarded links connecting pages on the same host, because these links, largely authored by the same person, did not confer authority in the same sense as an academic citation, and could therefore be regarded as "nepotistic."[2]

Soon after HITS was published, Bharat and Henzinger [18] found that the threat of nepotism was not necessarily limited to same-site links. Two-site nepotism (a pair of Web sites endorsing each other) was on the rise. In many trials with HITS, they found two distinct sites h_1 and h_2, where h_1 hosted a number of pages u linking to a page v on h_2, driving up $a(v)$ beyond what may be considered fair.

Two-host nepotism can also happen because of Web infrastructure issues, for example, in a site hosted on multiple servers such as `www.yahoo.com` and `dir12.yahoo.com`, or the use of the relative URLs with regard to a base URL specified with the `<a base=...>` HTML construct. If it is a simple case of mirroring, the algorithms in Section 3.3.2 will generally fix the problem, but deliberate nepotism also exists on the Web.

Clique attacks

Over time, two-host nepotism evolved into multihost nepotism, thanks to the culture of professional Web-hosting and "portal" development companies. It is now surprisingly common to encounter query response pages with elaborate

---

2. Page et al. do not discuss nepotistic links in their paper.

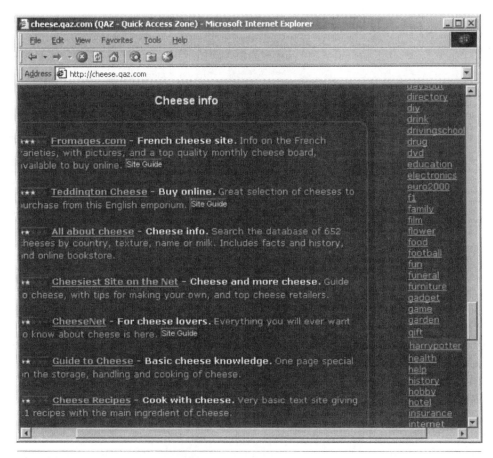

FIGURE 7.5   Hyperlinks generated from templates in navigation bars do not reflect content-based editorial judgment and often implement "clique attacks" that foil HITS-like algorithms. There are only a handful of links related to *cheese* on this page, but over 60 nepotistic links going to different hosts from *ads.qaz.com/* through *women.qaz.com/*.

navigation bars having links to other sites with *no* semantic connection, just because these sites are all hosted by a common business. I show one example in Figure 7.5, but the Web has plenty of such pages and sites.[3] These sites form a densely connected graph, sometimes even a completely connected graph, which

---

3. Although these sites might disappear with time, I will give some more examples: *www.411web.com/*, *www.depalma-enterprises.com/*, *www.cyprus-domains.com/*, and *www.usa.worldweb.com/*.

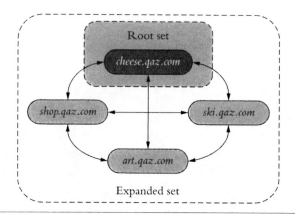

FIGURE 7.6 How a clique attack takes over link-based rankings.

led to my naming the phenomenon a "clique attack." Sometimes members of the clique have URLs sharing substrings, but they may map to different IP addresses. It is not easy to judge from the graph alone whether the clique is a bona fide, content-inspired link community or has been created deliberately. An example of a clique attack is shown in Figure 7.6. Both HITS and PageRank can fall prey to clique attacks, although by tuning d in PageRank, the effect can be reduced.

Mixed hubs

Another problem with decoupling the user's query from the link-based ranking strategy is that some hubs may be *mixed* without any attempt on the part of the hub writer to confound a search engine. Technically, this is hard to distinguish from a clique attack, but probably happens even more frequently than clique attacks. For example, a hub u containing links relevant to the query "movie awards" may also have some links to movie production companies. If a node v_1 relevant to movie awards gains authority score, the HITS algorithm (see Figure 7.2) would diffuse the score through u to a node v_2, which could be a movie production company homepage. Another example, in the form of a section of links about "Shakespeare" embedded in a page about British and Irish literary figures in general, is shown in Figure 7.7. Mixed hubs can be a problem for both HITS and PageRank, because neither algorithm discriminates between outlinks on a page. However, a system (such as Google) using PageRank may succeed at suppressing the ill effects by filtering on keywords at query time.

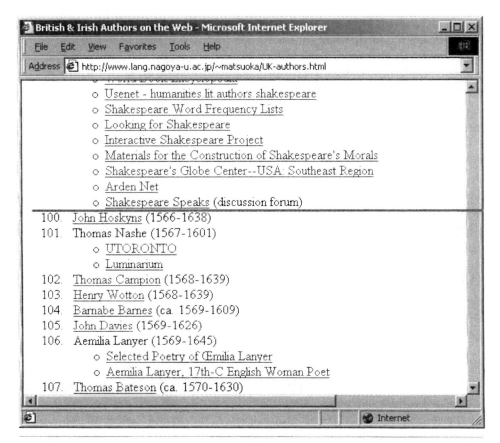

FIGURE 7.7 A mixed hub on British and Irish authors with one section dedicated to Shakespeare. (The horizontal line has been added by hand to demarcate the section.)

7.3.2 Topic Contamination and Drift

The expansion step in HITS was meant to increase recall and capture a larger graph G_q, which was subjected to eigen analysis. Why was this needed? Here is one reason. As of late 1996, the query "browser" would fail to include Netscape's Navigator and Communicator pages, as well as Microsoft's Internet Explorer page in the root set, because at that time these sites avoided a boring description like "browser" for their products. However, millions of pages included blurbs such as "this page is best viewed with a frames–capable *browser* such as . . ." and linked to these authoritative browser pages.

Conversely, sometimes good authorities would get included in the root set, but hubs linking to them might not be adequately represented in the root set for HITS to be able to estimate reliable authority scores for the former pages. The radius-1 expansion step of HITS would include nodes of both categories into the expanded graph G_q. Thus, the expansion step in HITS is primarily a recall-enhancing device. However, this boost in recall sometimes comes at the price of precision.

Consider a set of topics such as proposed by Yahoo!, and for simplicity assume that each Web page belongs to exactly one topic. Experimental evidence [45, 61] suggests that there is locality of content on the Web, that is, if a page is about cycling, following an outlink is more likely to lead to a page about cycling as well, compared to sampling a page uniformly at random from the Web. (The probability that the latter action will get us a page with a specific topic c is the fraction of pages in the Web belonging to topic c.)

This locality works in a very short radius, however. The probability of a page linking to another page of the same topic falls short of one for nontrivial topics, and the more specific the topic is, the smaller is this probability. Within a small number of links, the probability that all nodes have the same topic as the starting point vanishes rapidly.

Expansion by a single link was the maximum that could usually be tolerated by HITS; at radius two, most of the pages would be off-topic and the output of HITS would be largely unsatisfactory. (Indefinite graph expansion with HITS would make it degenerate to a PageRank-like scoring system with no connection to any specific query.) Even at radius one, severe contamination of the root set may occur, especially if pages relevant to the query are often linked to a broader, more densely linked topic. For example, at one time[4] the graph G_q corresponding to the query "movie awards" included a large number of movie company pages such as MGM and Fox, together with a number of hubs linking to them more densely than the subgraph that contained pages related to Oscar, Cannes, and so on. As a result, the hub and authority vectors have large components concentrated in nodes about movies rather than movie awards.

The above example is one of *topic generalization*. Another possible problem is that of *topic drift*. For example, pages on many topics are within a couple of

---

4. Both the Web and HITS have undergone significant evolution, so these specific anecdotes may be transient, although similar examples abound.

links of sites like Netscape, Internet Explorer, and Free Speech Online. Given the popularity of these sites, HITS (and PageRank) runs the danger of raising these sites to the top once they enter the expanded graph. Drift and contamination can sometimes be purposefully engineered, as in Figure 7.5. In effect, a Trojan horse page connected to a large clique can overwhelm any purely graph-based analysis (as in Figure 7.6).

An ad hoc fix is to list known *stop-sites* that would be removed from the expanded graph, but this could have undesirable effects as the notion of a "stop-site" is often context-dependent. For example, for the query "java," *www.java.sun.com/* is a highly desirable site, whereas for a narrower query like "swing," it may be considered too general.

Topic contamination may affect both HITS and PageRank. The top results from HITS may drift away from the query. The PageRank of irrelevant nodes may become unduly large because of membership or proximity to dense subgraphs. Again, a system (such as Google) using PageRank as one of many scores in ranking may be able to avoid problems by using a suitable relative weighting of scores.

7.4 Enhanced Models and Techniques

In this section we will consider hyperlink information in conjunction with text and markup information, model HTML pages at a finer level of detail, and propose enhanced prestige ranking algorithms.

The models that we have discussed thus far offer very simple and elegant representations for hypertext on the Web. Consequently, the mature fields of graph theory and matrix algebra can then be brought to bear. As we have seen in the previous section, such simple graph models break down in a variety of ways. This section offers solutions to some of the problems with the simplistic models.

7.4.1 Avoiding Two-Party Nepotism

Bharat and Henzinger [18] invented a simple and effective fix for two-site nepotism (the B&H algorithm). They observed that ascribing one unit of voting power to each page pointing to a given target may be too extreme, especially if those source pages are all on the same Web site. They proposed that a *site*, not a page, should be the unit of voting power. Therefore, if it is found that k pages on a single host link to a target page, these edges are assigned a weight of $1/k$. This is unlike HITS, where all edges have unit weight.

This modification changes E from a zero-one matrix to one with zeros and positive real numbers. However, EE^T and $E^T E$ remain symmetric, and the rest of the HITS computation goes through as before. In particular, all eigenvectors are guaranteed to be real, and higher-order vectors can be used to identify clusters and link-based communities. Bharat and Henzinger evaluated the weighted scheme with the help of volunteers, who judged the output to be superior to unweighted HITS.

Although it is easy to modify the PageRank formulation to take edge weights into account, it is not publicly known if the implementation of PageRank in Google uses edge weights to avoid two-party (or other forms of) nepotism. Another idea worth experimenting with is to model pages as getting endorsed by *sites*, not single pages, and compute prestige for sites as well, represented by some sort of aggregated supernodes.

Although the B&H edge-weighting scheme reduces the problems of two-host nepotism, multihost nepotism is harder to isolate from a genuinely authoritative Web community. We shall study one approach to reducing that problem in Section 7.4.4.

7.4.2 Outlier Elimination

Bharat and Henzinger [18] observed that keyword search engine responses are largely relevant to the query (even if they are not of the highest quality or popularity). It is the indiscriminate expansion of links that is mostly responsible for contaminating the expanded graph. They devised a content-based mechanism to reduce contamination and resulting drift. Before performing the link expansion, they computed the term vectors of the documents in the root set (using the TFIDF model described in Section 3.2.2) and the centroid μ of these vectors. When the link expansion was performed, any page v that was "too dissimilar" to the centroid μ (i.e., the cosine between the vector representation of v and μ was too small) was discarded, and HITS-like iterations were performed only over the surviving pages.

In HITS, expansion to a radius more than one could be disastrous. Outlier elimination in the B&H algorithm has quite a stabilizing effect on graph expansion, especially if the relevant root set is large. One may envisage a system that continues indefinite expansion and keeps pruning outliers in the vector space. However, the centroid *will* gradually drift, even if much more slowly than in HITS, and eventually the expanded set will bear little relevance to the query. In Chapter 8 we will study techniques to control the expansion of the graph by using supervised learning and other ideas.

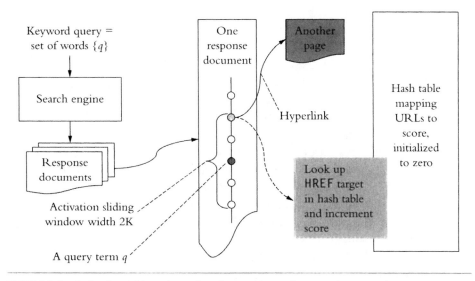

FIGURE 7.8 A simple ranking scheme based on evidence from words near anchors.

7.4.3 Exploiting Anchor Text

There is a simple if crude way in which the initial mapping from a keyword query to a root set followed by the graph expansion can be folded into a single step, in fact, one that does not involve power iterations. Consider each page in the root set not as a single node in a graph, but as a nested graph that is a chain of "micronodes." Each micronode is either a textual token or an outbound hyperlink. Tokens that appear in the query are called *activated*. (Assume for simplicity that the query has no negated token and a phrase is a compound token.)

Prepare a map from URLs to integer counters, initialized to all zeros. Pick a positive integer k. Consider all outbound URLs that are within a distance of k links of any activated node. Increment the counter associated with the URL once for every activated node encountered. Finally, sort the URLs in decreasing order of their counter values and report the top-rated URLs. The procedure, called *Rank-and-File* [36], is illustrated in Figure 7.8. Note that only the root set is required for the analysis.

With some tuning of k, the answers from Rank-and-File are astonishingly good for many broad queries. Note that although pages outside the root set are not fetched (and this makes the method substantially faster than HITS or B&H), URLs outside the root set are being rated. In effect, this method is like spreading an activation from terms to neighboring links.

Just like HITS may return better results than those obtained by sorting by in-degree, the simple one-step procedure above can be improved by bringing power iterations back into it. The simplest way to do this is to tweak the edge weights in the graph on which power iterations are performed. In HITS, all edges have unit weight. Taking the cue from Rank-and-File, we can increase the weights of those hyperlinks whose source micronodes are "close" to query tokens. This is how the Clever[5] project and search system [40] combined HITS and Rank-and-File.

Another modification is to change the shape of the activation window. In Rank-and-File, the activation window used to be a zero-one or rectangular window of width $2k$. Instead, we can make the activation window *decay* continuously on either side of a query token.[6] The activation level of a URL v from page u can be the sum of contributions from all query terms near the HREF to v on u.

The decay is an attempt to reduce authority diffusion, which works reasonably well, even though mixed hubs often have sharp section boundaries. For example, a personal bookmark hub may have a series of sections, each with a list of URLs with corresponding annotations. A query term matching terms in the first annotation of section i may activate the last few URLs in section $(i - 1)$. The heuristics in Clever work reasonably well, partly because not all multisegment hubs will encourage systematic drift toward a fixed topic different from the query topic.

A stock of queries with preranked answers and a great deal of human effort is necessary to make the best choices and tune all the parameters. This was indeed the case with the Clever project; three or four researchers spent a few hours per week over a year running experiments and inspecting results for anomalies.

7.4.4 Exploiting Document Markup Structure

I sketch below the key transitions in modeling Web content that characterize the discussion thus far in this chapter:

HITS: Each page is a node without any textual properties. Each hyperlink is an edge connecting two nodes with possibly only a positive edge weight property. Some preprocessing procedure outside the scope of HITS chooses what subgraph of the Web to analyze in response to a query.

---

5. *Clever* was intended to be an acronym for *client-side eigen vector enhanced retrieval*.

6. Negated terms can be used for the keyword search, but there seems to be no clear way to use them in the activation step.

B&H algorithm: The graph model is as in HITS, except that nodes have additional properties. Each node is associated with a vector-space representation of the text on the corresponding page. After the initial subgraph selection, the B&H algorithm eliminates nodes whose corresponding vectors are far from the typical vector computed from the root set.

Rank-and-File: This replaced the hubs-and-authorities model with a simpler one. Each document is a linear sequence of tokens. Most are terms, some are outgoing hyperlinks. Query terms *activate* nearby hyperlinks. No iterations are involved.

Clever: A page is modeled at two levels. The coarse-grained model is the same as in HITS. At a finer grain, a page is a linear sequence of tokens as in Rank-and-File. Proximity between a query term on page u and an outbound link to page v is represented by increasing the weight of the edge (u, v) in the coarse-grained graph.

All these models are approximations to what HTML-based hypermedia really is. A more faithful view is shown in Figure 7.9. HTML pages are characterized by tag-trees, also called the *document object model* (DOM). DOM trees are interconnected by regular HREFs. (For simplicity, I remove location markers indicated by a # sign from URLs, which occurs in a very small fraction of search engine responses. Therefore, all HREF targets are DOM tree roots.) I will call this the *fine-grained model*.

Segmenting DOM trees

Upon encountering the pages shown in Figures 7.5 or 7.7, a human surfer will have no problem in focusing on links appearing in zone(s) relevant to his interest and avoiding links in other zones. For uniformity, clique attack and mixed hubs will be collectively called *multitopic pages* in this section.

We can name at least two kinds of clues that help users identify relevant zones on a multitopic page. An obvious one is text. In Figure 7.5, the term "cheese" occurs in only a limited area, and likewise for "Shakespeare" in Figure 7.7. The other clue to a zone's promise is its density of links to relevant sites known to the user. I will focus on textual clues for the rest of this discussion.

Perhaps the first idea that comes to mind is to give preferential treatment to DOM subtrees where query terms occur frequently. This scheme will not work very well for some queries, even if we could somehow define what "frequently" means. For example, for the query "Japanese car maker," DOM subtrees with

```
<html> ... <body> ...
<table ...>
<tr><td>
        <table ...>
        <tr><td><a href="http://art.gaz.com">art</a></td></tr>
        <tr><td><a href="http://ski.gaz.com">ski</a></td></tr>...
        </table>
</td></tr>
<tr><td>
        <ul>
        <li><a href="http://www.fromages.com">Fromages.com</a>
        French cheese ... </li>
        <li><a href="http://www.teddingtoncheese.co.uk">Teddington...</a>
        Buy online...</li>
        ...
        </ul>
</td></tr>
</table>...
</body></html>
```

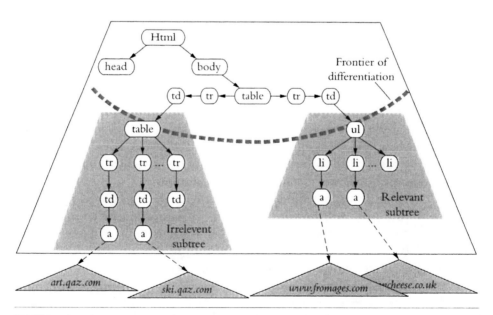

FIGURE 7.9 Characterization of hypertext as a collection of interconnected trees. The HTML tag-tree of a multitopic hub can be segmented into relevant and irrelevant subtrees.

sushi: sushi, japanese, restaurant, page, bar, rice, roll
gardening: garden, home, plants, information, organic, click
bicycling: bike, bicycle, page, site, ride, tour, new, sports
alcoholism: alcohol, treatment, drug, addiction, recovery, abuse
blues: blues, site, festival, jazz, music, new, society

FIGURE 7.10 Despite a few Web-specific words ("click," "site") and mild generalizations ("drug"), the largest components of root set centroid vectors are extremely intuitive.

links to *www.honda.com/* and *www.toyota.com/* rarely use any of the three query words; they instead use just the names of the companies, such as "Honda" and "Toyota." Therefore, depending on direct syntactic matches between query terms and the text in DOM subtrees can be unreliable.

One idea from the B&H algorithm comes to our aid. Even though query terms are difficult to find near good links, the centroid of the root set features "Honda" and "Toyota" with large weights. Other similar examples are shown in Figure 7.10. Therefore, to estimate the relevance of a DOM subtree rooted at node u with regard to a query, we can simply measure the vector-space similarity (like B&H) between the root set centroid and the text in the DOM subtree, associating u with this score.

For a multitopic page (such as the one in Figure 7.5, shown as a DOM in Figure 7.9), what kind of pattern can we expect to see in these scores? If we already knew the frontier of differentiation in Figure 7.9, we would expect the irrelevant subtree (containing the clique attack or nepotistic links) to have a small score and the subtree related to cheese to have a larger score. Above the frontier, these scores would be averaged out somewhat because of the cosine measure (the Jaccard measure described in Section 3.3.1 may do the same). The score at the root of the page in Figure 7.9 would be in between the scores at the relevant subtree root and irrelevant subtree root. By the same token, descendants of the relevant subtree root will also have scores distributed both above and below the subtree root score. So what is special about the frontier?

To answer this question, we need a generative model for the text embedded in the DOM tree. Atomic blocks of text occur only at some leaves in the DOM tree (e.g., between <A> and </A> or between <P> and </P>). We consider these *microdocuments*. Each internal node represents a collection of microdocuments, those that appear as leaves in the subtree rooted at that internal node. We can use any of the generative models discussed in Section 4.4.1 to characterize the

1: **Input:** DOM tree of an HTML page
2: initialize frontier F to the DOM root node
3: **while** local improvement to code length possible **do**
4:      pick from F an internal node u with children $\{v\}$
5:      find the cost of pruning at u (see text)
6:      find the cost of expanding u to all v (see text)
7:      **if** expanding is better **then**
8:          remove u from F
9:          insert all v into F
10:     **end if**
11: **end while**

FIGURE 7.11 Greedy DOM segmentation using MDL.

distribution of terms in a collection of microdocuments. I will represent such a generic term distribution as Φ.

Let the term distribution over all microdocuments over all Web pages in V_q be Φ_0. One may imagine a "superroot" node whose children are the DOM roots of all Web pages in V_q. Then Φ_0 is the term distribution associated with this superroot. Smaller sets of microdocuments about specific topics will have term distributions different from Φ_0. Subtrees concerning different topics in a multitopic page are expected to have somewhat different term distributions.

Given a DOM subtree with root node u, we can greedily decide if it is "pure" or "mixed" by comparing some cost measure for the following two options:

- The tree T_u rooted at u is pure, and a single term distribution Φ_u suffices to generate the microdocuments in T_u with large probability. In this case we *prune* the tree at u.

- u is a point of *differentiation* (see Figure 7.9), and each child v of u has a different term distribution Φ_v from which the microdocuments in their corresponding subtrees were generated. In this case we *expand* the tree at u.

We can start this process at the root and continue expansion until no further expansion is profitable as per the cost measure, as shown in Figure 7.11.

As with applications of the *Minimum Description Length* (MDL) principle (see Section 4.4.5), we can devise a model cost and data cost to drive the search for the frontier. The model cost at DOM node u is the number of bits needed to represent the parameters of Φ_u, denoted $L(\Phi_u)$, which is encoded with regard to some *prior* distribution Π on the parameters (similar to Section 5.6.1), approximately $-\log \Pr(\Phi_u | \Pi)$. The data cost at node u is the cost of encoding all the microdocuments in the subtree T_u rooted at u with regard to the model Φ_u at u, approximately $-\sum_{d \in T_u} \log \Pr(d | \Phi_u)$.

Fine-grained topic distillation

We will now integrate the segmentation step described before into a HITS/B&H-style topic-distillation algorithm.

There is a certain asymmetry between how people interpret hubs and authorities, despite the symmetric formulation of HITS. A good authority page is expected to be dedicated in its entirety to the topic of interest, whereas a hub is acceptable if it has a reasonable number of links relevant to the topic of interest, even if there are some irrelevant links on the page. The asymmetry is reflected in hyperlinks: unless used as navigational aids, hyperlinks to a remote host almost always point to the DOM *root* of the target page.[7]

We will use DOM segmentation to contain the extent of authority diffusion between co-cited pages (like v_1 and v_2 in Figure 7.2) through a multitopic hub u. If we believe that u should be segmented into unrelated regions, we should represent u not as a single node but with one node for each segmented subtree of u, which will have the desirable effect of *disaggregating* the hub score of u, preventing the relevant portion of hub scores from reinforcing the putative authorities linked from irrelevant regions of the hub DOM tree. For example, in Figure 7.9, two nodes would be created, one for the unwanted subtree and one for the favored subtree. We expect that the latter will take an active role in reinforcing good authorities, whereas the former's score will dwindle in comparison. Figure 7.12 illustrates this step.

The complete algorithm is given in Figure 7.13. We allow only the DOM tree roots of root set nodes to have a nonzero authority score when we start, unlike HITS and B&H, which set all scores to positive numbers. We believe that positive authority scores should diffuse out from the root set only if the connecting hub regions are trusted to be relevant to the query. Accordingly, the first half-iteration implements the $\mathbf{h} \leftarrow E\mathbf{a}$ transfer.

For the transfer steps, the graph represented by E does not include any internal nodes of DOM trees. The new steps **segment** and **aggregate** are the only steps

---

7. To be fair, authors avoid linking to internal regions of pages also because the HREF will break if the author of the target pages removes the `<a name...>` marker.

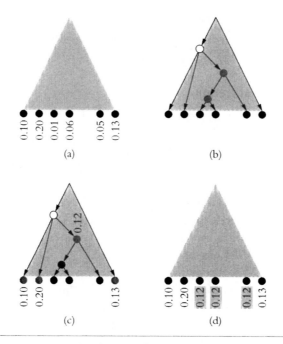

FIGURE 7.12   To prevent unwanted authority diffusion, we aggregate hub scores along the frontier nodes (no complete aggregation up to the DOM root) followed by propagation to the leaves. Initial values of leaf hub scores are indicated (a). Must-prune nodes are marked (b). Frontier microhubs accumulate scores (c). Aggregate hub scores are copied to leaves (d).

that involve internal DOM nodes. Therefore, only DOM roots have positive authority scores, and only DOM leaves (corresponding to HREFs) have positive hub scores.

I have focused on text-based DOM segmentation, but I said near the beginning of Section 7.4.4 that outlinks to known authorities can also help us segment a hub. Specifically, if all large leaf hub scores are concentrated in one subtree of a hub DOM, we may want to limit authority reinforcement to this subtree. At the end of an $\mathbf{h} \leftarrow E\mathbf{a}$ transfer step, we could use only the leaf hub scores (instead of text) to segment the hub DOMs. The general approach to DOM segmentation remains unchanged; we only have to propose a different Φ and Π. When only hub score–based segmentation is used in Figure 7.13, let us call the resulting algorithm DOMHITS. We can also combine clues from text and hub scores [42]. For example, we can pick the shallowest frontier or we can design a joint distribution combining text and hub scores. Let us call such an algorithm DOMTextHITS. We discuss the performance of DOMHITS and DOMTextHITS in the next section.

```
 1:  collect G_q for the query q
 2:  construct the fine-grained graph from G_q
 3:  set all hub and authority scores to zero
 4:  for each page u in the root set do
 5:      locate the DOM root r_u of u
 6:      set a_{r_u} = 1
 7:  end for
 8:  while scores have not stabilized do
 9:      perform the h ← Ea transfer
10:      segment hubs into "microhubs"
11:      aggregate and redistribute hub scores
12:      perform the a ← E^T h transfer
13:      normalize |a|
14:  end while
```

FIGURE 7.13   Fine-grained topic distillation. Note that the vertex set involved in E includes only DOM roots and leaves and *not* other internal nodes. Internal DOM nodes are involved only in the steps marked **segment** and **aggregate**.

7.5   Evaluation of Topic Distillation

The huge success of Google speaks for itself, but then, Google today is much more than just PageRank alone. From the perspective of controlled, reproducible research experiments, it is extremely difficult to evaluate HITS, PageRank, and other similar algorithms in quantitative terms, at least until benchmarks with the extent, detail, and maturity of IR benchmarks are constructed. Currently the evaluation seems largely based on an empirical and subjective notion of authority. As one example of the subjective nature of the formulation, there is no up-front reason why conferral of authority ought to be linear, or even compoundable. In this section I will discuss a few papers that have sought to measure, using human effort and/or machine learning techniques, the efficacy of various algorithms for social network analysis applied to the Web.

7.5.1   HITS and Related Algorithms

Kleinberg's original paper [122] and a follow-up experience report [89] describe a number of experiments with HITS. HITS has been found reasonably insensitive to the exact choice of the root set. This property was tested by picking a root set with 200 nodes and iterating HITS 50 times to derive the "ground truth" set of 10 hubs and 10 authorities, which we may call $C_{10}(200, 50)$, in general, $C_{10}(r, i)$ for r root set pages and i iterations. Figure 7.14 shows the size of intersections

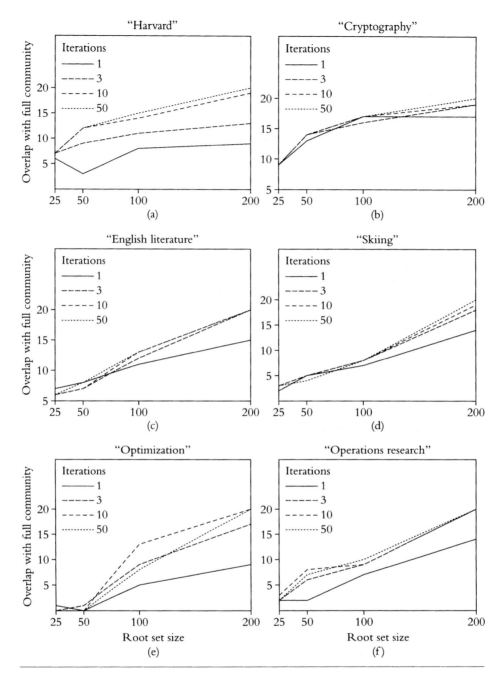

FIGURE 7.14 For six test topics HITS shows relative insensitivity to the root-set size r and the number of iterations i. In each case, the y-axis shows the overlap between the top 10 hubs and top 10 authorities (20 pages total) and the "ground truth" obtained by using $r = 200$ and $i = 50$.

between $C_{10}(200, 50)$ and $C_{10}(r, i)$ for $r = 25, 50, 100, 200$ and $i = 1, 3, 10, 50$ for six topics.

One may also use different search engines to generate the root set. A 1998 study by Bharat and Bröder [16] showed that the portions of the Web covered by major search engines have small overlap. When seeded from different search engines (AltaVista, Infoseek, and Excite) the principal communities (i.e., the communities corresponding to the largest eigenvalue) discovered by HITS were different. Ng et al.'s study [162] of the stability of HITS corroborates this observation. However, the principal community found using one search engine was often found as a nonprincipal community (corresponding to some other eigenvalue) using another search engine. Another way to perturb the root set is to ask the query in different languages, for example, "astrophysics" and "astrophysique." The top authorities in the principal community for the query "astrophysics" were found to largely overlap with the top authorities in a nonprincipal community for the query "astrophysique."

There are two recent careful empirical evaluations of the efficacy of various link-based ranking strategies. Amento et al. [5] chose five queries that corresponded to broad topics in Yahoo! They used Yahoo! to assemble the root set. Some of the rank orderings used were

PR: PageRank as computed over the expanded graph (not large crawls of the Web).

HITS: HITS with B&H edge weights, as described in Section 7.4.1.

IN: The number of sites that link to this site, computed on a coarse site-level graph.

Forty volunteers ranked URLs, which were then used to judge the quality of these orderings. Amento et al. first confirmed that there were large, significant correlations (in the range of 0.6 to 0.8) between the rankings produced by the volunteers, indicating that consistent notions of quality exist. (Otherwise the other measurements would have been pointless.)

From volunteer input, it was found that about a 0.32 fraction of all documents were of high quality, the precision at rank 5 is about 0.75, and the precision at rank 10 about 0.55 using the various link-based rankings, which were all comparable in performance. The correlation between the various ranking methods is shown in Table 7.1. Of course, these numbers do not mean that the notion of "all links are not equal" underlying the HITS family of algorithms is

Topic	IN and HITS	IN and PR	HITS and PR
Babylon 5	0.97	0.93	0.90
Buffy	0.92	0.85	0.70
Simpsons	0.97	0.99	0.95
Smashing Pumpkins	0.95	0.98	0.92
Tori Amos	0.97	0.92	0.88
Spearman average	0.96	0.93	0.87
Kendall average	0.86	0.83	0.75

TABLE 7.1 Authority rank correlation across different ranking strategies shows broad agreement.

invalidated. The queries and communities experimented with were quite different (compare the topics in Figure 7.14 with those in Table 7.1), as were the times of experimentation (1997 and 2000).

Surprisingly, a very simple scoring heuristic called *NumPages* performed quite close to the link-based strategies. NumPages simply set the score of page u to the number of pages published on the host serving the page u, which is a rough indication of how extensive the site is on the topic of the query. This measure was surprisingly strongly correlated with authority scores.

The second user study has been conducted by Singhal and Kaszkiel [195]. The National Institute of Standards and Technology (*trec.nist.gov/*) organizes an annual IR competition called the Text REtrieval Conference (TREC). Since 1998, TREC has added a "Web Track" featuring 500,000 to 700,000 pages from a 1997 Web crawl collected by the Internet Archive [99] and real-life queries collected from commercial search engine logs. The top 1000 results returned by competition participants are assessed by TREC personnel to generate precision scores (see Section 3.2.1). The goal in this competition is not to compile a collection of high-quality links about a topic, but to locate the obvious page/site from a keyword description. Although this task is not directly comparable to topic distillation, the results of the study are quite instructive, the main result being that link-based ranking strategies decisively beat a state-of-the-art IR system on Web workloads (see Figure 7.15).

7.5.2 Effect of Exploiting Other Hypertext Features

Clever [40] was evaluated using 26 queries first used in the *Automatic Resource Compilation* (ARC) system [38] and later by Bharat and Henzinger [18]. Clever,

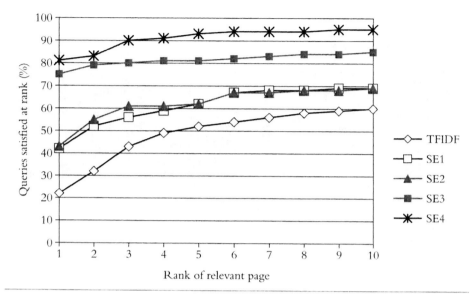

FIGURE 7.15 Link-based ranking beats a traditional text-based IR system by a clear margin for Web workloads. One hundred queries were evaluated. The x-axis shows the smallest rank where a relevant page was found, and the y-axis shows how many out of the 100 queries were satisfied at that rank. A standard TFIDF ranking engine is compared with four well-known Web search engines (Raging Search, Lycos, Google, and Excite). Their respective identities have been withheld in this chart by Singhal and Kaszkiel [195].

Yahoo!, and AltaVista were compared. AltaVista and Clever directly used the query as shown in Figure 7.16. For Yahoo!, the query was mapped manually to the best-matching leaf category. The top 10 pages were picked from AltaVista, the top 5 hubs and authorities were picked using Clever, and 10 random URLs were picked from Yahoo!. These were rated as bad, fair, good, and fantastic by 37 volunteers, with good and fantastic ratings regarded as relevant. Clever won in 50% of the queries; Clever and Yahoo! tied in 38% of the queries; Yahoo! won in 19% of the queries; and AltaVista never beat the others.[8]

---

8. Results today are likely to differ; since our experiments, most search engines appear to have incorporated some link-based ranking strategy.

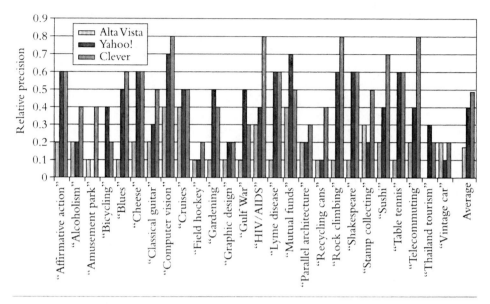

FIGURE 7.16 In studies conducted in 1998 over 26 queries and 37 volunteers, Clever reported better authorities than Yahoo!, which in turn was better than AltaVista. Since then, most search engines have incorporated some notion of link-based ranking.

Experiments based on the same query collection were also used for evaluating the B&H topic system, again using volunteer input. Results shown in Figure 7.17 show relative precision for HITS, HITS enhanced with edge weights to fight two-host nepotism, and this in turn enhanced with outlier elimination (documents with similarity better than median to the centroid of the base set were retained). Significant improvements are seen in the precision judgments.

DOMHITS and DOMTextHITS show visible resistance to topic drift as compared to HITS [42]. These experiments did not depend on volunteers. Instead, the following strategy was used:

1.   The Open Directory from *dmoz.org* (a topic taxonomy like Yahoo!) was massaged to form a classification system with about 250 classes covering most major topics on the Web, together with at least 1000 sample URLs per topic.

2.   A text classifier called Rainbow (see Chapter 5) was trained on these classes.

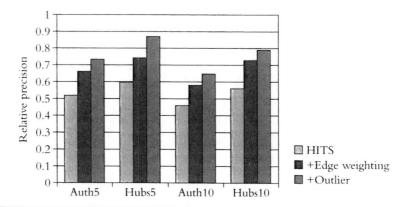

FIGURE 7.17 B&H improves visibly beyond the precision offered by HITS. ("Auth5" means the top five authorities were evaluated.) Edge weighting against two-site nepotism already helps, and outlier elimination improves the results further.

3. A few topics (/Arts/Music/Styles/classical/Composers, /Arts/Visual_Arts, /Business/Human_Resources, and /Computers/Security) were chosen from the complete set of topics for experimentation. For each chosen topic, 200 URLs were sampled at random from the available examples to form the root set.

4. HITS, DOMHITS, and DOMTextHITS were run starting from each of these root sets.

5. For each class/topic c, the top 40 authorities, excluding pages already in the root set, were submitted to the Rainbow classifier. For each such document d, Rainbow returned a Bayesian estimate of $\Pr(c|d)$, the posterior probability that document d was generated from (i.e., is relevant to) topic c.

6. By linearity of expectation, $\sum_d \Pr(c|d) = \sum_d E([d \in c]) = E(\sum_d [d \in c])$ is the expected number of authorities relevant to c, which is a measure of "staying on topic."

Figure 7.18 shows that across the topic, DOMTextHITS is more resistant to topic drift than DOMHITS, which is more resistant than HITS. How do DOMHITS and DOMTextHITS resist drift? Figure 7.19 shows the number of DOM nodes pruned (that is, judged to be on the frontier) and expanded in the first few iterations of the while-loop in Figure 7.13 (using DOMHITS). Two queries are shown. For the first query, "bicycling," there is no danger of drift, and the number of pruned nodes increases quickly, while the number of

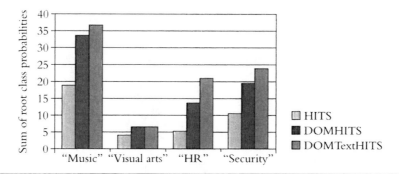

FIGURE 7.18   Top authorities reported by DOMTextHITS have the highest probability of being relevant to the Open Directory topic whose samples were used as the root set, followed by DOMHITS and finally HITS. This means that topic drift is smallest in DOMTextHITS.

expanded nodes falls. This means that DOMHITS accepts a large number of pages as pure hubs. For the other query, "affirmative action," there is a clique attack from popular software sites owing to a shareware of that name. In this case, the number of expanded nodes keeps increasing with subsequent iterations, meaning that DOMHITS rightly suspects mixed hubs and expands the frontier until they reach leaf DOM nodes, suppressing unwanted reinforcement.

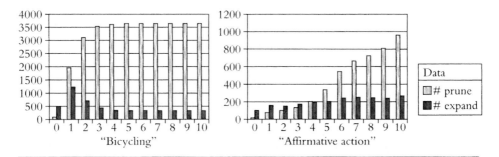

FIGURE 7.19   The number of nodes pruned vs. expanded may change significantly across iterations of DOMHITS, but stabilizes within 10–20 iterations. For base sets where there is no danger of drift, there is a controlled induction of new nodes into the response set owing to authority diffusion via relevant DOM subtrees. In contrast, for queries that led HITS/B&H to drift, DOMHITS continued to expand a relatively larger number of nodes in an attempt to suppress drift.

7.6 Measuring and Modeling the Web

So far in this chapter we have discussed a variety of techniques for analyzing the Web graph and exploiting it for better searches. Most of these techniques depend implicitly on *locality* in various guises, for example, textual similarity, link neighborhoods, and page structure. Furthermore, although actions such as adding or removing pages, terms, and links are local, they can be characterized by very robust global properties.

Early works on the theory of random graphs (with a fixed number of nodes n) have studied various properties such as the number of connected components and vertex connectivity under very simple edge creation models, a common one being that each of the $n(n - 1)$ potential edges is materialized with a fixed probability p. It is hardly surprising that these models are not very suitable for the Web: the Web graph was obviously not created by materializing edges independently at random.

7.6.1 Power-Law Degree Distributions

One of the earliest regularities in Web structure to be measured and modeled has been the *degree distribution* of pages, both in-degree and out-degree. To a first approximation, Web page degree follows the *power-law distribution:*

$$\Pr(\text{out-degree is } k) \propto 1/k^{a_{\text{out}}} \tag{7.19}$$

$$\Pr(\text{in-degree is } k) \propto 1/k^{a_{\text{in}}} \tag{7.20}$$

This property has been preserved modulo small changes in a_{out} and a_{in} as the Web has grown, and this has been experimentally verified by a number of people.

It is easy to fit data to these power-law distributions, but that does not explain how largely autonomous page and link creation processes can end up producing such a distribution. An early success in this direction came from the work of Barabási and Albert [13]. They proposed that the graph (let it be undirected to simplify the following discussion) continually adds nodes to increase in size, as is eminently the case with the Web. They also proposed a key property in their model called *preferential attachment*, which dictates that a new node is linked to existing nodes not uniformly at random, but with higher probability to existing nodes that already have large degree, a "winners take all" scenario that is not far removed from reality in most social networks.

The graph starts with m_0 nodes. Time proceeds in discrete steps. In each step, one node is added. This new node u comes with a fixed number of m edges $(m \le m_0)$, which connect to nodes already existing in the graph. Suppose at this timestep an existing node v is incident on d_v existing edges. Associate v with a probability $p_v = d_v / \sum_w d_w$, where w ranges over all existing nodes. Node u makes m choices for neighbors. For each trial, node v is chosen with probability p_v.

If this system evolves for t timesteps, the resulting graph has $m_0 + t$ nodes and mt edges, and therefore the total degree over all nodes is $2mt$. Let us approximate the degree $k_i(t)$ of node i at timestep t as a continuous random variable. Let $\kappa_i(t)$ be shorthand for $E(k_i(t))$. At time t, the infinitesimal expected growth rate of κ_i is $m \times \frac{\kappa_i}{2mt} = \frac{\kappa_i}{2t}$, by linearity of expectation. Thus we can write $\partial \kappa_i / \partial t = \kappa_i / 2t$, which leads to the solution

$$\kappa_i(t) = m \sqrt{\frac{t}{t_i}} \tag{7.21}$$

by enforcing the boundary condition $\kappa_i(t_i) = m$.

Next let us find the number of nodes i at time t that have $\kappa_i(t) > k$ for some fixed k. For $\kappa_i(t) > k$ to be true, we need $t_i < m^2 t / k^2$, and therefore the fraction of nodes that satisfies this condition is $\frac{m^2 t}{(m_0 + t)k^2}$ because the total number of nodes is $m_0 + t$ at this time. Approximating k to be a continuous variable as well, and differentiating with regard to k, we get that the fraction of nodes having expected degree k is roughly

$$-\frac{\partial}{\partial k} \frac{m^2 t}{(m_0 + t)k^2} = \frac{2m^2 t}{(m_0 + t)k^3} \tag{7.22}$$

This establishes the power law with an exponent of three. If the system runs for a long time ($t \to \infty$), the degree distribution of the resulting graph becomes independent of m_0, the only arbitrary parameter in the model.

Exponents from Web measurements differ from 3; they range between 2.1 and 2.5 (see Figure 7.20). One reason could be that the simple linear model for probability of attachment may not be very accurate. Power-law degree distributions have been confirmed by a number of other measurements, such as by Bröder and others [28].

Closer inspection of additional data showed that the pure power-law model does not fit well for low values of k. It appeared that winners did not quite take all—the degree distribution actually has a peak at a modest value of k. The preferential attachment model above does not explain this phenomenon.

A refinement that has been found to improve the fit is the following two-choice behavior in generating links: With some probability d, the newly generated node will link uniformly at random to an existing node. With probability $(1 - d)$, the earlier preferential attachment rule would be followed. Basically, the mixing parameter d gives as-yet unpopular pages a chance to eventually attain prominence.

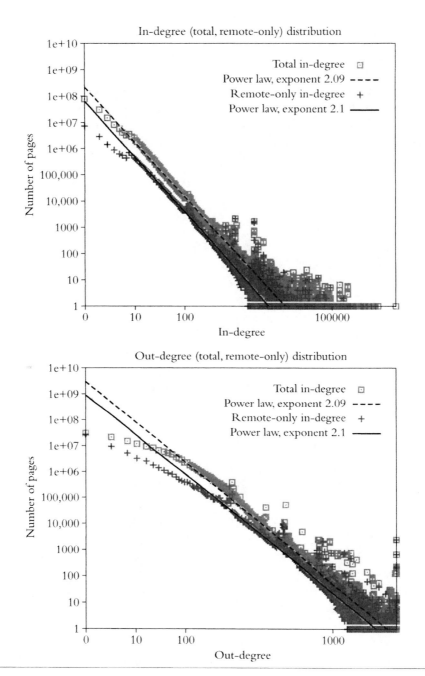

FIGURE 7.20   The in- and out-degree of Web nodes closely follow power-law distributions, except at low degrees.

7.6.2   The "Bow Tie" Structure and Bipartite Cores

In November 1999, Bröder et al. [28] mapped a large Web crawl containing over 200 million nodes to expose the large-scale structure of the Web graph as having a central, strongly connected core (SCC); a subgraph (IN) with directed paths leading into the SCC, a component (OUT) leading away from the SCC, and relatively isolated tendrils attached to one of the three large subgraphs. These four regions were each about a fourth the size of the Web, which led the authors to call this the "bow tie" model of the Web (see Figure 7.21). They also measured interesting properties like the average path lengths between connected nodes and the distribution of in- and out-degree. Follow-up work by Dill et al. [70] showed that subgraphs selected from the Web as per specific criteria (domain restriction, occurrence of keyword, etc.) also appear to often be bow tie–like, although the ratio of component sizes varies somewhat. There are no theories predicting the formation of a bow tie in a social network, unlike power-law degree distributions. We do not even know if the bow tie will be the most prominent structure in the Web graph 10 years from now.

Kumar et al. [128] wrote programs to search a large crawl of the Web for bipartite cores (e.g., those that take an active role in topic–distillation algorithms). They discovered tens of thousands of bipartite cores and empirically observed that a large fraction are in fact topically coherent. A small bipartite core is often an indicator of an emerging topic that may be too fine-grained to be cataloged manually into Web directories.

7.6.3   Sampling Web Pages at Random

Many of the measurements discussed in this section involve sampling the Web. The precision of some of the estimated parameters clearly depends on the uniformity of the sample obtained.

We must be careful how we define "sampling from the Web," because the Web has dynamic pages generated in response to an unlimited number of possible queries, or an unlimited variety of browser cookies. The Web also has malicious or accidental "spider traps," which are infinite chains and trees of pages generated by a combination of soft links, CGI scripts, and Web server mappings. Clearly, we need to settle on a finite graph before we can measure the quality of a sample.

As a result of an ongoing race, Web crawlers do a good job of avoiding such pitfalls while collecting pages to index, although this may mean that they leave out some safely indexable pages (see Chapter 2). We may use this notion of a

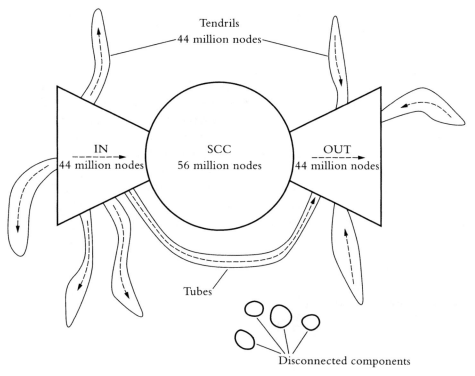

Region:	SCC	IN	OUT	Tendrils	Disconnected	Total
Size:	56,463,993	43,343,168	43,166,185	43,797,944	16,777,756	203,549,046

FIGURE 7.21 The Web as a bow tie [28].

public, indexable subset of the Web as our universe and consider sampling in the context of this universe. This is not a precise characterization either, because the Web is not strongly connected, and therefore what ground a crawler can cover depends on the starting point.

To make progress without getting bogged down by the above technicalities, let us set up the problem from a perspective of a fixed crawling strategy, starting from a fixed set of pages. Assume for simplicity that the Web does not change while the crawl completes. At the end of the crawl, the crawler may output the set of all URLs crawled. From this set, a URL may be readily sampled uniformly at random. The key question is: *Can a URL be sampled uniformly at random without undertaking a full crawl?*

Why is uniform sampling of URLs from the Web of interest? I will propose a few applications. Sampling may be used to quickly and approximately answer aggregate queries about the Web, such as "What fraction of Web pages are in the .co.jp domain?" Answering such a question may help balance crawling load across a distributed team of crawlers. Assuming one has a reasonably reliable classifier for a given topic taxonomy such as Yahoo!, one may ask what fraction of Web pages belongs to each of the topics. This may be useful for channeling effort toward cataloging topics for that the taxonomy is underrepresented in proportion to the Web. Such measurements can be extended to links. One may sample links and classify the two endpoints to estimate how often a page related to one topic links to a page on another topic. Clusters of densely connected topics may be used to redesign or reorganize topic taxonomies. In the rest of this section, we will study a progression of ideas for uniform sampling from the Web.

PageRank-like random walk

One way to approximate a random sample is to implement a suitable random walk on the graph to be crawled. If the graph satisfies certain properties, a random walk is guaranteed to visit nodes at a rate that quickly approaches the stationary distribution of prestige given in Equation (7.7), forgetting any effects of the starting point with high probability.

Henzinger and others [105] propose to use the "random surfer" notion underlying PageRank (see Section 7.2.1) directly to derive random samples. Recall the transition matrix L used there, and also recall the uniform jump to avoid getting trapped somewhere in the Web graph. The uniform jump can be modeled as a simple *jump matrix* $J = \frac{1}{N}\boxed{1_N}$, where $N = |V|$. As we discussed before, the random surfer uses J with probability d and L with the remaining probability $1 - d$. Thus, as in Equation 7.9,

$$\mathbf{p}_{i+1} = \left(dJ + (1-d)L^T\right)\mathbf{p}_i \tag{7.23}$$

or

$$p_{i+1}[v] = \frac{d}{|V|} + (1-d)\sum_{(u,v)\in E}\frac{p_i[u]}{N_u}$$

Because all elements of J are positive and $0 < d < 1$, $(dJ + (1 - d)L^T)$ represents an irreducible and aperiodic Markovian transition process with a unique, well-defined stationary distribution that is the principal eigenvector of $(dJ + (1 - d)L^T)$.

Unfortunately, in an actual implementation of the random surfer, there is no way to jump to a random node in V, because that is the problem we are trying to solve! Henzinger et al. approximate the jump by running 1000 walks at the same time that use a pooled collection of URLs visited thus far to implement the jump. This introduces what is called the *initial bias,* which tends to keep the surfer closer to the starting set of URLs than would be the case if a truly random jump were possible.

The basic approach here is to first run a random walk for some time, then sample from the page set thus collected. For any page v,

$$\Pr(v \text{ is sampled}) = \Pr(v \text{ is crawled})\ \Pr(v \text{ is sampled}|v \text{ is crawled}) \qquad (7.24)$$

We must set $\Pr(v \text{ is sampled}|v \text{ is crawled})$ in a way such that $\Pr(v \text{ is sampled})$ is the same for all v. To do this, we need to first estimate $\Pr(v \text{ is crawled})$.

Let the steady-state PageRank vector corresponding to Equation (7.23) be $\mathbf{p}^*$. In a sufficiently long walk that visits w nodes in all, we would expect node v to be visited $w\,p^*[v]$ times. Even much shorter walks of about $\sqrt{|V|}$ hops, if limited to the SCC of the Web, are also expected to suffice. Most nodes will appear at most once in short walks of length at most $\sqrt{|V|}$. (This is similar to the claim that you need about $\sqrt{365}$ people in a party before you get 2 people with the same birthday.) Under this assumption, we can approximate

$$\Pr(v \text{ is crawled}) = E(\text{number of times } v \text{ is visited}) \qquad (7.25)$$
$$= w\,p^*[v]$$

From Equations (7.24) and (7.25), it is clear that we must set

$$\Pr(v \text{ is sampled}|v \text{ is crawled}) \propto 1/p^*[v] \qquad (7.26)$$

Again, we cannot know $\mathbf{p}^*$ and must approximate it. The simple solution is to use the actual *visit ratio* of each page, that is, the number of visits to each page divided by the walk length. This is not perfect, because the visit ratio is discrete and has large jumps compared to the smallest PageRank values.

Given the approximations and biases involved, how can we evaluate the quality of such sampling algorithms? Since we cannot hope to "know" the whole Web graph, it is best to generate a finite, unchanging, artificial graph that resembles the

Web graph in some important properties (such as degree distribution). Now one can sample from this graph and thus generate, say, a sampled degree distribution. Comparing this with the true degree distribution will give an indication of the uniformity of the algorithm. In fact, any property can be arbitrarily assigned to each node (such as two colors, red and blue) and the sample properties compared with the global properties (e.g., fraction of red nodes).

Henzinger et al. generated synthetic graphs with controlled in- and out-degree distributions and compared the true degree distributions with those derived from their sampling algorithms. The results, shown in Figure 7.22, show negligible deviations for out-degree distribution and small deviations for in-degree distribution. They also explore a number of applications of random sampling, such as estimating the fraction of URLs in various top-level domains and estimating search engine coverage.

Random walk on a regular graph

The probability "inversion," Equation (7.26), is problematic with a large number of nodes that are never visited during short walks. In an attempt to reduce this

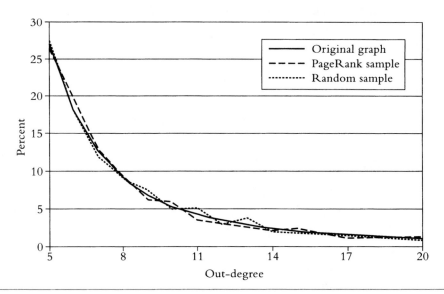

FIGURE 7.22 Random walks based on PageRank give sample distributions that are close to the true distribution used to generate the graph data, in terms of out-degree, in-degree, and PageRank.

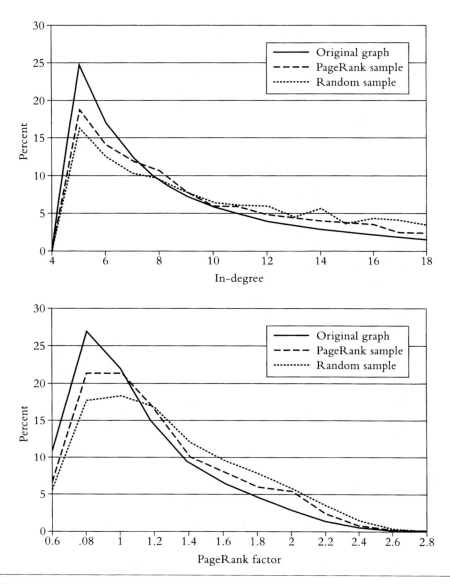

FIGURE 7.22   *(continued)*

problem, Bar-Yossef and others [12] seek to alter the graph in such a way that a sufficiently long random walk leads *directly* to a uniform sample.

It is easy to see that a vector with all elements set to $1/|V|$ is an eigenvector for the adjacency matrix of an undirected graph where every node has the same degree. It also turns out that this is the principal eigenvector [91]. Therefore, if only the Web graph were undirected and regular (i.e., all nodes have the same degree), we would be done.

Bar-Yossef et al. force these two properties to roughly hold for the graph they walk, in the following manner. First, when making a transition from one node u to the next, candidates are considered not only from out-neighbors of u but also in-neighbors of u. (This can be done by a "backlink" query interface, provided by many search engines.) Thus the Web graph is in effect rendered undirected. Second, the degree of all nodes is equalized by adding $N_{max} - N_v$ *self-loops* to node v, where N_{max} is the maximum degree.

You may immediately protest that using a search engine to find backlinks voids our goal stated on page 248. This criticism is valid, but for many applications, including crawling, an older crawl is available to approximately answer the backlink queries. That the backlink database is incomplete and out of date introduces yet other biases into the strategy, requiring empirical checks that their effects are mild. The "ideal" walk (if the backlink database were complete and up to date) and the realistic implementation WebWalker are shown in Figure 7.23. The key modification is that WebWalker maintains its own in- and out-neighbor list for each node, and this must not be modified once created, even if new paths are found to nodes as the crawl proceeds. It turns out that, like Henzinger's random walk, WebWalker also needs a random jump to take it out of tight cycles and cliques [14], but this is not shown in the pseudocode for simplicity.

As with the PageRank-based random walk, one can stage sampling problems where the answer is known. Bar-Yossef et al. used a real Web crawl with between 100 and 200 million nodes collected by Alexa Internet (*www.alexa.com*) in 1996. They sorted the nodes in that crawl by degree and computed the deciles of the degree distribution. Next they performed a random walk on this graph and collected the samples into buckets according to the same deciles. If the sample is unbiased, each bucket should have about one-tenth of the pages in the sample. Figure 7.24 shows that this is the case except for some bias toward high-degree nodes, which is expected.

1: Ideal Random Walk:
2: pick starting node
3: **for** given walk length **do**
4: consider current node v on the walk
5: self-loop at v a random number of times,
    which is distributed geometrically with mean $1 - \dfrac{N_v}{N_{\max}}$
6: pick the next node uniformly at random from in- and out-neighbors of v
7: **end for**

1: WebWalker:
2: pick start node u and set $I_u = O_u = \emptyset$
3: **for** given walk length **do**
4: consider current node v on the walk
5: **if** v has not been visited before **then**
6:   get in-neighbors of v using a search engine
7:   get out-neighbors of v by scanning for HREFs
8:   add new neighbors w to I_v and O_v only if w has not been visited already
9: **end if**
10: self-loop at v as in the Ideal Random Walk
11: pick the next node uniformly at random from $I_v \cup O_v$
12: **end for**

FIGURE 7.23 Random walks on regular graphs derived from the Web graph.

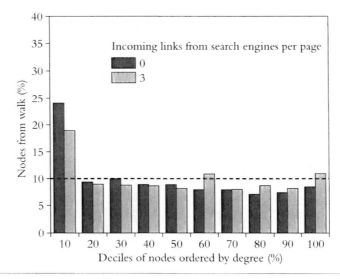

FIGURE 7.24 Random walks performed by WebWalker give reasonably unbiased URL samples; when sampled URLs are bucketed along degree deciles in the complete data source, close to 10% of the sampled URLs fall into each bucket.

7.7 **Bibliographic Notes**

An in-depth treatment of social network theory dating from the 1950s and prior to the growth of the Web can be found in the classic text by Wasserman and Faust [210]. Larson [132] and Pirolli and Pitkow [174] discuss document clustering based on combinations of text and link attributes. In the context of the Web, hyperlink-based authority rating systems were first reported by Page and Brin [26, 169] and Kleinberg [122]. Carriere and Kazman proposed an early system for visual searching and ranking using hyperlinks [33]. Kleinberg's HITS system was improved by a number of research efforts such as Clever [40] and topic distillation [18]. Gibson and others studied convergence properties of HITS, as well as graph clusters identified by multiple eigenvectors output by HITS [89]. Barabási and Albert were among the first to analyze the degree distribution of the Web graph and propose models to explain it [13]. Later work by Pennock and others [172] showed that winners do not take all; a slight modification to the model of Barabási and Albert shows a much better fit to Web data. Alternative models that explain the power-law degree distribution have been proposed by Kumar and others [128]. Bharat and Bröder were among the first to consider sampling Web pages systematically in order to find the sizes of and overlaps in the crawl graphs collected by major search engines [16]. The PageRank-based sampling technique is due to Henzinger and others [105]. The regular graph sampling idea is due to Bar-Yossef and others [12].

CHAPTER 8

RESOURCE DISCOVERY

General-purpose crawlers take a centralized, snapshot view of what is essentially a completely distributed hypermedium in uncontrolled flux. They seek to collect and process the entire contents of the Web in a centralized location, where it can be indexed in advance to be able to respond to any possible query. Meanwhile, the Web, already having two billion pages, keeps growing and changing to make centralized processing more difficult. An estimated 600 GB worth of pages changed per month in 1997 alone [120].

In its initial days, most of the Web could be collected by small- to medium-scale crawlers. From 1996 to 1999, coverage was a very stiff challenge: from an estimated coverage of 35% in 1997 [16], crawlers dropped to a coverage of only 18% in 1999 [131]. After 1999, the growth of the Web slackened and wide-area network connectivity improved, resulting in a 45% to 55% coverage by Google by 2000.

As we have seen in Chapter 2, hardware and software are not significant issues for Web-scale crawling. The bulk of the cost is in high-speed network access, reliable and scalable storage, and system administration. These costs have taken Web-scale crawling out of the reach of amateurs and individual researchers. Although the Internet Archive (*www.archive.org*) fetches hundreds of gigabytes a day and makes the collection available in the public domain, researchers still need to get the data shipped and arrange for local storage of several terabytes.

It has also been clear for some time that crawlers need not cover all corners of the Web to be effective. In fact, Chapter 7 indicates otherwise: when there is an abundance of information, we can afford to be choosy about which pages to index and how to rank them. In particular, for Google/PageRank, pages with very low prestige are largely useless in responding to queries. If we consider Google's most frequent queries, and compile the set of response URLs actually viewed by the users (or even the top ten responses presented to the user), this set might be a small fraction of Google's crawled collection.

Therefore, a natural question is, given finite crawling resources (time, network bandwidth, storage), is it possible to prioritize the crawl frontier to preferentially collect and/or refresh pages? A variety of goals may guide the priority assignment:

- We may prefer to crawl pages with high prestige, which would be the case with most modern search engines.

- Pages that change frequently may be preferable for some applications, like news portals.

- For a so-called vertical portal that intends to cater to queries pertaining to one or a few broad topics, we may wish to build only an index of pages relevant to these topics.

A general way of thinking about these settings is that we are given a few starting nodes in the Web graph, and our goal is to seek out and collect other nodes that satisfy some specific requirement of the form given in the list above. The computation required to figure out whether a page satisfies the requirement, or which links to follow next, may be centralized or distributed. If the system is centralized, it may still be considered in the same league as crawlers. A distributed design will generally be described as a federation of *agents*.

In this chapter, we will discuss some of the distinct paradigms for locating desired resources in distributed hypertext. We will not make a precise distinction between architecture choices, such as crawlers and agents. Our emphasis will be on the application of techniques from previous chapters to solve resource discovery problems. This chapter is mostly about synthesizing the basic ideas in previous chapters into working systems for resource discovery.

Notwithstanding the fact that the largest crawlers cover over half the public Web, recent years have seen a spate of research in resource discovery. This is partly because the statistics above tell an incomplete story. Three interrelated factors decide the efficacy of a search engine: the extent of coverage, the ability to react to rapid flux, and the depth of analysis of the collected contents for query processing. A crawler can have large coverage but rarely refresh its crawls. At the time of writing, Google refreshes its crawl at least once a month, but pages are generally refreshed at most as often as once every four hours. A crawler can have good coverage and fast refresh rates, but not have good ranking functions or support advanced query capabilities that need more processing power. Search engines do not reveal their ranking function, let alone allow advanced users to plug in personalized, experimental ranking functions. As vector-space ranking yields to link-assisted ranking, which in turn adds on more linguistic processing and feature extraction, researchers are increasingly turning to resource discovery systems to build custom document collections to evaluate their ideas.

8.1 Collecting Important Pages Preferentially

Search engines increasingly use link-based prestige measures to rank responses. Link-based ranking is central to Google's success. Other search engines do not publicize if and how their ranking strategies depend on links, but their ranking quality has clearly improved in similar ways. For a crawler that collects Web pages for such a search engine, it is more valuable to crawl a page that is likely to have a large PageRank as compared to an obscure page. More generally, one may want to collect Web pages with large in-degree (indicating authority), out-degree (generally indicating large coverage, although this may be useless for mixed hubs; see Section 7.4.4), PageRank (had the whole Web graph been available), or similarity to a driving query. The *importance* of a page u, which could be any of the above notions, is denoted $I(u)$.

8.1.1 Crawling as Guided Search in a Graph

A crawler may be modeled as starting from one page u_0, crawling K pages, and stopping. A perfect crawler would crawl those K pages with the largest importance reachable from u_0, called $u_1, \ldots, u_K$ with $I(u_1) \geq \ldots \geq I(u_K)$. An imperfect crawler will also crawl K pages, but only M out of those will have importance of at least $I(u_K)$. Then the measure of merit of the imperfect crawler will be defined as M/K. An alternative model may fix an importance threshold τ instead. Any page u with $I(u) > \tau$ is *hot*. If there are H hot pages and a crawler fetches K of them, the measure of merit is K/H. If a perfect crawler fetched at least H pages, its measure of merit will be one.

Some measures of importance (such as in-degree, out-degree, or PageRank) can be evaluated only after the page and some significant neighborhood has been fetched. Therefore, practical crawlers have to use heuristic guidance to decide what page to fetch next. In-degree can be approximated by the current number

```
 1:  enqueue starting URL into the URL frontier queue F
 2:  while F ≠ ∅ do
 3:     dequeue unvisited URL u from F
 4:     fetch the page corresponding to u and scan for outlinks
 5:     for each outlink URL v found do
 6:        add (u, v) to link database unless already there
 7:        if v is not already visited then
 8:           enqueue v into F
 9:        end if
10:     end for
11:     reorganize F according to priority ordering
12:  end while
```

FIGURE 8.1 The generic template used by Cho et al., with different ordering policies used in the reorganization of *F*.

of links known by the crawler to lead to the page, and PageRank can likewise be computed using the graph known by the crawler at the current moment. But out-degree or similarity to a driving query cannot be determined before fetching the page. (However, one can make intelligent guesses about the term distribution; see Section 8.3.)

Cho et al. [50] empirically studied the effect of various URL prioritization strategies on the measures of merit defined above. To perform controlled, repeatable experiments, they precrawled all Stanford University Web servers and collected roughly 200,000 pages in a hypertext repository as their "universe." This permitted them to compute the importance attributes and later quickly evaluate crawlers with various priority choices (see Figure 8.1).

Because many page/node properties cannot be determined before a page is fetched, approximations based on the graph fetched by the crawler must be used. The effects of approximate priorities on the quality of crawls is complex and sometimes unintuitive. Let us set our importance measure to in-degree. The crawler may use a number of approximate priority schemes to order page fetches:

- The number $I'(u)$ of inlinks to the target URL u currently known to the crawler.

- The PageRank $R'(u)$ of the target URL u computed using the graph collected so far by the crawler.

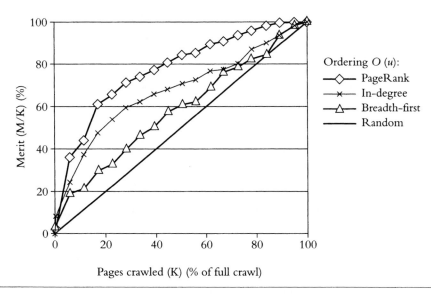

FIGURE 8.2 An approximate PageRank priority ordering helps the crawler find large in-degree nodes faster than an approximate in-degree priority ordering. Breadth-first or random priority are understandably worse. The importance threshold measure is used here.

As shown in Figure 8.2, I' and R' both collect hot pages faster than breadth-first crawling or random crawling, but surprisingly, R' performs better than I'.

More recently, Najork and Weiner [158] ran a crawler with a simple breadth-first prioritization to collect over 328 million pages from the entire Web, covering more than 7 million distinct hosts. They used PageRank as the importance measure and found that pages with the highest PageRank are found very quickly upon starting a breadth-first crawler from *www.yahoo.com*. A plot of normalized average PageRank per days of crawl is shown in Figure 8.3.

8.1.2 Keyword-Based Graph Search

The priority heuristics discussed so far used graph properties of pages, but one may also use IR-based properties of the pages, such as keywords that occur on the pages crawled. One may point to a specific page and look for pages in "the vicinity" (suitably defined) that contain a specified word. One may wish to preferentially collect and display a graph of the vicinity to highlight nodes matching the specified keywords.

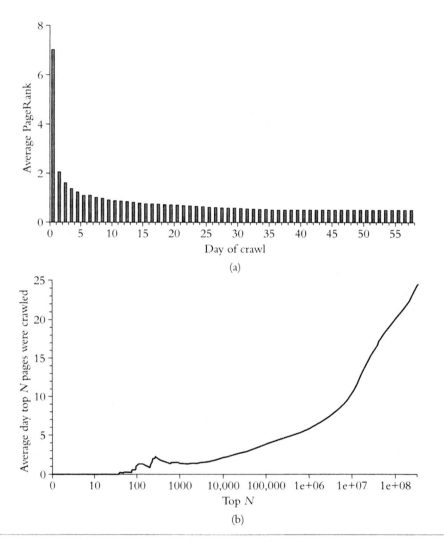

FIGURE 8.3 Pages fetched early by a breadth-first crawler have high PageRank. Average PageRank of each page is scaled to one, and daily average PageRank is plotted against the age of the crawl (a). The average day by which the N most important pages (with largest PageRank) were crawled is plotted against N (b).

A very early system for hypertext graph exploration driven by a query was the FISHSEARCH system designed by De Bra and Post [63, 64]. It can be run as a client-side search tool or provided as a central service similar to search engines.[1] The user provides a starting URL and a match condition, which could be a set of keywords or a regular expression (external page filters can also be installed). Instead of a user-provided start URL, a search engine may be used to obtain the start URL(s). The FISHSEARCH system simulates a school of fish, breeding and searching for food. Each page corresponds to a fish. If the page has "food," that is, it matches the search condition, the fish "breeds" and creates offsprings, which explore the neighborhood, breeding in turn if the neighborhood matches the driving query.

FISHSEARCH simulates the fish using a priority queue of unvisited URLs; at each step the first URL on the queue is fetched. As the text of a page becomes available, a scoring module decides whether to expand unvisited links from that page. A global depth bound is specified by the user. If a page u survives the scoring check, its outlinks are inserted into the priority queue with the same depth as u; otherwise, the outlink depth is set to one less than the depth of u. If the depth reaches zero, the outlink is discarded. FISHSEARCH capitalizes on the intuition that relevant documents often have relevant neighbors, an intuition I will formalize and use in Section 8.3.

Hersovici et al. [107] improved the FISHSEARCH algorithm to propose a more aggressive variant, the SHARKSEARCH algorithm. Rather than assign priority scores from a small set of discrete values, SHARKSEARCH used a standard TFIDF- and cosine-based relevance score (see Chapter 3), which is a continuous score between zero and one. Instead of using a discrete depth cutoff, SHARKSEARCH uses a continuous *fading* or *decay* factor $0 < \delta < 1$, which let an unvisited URL v "inherit" δ times the relevance of nodes u linking to v, δ^2 times the relevance of node w with a length-2 path to v, and so on. Figure 8.4 shows samples of FISHSEARCH and SHARKSEARCH in action.

Cho et al. [50] also experimented with keyword-sensitive crawling strategies. For the purpose of their application, they defined the following notion of importance: a page is hot if the word *computer* occurs in the title or at least 10 times in the text of the page. They argued that the earlier approach (see Figure 8.1) was

---

1. For bounded-depth keyword searches at a specific Web server, one can also use Webglimpse (*webglimpse.org/*).

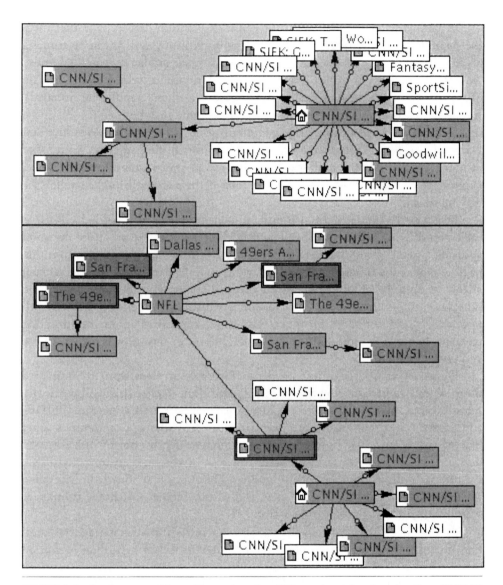

FIGURE 8.4   FISHSEARCH and SHARKSEARCH in action: Web graphs explored starting from CNN/SI with query "San Francisco 49ers." Relevant pages are shaded; highly relevant pages have a heavy border. (Images taken from [107].)

```
 1: enqueue the start URL into the cold queue C
 2: while at least one of C and the hot queue H is nonempty do
 3:     if H is nonempty then
 4:         obtain the new URL u to fetch by dequeuing from H
 5:     else
 6:         obtain the new URL u to fetch by dequeuing from C
 7:     end if
 8:     fetch u and scan for text and outlinks
 9:     for each outlink URL v found do
10:         add (u, v) to link database unless already there
11:         if v is not already visited then
12:             if the anchor text on the (u, v) link contains "computer"
                or the URL v contains the string "computer" then
13:                 enqueue v into H
14:             else
15:                 enqueue v into C
16:             end if
17:         end if
18:     end for
19:     reorganize H and C according to priority ordering
20: end while
```

FIGURE 8.5 A modified crawler driven by a keyword query, looking for pages related to computers.

clearly unsuited to deal with textual content[2] and proposed a modified algorithm where two separate queues were used (see Figure 8.5): a hot queue held URLs v such that some HREF targeting v had the word *computer* in its anchor text. The two queues were kept ordered individually, and the next page to fetch was taken from the hot queue in preference to the regular URL queue.

Again, a variety of reorganization priorities can be used in Figure 8.5. Interestingly, as Figure 8.6 shows, a breadth-first reorganization acquires hot pages faster than PageRank- or in-degree–based reorganization. (A breadth-first policy is implemented by using a FIFO queue and doing nothing in the reorganization step.) Under FIFO ordering of the hot queue, if a computer-related page is crawled earlier, then the crawler discovers and visits its outlinks earlier as well. These pages have a tendency to also be computer related, so the acquisition rate is higher.

---

2. A comparison might still be useful.

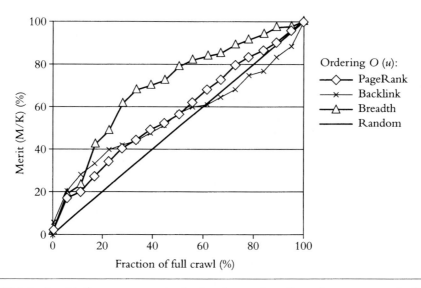

FIGURE 8.6   Breadth-first queue organization lets the crawler collect relevant pages at the fastest pace.

The experiments above show that mild variations in crawl prioritization, imposed on top of the basic crawler discussed in Chapter 3, can make a significant difference to targeted acquisition of pages with specific properties. The approaches proposed by Cho, De Bra, Hersovici and others, which I have discussed above, could be brittle in the same sense that simple IR systems deal poorly with synonymy. Relying on the anchor of a link to a computer science department to contain the word *computer* will let us down if "CS Division" is another common idiom used by anchor text writers. In Section 8.3 we will study more general and robust techniques based on machine learning that remove the brittleness of syntactic matching.

8.2   Similarity Search Using Link Topology

Links in social networks do not merely confer authority; they also hint at semantic connections between entities. A typical Web link is created because the link endpoints are about related concepts. Co-citations expose a slightly longer-range relation: two nodes frequently cited together from other nodes are most likely related. As we discussed in Chapter 7, analysis of the co-citation matrix brings out the structure of link-based communities.

For a number of years, many major search engines have supported a "find similar pages" function, which could be invoked on one Web page as argument and would return a set of similar or related pages. Early search engines used IR techniques to implement this feature. For example, they might find TFIDF document vectors having large cosine similarity with the page provided as argument, and eliminate mirrors before presenting the answers (see Section 3.3.2).

As with ad hoc searching, clustering, and classification, it gradually became clear that the "find-similar" operation, too, could benefit from paying attention to static hyperlink structure as well as dynamic click streams. Alexa (*www.alexa.com*) uses all these sources of information to derive a list of pages similar to a given page, but their exact algorithm is not published yet, to my knowledge. The Netscape browser (*www.netscape.com*) uses the Alexa system as a plug-in to provide the find-similar service.

The HITS family of algorithms has also been used successfully for find-similar searches. HITS, as discussed in Chapter 7, uses a keyword search engine to assemble its root set, but this is not the only way to do so; in principle, *any* subgraph of the Web can be used as a root set, although only specific root sets make semantic sense and produce coherent results when processed by HITS.

For some queries, a good set of examples is enough to bootstrap, even without running HITS at all. For example, at the time of writing, the query

```
link:http://www.lufthansa.com link:http://www.iberia.com
```

returns the page shown in Figure 8.7 as the second best response. It is an excellent hub on European airlines.

The example above explains why the following "query-by-example" style works quite well with HITS. We put the examples in the root set and invoke HITS. While constructing the base set (see Section 7.2.2), HITS uses a backlink query on each page u in the root set, that is, it fetches pages that link to u. Many search engines provide this service through the link:u query syntax. During this process, we expect several hubs, such as the one shown in Figure 8.7, to enter the base set. During the HITS iterations, such good hubs will rapidly accumulate large hub scores. The outlinks of some of the top hubs can be accumulated and presented as the answer to the query-by-example.

EUROPEAN AIRLINES		
|A|B|C|D|E|F|G|H|I|J|K|L|M|N|O|P|Q|R|S|T|U|V|W|X|Y|Z|		
A		
AB AIRLINES	ADRIA AIRWAYS	AER LINGUS
AERO LLOYD	AEROFLOT	AEROSWEET
AIR ATLANTA	AIR BALTIC	AIR BERLIN
AIR DOLOMITO	AIR ENGIADINA	AIR EUROPE
AIR EUROPA LINEAS	AIR FRANCE	AIR GEORGIA
AIR GREECE	AIR ICELAND	AIR JET
AIR LIBERTE	AIR LITTORAL	AIR MALTA
AIR MARIN	AIR MOLDOVA	AIR NOSTRUM
AIR ONE	AIR OSTRAVA	AIR SEYCHELLES
AIRE OYLE	AIRUK	ALITALIA
AOM MINERVE FRENCH AIRLINES	ARMENIAN AIRLINES	AURIGNY AIR SERVICES
AUSTRIAN AIRLINES	AVIO EXPRESS	AVIOIMPEX AIR COMPANY
B		
BALKAN - BULGARIAN AIRLINES	BINTER CANARIAS	BRAATHENS
BRITANNIA AIRWAYS	BRITISH AIRWAYS	BRITISH MIDLANDS AIRWAYS

FIGURE 8.7 Good hubs are easy to find using backlink search alone, provided some sample authorities are known. This is a view of *www.marsit.com/folders/usenm/airlines/european_airlines.htm*, titled *European Airlines*.

Dean and Henzinger [65] made this process more sophisticated by proposing two effective link–based, find-similar procedures, which they call the Co-citation and Companion algorithms. These algorithms use not only the coarse-grained graph structure but also proximity of outlinks on a page.

The degree of co-citation of nodes u and v is the number of nodes x that link to both u and v. Given seed node u, Co-citation picks up to B arbitrary nodes x that link to u, then for each such node x, up to BF children v other than u itself. The outlinks on x are arranged as a linear sequence, in that one outlink is the $x \rightarrow u$ link. Up to $BF/2$ outlinks before and $BF/2$ outlinks after the $x \rightarrow u$ outlink are chosen to select the nodes v. $B = 2000$ and $BF = 8$ were used by Dean and Henzinger. Co-citation assumes that links lexically close on x are more likely to be semantically related, a hunch we have seen confirmed in Section 6.2.2 as well as Section 7.4.4 (see Figure 8.8). Once all v have been collected thus, they are ordered in decreasing degree of co-citation and the best vs returned. Other minor details of the algorithm can be found in [65].

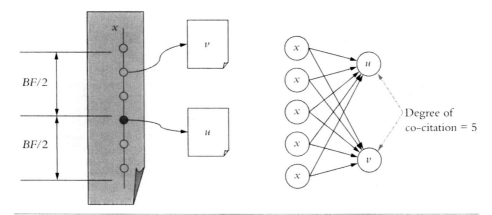

FIGURE 8.8   Exploiting link proximity in the Co-citation and Companion algorithms.

The Companion algorithm first builds a *vicinity graph* G_u from the given URL u. It assumes that four integer parameters, B, F, BF, and FB, have been defined. Up to B inlinks of u are included in G_u. For each of the inlinks, up to BF outlinks (different from u) are included in G_u as well (with a link proximity judgment, as in Co-citation). Up to F outlinks of u are included in G_u. For each of the outlinks, up to FB inlinks (excluding u) are included in G_u.

The next step is to collapse duplicates and near duplicates. If two nodes in the vicinity graph have at least 10 outlinks each and at least 95% of the links are common, these nodes are collapsed into one. These parameters were likely tuned by trial and error. Collapsing mirrored and aliased URLs makes the hub and authority scores denser and more reliable. Once the graph has been fixed, edge weights are assigned as in the B&H topic-distillation algorithm (see Section 7.4.1) [18]. Finally, the B&H iterative algorithm is run and the top several authorities reported.

Dean and Henzinger conducted a user study with 18 volunteers and 69 runs of the Companion and Co-citation algorithms, each starting from one distinct URL to find others similar to it. For each run, the top r authorities were reported to the volunteers in random order. For comparison, Netscape's "find-similar" feature (implemented by Alexa) was also invoked for each URL. The results, in Figure 8.9, show that of the top 10 responses provided by the three algorithms, Companion and Co-citation perform better than Netscape/Alexa. Since the Netscape/Alexa

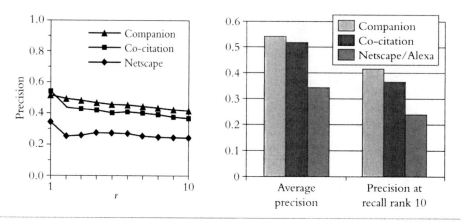

FIGURE 8.9 The Companion algorithm has higher precision than Co-citation, which has higher precision than Netscape/Alexa. Average precision and precision at recall rank 10 are shown.

algorithm is not published, it is not possible to perform a detailed analysis of the difference in performance.

8.3 Topical Locality and Focused Crawling

Suppose we sample two Web pages uniformly at random (see Section 7.6.3 on how to sample pages from the Web) and compute their vector-space cosine similarity. (We assume that a global IDF vector is available.) This expected pairwise similarity would be quite low, only noise-words making a contribution to the cosine. Now consider a slightly different experiment: sample one page at random, let the other page be a random out-neighbor from the first page, and measure the cosine similarity between these two pages. Suppose we repeat each experiment a number of times.

The Web graph was not constructed by connecting pairs of nodes selected at random, and therefore, we would naturally expect the second similarity to be higher than the first on average. Davison [61] conducted a scaled-down approximation of this experiment using 100,000 pages sampled from the repository of a research search engine called DiscoWeb. The following quantities were measured (the global IDF was approximated with one computed over these 100,000 pages).

Random: TFIDF cosine similarity between two pages sampled uniformly at random from the collection was measured.

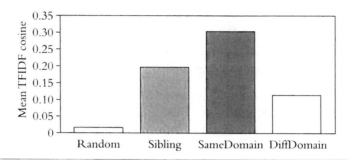

FIGURE 8.10 Cited or co-cited page pairs show about an order of magnitude more similarity (vector-space cosine) than randomly selected page pairs.

Sibling: Two random outlinks *u* and *v* were fetched from a random page in the collection and the TFIDF cosine similarity between *u* and *v* measured.

SameDomain: A random page *u* was sampled from the collection. A random outlink *v* was chosen such that *u* and *v* were from the same host (identified by name).

DiffDomain: A random page *u* was sampled from the collection. A random outlink *v* was chosen such that *u* and *v* were from *different* hosts (identified by name).

Figure 8.10 shows the results. SameDomain pairs showed the highest similarity, followed by Sibling, DiffDomain, and Random, in that order. Random similarity is an order of magnitude less than even DiffDomain similarity. The observations are quite intuitive, and reaffirm our faith that the Web network is topically clustered.

The notion of a vicinity graph is an important one, so let me quickly retrace how this notion evolved between 1996 and 1999.

1. In traditional IR, there is no notion of "vicinity" because there are no links. you may think of it as a vicinity graph of radius zero.

2. In PageRank there is no nontrivial notion of "vicinity" either; the whole Web graph (or whatever could be crawled) is used. (This is the opposite extreme: the radius is unlimited.)

3. In HITS, the notion of "vicinity" is limited to the Web subgraph within a single link of the IR notion of responses to the query.

4.   In B&H, the vicinity graph is a subgraph of that in HITS; nodes that are textually dissimilar from the IR responses are discarded.

5.   On the other hand, Companion *enlarges* the vicinity graph of HITS and B&H to include neighbors at distance two.

All the graph expansion strategies above are quite reticent about exploring out from the root set. They depend completely and implicitly on the locality property "DiffDomain" measured by Davison. Unfortunately, DiffDomain locality decays rapidly with distance: a random walk starting from a node related to bicycling rapidly loses its way amid pages pertaining to many different topics. This is what prevents all the algorithms above from aggressively growing the vicinity graph using DiffDomain locality alone. (A combination of DiffDomain, SameDomain, and Sibling would meet the same fate sooner or later, because every time a link is followed, there is a positive and not-too-small probability of "losing" the topic.) The algorithms are thus "passive beneficiaries" of locality.

Another way to interpret the observations presented so far is that a random walk over the Web graph may mix topics quite fast, but this does not rule out the existence of moderately long paths that are topic-coherent, that is, pertaining to one topic or a few strongly related topics.[3] The key question is, can one substitute the passive expansion by a possibly indefinite active expansion?

8.3.1   Focused Crawling

Figure 8.11 shows a simple modification to a crawler to implement active expansion. First, we collect a suitable sample of pages from the Web (using, say, the methods discussed in Section 7.6.3). Through human effort, we mark some of these samples "positive" and the rest "negative." In what follows, we will assume that the positive class shows locality of the form discussed before; in other words,

The radius-1 hypothesis: If page u is positive and u links to v, then the probability that v is positive is higher than the probability that a randomly chosen Web page is positive.

We will train a supervised classifier ahead of time with the positive and negative examples. When the crawler fetches a new page u, it will be submitted to the classifier as a test case. If the classifier judges that u is positive, outlinks from u

---

3. I have not defined topics yet, but a working definition may be a directory such as The Open Directory (*http://dmoz.org*) or Yahoo! (*www.yahoo.com*).

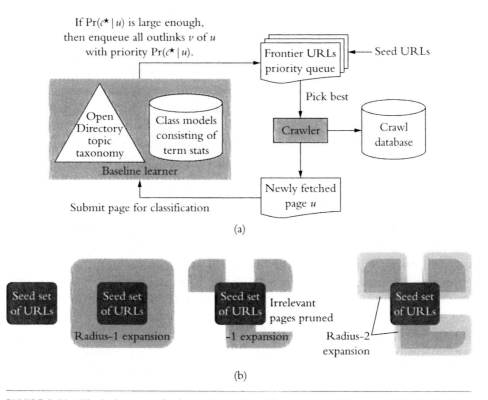

FIGURE 8.11 Block diagram of a focused crawler with a supervised learner guiding it (a). An operational view (b).

are added to the work pool as with standard crawlers (see Figure 2.2). Otherwise u is *pruned*, that is, its outlinks are not considered for further crawling. Such a system is called a *focused crawler*.

A "hard" binary decision regarding relevance may be somewhat draconian. Suppose a Bayesian classifier (described in Chapter 5) is used. There are two classes c_+ and c_-. Given a test page d just crawled, the classifier emits $\Pr(c_+|d)$ and $\Pr(c_-|d) = 1 - \Pr(c_+|d)$. A negative decision is taken whenever $\Pr(c_+|d) < 1/2$. This threshold of $1/2$ may be too severe; there may well be topics (the more specific ones) for which following a link "loses" the topic with a probability of more than half. One possible fix would be to reduce the acceptance threshold.

A better idea is to control the priority of the crawl frontier directly, using the probability scores. Let us call $\Pr(c_+|d)$ the *relevance* of d, written $R(d)$. Suppose page *u* links to page *v*. Page *u* has been fetched and classified, with relevance $R(u)$, but page *v* has not been fetched yet. Lacking any further information about *v*, we will assume, for the moment, that the relevance of *v* is the same as $R(u)$.

Thus, we add all[4] unvisited links to the work pool, but the work pool is prioritized by the guessed relevance of the unseen pages. This is a form of gambling, banking on the radius-1 hypothesis. When *v* comes to the head of the work pool and is finally fetched, we can evaluate the "true" relevance of *v*. At that time we know if our gamble paid off or not. This is the basic form of "soft" focused crawling first proposed by me [45]; we call this the *radius-1 crawler.* The average relevance of pages fetched in the recent past reflects the current health of the focused crawl; let us call this the *harvest rate.*

It is laborious to mark positive and negative examples from a Web sample for each focused crawling task. For most topics, the negative sets will have broad overlap: most Web pages are uninteresting to most of us. Furthermore, rare topics may be poorly represented in the sample. Can one reuse others' classification efforts and streamline the process of "seeding" a focused crawl?

I propose to use hierarchical topic directories like Yahoo! or the Open Directory, which I model as topic trees[5] under the obvious *is-a* relation: a page about /Arts/Painting and a page about /Arts/Photography are both about /Arts as well. All pages are "about" /, which represents "the whole Web." Sample data collected for all classes can be used to train a hierarchical classifier, as discussed in Section 5.7.

The user's focused crawling needs are communicated to the system by marking one or more nodes (classes) in the topic tree as *good*. A good node cannot be a descendant of another good node. Given that $\Pr(\text{root}|d) = 1$ by definition and Equation (5.24), which says that the probability of children adds up to the probability of the parent (i.e., a document belongs to exactly one leaf class), we can write

$$R(d) = \sum_{c \text{ is good}} \Pr(c|d) \tag{8.1}$$

We allow multiple nodes to be marked "good" so that user interests can be expressed as a union of topics. If the user's information need is not adequately

---

4. Other standard elimination criteria can be used.

5. Some directories have *cross-links* connecting similar topics across subtrees; I will ignore these links for simplicity.

represented in the topic hierarchy, we assume that the user first alters the directory suitably. Most often, this will constitute adding additional sample URLs to existing classes and specializing existing topics to finer topics.

Based on the preceding discussion, we can formalize the goal of focused crawling as follows. We are given a directed hypertext graph G whose nodes are physically distributed. In our context, G is potentially the entire Web. There is a cost for visiting any vertex (Web page) of G. There is also a tree-shaped hierarchical topic directory C such as Yahoo!. Each topic node $c \in C$ refers to some pages in G as examples. We denote the sample documents associated with topic c as $D(c)$. These pages can be preprocessed as desired by the system. The user's interest is characterized by a subset of topics $C^* \subset C$ that is marked "good." No good topic is an ancestor of another good topic. Given a Web page q, a measure of relevance $R_{C^*}(q)$ of q with regard to C^*, together with a method for computing it, must be specified to the system. (Usually, this would be a supervised learner, as in Chapter 5.) For a Bayesian classifier, or a TFIDF-cosine measure, $0 \leq R(q) \leq 1$. The system starts by visiting all the seed pages in $D(C^*)$. In each step, the system can inspect its current set V of visited pages and then choose to visit an unvisited page from the crawl frontier, corresponding to a hyperlink on one or more visited pages. Informally, the goal is to visit as many relevant pages and as few irrelevant pages as possible, that is, to maximize average relevance. Therefore, we seek to find a vertex set $V \supset D(C^*)$, where V is reachable from $D(C^*)$, such that the mean relevance $\left(\sum_{v \in V} R(v) \right) / |V|$ is maximized.

There are a variety of performance indicators that reflect the health of a focused crawl. By far the most important is the harvest rate, or the "true" relevance of fetched pages at any given time. The "true" relevance of a page can only be evaluated with human input, if at all. However, to evaluate a focused crawler, it would be nearly impossible to obtain human judgment on millions of pages. Instead, we can use the same classifier that guides the crawler in the first place. This may sound fishy, but there is really nothing wrong in using the same classifier. The crawler is basically gambling on a link (u, v) when u is very relevant, and, when v is fetched, we get to know if the gamble paid off. Note that the gambling exercise may well have been performed by a human, who also has a certain probability of classification error. As long as the classifier's errors are not somehow correlated with the local graph structure of v, evaluating a focused crawler using an automatic classifier is reasonable.

I measured the harvest rate of our focused crawler for over 20 topics selected from Yahoo!. Figure 8.12 shows a running average of the harvest rate for two

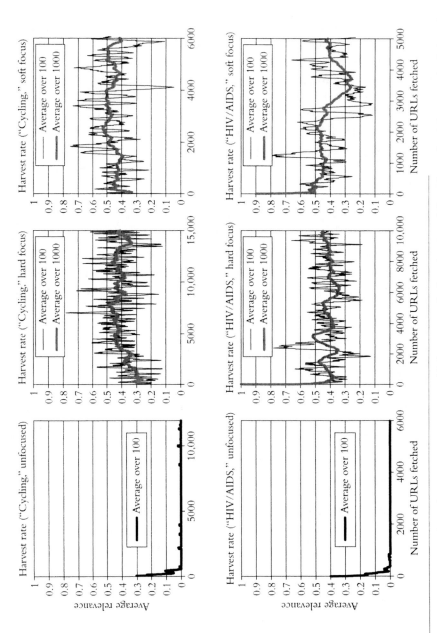

FIGURE 8.12 Focused crawlers can maintain a reasonable harvest rate for broad topics while unfocused crawlers completely lose their way, even though they start from the same set of URLs. The x-axis represents the number of URLs fetched (discrete time), and the y-axis plots a smoothed value for the relevance of fetched pages.

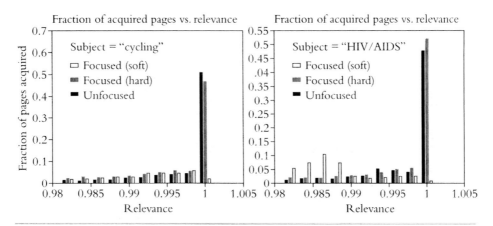

FIGURE 8.13 The distribution of relevance scores of pages collected by focused crawlers is sharply concentrated around one, whereas the relevance of pages fetched by the unfocused crawlers is not.

topics ("cycling" and "HIV/AIDS") and three crawlers: a standard (unfocused) crawler that picks a random frontier page for fetching, a hard-focused crawler, and a soft-focused crawler.

The unfocused crawler starts out from the same set of dozens of highly relevant links as the focused crawler, but is completely lost within the next 100 page fetches: the relevance goes quickly to zero. In contrast, the hard-focused crawls keep up a healthy pace of acquiring relevant pages over thousands of fetches, in spite of some short-range rate fluctuations, which is expected. On an average, between a third and a half of all page fetches result in success over the first several thousand fetches, and there seems to be no sign of stagnation. Given that none of the crawls approached stagnation, it is difficult to compare between hard and soft focusing; they both do very well. For the topic "cycling," the hard crawler takes a little while to warm up because it loses some good opportunities to expand near-match pages. Figure 8.13 shows that the distribution of relevance of pages collected by the soft-focused crawler is sharply peaked at the high end of the zero-to-one scale, the hard-focused crawler is mildly inferior, and the distribution for the unfocused crawler has no peak at one; in fact, it is concentrated near zero (not shown).

Improving recall by restricting scope is a key rationale for focused crawling, but it is rather difficult to evaluate focused crawlers for recall. One can follow Cho et al.'s strategy to collect and define a hypertext graph and the "universe" from that different crawlers collect subgraphs, but no single crawl is likely to collect

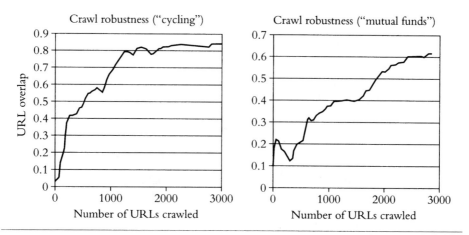

FIGURE 8.14 A large overlap is quickly developed in URLs between two instances of the focused crawler started from disjoint sets of seed URLs pertaining to the same topic.

a reasonable universe, given that the coverage of even the largest commercial crawlers is modest [16, 134].

We can get some indirect evidence of recall or coverage by evaluating the *robustness* in acquiring relevant pages, starting from different seed URLs. The idea is to collect (say, two) *disjoint* sets of sample URLs for a topic, and start distinct focused crawls A and B, which collect vertex sets $V_A(t)$ and $V_B(t)$ after fetching t pages each ($|V_A(t)| = |V_B(t)| = t$). Now we can measure $|V_A(t) \cap V_B(t)|/t$ as an indicator of overlap or consensus between the two crawlers. Figure 8.14 shows that overlap grows rapidly within a few thousand page fetches.

The large overlap is good news: it indicates that broad topics stake out a well-defined link community on the Web, and as long as this community is reachable from the seed URLs, a focused crawler guided by a supervised learner will reach it irrespective of the specific seed URLs used.

Discovering stable link communities pertaining to a query or topic is also important for topic distillation, discussed in Section 7.2. Researchers experimenting with the HITS family of algorithms have noted that the results are often sensitive to the construction of the base graph.

We also established that nontrivial graph exploration is involved in the discovery tasks that were undertaken. After fetching several tens of thousands of relevant pages, we ran the B&H edge-weighted version of topic distillation (see

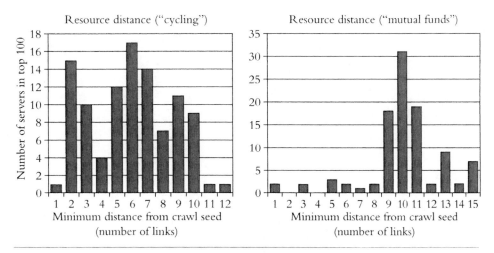

FIGURE 8.15 The best authorities are found several links away from the seed URLs; there are millions of accessible pages within such distances of the seed URLs. Goal-directed pruning and prioritization enables the crawler to ignore most of these pages and zoom in on the relevant subgraph.

Section 7.4.1) on the collected graph to determine the top 100 authorities. Next, the number of links that the crawler traversed to reach each authority, starting at some seed URL, was determined. (There may exist shorter paths from a seed to some of these nodes.) Finally, histograms of these link distances were plotted. Figure 8.15 shows two samples, for the topics "cycling" and "mutual funds."

The seed URLs were collected using AltaVista and HITS. Hence, the discovery of excellent resources as far as 10 to 12 links from the seeds also establishes the need to explore aggressively from the keyword-based root set and the limited-radius expansion to the base set. This resolves, at least empirically, the graph collection problem raised in the beginning of Section 8.3.

8.3.2 Identifying and Exploiting Hubs

Hubs are not treated well by the radius-1 focused crawler. They often contain relatively little descriptive text, making a perfect classification by the algorithms described in Chapter 5 less likely. Moreover, hubs may pertain to multiple topics (see Section 7.4.4), in that case a classifier may correctly claim that the hub has small relevance. This is unfortunate, because a great authority with no outlinks

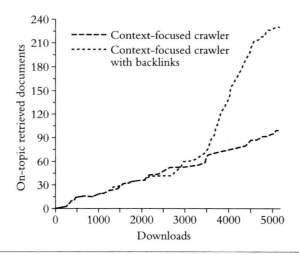

FIGURE 8.16   Assisting a focused crawler with backlinks from a standard search engine effectively increases the connectivity of the Web graph and increases the harvest rate.

may be a great catch for a focused crawler, but good hubs are critical to sustaining a healthy rate of collecting authorities.

The true worth of hubs is better recognized by

The radius-2 (co-citation) hypothesis: If u points to many pages v with large $R(v)$, then u is a good hub; an unvisited out-neighbor w of u is expected to have a higher relevance than a random sample from the Web.

When the harvest rate of a radius-1 crawler drops, we can try to shore it up by raising the priority of unvisited nodes pointed to by good hubs. We can find good hubs by running some variant of the HITS algorithm (Section 7.2.2) once in a while. We call this a *radius-2 crawler*.

For topics that are well represented on the Web, with large clustered subgraphs, the focused crawler described so far works quite well. Eventually, however, the typical relevance of newly fetched pages drops toward zero. Either the crawler has exhausted all that there is to collect from the Web (unlikely, and we will never know for sure), or it has collected a relevant subgraph that is hemmed in on all sides with pages of low relevance, separating the crawler from additional relevant clusters that ought to be collected.

As can be seen from Figure 8.16, the harvest rate generally improves if backlinks are used. This is not surprising, as the undirected connectivity of the

Web graph is expected to be better than the directed connectivity, a hunch empirically confirmed later by Bröder et al. [28]. However, since the effective degree of each node increases upon using backlinks, care must be taken to choose promising backlinks, as discussed in the next section.

8.3.3 Learning Context Graphs

Although they differ in cosmetic details, the positive-negative as well as the topic-hierarchy paradigms of focused crawling exploit the fact that pages pertaining to a topic tend to cite pages pertaining to the same topic. As we have seen in Chapter 6, relations between topics can be more complex. For example, if the crawler's goal is to collect papers about robotics, a page about a computer science department is likely to be useful; it is likely to point to faculty homepages, some of which are likely to point to papers, some of which could be about robotics. Trained to treat robotics papers as positive and everything else as negative, a classifier may rate a computer science department homepage as poorly as a page on philately.

How can we learn to distinguish between such situations? Given the seed URLs, we assume are all relevant, we can trace back various paths that lead to the relevant pages and try to learn features that indicate if relevant pages are a short link distance away. We can also do this for pages with high relevance scores found later in the crawl. As with random sampling (see Section 7.6.3), one may complain that depending on a standard crawler for backlink queries amounts to cheating, but various research proposals [41] as well as upcoming standards such as XLink (*www.w3.org/TR/xlink/*) make limited forms of bidirectional hyperlinks more likely to be implemented in the future.

Diligenti et al. [69] propose supervised learning on the structure of paths leading to relevant pages to enhance the focused crawlers discussed so far. The seed document is said to be at *layer 0*. Pages linking to documents at level zero are at layer 1, and so on. For simplicity, we will assume that pages with paths to multiple seeds are "named apart" so that they become distinct pages for the purpose of the following discussion.

A supervised learning problem (see Chapter 5) is set up as follows. The objects being classified are the pages (nodes in the context graph). The attributes of a page are the terms that occur in it. The novelty is in the class variable to be predicted; the class variable is the layer number of the page. That is, looking at the text on the page, the supervised learner tries to predict the number of hops at which a relevant page may be found. If the layers in the training set are $0, 1, \ldots, N$, we add a class called OTHER to reflect that a page does not seem to fit any of the existing layers. Diligenti et al. preprocess the training documents using a TFIDF representation to perform a kind of feature selection. Then they use a naive Bayes classifier (see Section 5.6.1) trained with $N + 1$ classes. It is not easy to train the OTHER class directly. Instead, when the winning class c^* is determined from the $N + 1$ candidates, the classifier compares $\Pr(c^*|d)$ against a tuned threshold; if $\Pr(c^*|d)$ is too small, d is placed in the OTHER class.

A block diagram of the complete *context-focused crawler* is shown in Figure 8.17. Rather than the single priority queue in the standard focused crawler, the context-focused crawler maintains $N + 1$ different pools of pages whose URLs need to be expanded, one pool for each class or layer. The pool numbered 0 corresponds to layer 0, the harvested output of the crawler. The pool for a lower layer (closer to zero) has priority over the pool of a higher layer. When out of work, the crawler picks (fetches) a page from the lowest positive layer possible, scans it for outlinks, and adds the outlinks to the to do list.

The context-focused crawler outperforms the "standard" focused crawler by a visible margin, especially when a page about the desired topic tends not to link directly to another page on that same topic, but takes a path through nodes pertaining to related topics. The paths may even follow some backward edges. For example, pages within the site *www.toyota.com* are unlikely to cite *www.mazda.com*, so following forward links alone would be quite restrictive. But there are thousands of pages co-citing them. Figure 8.18 shows examples of the superior harvest rate of the context-focused crawler.

8.3.4   Reinforcement Learning

Another technique that generalizes the radius-1 and radius-2 rules is *reinforcement learning* (RL), proposed by Rennie and McCallum [181]. Like context graphs, a focused crawler using RL has to be trained using *paths* leading to relevant goal nodes. For example, to collect papers on robotics, one may locate electrical, mechanical, and computer engineering departments, follow links to homepages of faculty and students, check them for evident involvement in robotics research, and then follow links on promising homepages to robotics papers. Such paths form the input to an RL crawler.

The RL crawler seeks to predict the *total benefit* from following a link (u, v) from page u. Different links on the same page u may lead to very different measures of benefit. In this respect the RL crawler is an improvement over the context-focused crawler, which estimates the distance to a goal but not which outlinks to follow to reach these goals. For the system administrator or user, the RL crawler's biggest attraction is that there is no need to spend time collecting or training the

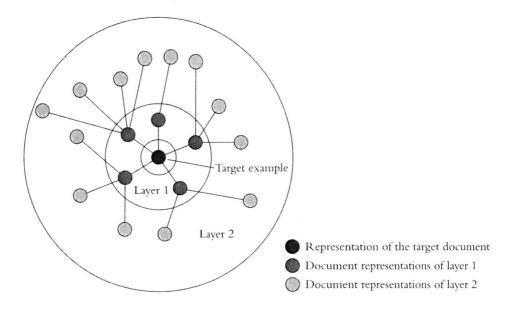

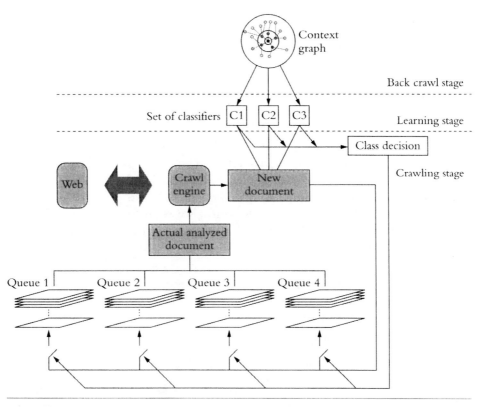

FIGURE 8.17 A context-focused crawler.

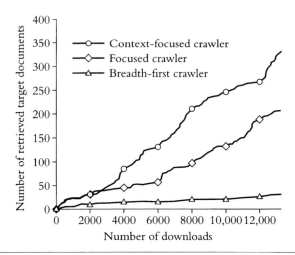

FIGURE 8.18   The context-focused crawler yields a higher harvest rate of relevant pages.

system with negative instances. However, more effort is needed to collect paths than simple page instances as with the first-generation focused crawlers.

Care is required to specify the *total benefit*. If v is itself a relevant goal node, then following (u, v) pays off immediately. This may not always be the case. Sometimes v may not be very relevant in itself, but may lead through short paths to many goal nodes. As with the context-focused crawler, links leading to immediate rewards should be rewarded (i.e., regarded with higher priority by the crawler) more than links leading to distant goals. In other words, we should *discount* the worth of distant goals while training. Rennie and McCallum set the reward for following (u, v) to 1 if v was relevant. A goal node ℓ links from v additively contributes $1/\gamma^{\ell}$ to the reward for crossing (u, v), where $0 < \gamma < \frac{1}{2}$ was a geometric discounting factor. This is reminiscent of hypertext search systems (e.g., by Savoy [188]) that score pages in the link vicinity of pages matching query keywords.

Using this notion of reward, Rennie and McCallum trained a classifier with the following characteristics:

- An *instance* was a single HREF link like (u, v).

- The *features* were terms from the title and headers (<h1>...</h1>, etc.) of u, together with the text in and "near" the anchor (u, v). Directories and pathnames were also used. (Their paper does not provide a precise definition of "near," or how these features were encoded and combined.)

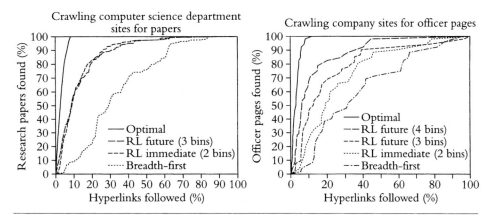

FIGURE 8.19 Reinforcement learning helps a crawler quickly locate goal nodes. Training on discounted rewards is essential to develop this capability.

♦ The *prediction* was a discretized estimate of the reward for following (u, v).

Although the learner really needs a regression from the discrete features to a continuous "promise" estimate, it is often simpler and faster to use a classification (rather than a regression) strategy by suitably discretizing the predicted variable into a few bins. They used a simple naive Bayes classifier (see Section 5.6.1).

Rennie and McCallum experimented with a few crawl specifications. One of them was to find research papers within a handful of computer science department Web sites, starting from the departmental homepages. Another was to find pages listing the executive officers of companies, starting with their respective homepages. Because of the precisely defined crawling domains, it was possible for them to exhaustively mark all relevant pages. For research papers they wrote a script that checked for an abstract and reference section. For the second task, 26 company homepages were identified as the starting points, and one page for each company was manually identified as a goal node.

Figure 8.19 shows some of their results. As with the focused crawlers discussed before, the RL crawler acquires goal nodes much faster than a breadth-first crawler. More interesting, the discounted reward scheme for distant goals pays off, especially for the task of finding company officer pages. Finding computer science papers might have been easier because most of them are PostScript or PDF files, a "feature" that would show up in the URL. Therefore, a goal at distance one is easy to find.

8.4 Discovering Communities

I have discussed a number of related approaches to topic-specific resource discovery. An administrator needs to "seed" all of these systems with a fixed set or taxonomy of topics, together with examples for all the topics. Although broad topics evolve only slowly, more specific topics may be quite ephemeral on the Web. (At least, the fastest rate of growth in the number of relevant pages is often a spike on the time line, even if old pages on specialized topics may linger beyond the time of maximum general interest.)

The previous sections have characterized communities as a phenomenon characterized by both link proximity and content coherence, but there has been significant success in detecting communities on the basis of link structure alone. I will discuss two such techniques in this section. The first one, inspired by HITS (see Section 7.2.2), searches for small, complete, bipartite subgraphs (called *cores*). The second approach is inspired by notions of network separability and graph clustering: it finds a densely connected subgraph isolated from the remainder of the Web by a sparse cut.

8.4.1 Bipartite Cores as Communities

Random graph models materialize edges independently with a fixed probability. If the Web were a random graph, large, densely connected components and bipartite cores would be extremely unlikely. The Web is not random, and such subgraphs abound on it.

In particular, the success of HITS-like algorithms for many broad topics suggests that bipartite cores relevant to these topics grow in an organic manner on the Web (see Section 7.2.3). A small bipartite core is often an indicator of an *emerging* topic, which may be too specific at the moment to draw the attention of human catalogers on the Web.

An interesting question is, can we hunt for bipartite cores *efficiently* from a Web crawl? Finding large bipartite cores amid a graph with billions of nodes is clearly impractical. Large cores represent communities that are already well established. Small, emerging cores may represent communities that are most novel.

The search for cores will proceed by identifying and/or eliminating *fans* and *centers*. In a bipartite graph (L, R, E) where directed edges go from L to R, nodes in L are fans and nodes in R are centers. An (i, j) core has $|L| = i$ and $|R| = j$.

Duplicate and near duplicate hubs (see Section 3.3.2) must be eliminated before we get started. Otherwise many cores will have near duplicate hubs as fans. We already know from Section 3.3.3 how to weed out pages with nearly identical outlink sequences. Kumar et al. [128] observed a 60% reduction in graph size using shingling on the link sequence as described in Section 3.3.3; some pages from Yahoo! were duplicated as many as 50 times.

Based on the preceding discussion, we may also want to eliminate fans with very large degree. Pruning fans with large out-degree will also make it easier to report nonoverlapping cores (otherwise, they could be subgraphs of larger dense cores). What should be the threshold degree above which we eliminate fans? One crude heuristic to set this policy is to note that well-known (therefore, likely to be largest) communities indexed by Web directories cover (as a rough ballpark estimate) 1/200 to 1/100 of the Web [128]. We can pick a degree k from the power-law graphs in Figure 7.20 such that the fraction of nodes with degree larger than k is 1/200. This threshold k turns out to be around 40 to 80.

No fan with out-degree less than j can belong to an (i, j) core, and no center with in-degree less than i can belong to an (i, j) core. Eliminating a fan or center may reduce the degree of a center or fan below these thresholds and help prune the latter in cascade. We sort the edge list by source, then scan the data eliminating fans that have out-degree less than j. Next we sort the result by destination and eliminate centers that have in-degree less than i. We continue this process until the rate of elimination slows down. A host of other pruning techniques can be used.

After pruning away as many candidates as we can, we can directly search for (i, j) cores in the surviving graph in a bottom-up fashion. We start with all $(1, j)$ cores, which is simply the set of all nodes with out-degree at least j. Next we construct all $(2, j)$ cores by checking every fan that also cites any center in a $(1, j)$ core. We find all $(3, j)$ cores by checking every fan that cites any center in a $(2, j)$ core, and so on.

Kumar et al. [128] discovered tens of thousands of $(3, 3)$ to $(3, 5)$ bipartite cores and observed (through manual inspection) that a large fraction of the cores were, in fact, topically coherent (the definition of "topic" was left informal). In some cases, an emerging community found from an old crawl was found to be well established in the Web graph at a later date.

8.4.2 Network Flow/Cut-Based Notions of Communities

Dense bipartite subgraphs are an important indicator of community formation, but they may not be the only one. In this section, we will study a general definition (due to Flake et al. [77]) of a community as a subgraph whose internal link density exceeds the density of connection to nodes outside it by some margin.

Formally, we can define a *community* as a vertex subset $C \subset V$ such that each $v \in C$ has at least as many neighbors in C as in $V - C$. This problem is NP-complete owing to reductions from various graph-partitioning problems. Hence we will come up with a less stringent definition, based on network flows.

The max-flow/min-cut problem [56] is posed as follows. We are given a graph $G = (V, E)$ with a source node $s \in V$ and a target node $t \in V$. Each edge (u, v) is like a water pipe with a positive integer maximum flow capacity $c(u, v) \in \mathbb{Z}^+$. The max-flow algorithm finds the maximum rate of flow from s to t without exceeding the capacity constraints on any edge. It is known that this maximum flow is the same as a minimum-capacity cut (min-cut) separating s and t.

Suppose we are given the Web graph $G = (V, E)$ with a node subset $S \subset V$ identified as *seed* URLs, which are examples of the community the user wishes to discover. We create an artificial source s and connect it to all seed nodes $u \in S$, setting $c(s, u) = \infty$. We connect all $v \in V - S - \{s, t\}$ to an artificial target t with $c(v, t) = 1$. Each original edge is made undirected and heuristically assigned a capacity of k (I will discuss k shortly). Now we run an $s \rightarrow t$ max-flow algorithm and define all nodes on the s-side of the min-cut as being part of the community C. Thanks to all $c(s, u)$ being infinite, we are guaranteed that $S \subseteq C$ as well.

In reality, we are not given the whole Web graph and must collect necessary portions of it by crawling. We are only given S and, if the community found using the *whole* Web graph is $C \supseteq S$, then we wish to collect as few nodes outside C as possible while computing C. To this end, we will do a different form of focused crawling that is driven not by textual content but purely by hyperlink (density) considerations.

The crawler begins with the seed set S, shown as (b) in Figure 8.20, and finds all in-[6] and out-neighbors of the seed nodes (layer (c)). It can continue to any fixed depth; the figure shows two such steps. Once we have collected layers (c) and (d), say, we can set up a max-flow problem as described above by connecting all nodes in (c) and (d) (in general, $V - S - \{s, t\}$) to a virtual sink t, creating s, and assigning edge capacities. Let C be the community found by this procedure.

If S is too small, C may turn out to be too close to S, that is, bring in very few new example nodes. In that case, we can consider some nodes in C with the largest number of neighbors in C as new seeds and repeat the process. There is no guarantee that C (after each round of crawling followed by max-flow) will not

---

6. Using the "link:. . ." query on most search engines.

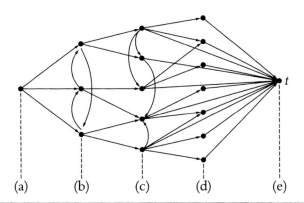

(a)   (b)   (c)   (d)   (e)

FIGURE 8.20 Flow-based definition of a community. The artificial source (a) is connected with infinite capacity edges to the source nodes (b). The next two levels of the crawl are represented by (c) and (d). An artificial sink node helps compute max-flow (e).

grow without bound. In practice, for many trials, C stabilized once the collected graph grew beyond a certain size.

k is set empirically. If k is very large, the min-cut will be pushed out to the periphery of the crawled graph, where the unit-capacity (v, t) links are to be found. If k is too small, we will discover a small cut close to S. Since we believe that nodes close to S are more likely to be on-topic than nodes far away in the link graph, k can be used to tune a recall-precision–like trade-off. In practice, the simple choice $k = |S|$ seems to work well.

Table 8.1 shows the most popular nodes found by crawling out from the homepage of Ronald Rivest, inventor of the RSA cryptosystem and coauthor of a well-known textbook on algorithms with Thomas Cormen.

Defining a focused community in terms of network flows makes the focused crawler much simpler to operate, compared to content-based focused crawlers. In

Degree in C	URL, Title or Description
86	Ronald L. Rivest: Homepage
29	Chaffing and Winnowing: Confidentiality without Encryption
20	Thomas H. Cormen's homepage at Dartmouth
9	The Mathematical Guts of RSA Encryption
8	German News Story on Cryptography

TABLE 8.1 The highest-degree members of C after crawling out from S set to a single URL: Ronald Rivest's homepage.

particular, it is not necessary to collect negative examples or to train a classification system. However, we cannot claim that either the content-based system or the link-based system finds the "right" answer in all cases. It would be interesting to compare communities found by these systems, as well as evolve a formal evaluation procedure for systems that collect community graphs.

8.5 **Bibliographic Notes**

The need for decentralized searching that integrates link proximity and textual content has been felt for a number of years. The Webglimpse system (*web-glimpse.org/*) lets the user specify a seed page, a depth bound, and a keyword query and will return hypertext nodes within the specified link distance of the seed that satisfy the query. FISHSEARCH and SHARKSEARCH [63, 64, 107] are client-side tools with similar goals. The "distributed agents" literature provides similar approaches to resource discovery. A well-known and representative system of that flavor is InfoSpiders by Menczer and Belew [149].

By 1998, commercial crawlers were very sophisticated, but their queuing discipline and priority strategies remained unpublished. Cho et al.'s work [50] is an early public report on the effect of various crawling strategies on the acquisition rate of "desirable" pages, defined in a variety of ways. Najork and Weiner [158] report on more extensive experiments of a similar nature over much larger crawls of the Web at large.

Although co-citation has been used in bibliometry for a long time to find related publications [132], Dean and Henzinger's work [65] is an early and influential application to the Web. In the entire lineage of topic-distillation research, from Kleinberg's HITS algorithm [122] to the D&H algorithm, the issue of collecting a suitable graph for distillation has been left to radius-1 or radius-2 expansion heuristics. The subsequent research on focused crawling by van den Berg, Dom, and me, as well as by Diligenti et al. [45, 69], provide some solutions to this issue.

Focused crawlers produce what are sometimes called *vertical portals* because they address the information needs related to just one or a few topics. Focused resource discovery seems to be at the heart of many new information management companies, where its output feeds into custom search engines and information extractors. CoRA (*cora.whizbang.com/* [146]) and CiteSeer/ResearchIndex (*citeseer.nj.nec.com/*) are examples of vertical portals collected by semiautomatic resource discovery in various forms.

CHAPTER 9

THE FUTURE OF WEB MINING

The Web continues to grow, but the pace has slackened since the early years (1994–1999). There is a relatively steady flux and turnover. Search engines started from their IR ancestors but made a substantial technological leap, as we have seen in this book. Other operations on hypertextual documents, such as crawling, clustering, and classification, have also been enhanced by the research described here.

Information foraging on the Web is now vastly easier than in the initial years of crawlers and search engines, but it is running up against the "syntactic search" barrier. Large search engines rarely get into in-depth linguistic analysis of document collections because many processes in automatic language processing are much more complex and therefore somewhat slower than regular crawling and indexing. Many components of automatic language processing have been intensely researched for decades [4, 55], and I predict increasing adoption of these components for Web searching and analysis. I will discuss some techniques to exploit "ankle-deep semantics" in this chapter.

The macroscopic structures and idioms on the Web are well entrenched and already exploited to a great extent in searching and pattern discovery. We are seeing a steady migration of research effort to disassembling pages and page regions into finer structures until we can deal with phrases and sentences, taking them apart into finer linguistic units. The extracted information is being integrated with other knowledge bases, such as dictionaries and domain-specific catalogs, and data extracted from multiple sources is being combined to address information needs. Uniform description and interchange formats are being designed using

XML and its associated metadata description standards to exchange and combine knowledge bases more easily.

In this chapter, I will describe a few techniques for analyzing documents at the level of tokens, their proximity, and their relationships with each other. For some applications, understanding the relationships between tokens at a syntactic level suffices. For example, we may be interested in populating a standardized database of academic citations from the bibliography found in online research papers (e.g., *www.citeseer.com/*), which are typeset in a variety of styles, the fields appearing in many orders, some abbreviated and some missing. For other applications, a deeper understanding of language is involved, which may include assigning parts of speech to tokens, attempting a parse, and generating a parsed graph of entities and relationships. Although these sound like disparate techniques, we shall see that they are often based on ideas explored in the previous chapters. Finally I will discuss the drive toward profiling Web users and tuning their Web experience to their interests.

9.1   Information Extraction

Suppose an analyst needs to keep an up-to-date database of corporate acquisitions in the format "*A* acquired *B* for *x* dollars, of which *y* percent was in the form of equity." It would be difficult to express such an information need as a keyword query. Keyword search engines work best for the class of queries that seek information *about* an entity specified using a noun or noun phrase, not for queries that seek to match a template of *relationships* between entities whose names are to be extracted from documents. Here are some more examples.

- An HR firm may wish to monitor the Web sites of businesses in a specific sector for available job positions with salaries and locations, and build and maintain a structured database containing this data to help design their pay packages.

- A market analyst may wish to monitor management changes in companies from a specified sector and get updates of the form "*X* replaced *Y* in position *P* of company *C*."

- A researcher may wish to monitor a set of university and journal Web sites for articles that claim to improve on a specific technique and to be notified with the title, authors, and a URL where the article is available online.

- An academic department may wish to monitor other universities for promising doctoral candidates to hire in specified areas, with related faculty being notified about significant publications by the candidates.

- A small company that assembles PCs may wish to monitor online catalogs from wholesalers of system boards, cabinets, and CPUs to detect any significant change in prices from current suppliers and bidders.

These are all *information extraction* (IE) problems. Clearly, applications of IE abound. Generally speaking, IE problems are specified as long-standing or continuous queries in the face of a growing and changing corpus. Each "query" is like a template with empty slots that must be filled by matching the template to (new) documents.

The difficulty of IE tasks varies a great deal depending on how well behaved the input is, as do techniques that are brought to bear. I shall informally name IE tasks as *screen scraping, record extracting,* and *message understanding,* in order of increasing difficulty.

A trivial IE problem is solved routinely by metasearch engines (see Section 3.2.5) using ad hoc means: they have to extract the query responses (URL, title, blurb with query terms highlighted, and possibly a score) from the pages returned by a fixed set of search engines, an activity befittingly called *screen scraping*. Here there is a reliable record structure that is very regular and predictable; markup tags are also a great help in this task.

Record extraction tasks are more difficult than screen scraping. Academic citations provide an example: a typical citation may contain author names, editor names, article title, book title, page numbers, volume number, and year. Written in BibTeX, these fields are labeled explicitly, but in a formatted paper, the fields may be reordered or dropped and names abbreviated. Fonts and punctuation may be used to delimit fields. There is no single standard for choosing field orders, fonts, punctuation, or abbreviations. International mailing addresses provide another challenging example.

Message understanding is the more difficult task of populating slots from a diversity of sources of completely free-format text. A common application is to extract structured "stories" of a specific genre from news articles. An insurance company may wish to collect multiple accounts of tornado damage or auto accidents, or a security agency may wish to file away crime incidents in a manner amenable to structured queries and statistics collection. There is an entire conference, the Message Understanding Conference[1] (MUC), dedicated to IE of this genre.

It has been argued that the easier IE tasks amount to reverse engineering, which has been made necessary by a lack of authoring formats and standards, a "transient" problem that will be readily remedied as semistructured data (e.g., XML) and metadata (e.g., RDF) standards become mainstream. While format standardization will be driven by commercial motives in specific vertical sectors, I believe that there will always be a need to perform IE in domains that are not standardized.

IE techniques can be based on rule induction (see Section 5.10.2) [30, 84, 198] or statistical learning, generally using hidden Markov models (HMMs). I will cover the latter briefly. An HMM is a finite-state machine with probabilistic transitions between a set of states Q. The machine starts from an initial state q_I, moves randomly from state to state, and finishes at the final state q_F. In any state, it tosses a biased multiway coin (i.e., invokes a multinomial distribution) to decide which outlink to follow out of the current state. $\Pr(q \rightarrow q')$ gives the probability of moving from state q to q'. There is also a multinomial term distribution (see Section 4.4.1) associated with each node over a global set Σ of output symbols. $\Pr(q \uparrow \sigma)$ is the probability of emitting symbol $\sigma \in \Sigma$ while in state q. Let the output string of symbols emitted by the HMM be called $\mathbf{x} = x_1 x_2 \ldots x_\ell \$$ ("$" is an end-of-string marker that is emitted with probability one by the final state q_F). A sample state transition diagram for the masthead of a research paper, comprising the title, authors, their affiliations, their emails, and the abstract, is shown in Figure 9.1.

There are two steps for using HMMs for IE. First, we induce an HMM from training data. Next, given new text, we apply the HMM to the text to estimate the state transition sequence for that text. Generally, HMM states correspond to fields or slots to be extracted in some natural way, as Figure 9.1 shows.

Given a string $\mathbf{x}$, our task is to recover the state sequence that is most likely to emit $\mathbf{x}$, written as

$$\underset{(q_1,\ldots,q_\ell) \in Q^\ell}{\arg\max} \prod_{i=1}^{\ell+1} \Pr(q_{i-1} \rightarrow q_i) \Pr(q_i \uparrow x_i) \tag{9.1}$$

---

1. See, for example, *www.itl.nist.gov/iaui/894.02/related_projects/muc/*.

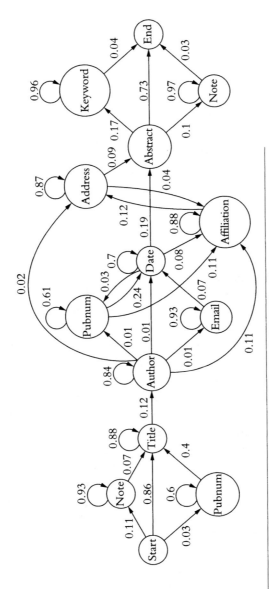

FIGURE 9.1 A hidden Markov model (HMM) for the title page of a research paper [193].

where $q_0 = q_I$ and $q_{\ell+1} = q_F$. The Viterbi algorithm [81] can be used to estimate the most likely state sequence $\mathbf{q} = q_I, q_1, \ldots, q_\ell, q_F$ given an HMM M (characterized by Q, $\Pr(q \to q')$, Σ, and $\Pr(q \uparrow \sigma)$) and x. I will describe the Viterbi algorithm briefly. Let us define

$$L(\mathbf{q}) = -\sum_{i=1}^{\ell+1} \log \left(\Pr(q_{i-1} \to q_i) \Pr(q_i \uparrow x_i) \right) \tag{9.2}$$

Then $\Pr(\mathbf{x}, \mathbf{q}|M) = e^{-L(\mathbf{q})}$, so our goal of maximizing $\Pr(\mathbf{x}, \mathbf{q}|M)$ is the same as minimizing $L(\mathbf{q})$. We can now think of

$$- \log \Pr(q \to q') - \log \Pr(q' \uparrow x_i) \tag{9.3}$$

as the *cost* of making a transition from q to q' and emitting x_i. Because we would like to consider all possible state pairs for q and q' for each timestep i, we construct the layered graph shown in Figure 9.2. It is possible that not all transitions are possible in all timesteps. With edge weights set as indicated above, the best state sequence can be estimated by finding the shortest path from q_I in the topmost layer to q_F in the bottom-most layer. (I have simplified the example by magically claiming that multitoken substrings are emitted from one state. In practice, these states need self-loops to generate more than one token, and/or we must use some notion of a "mini"-HMM within these states.)

We return to estimating M from training data. If the structure of the HMM is known and all lexical units are manually labeled with states, it is simple, in principle, to estimate the parameters $\Pr(q \to q')$ and $\Pr(q \uparrow \sigma)$. Some smoothing of parameters may be useful, as described in Section 5.6.1.

It is more difficult to design which state transitions $q \to q'$ are at all possible (i.e., with $\Pr(q \to q') > 0$). A simple approach is to initialize one state for each token, with a transition to the following token. Next, a variety of state-merging steps are applied. For example, if $q_1 \to q_2$ and the labels of q_1 and q_2 are the same, we merge them. This will introduce self-loops. Another transformation is to merge q_1 and q_2 if some $q \to q_1$ and $q \to q_2$ (or $q_1 \to q$ and $q_2 \to q$) and the labels on q_1 and q_2 are the same.

HMM-based IE is fairly accurate; for the model shown in Figure 9.1 the accuracy was over 90%. Obviously, the performance depends on the problem domain.

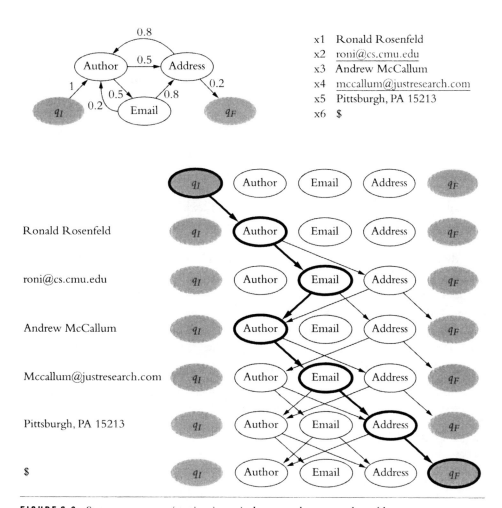

FIGURE 9.2 State sequence estimation is equivalent to a shortest-path problem.

9.2 Natural Language Processing

In the long run, hypertext information retrieval and mining must embrace and extend natural language (NL) representation and analysis, which have been researched intensively by a large body of computational linguists for several decades. NL techniques can now parse relatively well-formed sentences in many languages [80, 95, 203, 214], disambiguate words with multiple senses with high accuracy [4, 31, 185], tag words in running text with part-of-speech information [4, 88], represent NL documents in a canonical machine-usable form [205, 189, 199], and perform NL translation [8, 10, 113]. A combination of NL and IR techniques have been used for creating hyperlinks automatically [3, 21, 34, 93, 129] and expanding brief queries with related words for enhanced searches.

9.2.1   Lexical Networks and Ontologies

Humans acquire language understanding skills through constant learning during the first several years of their lives. Two key elements of language acquisition are building a *lexicon* and relating entries in the lexicon through a *lexical network* and/or an *ontology*. These initial steps of human language acquisition have now been captured digitally.

WordNet [151] is an English dictionary and an associated lexical network. Unique concepts are represented by nodes called *synsets* (synonym sets) in a number of graphs, one for each part of speech. In each graph, synsets are connected by a variety of labeled, generally directed edges. The noun graph has the richest link structure, featuring relations such as *is a kind of* (hyponymy) and *is a part of* (meronymy). For example, we can start from the noun *bronco* and walk up the hyponymy relation to find the path

> bronco, mustang, pony, horse, equine, odd-toed ungulate, placental mammal, mammal, vertebrate, chordate, animal, organism, entity

Interestingly, the *opposite of* (antonymy) relation is not between synsets but between words. Although

> watery, damp, moist, humid, soggy

are similar to *wet* and

> parched, arid, anhydrous, sere

are similar to *dry*, only *dry* and *wet* are antonyms.

Lexical networks, specifically the noun hierarchy of WordNet, are useful for a number of applications. They have been used for *query expansion*: padding a query with words in the same or closely related synsets to improve recall, as well as to better match the query to candidate answers in *question answering* (QA) systems (see Section 9.3). An ambiguous query term can be recognized using a dictionary or a lexical network, and it can be disambiguated by either asking the user or automatically from the context information in the query.

An ontology is a kind of schema describing specific roles of entities with regard to each other. Although there are large, general-purpose ontologies like CYC and OpenCYC [136], it is usually easier to design custom ontologies for specific applications. For example, a PC troubleshooting site may use a custom ontology where concepts like a hard disk, PCI bus, CPU, CPU fan, SCSI cables, jumper settings, device drivers, CD-ROMs, software, installation, and so on are represented and interconnected carefully through relations (e.g., the CPU fan is *attached* to the CPU to keep it *cool*). As another example, we can design an ontology for a university department comprising entities like faculty, student, administrative staff, research project, sponsor organization, research paper, journal, conference, and the like, together with relations like "a faculty advises a student," "a research project is sponsored by an organization," "a paper appears in a journal," and so on.

Deep knowledge of language, detailed design considerations, and a great deal of manual labor are needed to build lexical networks and ontologies. But the benefits of this investment are cumulative, and the process seems unavoidable for automatic language processing. Software and tools for maintaining, extending, and merging such knowledge bases are an attractive area of research.

9.2.2 **Part-of-Speech and Sense Tagging**

The extent of ambiguity in common words may surprise even a native speaker of a language. The word *run* has at least 11 senses as a noun (score, trial, sequence, trip, rivulet, etc.) and at least 42 senses as a verb (operate, flow, campaign, hunt, etc.)! Delimiting regions of sentences with *part-of-speech* (POS) and sense information for each token or token sequence is clearly the first step toward processing language with computers.

POS tagging can be done in a supervised or unsupervised fashion. A manually designed tag set and a collection of hand-tagged documents are needed for training a supervised tagger. Some sample tags are article, noun, verb, adverb, past-tense verb, object pronoun, and possessive pronoun. Since manual tagging is laborious, we can also use unsupervised techniques to cluster tokens that are likely to have similar functions in sentences, but unsupervised POS tagging may not have the precision needed to support subsequent linguistic operations such as parsing. Let us concentrate on supervised POS tagging.

Approaches to IE and supervised POS tagging are very similar because they both exploit proximity between tokens and labeling with token classes. Consider the following example by DeRose [67].

Word	Possible POS
The	article
man	noun, verb
still	noun, verb, adjective, adverb
saw	noun, past-tense verb
her	object pronoun, possessive pronoun

Similar to IE tasks, HMMs can be used for POS tagging. (In fact, HMMs were used for POS tagging before they were widely applied to IE scenarios.) The states of the HMM correspond to parts of speech. There are over 130 POS used regularly (see *www.comp.lancs.ac.uk/ucrel/claws1tags.html*). From a manually tagged training corpus, we estimate

- The matrix of transition probabilities from one POS state to another

- For each POS, a multinomial distribution over terms that can occur with that POS

We can now apply the Viterbi algorithm to find the best-state (POS) sequence for the sentence. Accuracy of 96% to 99% is not uncommon in statistical POS tagging. Once the model has been estimated, tagging can be performed at hundreds of megabytes per hour. Brill's tagger [25] and the CLAWS tagger [87] are two very well-known POS taggers.

Word sense disambiguation (WSD) is initiated after POS tagging is completed, which mostly limits ambiguity to within the correct POS. Much ambiguity may remain even after POS resolution. For example, the noun *interest* has at least six senses, the more frequent being

Usage	Sense
53%	money paid for use of money
21%	a share in a business or company
18%	readiness to give attention

Similar to the topic-distillation techniques we studied in Section 7.4, where anchor text and terms in nearby DOM nodes were used to qualify a hyperlink, most WSD techniques are based on learning from tokens *near* a target token. The training set consists of a sequence of sentences. Ambiguous tokens are tagged with a *sense identifier*, which can be a node ID from the WordNet graph. Consider a word w in the training text, which may be represented using a set of features extracted from

- The POS of words surrounding w within some window
- The stemmed form of w (see Section 3.1.1)
- Words that frequently co-occur with w in the same sentence

Each sense ID, which may be regarded as a class label (see Chapter 5), is thus associated with a number of instances, each being a suitable feature vector. At this point, a variety of supervised learning techniques can be used. Variants of NN classifiers are reported to perform very well [163]. I believe WSD would be a great feature for all but the most trivial queries, but WSD is not common in Web search engines. The only reason I can offer is that training a WSD system requires manual labeling and considerably more processing than inverted indexing.

9.2.3 Parsing and Knowledge Representation

Morphological and syntactic analyses are only the initial steps of the long path to parsing the input and then representing natural language in a form that can be manipulated and searched by a computer. For example, we would ideally like to map the sentences

Raja broke the window. I saw him running away.

into the graph structure shown in Figure 9.3. The sentences are quite simple, but it is nontrivial (and uncertain) to infer that *him* refers to *Raja* in the passage. Pronoun resolution is a special case of general resolution of references in sentences ("On the other hand, . . ."). *Pragmatics* also play an important role in correct parsing, as this (somewhat contrived) example shows:

Raja ate bread with jam.
Raja ate bread with Ravi.

Syntactic analysis can offer clues but not completely resolve such ambiguity.

Current parsing technology suitable for the Web can deal with single-sentence parses for restricted forms of sentences. Most grammar for natural language is ambiguous (e.g., "He saw the actor with a telescope"). The parsers are not always

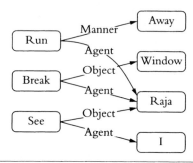

Raja broke the window.
I saw him running away.

FIGURE 9.3   A passage and its parsed graph.

context-free, and some might backtrack in the source. The "tree-adjoining grammar" (see *www.cis.upenn.edu/~xtag/*) approach [216] has succeeded in capturing a large subset of English in common usage. A detailed study of NL parsing is beyond the scope here, but I will touch upon the Link Parser by Sleator and Temperley [196]. The Link Parser has a dictionary that stores terms associated with one or more linking requirements or constraints, shown as polarized connectors in Figure 9.4. A successful parse introduces links among the terms in the sentence so three properties hold:

Satisfaction: Each linking requirement for each term in the sentence needs to be satisfied by some connector of the opposite polarity emerging from some other word in the sentence.

Connectivity: The links introduced should be able to connect all the terms in the sentence.

Planarity: The links introduced by the parser cannot cross when drawn above the sentence written on a line.

If a connector points to the right, its mate must point to the left. Exactly one connector wired to a black dot must be satisfied. The linking requirements are designed from linguistic considerations such as subject (S), object (O), determiner (D), modifier (M), preposition (J), and adverb (EV).

The parses produced by the Link Parser or some other parser can be a foundation for representing textual content in a uniform graph formalism (as in

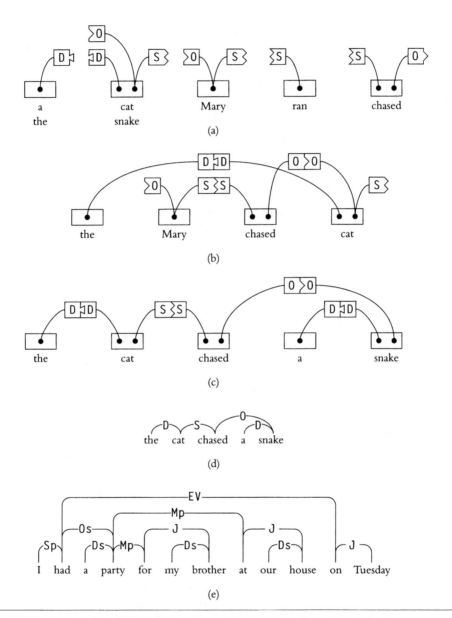

FIGURE 9.4 Examples of the Link Parser at work [196]. A set of words from the dictionary, each with one or more linking requirements (a). An illegal sentence and its unsuccessful parse (b). A legal sentence and its successful parse (c). A simpler way to show a legal parse graph (d). A relatively complex sentence parsed by the Link Parser (e).

Figure 9.3). Once this is accomplished, the challenge would be in matching parse graphs to query graphs and ranking the responses. Suitably annotated parse graphs can also be used as an interlingua for translation between many languages. The Universal Networking Language (*www.unl.ias.unu.edu/*) [206], being developed by the United Nations University in cooperation with a number of countries, is a promising step toward universal knowledge representation, translation, and searching.

9.3   Question Answering

IR systems and Web search engines return lists of documents in response to queries. Sometimes these queries are well-formed natural language questions that deserve short, accurate replies. Some examples of such queries are

- What is the height of Mount Everest?
- After which animal is the Canary Island named?
- What chemicals are used in the surface of writable compact disks?
- How many liters are there to a gallon?

The following questions also fall within the scope of QA systems, provided the answer appears directly in some document:

- How many people have set foot on the moon? (A QA system usually cannot make a list of all such people and return the length of the list.)
- Who was the most frequent coauthor with Gerald Salton? (A QA system cannot aggregate paper counts with each coauthor.)
- Is the distance between Tokyo and Rome more than 6000 miles? (Even if a document mentions the distance, a QA system generally will not do arithmetic.)

QA systems can be classified into the following grades of sophistication.

Slot-filling: The easiest kinds of questions, like "Who was the first human to set foot on the moon?," can be answered in the same way as slot-filling IE systems. There is a difference in the mode of operation: IE systems can use very sophisticated extraction logic because the set of queries is relatively static, whereas QA systems must take on ad hoc queries.

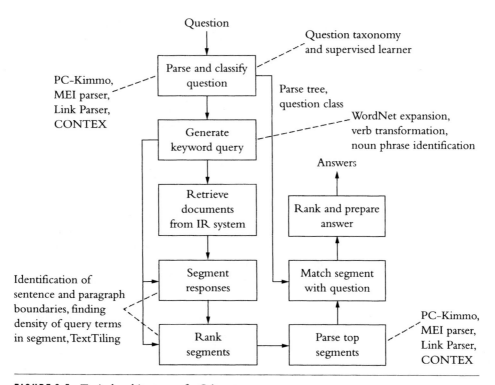

FIGURE 9.5 Typical architecture of a QA system.

Limited-domain: One way to retain the sophistication of the scanners is to limit the scope of the QA system to specific domains with handcrafted dictionaries and ontologies. The restriction lets the QA system do better knowledge representation and inferencing, and therefore answer deeper questions.

Open-domain: Without the luxury of domain restriction, QA systems have to be very sophisticated, bringing together IR, IE, NL parsing, and inferencing. This is still an intensely researched area.

START (*www.ai.mit.edu/projects/infolab/*) [121], Ask Jeeves (*www.ask.com/*, Mulder [131], Webclopedia [112], and MURAX [130] are some well-known QA systems.

The broad architecture of a typical QA system is shown in Figure 9.5. (The diagram follows the Webclopedia and Mulder systems.) Initially, documents are indexed using an IR system as usual. Using corpus knowledge, the system designers also compile a set of *answer types* and a (usually supervised) means of classifying a question into the most likely answer type(s). This step is called *question classification*. For example, answer types may include *date* (When was television invented?), *city name* (What is the capital of Uganda?), *definition* (What is a solenoid?), *countable number* (How many players form a football team?), *relative time* (How long does it take to fly from Rome to Tokyo?), and so on.

The main steps in processing a question are as follows. A question is generally assumed to be a coherent sentence that can be properly parsed. A variety of parsers, for example, MEI [46], the Link Parser [196], or CONTEX [106], may be used. Additional morphological analysis to guess the POS of unknown words may also help in open-domain QA systems (e.g., PC-Kimmo [6]).

The parsed question is first used for question classification. The question class and the original question are combined to generate a keyword query for the IR system. For example, if we know that the answer to the question "How long does it take to fly from Rome to Tokyo?" is a relative time, we can pad the IR query with terms preassociated with the concept of relative time, such as "hours," "weeks," and "months."

A basic premise in QA systems is that answers are contained within relatively small segments of single documents. Accordingly, once the IR system returns with response documents, the QA system has to segment the documents and score each segment with regard to the query. The segmenting approach stems from the fact that a short query and short segments can be subjected to sophisticated parsing, but it would be too time-consuming to subject the entire corpus, much of which may never be required by queries, to detailed parsing. The high speed of syntactic IR, compared to parsing, induces this basic asymmetry in the treatment of documents and queries in QA systems, compared to the largely symmetric treatment in vector-space IR systems.

Segments are initially chosen to contain all/most of the query terms within sentence or paragraph boundaries, and then scored, typically by computing some measure of the density with which query terms appear in them. Once the most promising segments are identified, they must be scored off with regard to the query for their final presentation to the user. Matching and scoring could be done through purely syntactic means, as in traditional IR, but increasingly, linguistic techniques are being brought to bear. The necessity of better matching becomes clear from the following question and answer:

Q: What is the color of grass?
A: Green.

The answer may come from a document that simply says "grass is green" without mentioning *color*. However, the hypernym hierarchy for *green* in WordNet reads

> green, chromatic color, color, visual property, property

Therefore, we need to integrate proximity search in lexical networks into the answer segment–matching step.

The highest-scoring segments are parsed to extract the specific information need expressed in the question. For example, for a question starting with "who," we should look for proper nouns (person names) in the parsed segments. If a question seeks a number, we should look for quantities, and so on. One advantage of QA on the Web (as opposed to QA on traditional IR corpora) is that many pages may contain the same information in slightly different linguistic forms, and the aggregation of data from different pages can weed out noise from erroneous parsing through majority voting. Finally, the matched lexical units are presented to the user.

9.4   Profiles, Personalization, and Collaboration

Despite their increasing sophistication, the most popular Web search engines remain impersonal. They definitely make use of aggregated query logs to improve indexing and ranking, but most do not keep track of users or sessions, which might help them build some representation of a user profile and use it for later searches by the same user, or implement some sort of collaborative searching by users with related information needs.

Personalization sounds appealing in principle, but is challenged with a number of issues, privacy being an important concern. Even if we overlooked the privacy issue for the time being, it is unclear how to represent user profiles or how to use them for subsequent searches. In terms of the data that can be collected easily from a user, the browsing history and bookmark files from a Web browser seem like a reasonable starting point. Bookmark files are sometimes organized into topic-based folders: these folders reflect the users' views of topics on the Web that are important to them.

Profiles can be used in at least two ways: to modify the behavior of search engines to ad hoc queries and to implement collaborative recommendation. For both applications, it will be useful to represent interest profiles as *mixtures* of topics (see Sections 4.4.2 and 4.5.2). Mixture modeling will help us compare people at a finer grain than aggregates, enabling better collaborative recommendations [44].

FreeNet (*freenet.sourceforge.net/*), Gnutella (*www.gnutella.com/*), and Napster (*www.napster.com/*) have hit the headlines by designing Web-enabled, large-scale, peer-to-peer systems for robust, decentralized file sharing. These systems are highly survivable. They pool storage from peer computers around the world to provide a repository of shared files. There is no central point of control, making it virtually impossible for an attacker to destroy information or take control of the system. These systems dynamically replicate and move information in response to demand, protecting the integrity of copies using strong cryptography against malicious tampering or counterfeiting. Some of these systems also provide private, anonymous access.

Just as the hyperlink graph of the Web is an overlay on the Internet graph, peer networks are an overlay on the Internet and the Web. To date, peer overlays have been used largely for file sharing, with no "deep" matching of information needs to content over the peer network. I envisage more content analysis (using techniques described in this book) to be integrated into peer networks.

REFERENCES

To make references as accessible as possible, we have included URLs where possible. Unfortunately, over time, Web sites disappear, accounts are reorganized, and hyperlinks break. If you find a broken link, you may be able to find the paper by pasting the title and author names into a general search engine such as *www.google.com* or an academic paper collection such as *citeseer.com,* or pasting the broken URL into the *Wayback Machine* at *www.archive.org.*

[1]   R. Agrawal, R. J. Bayardo, and R. Srikant. Athena: Mining-based interactive management of text databases. In *7th International Conference on Extending Database Technology (EDBT)*, Konstanz, Germany, March 2000. *www.almaden.ibm.com/cs/people/ragrawal /papers/athena.ps.*

[2]   R. Agrawal, J. Gehrke, D. Gunopulos, and P. Raghavan. Automatic subspace clustering of high dimensional data for data mining applications. In *SIGMOD Conference on Management of Data*, Seattle, WA, June 1998. *www.almaden.ibm.com/cs/quest/papers/sigmod98 _clique.pdf.*

[3]   J. Allan. Automatic hypertext link typing. In *7th ACM Conference on Hypertext, Hypertext '96*, pages 42–51, 1996.

[4]   J. Allen. *Natural Language Understanding*. Benjamin Cummings, 1987, 1995.

[5]   B. Amento, L. G. Terveen, and W. C. Hill. Does "authority" mean quality? Predicting expert quality ratings of Web documents. In *SIGIR*, pages 296–303. ACM, 2000. *citeseer.nj.nec.com/417258.html.*

[6]   E. L. Antworth. PC-KIMMO: A two-level processor for morphological analysis. Summer Institute of Linguistics, International Academic Bookstore, Dallas, 1990. *www.sil.org/pckimmo/pc-kimmo.html.*

[7]   C. Apte, F. Damerau, and S. M. Weiss. Automated learning of decision rules for text categorization. *ACM Transactions on Information Systems*, 1994. Also published as IBM Research Report RC18879.

[8]   D. J. Arnold, L. Balkan, R. L. Humphreys, S. Meijer, and L. Sadler. Machine translation: An introductory guide, 1995. *clwww.essex.ac.uk/~doug/book/book.html, clwww.essex.ac.uk/MTbook/, www.essex.ac.uk/linguistics/clmt/MTbook/.*

[9]   Y. Azar, A. Fiat, A. Karlin, F. McSherry, and J. Saia. Spectral analysis for data Mining. In *STOC*, vol. 33, pages 619–626, 2001.

[10]   Babelfish Language Translation Service. *www.altavista.com*, 1998.

[11]   F. Bacon. *The Advancement of Learning*. Clarendon Press, 1873.

[12]   Z. Bar-Yossef, A. Berg, S. Chien, J. Fakcharoenphol, and D. Weitz. Approximating aggregate queries about Web pages via random walks. In *Proceedings of the 26th International Conference on Very Large Databases (VLDB)*, pages 535–544, 2000. *www.cs.berkeley.edu/~zivi/papers/webwalker/webwalker.ps.gz.*

[13]   A.-L. Barabási and R. Albert. Emergence of scaling in random networks. *Science*, 286, pages 509–512, 1999.

[14]   A. Berg. Random jumps in WebWalker. Personal communication, April 2001.

[15]   M. W. Berry, S. T. Dumais, and G. W. O'Brien. Using linear algebra for intelligent information retrieval. *SIAM Review*, 37(4), pages 573–595, 1995. *www.cs.utk.edu/~library/TechReports/1994/ut-cs-94-270.ps.Z.*

[16]   K. Bharat and A. Bröder. A technique for measuring the relative size and overlap of public Web search engines. In *7th World Wide Web Conference (WWW7)*, 1998. *www7.scu.edu.au/programme/fullpapers/1937/com1937.htm*; also see update at *www.research.digital.com/SRC/whatsnew/sem.html.*

[17]   K. Bharat, A. Z. Bröder, J. Dean, and M. R. Henzinger. A comparison of techniques to find mirrored hosts on the WWW. *Journal of the American Society for Information Science and Technology*, 51(12), pages 1114–1122, 2000. *www.research.digital.com/SRC/personal /monika/papers/wows.ps.gz.*

[18]   K. Bharat and M. R. Henzinger. Improved algorithms for topic distillation in a hyperlinked environment. In *21st International ACM SIGIR Conference on Research and Development in Information Retrieval*, pages 104–111, August 1998. *www.henzinger.com/monika/mpapers/sigir98_ps.ps.*

[19]   S. Blackmore. *The Meme Machine*. Oxford University Press, 1999.

[20] C. L. Blake and C. J. Merz. UCI repository of machine learning databases, 1998. *www.ics.uci.edu/~mlearn/MLRepository.html*.

[21] W. J. Bluestein. Hypertext versions of journal articles: Computer aided linking and realistic human evaluation. Ph.D. thesis, University of Western Ontario, 1999.

[22] A. Blum and T. M. Mitchell. Combining labeled and unlabeled data with co-training. *Computational Learning Theory*, pages 92–100, 1998.

[23] P. Bradley, U. Fayyad, and C. Reina. Scaling clustering algorithms to large databases. In *4th International Conference on Knowledge Discovery and Data Mining*, August 1998. *www.ece.nwu.edu/~harsha/Clustering/scaleKM.ps*.

[24] B. E. Brewington and G. Cybenko. Keeping up with the changing Web. *IEEE Computer*, 33(5), pages 52–58, 2000.

[25] E. Brill. A simple rule-based part of speech tagger. In *Proceedings of the 3rd Conference on Applied Natural Language Processing*, pages 152–155, 1992. *www.cs.jhu.edu/~brill/acadpubs.html* and *citeseer.nj.nec.com/brill92simple.html*.

[26] S. Brin and L. Page. The anatomy of a large-scale hypertextual Web search engine. In *Proceedings of the 7th World Wide Web Conference (WWW7)*, 1998. *decweb.ethz.ch/WWW7/1921/com1921.htm*.

[27] A. Bröder, S. Glassman, M. Manasse, and G. Zweig. Syntactic clustering of the Web. In *Proceedings of the 6th International World Wide Web Conference*, pages 391–404, April 1997. Also appeared as SRC Technical Note 1997-015; see *research.compaq.com/SRC/WebArcheology/syntactic.html*.

[28] A. Bröder, R. Kumar, F. Maghoul, P. Raghavan, S. Rajagopalan, R. Stata, A. Tomkins, and J. Wiener. Graph structure in the Web: Experiments and models. In *WWW9*, pages 309–320, Amsterdam, May 2000. Elsevier Science. *www9.org/w9cdrom/160/160.html*.

[29] V. Bush. As we may think. *The Atlantic Monthly*, July 1945. *www.theatlantic.com/unbound/flashbks/computer/bushf.htm*.

[30] M. E. Califf and R. J. Mooney. Relational learning of pattern-match rules for information extraction. In *Proceedings of the 16th National Conference on Artificial Intelligence (AAAI-99)*, pages 328–334, July 1999.

[31] C. Cardie and D. Pierce. The role of lexicalization and pruning for base noun phrase grammars. In *AAA1 99*, pages 423–430, July 1999.

[32]   B. Carlin and T. Louis. *Bayes and Empirical Bayes Methods for Data Analysis*. Chapman and Hall, 1996.

[33]   J. Carriere and R. Kazman. WebQuery: Searching and visualizing the Web through connectivity. In *WWW6*, pages 701-7-11, 1997. *www.cgl.uwaterloo.ca/Projects/Vanish /webquery-1.html*.

[34]   N. Catenazzi and F. Gibb. The publishing process: The hyperbook approach. *Journal of Information Science*, 21(3), pages 161–172, 1995.

[35]   S. Chakrabarti and Y. Batterywala. Mining themes from bookmarks. In *ACM SIGKDD Workshop on Text Mining*, Boston, August 2000. *www.cse.iitb.ac.in/~soumen/doc/kdd2000 /theme2.ps*.

[36]   S. Chakrabarti and B. E. Dom. Feature diffusion across hyperlinks. U.S. Patent No. 6,125,361, April 1998. IBM Corp.

[37]   S. Chakrabarti, B. Dom, R. Agrawal, and P. Raghavan. Scalable feature selection, classification and signature generation for organizing large text databases into hierarchical topic taxonomies. *VLDB Journal*, August 1998. *www.cse.iitb.ac.in/~soumen/doc /vldbj1998/*.

[38]   S. Chakrabarti, B. Dom, D. Gibson, J. Kleinberg, P. Raghavan, and S. Rajagopalan. Automatic resource compilation by analyzing hyperlink structure and associated text. In *7th World Wide Web Conference (WWW7)*, 1998. *www7.scu.edu.au/programme/fullpapers /1898/com1898.html*.

[39]   S. Chakrabarti, B. Dom, and P. Indyk. Enhanced hypertext categorization using hyperlinks. In *SIGMOD Conference*. ACM, 1998. *www.cse.iitb.ac.in/~soumen/doc/sigmod98/*.

[40]   S. Chakrabarti, B. E. Dom, S. R. Kumar, P. Raghavan, S. Rajagopalan, A. Tomkins, D. Gibson, and J. Kleinberg. Mining the Web's link structure. *IEEE Computer*, 32(8), pages 60–67, August 1999.

[41]   S. Chakrabarti, D. A. Gibson, and K. S. McCurley. Surfing the Web backwards. In *WWW*, vol. 8, Toronto, May 1999.

[42]   S. Chakrabarti, M. M. Joshi, and V. B. Tawde. Enhanced topic distillation using text, markup tags, and hyperlinks. In *SIGIR*, vol. 24. ACM, New Orleans, September 2001.

[43] S. Chakrabarti, K. Punera, and M. Subramanyam. Accelerated focused crawling through online reference feedback. *WWW,* pages 148–159. ACM, Honolulu, May 2002. *www2002.org/CDROM/refereed/336/index.html.*

[44] S. Chakrabarti, S. Srivastava, M. Subramanyam, and M. Tiwari. Using Memex to archive and mine community Web browsing experience. *Computer Networks*, 33(1–6), pages 669–684, May 2000. *www9.org/w9cdrom/98/98.html.*

[45] S. Chakrabarti, M. van den Berg, and B. Dom. Focused crawling: A new approach to topic-specific Web resource discovery. *Computer Networks*, 31, pages 1623–1640, 1999. First appeared in the 8th International World Wide Web Conference, Toronto, May 1999. *www8.org/w8-papers/5a-search-query/crawling/.*

[46] E. Charniak. A maximum-entropy-inspired parser. Computer Science Technical Report CS-99-12, Brown University, August 1999. *www.cs.brown.edu/people/ec/.*

[47] P. Cheeseman and J. Stutz. Bayesian classification (AutoClass): Theory and results. In U. M. Fayyad, G. Piatetsky-Shapiro, P. Smyth, and R. Uthurusamy, editors, *Advances in Knowledge Discovery and Data Mining.* AAAI Press/The MIT Press, 1996. *ic.arc.nasa.gov/ic/projects/bayes-group/images/kdd-95.ps.*

[48] C. Chekuri, M. Goldwasser, P. Raghavan, and E. Upfal. Web search using automatic classification. In *6th World Wide Web Conference*, San Jose, CA, 1996.

[49] R. Chellappa and A. Jain. *Markov random fields: Theory and applications.* Academic Press, 1993.

[50] J. Cho, H. Garcia-Molina, and L. Page. Efficient crawling through URL ordering. In *7th World Wide Web Conference*, Brisbane, Australia, April 1998. *www7.scu.edu.au/programme/fullpapers/1919/com1919.htm.*

[51] J. Cho, N. Shivakumar, and H. Garcia-Molina. Finding replicated Web collections. In *ACM International Conference on Management of Data (SIGMOD)*, May 2000. *www-db.stanford.edu/~cho/papers/cho-mirror.pdf.*

[52] E. Cohen and D. D. Lewis. Approximating matrix multiplication for pattern recognition tasks. *Journal of Algorithms*, 30, pages 211–252, 1999. Special issue of selected papers from SODA'97. *www.research.att.com/~edith/publications.html.*

[53] W. W. Cohen. Fast effective rule induction. In *12th International Conference on Machine Learning*, Lake Tahoe, CA, 1995. *www.research.att.com/~wcohen/postscript/ml-95-ripper.ps* and *www.research.att.com/~wcohen/ripperd.html.*

[54]   W. W. Cohen and Y. Singer. Context-sensitive learning methods for text categorization. In *SIGIR*. ACM, 1996.

[55]   R. A. Cole, J. Mariani, H. Uszkoreit, A. Zaenen, V. Z. G. B. Varile, A. Zampolli, et al., editors. *Survey of the State of the Art in Human Language Technology*. Cambridge University Press, National Science Foundation and European Commission, 1996. *cslu.cse.ogi.edu/HLTsurvey/*.

[56]   T. H. Cormen, C. E. Leiserson, R. L. Rivest, and C. Stein. *Introduction to Algorithms*, second edition. McGraw-Hill, 2002.

[57]   T. M. Cover and J. A. Thomas. *Elements of Information Theory*. John Wiley & Sons, 1991.

[58]   M. Craven, S. Slattery, and K. Nigam. First-order learning for (Web) mining. *10th European Conference on Machine Learning*, pages 250–255, 1998. *citeseer.nj.nec.com/craven98firstorder.html*.

[59]   D. R. Cutting, D. R. Karger, and J. O. Pedersen. Constant interaction-time scatter/gather browsing of very large document collections. In *Annual International Conference on Research and Development in Information Retrieval (SIGIR)*, 1993.

[60]   D. R. Cutting, D. R. Karger, J. O. Pedersen, and J. W. Tukey. Scatter/gather: A cluster-based approach to browsing large document collections. In *Annual International Conference on Research and Development in Information Retrieval (SIGIR)*, Denmark, 1992.

[61]   B. D. Davison. Topical locality in the Web. In *Proceedings of the 23rd Annual International Conference on Research and Development in Information Retrieval (SIGIR 2000)*, pages 272–279. ACM, Athens, July 2000. *www.cs.rutgers.edu/~davison/pubs/2000/sigir/*.

[62]   R. Dawkins. *The Selfish Gene*, second ed. Oxford University Press, 1989.

[63]   P. M. E. De Bra and R. D. J. Post. Information retrieval in the World Wide Web: Making client-based searching feasible. In *Proceedings of the 1st International World Wide Web Conference*, Geneva, 1994. *www1.cern.ch/PapersWWW94/reinpost.ps*.

[64]   P. M. E. De Bra and R. D. J. Post. Searching for arbitrary information in the WWW: The fish search for Mosaic. In *2nd World Wide Web Conference '94: Mosaic and the Web*, Chicago, October 1994. *archive.ncsa.uiuc.edu/SDG/IT94/Proceedings/Searching/debra/article.html* and *citeseer.nj.nec.com/172936.html*.

[65]   J. Dean and M. R. Henzinger. Finding related pages in the World Wide Web. *8th World Wide Web Conference*, Toronto, May 1999.

[66]   S. Deerwester, S. T. Dumais, T. K. Landauer, G. W. Furnas, and R. A. Harshman. Indexing by latent semantic analysis. *Journal of the Society for Information Science*, 41(6), pages 391–407, 1990. *superbook.telcordia.com/~remde/lsi/papers/JASIS90.ps.*

[67]   S. J. DeRose. Grammatical category disambiguation by statistical optimization. *Computational Linguistics*, 14(1), pages 31–39, 1988.

[68]   M. Dewey. *Dewey Decimal Classification and Relative Index*, 16th edition. Forest Press, 1958.

[69]   M. Diligenti, F. Coetzee, S. Lawrence, C. L. Giles, and M. Gori. Focused crawling using context graphs. In A. E. Abbadi, M. L. Brodie, S. Chakravarthy, U. Dayal, N. Kamel, G. Schlageter, and K.-Y. Whang, editors, *Proceedings of 26th International Conference on Very Large Data Bases (VLDB), September 10–14, 2000, Cairo*, pages 527–534. Morgan Kaufmann, 2000. *www.neci.nec.com/~lawrence/papers/focus-vldb00/focus-vldb00.pdf*.

[70]   S. Dill, S. R. Kumar, K. S. McCurley, S. Rajagopalan, D. Sivakumar, and A. Tomkins. Self-similarity in the Web. In *VLDB*, pages 69–78, Rome, September 2001. *www.almaden.ibm.com/cs/k53/fractal.ps.*

[71]   P. Domingos and M. Pazzani. On the optimality of the simple Bayesian classifier under zero-one loss. *Machine Learning*, 29, pages 103–130, 1997.

[72]   R. Duda and P. Hart. *Pattern Classification and Scene Analysis.* John Wiley & Sons, 1973.

[73]   S. T. Dumais. Using SVMs for text categorization. *IEEE Intelligent Systems*, 13(4), pages 21–23, July 1998.

[74]   S. T. Dumais, J. Platt, D. Heckerman, and M. Sahami. Inductive learning algorithms and representations for text categorization. In *7th Conference on Information and Knowledge Management*, 1998. *www.research.microsoft.com/~jplatt/cikm98.pdf*.

[75]   T. E. Dunning. Accurate methods for the statistics of surprise and coincidence. *Computational Linguistics*, 19(1), pages 61–174, 1993.

[76]   C. Faloutsos and K.-I. Lin. FastMap: A fast algorithm for indexing, data-mining and visualization of traditional and multimedia datasets. In M. J. Carey and D. A. Schneider, editors, *Proceedings of the 1995 ACM SIGMOD International Conference on Management of Data*, pages 163–74, San Jose, CA, 1995.

[77]   G. W. Flake, S. Lawrence, C. Lee Giles, and F. M. Coetzee. Self-organization and identification of Web communities. *IEEE Computer*, 35(3), pages 66–71, 2002. *www.neci.nec.com/~lawrence/papers/web-computer02/bib.html*.

[78]   R. Flesch. A new readability yardstick. *Journal of Applied Psychology*, 32, pages 221–233, 1948.

[79]   D. Florescu, D. Kossman, and I. Manolescu. Integrating keyword searches into XML query processing. In *WWW*, vol. 9, pages 119–135, Amsterdam, May 2000. Elsevier Science. *www9.org/w9cdrom/324/324.html*.

[80]   S. Fong and R. Berwick. *Parsing with Principles and Parameters*. The MIT Press, 1992.

[81]   G. D. Forney, Jr. The Viterbi algorithm. In *Proceedings of IEEE*, 61(3), pages 263–278, March 1973.

[82]   W. B. Frakes and R. Baeza-Yates. *Information Retrieval: Data Structures and Algorithms*. Prentice Hall, 1992.

[83]   P. Frankl and H. Maehara. The Johnson-Lindenstrauss lemma and the sphericity of some graphs. *Journal of Combinatorial Theory*, B 44, pages 355–362, 1988.

[84]   D. Freitag. Information extraction from HTML: Application of a general machine learning approach. In *Proceedings of the 15th National Conference on Artificial Intelligence*, pages 517–523, 1998.

[85]   J. H. Friedman. On bias, variance, 0/1 loss, and the curse of dimensionality. *Data Mining and Knowledge Discovery*, 1(1), pages 55–77, 1997. Stanford University Technical Report. *ftp://playfair.stanford.edu/pub/friedman/curse.ps.Z*.

[86]   N. Fuhr and C. Buckley. A Probabilistic Learning Approach for Document Indexing. *ACM Transactions on Information Systems*, 9(3), pages 223–248, 1991.

[87]   R. Garside and N. Smith. A hybrid grammatical tagger: CLAWS4. In R. Garside, G. Leech, and A. McEnery, editors, *Corpus Annotation: Linguistic Information from Computer Text Corpora*, pages 102–121. Longman, 1997. *www.comp.lancs.ac.uk/computing/research/ucrel/claws/*.

[88]   G. Gazder and C. Mellish. *Natural Language Processing in LISP*. Addison-Wesley, 1989.

[89]   D. Gibson, J. M. Kleinberg, and P. Raghavan. Inferring Web communities from link topology. In *ACM Conference on Hypertext*, pages 225–234, 1998.

[90] A. Gionis, P. Indyk, and R. Motwani. Similarity search in high dimensions via hashing. In *VLDB*, pages 518-529, 1999. *citeseer.nj.nec.com/gionis97similarity.html*.

[91] G. H. Golub and C. F. van Loan. *Matrix Computations*. Johns Hopkins University Press, 1989.

[92] N. Govert, M. Lalmas, and N. Fuhr. A Probabilistic Description-Oriented Approach for Categorizing Web Documents. In *CIKM*, pages 475–482, 1999. *citeseer.nj.nec.com/govert99probabilistic.html*.

[93] S. G. Green. Building newspaper links in newspaper articles using semantic similarity. In *Natural Language and Data Bases Conference,* pages 178–190, 1997. *citeseer.nj.nec.com/Stephen97building.html*.

[94] S. Guiasu and A. Shenitzer. The principle of maximum entropy. *The Mathematical Intelligencer*, 7(1), pages 42–48, 1985.

[95] L. Haegeman. *Introduction to Government and Binding Theory*. Basil Blackwell Ltd., 1991.

[96] J. Han and M. Kamber. *Data Mining: Concepts and Techniques*. Morgan Kaufmann, 2000.

[97] D. Hand, H. Manilla, and P. Smyth. *Principles of Data Mining*. The MIT Press, 2001.

[98] T. H. Haveliwala. Topic-sensitive PageRank, *WWW,* pages 517–526. ACM, Honolulu, May 2002. *www2002.org/CDROM/refereed/127/index.html*.

[99] D. Hawking, E. Voorhees, N. Craswell, and P. Bailey. Overview of the TREC-8 Web track. In E. Voorhees and D. Harman, editors, *Proceedings of the 8th Text REtrieval Conference (TREC-8)*, NIST Special Publication 500-246, pages 131–150, 2000.

[100] M. Hearst. Multi-paragraph segmentation of expository text. In *Proceedings of the 32nd Annual Meeting of the Association for Computational Linguistics*, Las Cruces, NM, June 1994. *www.sims.berkeley.edu/~hearst/publications.shtml*.

[101] M. Hearst and C. Karadi. Cat-a-Cone: An interactive interface for specifying searches and viewing retrieval results using a large category hierarchy. In *Proceedings of the 20th Annual International ACM/SIGIR Conference*, Philadelphia, July 1997. *ftp://parcftp.xerox.com/pub/hearst/sigir97.ps*.

[102] D. Heckerman. A tutorial on learning with Bayesian networks. In *12th International Conference on Machine Learning*, Tahoe City, CA. July 1995. *ftp://ftp.research.microsoft.com/pub/dtg/david/tutorial.PS* and *ftp://ftp.research.microsoft.com/pub/tr/TR-95-06.PS*.

[103] D. Heckerman. Bayesian networks for data mining. *Data Mining and Knowledge Discovery*, 1(1), 1997. *ftp://ftp.research.microsoft.com/pub/dtg/david/tutorial.PS* and *ftp://ftp.research.microsoft.com/pub/tr/TR-95-06.PS*.

[104] B. Hendrickson and R. W. Leland. A multi-level algorithm for partitioning graphs. In *Supercomputing*, 1995.

[105] M. R. Henzinger, A. Heydon, M. Mitzenmacher, and M. Najork. On near-uniform URL sampling. In *WWW9*, Amsterdam, May 2000. *www9.org/w9cdrom/88/88.html*.

[106] U. Hermjakob and R. J. Mooney. Learning parse and translation decisions from examples with rich context. In P. R. Cohen and W. Wahlster, editors, In *Proceedings of the 35th Annual Meeting of the Association for Computational Linguistics and 8th Conference of the European Chapter of the Association for Computational Linguistics*, pages 482–489, Somerset, NJ, 1997.

[107] M. Hersovici, M. Jacovi, Y. S. Maarek, D. Pelleg, M. Shtalhaim, and S. Ur. The shark-search algorithm—an application: Tailored Web site mapping. In *WWW7*, 1998. *www7.scu.edu.au/programme/fullpapers/1849/com1849.htm*.

[108] A. Heydon and M. Najork. Mercator: A scalable, extensible Web crawler. *World Wide Web Conference*, 2(4), pages 219–229, 1999.

[109] T. Hofmann. Probabilistic latent semantic analysis. In *Uncertainty in Artifical Intelligence*, 1999. *www.cs.brown.edu/people/th/publications.html*.

[110] T. Hofmann. Probabilistic latent semantic indexing. In *SIGIR*, 1999. *www.cs.brown.edu/people/th/publications.html*.

[111] T. Hofmann and J. Puzicha. Unsupervised learning from dyadic data. Technical Report TR-98-042, University of California, Berkeley, 1998.

[112] E. Hovy, L. Gerber, U. Hermjakob, M. Junk, and C.-Y. Lin. Question answering in Webclopedia. In *Proceedings of the 9th Text REtrieval Conference (TREC-9)*. NIST, 2001. *trec.nist.gov/pubs/trec9/papers/webclopedia.pdf*.

[113] W. J. Hutchins and H. L. Somers. *An Introduction to Machine Translation*. Academic Press, 1992.

[114] A. K. Jain and R. C. Dubes. *Algorithms for Clustering Data*. Prentice Hall, 1988.

[115] W. James and C. Stein. Estimation with quadratic loss. In *Proceedings of the 4th Berkeley Symposium on Mathematical Statistics and Probability*, vol. 1, pages 361–379. University of California Press, 1961.

[116] E. T. Jaynes. Notes on present status and future prospects. In W. T. Grandy and L. H. Schick, editors, *Maximum Entropy and Bayesian Methods*, pages 1–13. Kluwer, 1990.

[117] T. Joachims. Making large-scale SVM learning practical. In B. Schölkopf, C. Burges, and A. Smola, editors, *Advances in Kernel Methods: Support Vector Learning*. The MIT Press, 1999. *www-ai.cs.uni-dortmund.de/DOKUMENTE/joachims_99a.pdf*.

[118] T. Joachims. A statistical learning model of text classification for support vector machines. In W. B. Croft, D. J. Harper, D. H. Kraft, and J. Zobel, editors, *International Conference on Research and Development in Information Retrieval*, vol. 24, pages 128–136. SIGIR, ACM, New Orleans, September 2001.

[119] T. Joachims. Text categorization with support vector machines: Learning with many relevant features. In C. Nédellec and C. Rouveirol, editors, *Proceedings of ECML-98, 10th European Conference on Machine Learning*, no. 1398 in LNCS, pages 137–142, Chemnitz, Germany, 1998. Springer-Verlag.

[120] B. Kahle. Preserving the Internet. *Scientific American*, 276(3), pages 82–83, March 1997. *www.sciam.com/0397issue/0397kahle.html* and *www.alexa.com/~brewster/essays/sciam_article.html*.

[121] B. Katz. From sentence processing to information access on the World Wide Web. In *AAAI Spring Symposium on Natural Language Processing for the World Wide Web*, pages 77–94, Stanford, CA, 1997. Stanford University. *www.ai.mit.edu/people/boris/webaccess/*.

[122] J. M. Kleinberg. Authoritative sources in a hyperlinked environment. In *Proceedings of ACM-SIAM Symposium on Discrete Algorithms*, 1998. Also appears as IBM Research Report RJ10076(91892). *www.cs.cornell.edu/home/kleinber/auth.ps*.

[123] J. M. Kleinberg. Two algorithms for nearest-neighbor search in high dimensions. In *ACM Symposium on Theory of Computing*, pages 599–608, 1997.

[124] J. M. Kleinberg and E. Tardos. Approximation algorithms for classification problems with pairwise relationships: Metric labeling and Markov random fields. In *IEEE Symposium on Foundations of Computer Science*, pages 14–23, 1999.

[125] T. Kohonen, S. Kaski, K. Lagus, J. Salojärvi, V. Paatero, and A. Saarela. Self organization of a massive document collection. *IEEE Transactions on Neural Networks (Special Issue on*

Neural Networks for Data Mining and Knowledge Discovery), 11(3), pages 574–585, May 2000. *websom.hut.fi/websom/doc/publications.html*.

[126] D. Koller and M. Sahami. Hierarchically classifying documents using very few words. In L. Saitta, editor, *International Conference on Machine Learning*, vol. 14. Morgan Kaufmann, 1997. *robotics.stanford.edu/users/sahami/papers-dir/ml97-hier.ps*.

[127] D. Koller and M. Sahami. Toward optimal feature selection. In L. Saitta, editor, *International Conference on Machine Learning*, vol. 13. Morgan Kaufmann, 1996.

[128] S. R. Kumar, P. Raghavan, S. Rajagopalan, and A. Tomkins. Trawling the Web for emerging cyber-communities. *WWW8 / Computer Networks*, 31(11–16), pages 1481–1493, 1999. *www8.org/w8-papers/4a-search-mining/trawling/trawling.html*.

[129] K. S. Kumarvel. Automatic hypertext creation. M.Tech thesis, Computer Science and Engineering Department, IIT Bombay, 1997.

[130] J. Kupiec. MURAX: A robust linguistic approach for question answering using an on-line encyclopedia. In R. Korfhage, E. M. Rasmussen, and P. Willett, editors, *SIGIR*, pages 181–190. ACM, 1993.

[131] C. Kwok, O. Etzioni, and D. S. Weld. Scaling question answering to the Web. In *WWW*, vol. 10, pages 150–161, Hong Kong, May 2001. IW3C2 and ACM. *www10.org/cdrom/papers/120/*.

[132] R. Larson. Bibliometrics of the World Wide Web: An exploratory analysis of the intellectual structure of cyberspace. In *Annual Meeting of the American Society for Information Science*, 1996. *sherlock.berkeley.edu/asis96/asis96.html*.

[133] S. Lawrence and C. Lee Giles. Accessibility of information on the Web. *Nature*, 400, pages 107–109, July 1999.

[134] S. Lawrence and C. Lee Giles. Searching the World Wide Web. *Science*, 280, pages 98–100, April 1998.

[135] R. Lempel and S. Moran. SALSA: The stochastic approach for link-structure analysis. *ACM Transactions on Information Systems (TOIS)*, 19(2), pages 131–160, April 2001. *www.cs.technion.ac.il/~moran/r/PS/lm-feb01.ps*.

[136] D. B. Lenat. Cyc: A large-scale investment in knowledge infrastructure. *Communications of the ACM*, 38(11), pages 32–38, November 1995. *www.cyc.com/* and *www.opencyc.org/*.

[137] D. D. Lewis. Evaluating text categorization. In *Proceedings of the Speech and Natural Language Workshop*, pages 312–318. Morgan Kaufmann, 1991.

[138] D. D. Lewis. Naive (Bayes) at forty: The independence assumption in information retrieval. In C. Nedellec and C. Rouveirol, editors, *10th European Conference on Machine Learning*, pages 4–15, Chemnitz, Germany, April 1998. Springer.

[139] D. D. Lewis. The Reuters-21578 text categorization test collection, 1997. *www.research .att.com/lewis/reuters21578.html*.

[140] W.-S. Li, Q. Vu, D. Agrawal, Y. Hara, and H. Takano. PowerBookmarks: A system for personalizable Web information organization, sharing and management. *Computer Networks*, 31, May 1999. First appeared in the *8th International World Wide Web Conference,* Toronto, May 1999. *www8.org/w8-papers/3b-web-doc/power/power.pdf* .

[141] Y. S. Maarek and I. Z. Ben Shaul. Automatically organizing bookmarks per content. In *5th International World Wide Web Conference*, Paris, May 1996.

[142] S. Macskassy, A. Banerjee, B. Davidson, and H. Hirsh. Human performance on clustering Web pages: A performance study. In *Knowledge Discovery and Data Mining*, vol. 4, pages 264–268, 1998.

[143] O. A. McBryan. GENVL and WWWW: Tools for taming the Web. In *Proceedings of the First International World Wide Web Conference*, pages 79–90, 1994.

[144] K. W. McCain. Core journal networks and cocitation maps in the marine sciences: Tools for information management in interdisciplinary research. In D. Shaw, editor, *ASIS'92: Proceedings of the 55th ASIS Annual Meeting*, pages 3–7, Medford, NJ, 1992. American Society for Information Science.

[145] A. McCallum and K. Nigam. A comparison of event models for naive Bayes text classification. In *AAAI/ICML-98 Workshop on Learning for Text Categorization*, pages 41–48. AAAI Press, 1998. Also Technical Report WS-98-05, CMU. *www.cs.cmu.edu/~knigam/papers/multinomial-aaaiws98.pdf* .

[146] A. McCallum, K. Nigam, J. Rennie, and K. Seymore. Building domain-specific search engines with machine learning techniques. In *AAAI-99 Spring Symposium*, 1999. *www.cs.cmu.edu/~mccallum/papers/cora-aaaiss99.ps.gz*.

[147]   A. McCallum, R. Rosenfeld, T. Mitchell, and A. Ng. Improving text classification by shrinkage in a hierarchy of classes. In *15th International Conference on Machine Learning*, pages 350–367, 1998. *www.cs.cmu.edu/~mccallum/papers /hier-icml98.ps.gz*.

[148]   F. Menczer. Links tell us about lexical and semantic Web content. Technical Report Computer Science Abstract CS.IR/0108004, arXiv.org, August 2001. *arxiv.org/abs/cs.IR/0108004*.

[149]   F. Menczer and R. K. Belew. Adaptive retrieval agents: Internalizing local context and scaling up to the Web. *Machine Learning*, 39(2/3), pages 203–242, 2000. Longer version available as Technical Report CS98-579, University of California, San Diego, *dollar.biz.uiowa.edu/~fil/Papers/MLJ.ps*.

[150]   D. Meretakis and B. Wuthrich. Extending naive Bayes classifiers using long itemsets. In *5th ACM SIGKDD International Conference on Knowledge Discovery and Data Mining*, San Diego, CA, August 1999.

[151]   G. Miller, R. Beckwith, C. FellBaum, D. Gross, K. Miller, and R. Tengi. Five papers on WordNet. Princeton University, August 1993. *ftp://ftp.cogsci.princeton.edu/pub/wordnet /5papers.pdf*.

[152]   T. M. Mitchell. Conditions for the equivalence of hierarchical and flat Bayesian classifiers. Technical note, 1998. *www.cs.cmu.edu/~tom/hierproof.ps*.

[153]   T. M. Mitchell. *Machine Learning*. McGraw-Hill, 1997.

[154]   M. Mitra, C. Buckley, A. Singhal, and C. Cardie. An analysis of statistical and syntactic phrases. In *Proceedings of RIAO-97, 5th International Conference* "Recherche d'Information Assistee par Ordinateur," pages 200–214, Montreal, Quebec, 1997.

[155]   D. Mladenic. Feature subset selection in text-learning. In *10th European Conference on Machine Learning*, vol. 1398, pages 95–100, 1998.

[156]   F. Mosteller and D. L. Wallace. *Inference and Disputed Authorship: The Federalist*. Addison-Wesley, 1964.

[157]   R. Motwani and P. Raghavan. *Randomized Algorithms*. Cambridge University Press, 1995.

[158]   M. Najork and J. Weiner. Breadth-first search crawling yields high-quality pages. In *WWW 10*, Hong Kong, May 2001. *www10.org/cdrom/papers/208*.

[159] National Archives and Records Administration. Using the census soundex. General information leaflet 55. Washington, DC, 1995. Free brochure available from *inquire@nara.gov*.

[160] T. Nelson. A file structure for the complex, the changing, and the indeterminate. In *Proceedings of the ACM National Conference*, pages 84–100, 1965.

[161] T. H. Nelson. *Literary Machines*. Mindful Press, 1982.

[162] A. Ng, A. Zheng, and M. Jordan. Stable algorithms for link analysis. In *24th Annual International ACM SIGIR Conference*. ACM, New Orleans, September 2001. *www.cs.berkeley.edu/~ang/*.

[163] H. T. Ng and H. B. Lee. Integrating multiple knowledge sources to disambiguate word sense: An exemplar-based approach. In A. Joshi and M. Palmer, editors, *Proceedings of the 34th Annual Meeting of the Association for Computational Linguistics*, San Francisco, pages 40–47. Morgan Kaufmann, 1996.

[164] B. Nichols, D. Buttlar, and J. P. Farrell. *Pthreads Programming*. O'Reilly and Associates, 1996.

[165] J. Nielsen. *Multimedia and Hypertext: The Internet and Beyond*. Morgan Kaufmann, 1995. (Originally published by AP Professional.)

[166] K. Nigam and R. Ghani. Analyzing the effectiveness and applicability of co-training. In *9th International Conference on Information and Knowledge Management (CIKM)*, 2000. *www.cs.cmu.edu/~knigam*.

[167] K. Nigam, J. Lafferty, and A. McCallum. Using maximum entropy for text classification. In *IJCAI'99 Workshop on Information Filtering*, 1999. *www.cs.cmu.edu/~mccallum/papers/maxent-ijcaiws99.ps.gz*.

[168] K. Nigam, A. McCallum, S. Thrun, and T. Mitchell. Text classification from labeled and unlabeled documents using EM. *Machine Learning*, 39(2/3), pages 103–134, 2000. *www-2.cs.cmu.edu/~mccallum/papers/emcat-mlj2000.ps.gz*.

[169] L. Page, S. Brin, R. Motwani, and T. Winograd. The PageRank citation ranking: Bringing order to the Web. Unpublished manuscript. *google.stanford.edu/~backrub/pageranksub.ps, 1998*.

[170] C. H. Papadimitriou, P. Raghavan, H. Tamaki, and S. Vempala. Latent semantic indexing: A probabilistic analysis. *JCSS*, 61(2), pages 217–235, 2000. A preliminary version appeared in *ACM PODS,* pages 159–168, 1998.

[171] L. Pelkowitz. A continuous relaxation labeling algorithm for Markov random fields. *IEEE Transactions on Systems, Man and Cybernetics*, 20(3), pages 709–715, May 1990.

[172] D. M. Pennock, G. W. Flake, S. Lawrence, C. L. Giles, and E. J. Glover. Winners don't take all: Characterizing the competition for links on the Web. *Proceedings of the National Academy of Sciences*, 2002. Preprint available: *www.neci.nec.com/homepages/dpennock /publications.html*.

[173] S. D. Pietra, V. D. Pietra, and J. Laferty. Inducing features of random fields. *IEEE Transactions on Pattern Analysis and Machine Intelligence*, 19(4), pages 380–393, April 1997.

[174] P. Pirolli, J. Pitkow, and R. Rao. Silk from a Sow's Ear: Extracting Usable Structures from the Web. In *ACM CHI*, 1996.

[175] J. Platt. Probabilities for SV machines. In A. Smola, P. Bartlett, B. Schölkopf, and D. Schuurmans, editors, *Advances in Large Margin Classifiers*, pages 61–74. The MIT Press, 1999. *research.microsoft.com/~jplatt/SVMprob.ps.gz*.

[176] J. Platt. Sequential minimal optimization: A fast algorithm for training support vector machines. Technical Report MSR-TR-98-14, Microsoft Research, 1998. *www.research.microsoft.com/users/jplatt/smoTR.pdf*.

[177] J. M. Ponte and W. B. Croft. A language modeling approach to information retrieval. In *SIGIR*, pages 275–281. ACM, 1998. *cobar.cs.umass.edu/pubfiles/ir-120.ps*.

[178] A. Popescul, L. H. Ungar, D. M. Pennock, and S. Lawrence. Probabilistic models for unified collaborative and content-based recommendation in sparse-data environments. In *Proceedings of the 17th Conference on Uncertainty in Artificial Intelligence (UAI-2001)*, Seattle, WA, August 2001, pages 437–444. *www.neci.nec.com/homepages/dpennock/publications .html*.

[179] M. F. Porter. An algorithm for suffic stripping. *Program*, 14(3), pages 130–137, 1980.

[180] E. Rasmussen. Clustering algorithms. In W. B. Frakes and R. Baeza-Yates, editors, *Information Retrieval: Data Structure and Algorithms*, Chap. 16. Prentice Hall, 1992.

[181] J. Rennie and A. McCallum. Using reinforcement learning to spider the Web efficiently. In *16th International Conference on Machine Learning*, pages 335–343, 1999. *www.cs.cmu.edu/~mccallum/papers/rlspider-icml99s.ps.gz*.

[182] J. Rissanen. Stochastic complexity in statistical inquiry. In *World Scientific Series in Computer Science*, vol. 15. World Scientific, 1989.

[183] S. E. Robertson and S. Walker. Some simple effective approximations to the 2-Poisson model for probabilistic weighted retrieval. In *SIGIR*, pages 232–241, 1994.

[184] M. Sahami, M. Hearst, and E. Saund. Applying the multiple cause mixture model to text categorization. In L. Saitta, editor, *International Conference on Machine Learning*, vol. 13, pages 435–443. Morgan Kaufmann, 1996. *robotics.stanford.edu/users/sahami/papers-dir/ml96-mcmm.ps*.

[185] G. Salton. *Automatic Text Processing*. Addison-Wesley, 1989.

[186] G. Salton and M. J. McGill. *Introduction to Modern Information Retrieval*. McGraw-Hill, 1983.

[187] E. Saund. A multiple cause mixture model for unsupervised learning. *Neural Computation*, 7(1), pages 51–71, 1995.

[188] J. Savoy. An extended vector processing scheme for searching information in hypertext systems. *Information Processing and Management*, 32(2), pages 155–170, March 1996.

[189] R. G. Schank and C. J. Rieger. Inference and computer understanding of natural language. In R. J. Brachman and H. J. Levesque (editors), *Readings in Knowledge Representation*, Morgan Kaufmann, 1985.

[190] B. Schölkopf and A. Smola. *Learning with Kernels*. The MIT Press, 2002.

[191] H. Schütze and C. Silverstein. A comparison of projections for efficient document clustering. In *Proceedings of the 20th Annual ACM SIGIR Conference on Research and Development in Information Retrieval*, pages 74–81, July 1997. *www-cs-students.stanford.edu/~csilvers/papers/metrics-sigir.ps*.

[192] J. R. Seeley. The net of reciprocal influence: A problem in treating sociometric data. *Canadian Journal of Psychology*, 3, pages 234–240, 1949.

[193] K. Seymore, A. McCallum, and R. Rosenfeld. Learning Hidden Markov Model structure for information extraction. In *Papers from the AAAI-99 Workshop on Machine Learning*

for Information Extraction, pages 37–42, 1999. *www-2.cs.cmu.edu/~kseymore/papers/ie_aaai99.ps.gz*.

[194] A. Shashua. On the equivalence between the support vector machine for classification and sparsified Fisher's linear discriminant. *Neural Processing Letters*, 9(2), pages 129–139, 1999. *www.cs.huji.ac.il/~shashua/papers/fisher-NPL.pdf*.

[195] A. Singhal and M. Kaszkiel. A case study in Web search using TREC algorithms. In *WWW 10*, Hong Kong, May 2001. *www10.org/cdrom/papers/317*.

[196] D. Sleator and D. Temperley. Parsing English with a link grammar. Computer Science Technical Report CMU-CS-91-196, Carnegie Mellon University, October 1991. *www.link.cs.cmu.edu/link/papers/index.html*.

[197] P. Smyth. Clustering using Monte Carlo cross-validation. In *Second International Conference on Knowledge Discovery and Data Mining (KDD-96)*, pages 126–133, Portland, OR, August 1996. AAAI Press.

[198] S. Soderland. Learning information extraction rules for semi-structured and free text. *Machine Learning*, 34(1–3), pages 233–272, 1999. *www.cs.washington.edu/homes/soderlan/WHISK.ps*.

[199] J. F. Sowa. *Conceptual Structures: Information Processing in Mind and Machines*. Addison-Wesley, 1984.

[200] K. Sparck Jones, S. Walker, and S. E. Robertson. A probabilistic model of information retrieval: Development and comparative experiments. *Information Processing and Management*, 36(1–2):1, pages 779–808, and 2, pages 809–840, 2000.

[201] C. Stein. Inadmissibility of the usual estimator for the mean of a multivariate normal distribution. In *Proceedings of the 3rd Berkeley Symposium on Mathematical Statistics and Probability*, vol. 1, pages 197–206. University of California Press, 1955.

[202] W. R. Stevens. *TCP/IP Illustrated: TCP for Transactions, HTTP, NNTP, and the UNIX Domain Protocols*, vol.3. Addison-Wesley, 1996.

[203] D. Temperley. An introduction to link grammar parser. Technical report, April 1999. *www.link.cs.cmu.edu/link/dict/introduction.html*.

[204] H. R. Turtle and W. B. Croft. Evaluation of an inference network-based retrieval model. *ACM Transactions on Information Systems*, 9(3), pages 187–222, 1991.

[205] U. N. U. Institute of Advanced Studies. The Universal Networking Language: Specification document. *Internal Technical Document*, 1999. *www.unl.ias.unu.edu/*.

[206] H. Uchida, M. Zhu, and T. D. Senta. *The UNL: A gift for a millennium*. Institute of Advanced Studies, United Nations University, pages 53–67, Tokyo, November 1999. *www.unl.ias.unu.edu/*.

[207] S. Vaithyanathan and B. Dom. Generalized model selection for unsupervised learning in high dimensions. In *Neural Information Processing Systems (NIPS)*, Denver, CO, 1999. *www.almaden.ibm.com/cs/k53/papers/nips99.ps*.

[208] L. G. Valiant. A theory of the learnable. *Communications of the ACM*, 27(11), pages 1134–1142, 1984.

[209] V. Vapnik. *Statistical Learning Theory*. John Wiley & Sons, 1998.

[210] S. Wasserman and K. Faust. *Social Network Analysis: Methods and Applications*. Cambridge University Press, 1994.

[211] R. Weiss, B. Velez, M. A. Sheldon, C. Nemprempre, P. Szilagyi, A. Duda, and D. K. Gifford. HyPursuit: A hierarchical network search engine that exploits content-link hypertext clustering. In *Proceedings of the 7th ACM Conference on Hypertext*, Washington, DC, March 1996.

[212] S. Weiss and N. Indurkhya. Optimized rule induction. *IEEE Expert*, 8(6), pages 61–69, 1993.

[213] P. Willett. Recent trends in hierarchic document clustering: A critical review. *Information Processing and Management*, 24(5), 1988.

[214] T. Winograd. *Language as a Cognitive Process, Vol. 1: Syntax*. Addison-Wesley, 1983.

[215] I. H. Witten, A. Moffat, and T. C. Bell. *Managing Gigabytes: Compressing and Indexing Documents and Images*. Multimedia Information and Systems. Morgan Kaufmann, 1999.

[216] XTAG Research Group. A lexicalized tree adjoining grammar for English. Technical Report IRCS-01-03. IRCS, University of Pennsylvania, 2001.

[217] Y. Yang and X. Liu. A re-examination of text categorization methods. In *Annual International Conference on Research and Development in Information Retrieval (SIGIR)*, pages 42–49. ACM, 1999. *www-2.cs.cmu.edu/~yiming/publications.html*.

[218] Y. Yang and J. Pedersen. A comparative study on feature selection in text categorization. In *International Conference on Machine Learning*, pages 412–420, 1997.

[219] J. Yi and N. Sundaresan. A classifier for semi-structured documents. In *KDD 2000*, pages 340–344. ACM SIGKDD, Boston, August 2000.

[220] T. Zhang, R. Ramakrishnan, and M. Livny. BIRCH: An efficient data clustering method for very large databases. In *SIGMOD*, pages 103–114. ACM, 1996. *www.ece.nwu.edu/~harsha/Clustering/sigmodpaper.ps*.

INDEX

ABOUT THE AUTHOR

Soumen Chakrabarti is assistant professor in Computer Science and Engineering at the Indian Institute of Technology, Bombay. Prior to joining IIT, he worked on hypertext information retrieval and mining at IBM Almaden Research Center. He has developed several systems for Web mining, published extensively, and acquired eight U.S. patents on his inventions to date. Chakrabarti has served as a vice-chair or program committee member for many conferences, including WWW, SIGIR, ICDE, VLDB, KDD, and SODA, and was a guest editor of the IEEE TKDE special issue on mining and searching the Web. His work on focused crawling received the Best Paper award at the 1999 WWW Conference. He holds a Ph.D. from the University of California, Berkeley.

Edwards Brothers Malloy
Ann Arbor MI. USA
April 10, 2012